Daughters of the Shtetl

"How could a person, a woman not even five feet tall, change the world?

"I'll tell you. It's a good story . . ."

—Rose Chernin, as quoted in Kim Chernin,
In My Mother's House

Daughters of the Shtetl

Life and Labor in the Immigrant Generation

Susan A. Glenn

Cornell University Press

ITHACA AND LONDON

First published 1990 by Cornell University Press.
First printing, Cornell Paperbacks, 1991.
Second printing 1993.

International Standard Book Number 0-8014-1966-2 (cloth)
International Standard Book Number 0-8014-9759-0 (paper)
Library of Congress Catalog Card Number 90-1557
Printed in the United States of America
Librarians: Library of Congress cataloging information
appears on the last page of the book.

⊗ The paper in this book meets the minimum requirements of the American National Standard for Information Sciences—Permanence of Paper for Printed Library Materials, ANSI Z39.48-1984.

For my daughter, Rachel,
my mother, Rhoda,
and in memory of
my grandmother, Jennie

Contents

Illustrations

Preface

This book brings together three topics that have long engaged me: immigration and its consequences both for the migrants and for the society they entered; working-class life and the labor movement; and the ways in which gender-role socialization has informed all of these issues.

To study the experiences of Jewish immigrant workers in the American garment industry is hardly to enter uncharted territory. Yet to reexamine this topic within the contexts of immigration and women's history has presented me with a significant set of challenges. Although our understandings of acculturation and adaptation have been shifting as new studies contest older models of immigration history, and scholarship in women's history has been steadily breaking new ground, the disparate subfields of social history have not been well integrated. My goal has been to bring these subfields together with an eye to a deeper understanding of how ethnicity, class, and gender have informed one another and informed the consciousness and behavior of a particular group of immigrant working women.

Many generous people and institutions helped to make this book possible. For financial support I am grateful to the American Council of Learned Societies, the National Endowment for the Humanities Summer Research Program, the Memorial Foundation for Jewish Culture, and the Mabelle McLeod Lewis Memorial Foundation.

Among the many archivists and librarians who facilitated my research, I especially thank Marek Web and Fruma Mohrer at the YIVO

Institute for Jewish Research in New York; Richard Strassberg and Martha Hodges at the Labor-Management Documentation Center, Catherwood Library, Cornell University; Debra Bernhardt at the Robert F. Wagner Labor Archives, Bobst Library, New York University; the staff of the ILGWU Research Department in New York; and Ida Cohen Selavan at the American-Jewish Periodical Center, who saved me a trip to Cincinnati by helping locate and translate articles from the *Yiddishes Tageblatt.*

I owe special debts of gratitude to the late Arcadius Kahan, economist and historian of eastern European Jewish life, who drew my attention to unpublished interviews collected in 1947–48 by the Columbia University Research in Contemporary Cultures, a little-known and extraordinarily rich source on early twentieth-century immigrant folklife; and to Sherna Gluck for allowing me to use interviews from the Feminist History Research Project.

Various scholars read this book at different stages of its evolution, and I am grateful for their comments. I thank Nancy A. Hewitt and Steve Fraser for giving the manuscript thoughtful and critical readings and for making suggestions that helped me improve the final version. Thanks also go to Roger Daniels, Lynn Dumenil, James R. Grossman, Jack Potter, Ann Schofield, and Robert Weyeneth for their valuable criticisms. Lizabeth Cohen, Jon Gjerde, Gerda Lerner, Alexander Saxton, Gerald Surh, and Kim Voss provided insightful critiques of individual chapters. Reginald Butler, Myron Greene, Barbara Loomis, and Richard Pells gave me advice, support, and encouragement. Peter Agree, my editor at Cornell University Press, has enthusiastically supported this project, offering sound advice at every step. Roger Haydon's careful copyediting saved me from numerous errors in the final draft.

I owe a different kind of debt to my teachers at the University of California, Berkeley. Paula Fass continually forced me to confront the difficult questions in social history and pushed me toward greater complexity of analysis. Leon Litwack has been more than a scholarly adviser. His warmth, generosity, and unflagging support have eased my way over the years this book has been evolving.

Finally I thank Jim Gregory for patiently reading, listening, discussing, criticizing, nurturing, and much much more.

SUSAN A. GLENN

Austin, Texas

Daughters of the Shtetl

Introduction

  Seventy-four years old when she was interviewed in the mid-1970s, Mollie Linker, a grandmother living in Chicago, recounted her life history in terms that were familiar to a generation of Jewish immigrant women. "When I came here I was thirteen and a half. . . . At fifteen I took almost three hundred people [out] on strike. . . . I got married at eighteen. . . . Then the babies came." Like thousands of other immigrant girls, she had left her home in Russia during the early part of this century to begin life anew in America. Forced to leave the American schoolroom because her family needed additional income, in 1915 she found a job sewing men's clothing at the giant Hart, Schaffner & Marx factory in Chicago. There she joined the Amalgamated Clothing Workers of America, a socialist-led industrial union, and helped organize the workers in her factory. Not long afterward she left the factory and the union for marriage and motherhood. But hers was not to be the standard American middle-class version of domesticity. As Linker described it, her honeymoon was spent in the back of a candy store, where she and her husband would work side by side for the next fifty-five years.[1]

  Her story is not unique, and in many ways it encapsulates some of the most compelling themes in the experiences of Jewish immigrant women who came to the United States in the first two decades of this century. Wage labor, participation in the union movement, marriage and motherhood sometimes accompanied by "helping" in a family business or by a temporary return to the factory to bring in extra income—these were the familiar cycles of immigrant women's lives.

  This book examines the experiences of a particular group of Jewish immigrants, European-born daughters who, early in this century, went to work in the American garment industry. It explores the life of Mollie Linker's generation, and the ways these women understood and integrated the worlds of work, politics, and family, creating a Jewish version of what early twentieth-century contemporaries called New Womanhood.

Their story begins in the Old World—the world of the Jewish *shtetl* (small town) and the burgeoning industrial cities of eastern Europe—where political, economic, and cultural upheavals were beginning to challenge long-standing customs and ways of thinking. Emigration represented both a response to and a symptom of those upheavals. Between 1880 and the outbreak of World War I, an estimated two million Jews left Russia, Poland, and other parts of eastern Europe and emigrated to America.

Many of the migrants were unmarried women in their teens and twenties. For countless Jewish immigrant women, the American garment industry became a home away from home, a place where they spent eight, ten, even fourteen hours a day, six and sometimes seven days a week. Many probably knew the garment workroom more intimately than any other aspect of their new American environment. For immigrant garment workers, one Jewish unionist would write, "the sweatshop *was* America."[2] Even if that assertion is only partially true, there is little doubt that the work experience provided an important prism through which Jewish daughters viewed the world around them and understood their own position in society. The centrality of the work experience to women's identity emerges in the poetry of a female garment worker:

> I would like to write a poem
> But I have no words.
> My grammar was ladies waists
> And my schooling skirts.[3]

These young women do not fit neatly into the established models of immigration, labor, and women's history. A substantial and growing literature on the female experience has provided many excellent histories of both middle- and working-class women in the United States. But the implications of immigration and ethnicity for women's culture and experience have not been adequately explored.[4] Even the growing literature on wage-earning women, which acknowledges the important role that immigrants played in early twentieth-century industrial life, focuses mainly on questions of gender roles and relations, paying only passing attention to the ways in which immigration and ethnic group culture informed the lives of women at work, at play, and in protest and political activity.[5] One of the goals of this book is to bring together the study of work, gender, and ethnicity and to describe working women's particular experience as it was mediated not only by sex and class but also by the ways in which ethnic group culture shaped female culture and consciousness.

The distinctiveness of eastern European Jewish culture was critical for these women, especially in two related contexts. The first is the broad cultural orientation that Jews brought with them to the United States and its bearing upon questions of acculturation and social change. The second involves the particular understandings of gender that distinguished Jews from other groups.

Jews were neither the "uprooted," culturally dislocated immigrants portrayed by Oscar Handlin and other historians writing in the 1950s nor the stubborn traditionalists romanticized by more recent studies of immigration and labor history. Neither of these polarities is complex enough to capture the enormous range of Jewish immigrants' attitudes and responses or the profoundly ambivalent nature of their cultural adaptation.[6] Many immigrants attempted to transplant and conserve Old World traditions. Yet the very act of emigration symbolized a willingness to take risks and a receptivity toward change.

Throughout this book I have identified this receptivity as an orientation toward "modernity." By that I mean an openness to experimentation and sometimes even a conscious rebellion against the traditions of the Old World. I use the term deliberately, so as to distinguish it from the concept of "Americanization." The latter implies a wholesale acceptance of American values and institutions, a process that did not characterize the experience of most of these women until the period after 1930. "Modernity" is more neutral in terms of specific national values and includes a constellation of symbols and opportunities denied or limited by the traditional boundaries of Jewish life in the Old World: political participation, education, freedom of movement and choice of residence, and secular as opposed to theocratic concepts of authority and status.[7]

For women, in particular, modernity meant breaking down traditional negative female stereotypes and expanding the feminine presence and voice beyond the customary spheres of home and marketplace. America offered various opportunities to step into the modern world, but immigrant women embraced these opportunities selectively and adopted them within a largely Jewish social and cultural orbit.

As the chapters that follow make clear, this orientation was not simply a product of emigration and resettlement, not simply the result of the Old World confronting the economic and cultural currents of urban-industrial life in the United States. Traditional understandings were being reexamined within Jewish society even before Mollie Linker and her generation crossed the ocean. The shtetl was neither a culturally stagnant nor a culturally insulated world, and many of the dilemmas that immigrants faced in the United States—physical uprooting, proletarianization, class conflict, politicization, generational conflict, and emerging redefinitions of gender roles—occurred on both sides of the Atlantic. Thus we should think of the cultural renegotiations that took place among eastern European Jews in the decades after 1880 as part of a trans-Atlantic phenomenon, a process that began in the Old World but accelerated and took on new dimensions for immigrants in the United States.

Jewish daughters' experiences in the American garment industry and the union movement were central to this renegotiation. Yet the specific nature of their factory and union experience, especially as a crucible for feminine identity, has not received nearly the attention it deserves. To argue, as one historian has, that Jewish immigrant women defined themselves exclusively within the domestic sphere is to ignore the formative influence of external activities in shaping their female consciousness.[8] Indeed, for wage-earning daughters one of the central issues was the relationship between domestic and nondomestic life, a relationship that had particular relevance for the emergence of a specifically Jewish immigrant version of New Womanhood.

The ways in which Jewish immigrant women understood their place in the industrial setting were in some respects unique. As Jews, they brought to their work a set of concerns, expectations, and values that grew out of the peculiar historical circumstances of their east European past and reflected their hopes for the future. As females, their situation differed in many respects from that of Jewish men. Feminine socialization and the special status of women affected their understandings, identities, and purposes, as well as their position within the industrial system. And to a considerable degree these two identities—Jewish and female—together defined immigrant women's special place in the history of working-class America.[9]

The work experience of Jewish daughters resembled but also differed from the patterns described by recent scholarship in women's labor history, much of which tends to dichotomize the shopfloor and union experiences of women and men. Most histories have described the working lives of women and men as essentially separate and distinct, both in their job structures and in their work cultures.[10] A gendered division of work shaped the labor market in the garment factories and shops, reinforcing patterns of patriarchal dominance. Nevertheless, as this book makes clear, women filled a range of positions and skill levels within the several branches of the clothing industry, from relatively highly paid status-bearing occupations to the most exploited realm of the unskilled "learner." Moreover, Jewish women in the garment industry lacked neither craft traditions nor an identification with their work. Many Jewish daughters came to America as highly skilled needle workers—dressmakers, seamstresses, and tailors. They brought with them a well-developed craft pride and a sense of competence that stood in sharp contrast to the stereotypic images of female workers as insecure, unambitious, and apathetic toward their jobs. Understandings about the legitimacy and necessity of female labor provided a sense of entitlement to this group of wage earners.[11]

That sense of entitlement helps us explain why Jewish women played such a highly visible role in the early twentieth-century labor movement. On the lookout for higher wages, interested in opportunities to implement their skills, deeply concerned about the plight of less fortunate workers in their industry, they not only spearheaded a campaign for union organization but earned a reputation for being among the most dedicated and idealistic participants in the labor movement. This book attempts to understand why the same young immigrant women who—like other female laborers in America—considered themselves only temporary wage earners took more than a passing interest in their jobs and fought to improve the conditions of employment they would eventually leave behind. Several writers who have sought to account for the militance of these women correctly attribute it to their Old World socialist and class backgrounds. Jews in Russia were exposed to and affected by socialism and were experienced in class struggle, the argument goes, and thus were better prepared than many other groups for union organization.[12] But that is only a partial explanation. Other factors helped shape their activism, including family and communal dynamics and the compelling new opportunities for public recognition, dignity, and respectability that young women saw in the union movement.

For Jewish women labor protest also represented a form of civic participation—a vehicle for exercising a political voice not only in their own behalf but also in defense of their families, their class, and their ethnic group. Here once again, group experience and understanding fit uncomfortably within the established paradigms of women's history. Jewish women exhibited what feminist scholars have called "female consciousness" and looked to other women for support and emotional sustenance. Yet their activism sprang not from an idealized gender-specific sense of "sisterhood" but rather from an evolving notion of partnership and coparticipation with men along class and community lines. Partnership with men in the struggle to earn a living, new ideas about romantic and companionate marriage, and community and radical socialist support for female activism all helped break down the barriers between the sexes, even if it did not dissolve them. It was this orientation toward partnership that gave Jewish women's activism its distinctive cast and its strongest contrast to the woman-centered politics of American middle-class reformers.

The search for self-esteem through political involvement was part of a larger transformation of feminine social identity, one that was evolving even before Jewish daughters had left their homes in eastern Europe. Emigration to America represented an opportunity to extend that process. In traditional eastern European Jewish culture, women were viewed as inferior beings. At the same time, however, both married and single women received positive social recognition for their abilities as breadwinners. But Jewish women who emigrated to America moved into a cultural environment where female labor was seen as a necessary evil, an activity to be tolerated only when the family was in difficult economic circumstances or, for single women, a brief interval between adolescence and marriage. In America a woman's social role was more exclusively domestic than it had been for females in Jewish culture. And far from viewing the female sex as inherently inferior, Americans tended to idealize and elevate womanhood and its distinctly feminine qualities.

Elements of both of these cultural models entwined themselves in the emerging identities and self-perceptions of Jewish daughters in America. As they made the transition from the Old World to the New, young women drew upon the most positive and complimentary features of womanhood in each setting. They took strength from Old World traditions of women's work, which included a sense of artisanal pride and self-sufficiency, while rejecting Jewish notions of female inferiority. They aspired to the respect and admiration they believed was the birthright of American women. Yet what they borrowed from American culture they altered and made uniquely their own. Although most of these young wage earners did not consider themselves "feminists," their public behavior—as workers, consumers of mass culture, and political activists—clashed with conventional American and "Victorian" doctrines of woman's proper place. Even their version of domesticity brought together elements from several cultural frameworks.

This melding of images partially explains why the motivations and aspirations of Jewish women sometimes appeared contradictory. Like Mollie Linker, most Jewish immigrant daughters aspired to conceptions of womanhood which stressed that their primary role after marriage would be domestic. Thus they planned to marry out of the factory into a home-centered existence. At the same time many were highly motivated and ambitious wage workers, militant participants in garment strikes and active union members. And they saw little contradiction in this mixture of womanly pursuits. What enabled Mollie Linker and other immigrant women to move easily from the arena of wage work and activism to the world of domesticity was the fluidity of their value system. As a transitional generation they were still defining the terrain of Jewish womanhood.

By focusing upon Jewish immigrant women in the garment industry, this book seeks to illustrate the significance of gender and culture in the lives of industrial workers and to illuminate the diversity of working-class experience in America. This is not a comparative study, but I have included discussions of women from southern Italy who played a major role in the garment industry and its unions. Where their lives and values intersected with or differed from those of Jews, I have attempted to explain why. For the most part, however, I have chosen to probe the meanings of work experience in the lives of one particular group of women.

Wherever possible I have drawn upon the personal testimonies of immigrant women themselves. These women included some of the most articulate members of the immigrant generation. Some recorded their experiences and memories in autobiographies, both published and unpublished. Others told the details of their lives to contemporary investigators. Still others recounted their personal histories to interested scholars in later years. Some of these immigrants had once occupied positions of leadership within their unions; others had helped organize important strikes. Many more were ordinary women who led unspectacular and undistinguished lives but shared features of a common background and had many of the same aspirations and goals as their more illustrious sisters.

I "A Girl Wasn't Much"

Jewish Womanhood in Eastern Europe

Women occupied a paradoxical place in eastern European Jewish society in the late nineteenth and early twentieth centuries. On the one hand, they were excluded from the main lines of public authority in matters civic and religious; on the other, they played a central role in economic life and were charged with the important task of maintaining the fundamental religious rituals of private life. Women's work, economic and domestic, was acknowledged as an essential component of physical and cultural survival, but women as a sex were considered inferior to men.

This paradox had both constraining and liberating consequences for Jewish women. It freed them to participate as quasi-independent brokers in the public world of the marketplace and vested them with the rights and responsibilities of breadwinners. But it limited their activities to work and domestic cares, privileging higher pursuits, such as education, for men. The result was that although women were looked upon as breadwinning partners in the Jewish family, they remained second-class citizens in the larger society.

Before they left the Old World, many Jewish women worked in artisan's shops or ready-made clothing factories. Others made cigars, cigarettes, stockings, and various consumer goods. Thousands worked in a family business or as a last resort went into domestic service. Although not all Jewish women in eastern Europe worked, the vast majority had been raised in a social environment in which the labor of wives and daughters was considered a vital part of the family economy.

Thus the Jewish immigrant women who went to work in America's garment industry were not peasants who moved from the Russian field to the American factory. Nor were they strangers to the workplace. Their childhoods and young adult years had been spent in eastern European towns and cities undergoing economic change. By the 1880s industrialization, commercialization of the economy, and a shifting political climate had created the conditions that drew increasing numbers of young Jewish women into workshops and factories. Along with these changes came the spread of new, Western, ideas. By the turn of the century female roles too were poised for change. The powerful transformations that would encourage a massive out-migration of eastern European Jews would also open the possibilities for reconstructing the relationships between women and men and between women and Jewish society.

Women's Status, Women's Work

The tradition of women's work in eastern European Jewish society was well established generations before the mass migration of Jews to America. In the *shtetlekh*—the small Russian and Polish towns where millions of Jews made their homes—Jewish men were legally responsible for supporting their families, but women took an active part in breadwinning, sometimes assuming entire responsibility for the family's welfare. This pattern reflected cultural as well as economic imperatives. Although women in the preindustrial and industrializing economies of western Europe commonly shared economic tasks with men, Jewish women in eastern Europe were expected to work not only as a practical matter but as an extension of their religious duties.[1]

In the shtetlekh of eastern Europe the social system was organized along religious lines with authority based in Jewish law and leadership. Although Jews officially lived under the jurisdiction of state authorities, within their own communities they maintained a large degree of autonomy. A Jewish community council, made up of prominent members of the local synagogue, oversaw both civil and religious affairs: collecting taxes, dispensing charity, establishing local policy for Jews. Although Jews did not live an isolated existence and had frequent commercial contact with Russians, Poles, Lithuanians, and other gentiles, in many ways their lives were circumscribed by separate cultural, religious, and communal concerns.[2]

Nineteenth- and early twentieth-century east European Jewish society was highly stratified and highly patriarchal. Within Jewish culture, religious scholars, almost without exception men, were the most respected people in the social order. Jews knew no loftier goal than the pursuit of religious learning, and no sacrifice was too great to send a son to *Yeshiva*—advanced religious school. Parents hoped their sons might become rabbis and bring great prestige to the family name.[3] Women, who could not become rabbis and whose place in the community depended upon their husband's or father's status, considered it a mark of great success to marry a learned man. "Learned people were more important than rich people and a girl would be happy to marry a boy that does nothing—that sits and studies" all day, one Russian Jewish woman recalled.[4]

Religious scholars received the support of the community and the family. When a boy went away to attend Yeshiva, the townspeople provided free board or, as it was called, "eating days."[5] A small number of men became rabbis after they left Yeshiva and had their salaries paid by the community. But most simply acquired the title of "reb" (teacher) and continued their studies in the *besmedresh* (study house) of the shtetl, serving as unpaid community leaders, taking part in the religious activities of the town, and acting as authorities on Jewish law. Yet without a subsidized rabbinical post, scholars had to find a means of support. Most looked for a wife who could manage the household and earn enough to free her husband from major economic responsibilities.

Jews considered it something of a religious obligation for the wife of a Torah scholar to work while her husband devoted most of his time to study and prayer. Jewish folk culture acknowledged that a woman might even earn a place in Paradise if she labored to support a religious man. This belief reflected women's inferior status in the traditional culture, for once she arrived in Paradise, according to Jewish lore, she served as her husband's "footstool."[6] As Ida Richter, an immigrant from a small town near Minsk put it, "In Russia, a [Jewish] woman was nothing. [But] A boy was very important in Jewish life for a lot of things. When my father used to pray in the morning with his prayer shawl, I used to hear him say in Hebrew, 'Thank God I'm not a woman.' A girl wasn't much."[7] Barred from playing any important role in religious leadership and excluded from positions of authority in the community, women found their "sphere" confined to domestic and economic functions.

In contrast to western Victorian ideas, which stressed the piety and purity of womanhood, Jews freely acknowledged woman's sexuality, her earthiness, even her ability to corrupt a man's morals. And while middle-class Victorians argued that woman's moral and domestic responsibilities should take precedent over any income-producing role, eastern European Jews, who expected females to be both pious and worldly, thought it perfectly proper for women to help earn a living while the men pursued a life of religious scholarship.[8]

In Tarnoruda, a small town in Galicia (a region of the Austro-Hungarian Empire bordering on the Ukraine), Fannie Edelman's parents lived in a manner common to the scholarly class. "My father was a learned Jew . . . . When he married my mother he was promised a year's free board so that he could sit in the synagogue and study the Torah." With the money from her dowry, her mother opened "a little store" and sold flour, salt, and barley to support her husband after the year was over.[9] A Jewish woman from Sandemish, a small shtetl near Warsaw, explained that most women felt "happy" and "proud" to support a man of learning: "There were thousands like that who worked very hard while their husbands sat and studied. . . . They were pregnant, gave birth, breast-fed children, carried on the business, and served him as well. . . . They used to take young boys from the Yeshivas, marry them off and give them room and board with a wife to work for them while they studied further." But she claimed that the women "didn't complain because it was already a form of life for many generations and they were used to it."[10]

In the Lithuanian countryside of her youth, Eva Broido, who would later become a revolutionary, saw her father only rarely. With some bitterness, Broido recalled his detachment from the family and her mother's almost heroic struggle to earn a living.

> There were three of us children living in the country. . . . Our mother was the head of the family, its driving force and its breadwinner. Our father, a kind and not unintelligent man, looked upon us children as something extraneous, with which he would not concern himself. He was an unworldly Talmudic scholar, who needed little for himself and knew nothing of our needs. He was on his own and we were on our own. It was left to our mother to provide for us all. It was left to her . . . to toil and to worry, to run the forest holding . . . while he remained in town throughout.[11]

Whatever status a woman's family gained by her marriage to a scholar, she paid dearly with her own labor. Although most women who supported religious scholars accepted their duties without much overt complaint, clearly it was not because their lives were easy. Burdened with domestic as well as economic tasks, a scholar's wife might hope to go to Paradise in the next world but had little earthly pleasure in this one. Miriam Shomer Zunser, recalling her girlhood in Russia, told of one humorously bitter Yiddish song that no doubt provided a certain psychic release to such women. As the song suggests, the scholar often had his head in the clouds while his wife worried about more mundane matters.

> He runs to the synagogue
> And reads all the laws,
> He runs here and there
> Growling like a bear.
>
> * * *
>
> To market she must hurry
> Wood to buy and worry
> Bread she must bake
> Kindling she must break;
> The children she must care for
> That's what she's there for,
> Put this one to bed,
> Smear up that one's head;
> Soothe this one's ache
> To the out-house that one take,
> And for measure full or near
> A baby every year.[12]

The Breadwinning Partnership

Women's economic obligation reached its most extreme degree in the families of religious scholars, where wives performed a religious *mitzvah* (good deed) by working so their husbands might pursue a higher purpose. And although the scholarly class was only a tiny segment of the society, as the cultural elite they set the tone for the society as a whole. The hard-working scholar's wife acted as a legitimating symbol of the female breadwinner for the masses of east European Jews. If the scholar's wife worked, then why not the merchant's, the trader's, the watchmaker's, or the tailor's? And that was the pattern. In every stratum of Jewish society the work of women was considered both necessary and respectable. The hundreds of thousands of Jews who eked out a living in small commercial enterprises and artisanal trades relied upon the labor of all family members, including wives and daughters.

Throughout the nineteenth and early twentieth centuries, Jewish families made their living mainly from various forms of commerce and handicrafts. By the 1880s larger industrial enterprises also provided work but still had not supplanted the small, home-centered producer. In addition to work in handicrafts and petty commerce, Jews supported themselves by running taverns and inns, dealing in various commodities such as grain and alcohol, and working as teamsters, draymen, and coachmen. Thousands of others were unskilled laborers, often without a regular occupation, drifting from job to job.[13] Although Jews traded in agricultural products, theirs had never been a peasant economy. Legal restrictions kept most Jews from working the land. In the early nineteenth century only 8 percent of the Jews in Russia were farmers, most of them living in government-sponsored agricultural colonies. By 1900, with the imposition of new restrictions on Jewish residence, fewer than 3 percent of Jews in Russia were earning a livelihood from the land.[14]

Most Jews lived in villages, small towns, and cities in what was known as the Pale of Settlement. Ever since the partition of Poland at the end of the eighteenth century, Jews living under Russian rule had been confined to fifteen provinces in western and southwestern Russia and ten eastern Polish provinces designated as the Pale. Permission to live in cities and towns outside the Pale of Settlement had been granted only to master artisans, merchants of the first guild, university students, professionals, and prostitutes. At the end of the nineteenth century all of these groups, with the exception of Jewish prostitutes, saw their special residential privileges revoked by the Czarist government.[15] Over the thirty-year period from 1880 to 1910, the Pale was a world squeezed ever more tightly by political restrictions and by the economic consequences of industrial change.

Women played a major role in this economy. Although statistics on Jewish working women in the Pale are not completely reliable, they provide important insights into women's economic role at the end of the nineteenth century. The Russian census of 1897 counted 307,038 Jewish women in the Pale who were considered "economically active." This represented roughly 21 percent of Jewish females in the 14-to-59-year old age group, the cohort likely to be engaged in some sort of breadwinning activity. Economist Arcadius Kahan, however, challenged this figure, noting that the census failed to count women working in small home-based workshops and omitted thousands of females laboring in the industries of several large cities. Kahan estimated that the total number of working women was undercounted by at least a hundred thousand, which would raise the portion of economically active females to between 27 and 28 percent.[16] Such statistics also hide an important feature of women's work experience—the fact that female breadwinning roles were sometimes part-time or intermittent, geared to particular phases of the life cycle as well as to times of family need. After marriage some women worked continuously, leaving the care of children to other members of the household or to servants. Others made their economic contribution as various domestic responsibilities permitted and when needs and opportunities were greatest.[17] But overall the frequency of married women's work was high enough and had sufficient cultural support to make it something of a norm.

All of this had important implications for the position of women in the family and the society. The paradigm of Jewish marriage, with the exception of those in which scholars' wives supported their husbands, involved some expectation of a male-female partnership in the responsibilities of breadwinning. Even though women remained in a decidedly subordinate position in Jewish society and enjoyed little of the moral religious authority of their western bourgeois counterparts, the breadwinning partnership gave Jewish wives some family authority, a knowledge of the marketplace, and a certain worldliness. In the absence of a husband, a woman could assume most of his duties, except, of course, his formal role in the synagogue. This flexibility in gender roles along with the shared responsibilities for earning a living helped modify patriarchal dominance and blurred the lines between gender roles.[18]

Although many women pursued their own trades, a woman's work frequently depended upon her husband's occupation.[19] As in most artisanal economies, a wife typically assisted her husband with the ancillary tasks of his trade. A traditional Yiddish marriage song spelled out the pattern:

> Cobblers' wives must make the thread ...
> Tailors' wives must sit up late ...
> Coachmen's wives must tar the axles ...
>
> * * *
>
> Butchers' wives must carry the meat ...
> Weavers' wives must throw the spindle ...
> Filers' wives must turn the wheel ...
> Painters' wives must mix the paint ...
> Carpenters' wives must saw the boards ...[20]

And if her husband engaged in some form of commercial enterprise, she assisted him there as well.

Large numbers of married women worked in business or trade, either helping in a store formally run by their husbands or keeping a store or stall on their own. Women ran produce stores, dry goods stores, sold home-baked goods and various home-produced items, and traded herring, chickens, and other products in the marketplace. Other women ran timber businesses, sold grain and flour, and operated taverns and inns.[21] Even the most prosperous male members of a community often depended upon the labor of their wives. In Vilna, for example, Abraham Cahan recalled that one herring dealer in his neighborhood prospered largely because of his wife's business acumen.[22] In Nieszawa, Lottie Spitzer's family considered their jewelry business a joint enterprise shared by husband and wife. In reality, however, Lottie's mother kept the business going.

> My father was a jeweler, but he did not make a living only from jewelry . . . he used to be an interpreter in court . . . he used to write for the Hebrew paper. Poetry. So he was always busy in those things. My father used to be in the back of the store doing a lot of writing. And my mother was the business woman. He was really the buyer of the store, but my mother took care of the store. . . . We had a maid in the house. The maid used to dress us. Mother used to make breakfast and send us out to school. And mother spent the whole day in the store.[23]

A woman's ability to run the family business or to oversee her own small business enterprise was sometimes necessitated by the peculiar structure of Jewish economic life. Jewish men often engaged in occupations that required them to travel. Artisans such as tailors and cobblers as well as commercial peddlers left the shtetl for long periods of time to sell their products in the surrounding countryside. In their absence women had to learn a certain degree of economic independence. Fannie Edelman recalled the regular disruptions of family life after her father became a "custom peddler." While he traveled through the countryside selling prayer shawls and other religious articles, her mother sold flour and other staples in the family store: "My father would come home only for the Jewish High Holy Days, that is, a few times a year. The rest of the time he traveled around with his merchandise—but my mother could not depend too much upon his earnings, and therefore kept the store going."[24]

In 1868 Yiddish novelist Isaac Meier Dick, who was critical of these practices, described in somewhat exaggerated terms the quality of shtetl life when men like Fannie Edelman's father were away peddling their wares: "The hamlet looks dead during the whole week; it has the semblance of a gynocracy, that is a kingdom inhabited only by women.

Men spend the week until Friday in the country, they wander from village to village. . . . In the hamlet itself remain only women, children, communal officials, students and a few . . . unemployed men."[25]

By the end of the century, as the economy diversified and middlemen took over much of the distribution for artisans, fewer men took to the road. Nevertheless, women continued to play a key role in the family commercial enterprises that made up such an important part of the Jewish economy.

Daughters, as well as wives, assisted in the workshops and businesses of their parents. Not only did girls help their mothers with domestic and child-rearing tasks, but they were also expected to share in the process of earning a living. Beginning at an early age, some middle-class daughters—the children of merchants—were groomed for a career in commerce.[26] As young girls, they spent time waiting upon customers in the family store or helping with the accounting. By the time she was nine years old, Rose Pesotta's Ukrainian-born mother had been inducted into the family business: "Aunt Sheba set out to train her charge to become a business woman. Thus . . . my mother became the bookkeeper in Aunt Sheba's flour, grain and cereal store." By the age of sixteen, when Rose's mother married, she was running the store by herself.[27]

The Hierarchy of Female Occupations

Because business provided a degree of economic independence, Jews in eastern Europe favored it over all other occupations. As anthropologists of the shtetl have observed, Jews felt that it was better to "work for oneself than for someone else" even if this independence meant smaller incomes and less security. Moreover, business was attractive because it required that one use one's head and was identified with intellectual activity.[28]

If business ranked highest in the hierarchy of occupations, domestic service was one of the lowest and least desirable positions for a Jewish woman. Whatever material comforts and security were afforded to domestics, the benefits scarcely compensated for the humiliation associated with servitude. Not only did it imply a loss of independence and an acknowledgment of inferiority, but it meant cleaning, sweeping, laundering, and other tasks labeled "dirty" work. Given Jewish concerns with ritual forms of cleanliness—especially the preoccupation with kosher foods and the separation of clean from *treyf* (unclean) dishes and pots—it is not surprising that domestic service seemed demeaning. As one Jew from the Ukraine explained, "the dirtier the work, or the more physical strength was required for it, the more *proste* [lowly] it was."[29] Unlike women in some western European societies, who viewed domestic service as an acceptable occupation because of its protective social surroundings and the preparation it provided for future marital duties, Jews saw the occupation as decidedly odious. "For a Jewish girl to become a maid—there's a tragic story behind it," another immigrant insisted.[30] Reflecting upon the number of Russian-Jewish girls who became domestics despite the low status of the position, one woman explained "they had no profession and the only thing was, to go for a maid." Yet because they were humiliated by the prospect, many left their home villages, instead finding domestic work in another community. There, if fortunate, a servant would save money for a dowry and eventually marry a worker or a man from a poor family.[31]

Symbolic factors aside, the occupation had practical drawbacks. Domestic service had limited utility as an occupation for wives. A woman might continue to carry on a business or work at her own trade after marriage, but working as a live-in servant was not feasible once she started her own family. Many women, however, had little choice in the matter. Unlike dressmaking or other trades, domestic service required no prior training or skill, and a poor woman could at least find immediate employment as a maid. Sheer poverty no doubt accounts for the substantial number of Jewish women who became household servants. The Russian census of 1897 reveals that 35 percent of gainfully employed Jewish women worked as domestic or personal servants. But as Arcadius Kahan suggests, this figure was probably exaggerated. Many women listed as domestic servants were more likely to have been live-in apprentices in the skilled trades, performing household labor for their master's or mistress's family.[32]

Lower still in status than domestic servants, and harder to count, were the prostitutes. Usually associated with big city life, the *burdak* (brothel) provided a source of income for poor Jewish women in the villages as well. As one Jewish immigrant from Galicia remarked, "Sure we had a brothel. What shtetl and town didn't?" And added, rhetorically, "What's the matter, a Jewish girl can't become a prostitute?"[33] A Russian-Jewish immigrant woman from Lida remembered that in her town the burdak was run by a Jew and that most of the prostitutes were Jewish. Her own aunt ran a grocery store and a saloon, where local prostitutes sold their favors. "All the soldiers used to come in there," she recalled. "Naturally when there were soldiers, there were girls who used to wait for them."[34] "There were a lot of girls that couldn't succeed in the small towns," recalled Dora Bayrack. Bobruisk, where she grew up, had little industry, and those factories which did exist were very small. Aside from cigar and cigarette making, and a few bakeries and dress-making shops, there were few jobs open to shtetl girls. Some of the most desperate women in her town went off to the interior of Russia and became prostitutes in the big cities. Although off limits to most other Jews, cities outside the Pale opened their gates to prostitutes who obtained the infamous "yellow ticket."[35]

Manufacturing and the Needle Trades

Much preferred over domestic service and other disreputable occupations were handicrafts and manufacturing work. As Russia experienced the early stages of industrialization in the 1880s, women found work in a range of industrial trades. Factory work provided some of these jobs. Pressing economic need in Jewish families and manufacturers' desire for cheap labor opened the way for a small but growing Jewish female factory proletariat at the end of the nineteenth century, mainly consisting of unmarried women. In workshops that manufactured cigarettes, cigars, knit goods, gloves, textiles, artificial flowers, buttons, glass, bricks, soap, candy, and other products, women and children worked at unskilled and semiskilled jobs, sometimes as helpers to the men. Typical was Handler's cloth factory in Bialystok, where unskilled girls worked for half the wages paid to skilled male weavers.[36]

Most of these "factories" were unmechanized workrooms employing between eleven and seventeen workers. Even those with machinery usually had only between twenty and forty employees.[37] There were some notable exceptions, however. Match, tobacco, and glove factories sometimes employed hundreds of Jewish women under one roof. Tobacco workers, more than others, resembled a modern industrial work force. Shereshevsky's tobacco factory in Grodno, one of the largest in the Pale, employed about a thousand people, most of them women and children.[38]

More important than factory production was the home-based putting-out system. At the end of the century, thousands of married and single women were employed on an outwork basis, performing both skilled and unskilled labor in their own homes. In the match industry, for example, the matches were made in large-scale factories, but packing was done by other female employees at home.[39] In Vilna province, the center of the stocking industry in the late nineteenth century, and in the great textile centers of Lodz and Bialystok, thousands of Jewish female homeworkers produced goods for contractors who provided them with machinery and yarn and paid them by the piece.[40]

Married women usually considered industrial homework a more appropriate source of income than factory labor. The putting-out system offered them some definite advantages. It allowed the whole family to work together as a unit and did not disrupt a woman's domestic responsibilities. Equally important, unlike factory work, which was generally disapproved of for Jewish wives, homework did not violate family norms. It preserved a husband's authority over his wife because it did not require women to labor all day under the direction of other men, and it gave women a great deal of freedom to arrange their own work schedules and thus had a strong appeal to many Jews.[41]

Neither outwork nor factory labor was as attractive as a skilled trade, and in the turn-of-the-century Pale independent and semi-independent artisans, most of them working out of their own homes, still outnumbered other laborers in the manufacturing sector. Families that depended upon women's earnings, and whose circumstances permitted it, hoped their daughters would become artisans. Outside of commercial business enterprise, a skilled trade was the most highly regarded form of women's work. Many young women learned crafts such as shoe- and bootmaking, baking, weaving, and lacemaking. Some also became glaziers, bookbinders, even butchers. But the chief trade for women (as for men) was garment making. In 1898, when the Jewish Colonization Association, a private philanthropic agency, conducted a massive investigation of the economic condition of the Jews in Russia, it discovered that over fifty thousand women in the Pale of Settlement were engaged in some branch of the sewing trades. They constituted 70 percent of the registered female artisans in the Pale.[42] In reality, the number of needleworkers was probably much larger, since many women for one reason or another did not register their occupations with local authorities.

The predominance of Jews in the needle trades apparently dates back centuries and seems to have been an outgrowth of religious customs. In the eighteenth century more than half of the Jewish artisans in Poland were working in the clothing trades, and it is likely that even then a large percentage of eastern European garment workers were Jewish.[43] Orthodox Jews were forbidden to wear clothing made of mixed wool and linen, and consequently came to trust only Jewish tailors to follow this rule.[44] Even in the early twentieth century, as one man from Bragin, Russia, explained, many Jews refused to wear clothes that were not "kosher"—that is, clothes that were not made according to Jewish law.[45] But Jewish needleworkers also made clothes for gentiles, and in the Pale of Settlement they sewed for the peasantry as well as village and urban populations. By the end of the nineteenth century more Jews of both sexes worked in the garment trades than in any other occupation except commerce and trade. The Russian census of 1897 shows that 17 percent of all gainfully employed Jews in the empire listed their occupation as the manufacture of clothing. This was nearly 50 percent of all Jews engaged in manufacturing or mechanical pursuits.[46]

The garment industry in eastern Europe was in a state of transition. As late as World War I, much of the clothing was still produced by independent artisans in their own shops. Most towns had tailors, tailoresses, dressmakers, and seamstresses who produced for individual customers, the former making men's and women's suits and coats, the dressmakers sewing bridal wardrobes and fancy gowns, and the seamstresses making blouses, skirts, underclothing, and linens. Some of these highly skilled needleworkers catered to a middle-class and wealthy Jewish and gentile clientele; others served the general urban population. A lower stratum of artisans sewed primarily for the local peasants, making cheaper garments and generally receiving less money for their work. In addition to filling orders for individual customers, some sold clothing in the marketplace or peddled their goods in the surrounding countryside. The least skilled and most poorly remunerated artisans were the "repairers" who patched, mended, and reconstructed old clothing for the poor.[47]

After 1890 this traditional system of artisanal production and distribution existed side by side with a growing ready-made clothing industry. In some locales the line between independent artisan and employee became increasingly blurred. Many needleworkers were artisans in name only: working independently in their own homes, they actually produced under contract for middlemen who distributed garments to stores.[48] Factories that mass-produced ready-made clothing for the stores or for export were also beginning to appear. Most of the new factories were still relatively small, commonly employing fewer than a dozen workers, but a few larger establishments had emerged as well. In Vilna and Pinsk, for example, ready-made tailoring factories employing as many as forty workers competed with the tiny artisans' shops. However, large-scale production was still very much the exception. For the most part the Jewish clothing industry remained concentrated in thousands of tiny enterprises employing no more than a couple of assistants or in home workshops.[49]

1. Modern factory production threatened traditional Jewish crafts and trades in Russia and Poland. Brandsteter's clothing factory, Tarnów, Poland, 1910. YIVO Institute for Jewish Research.

This production system made the needle trades an ideal occupation for women, combining respectable work with the ability to carry out domestic responsibilities. Motivated by hopes for a secure economic future, thousands of Jewish women learned dressmaking, tailoring, and other kinds of needlework. Especially after the 1870s, when the first sewing machines arrived in Russia and Poland, it was commonly believed that "those who could afford to buy a Singer machine were assured of a good livelihood." Journalist Abraham Cahan recalled that many parents, impressed by the economic potential of the new technology, hurried to apprentice their children to the "golden" trade.[50] Like so many other young Jewish women, Brucha Gutrajman was taught that sewing was a good trade for a girl, "a trade with a future," something she could depend upon to earn a living.[51] Indeed, a girl might take pride in the seamstresses' craft for it gave her a certain independence, a feeling of accomplishment, and some security against hard times. In a song that traveled from the workshops of Russia to the garment factories of New York, Jewish women expressed this confidence:

> Seamstress am I,
> The needle's my possession
> I need no longer worry
> For the coming days.
> Stitch, stitch, girly,
> See the seams are straight.
> Each pretty little dress
> Must be a perfect fit.[52]

The image of the independent seamstress also appeared in the writings of novelist Sholem Asch. In his 1925 novel *The Mother* he describes a poor girl's rise to respectability in a small town where she has become a seamstress: "Dvoyrele was sixteen years old then. Because she had set up her own little dressmaking establishment, she earned for herself an enviable social distinction among the other girls of the town. The older girls were therefore anxious to be her friends."[53]

To listen to young women who grew up in small towns in eastern Europe is to understand how in their eyes the seamstress could inspire respect. Fannie Shapiro, who grew up in an isolated village in White Russia, recalled how exciting the life of dressmaker seemed to her when she was a girl.

> I used to come to the small town and they had these little shops . . . 2, 3, 4, or 5 girls in a house, working . . . making dresses and things. . . . And they had a Singers, a sewing machine. . . . I used to . . . envy [them], and the girls would be sitting and working and *singing*, I thought it was so much *fun*. Singing . . . I says to myself, 'That's just what I want!' Oh but I thought it was a lot of fun, sitting and singing. They worked about ten hours a day, and were sitting on these chairs, and sewed by hand, and some—those [who] knew how to work by machine, those were the big shots.[54]

To learn how to be a seamstress or a dressmaker provided a woman not only with skills she could use to earn a living for her parents but also the means to help support a husband and children later on. Knowing the trade thus improved a woman's marriage prospects. Abraham Bisno, who grew up in a small village near Kiev, recalled how helpful a woman could be to her household if she could continue to follow her trade after she married. Bisno's father, a tailor whose trade had been passed down from his father, had grown up in the desperate poverty that often stalked an artisan's family. But because of his wife's ability to sew, economic conditions in his own family were improved. "My father was perhaps a little more fortunate, since Mother had learned the trade of making peasants' bonnets. She would embroider lengths of cloth, make them up into women's bonnets and sell them in the open market."[55] Indeed, if a woman came from a poor family with little to contribute in the way of a dowry, her earning power as a seamstress became an important asset to a potential husband. Moreover, girls from poor families went to work in the needle trades in order to save money for the dowry that was essential to marriage arrangements.[56]

A Yiddish love song, sung by young seamstresses in Russia, related a young girl's longing for the return of her sweetheart from the army and her willingness to toil at her trade in order to make money, perhaps for a dowry but in any case to provide an inducement for him to marry her.

> Let us fall in love,
> Let us be a pair by heaven blessed
> I swear to you by shear and iron
> I'll wait for you two, three years
> I'll wait for you two, three years
> Even four's worth while.
> I'll send you money to the regiment
> And myself will bear with tailoring.
> I will bear with tailoring
> And live here in great want.
> But when you return
> Don't say I'm an old maid.[57]

Jews regarded the needle trades differently for men and women. Gender mediated definitions of occupational status among the masses of Jews who generally held the seamstress in higher regard than her male counterpart, the tailor. This distinction reflected the inequality between men and women in the culture, particularly the stress upon the higher goal of learning for men and the correspondingly limited expectations for women. Jews assigned a low social status to male tailors and viewed the seamstress with greater respect because women did not compete for social prestige on the same basis as men. Women were supposed to aspire not to religious learning but to marriage. Consequently women's position in the social order depended less upon their occupation than upon whom they married. Although scholarly men and tailors stood at opposite ends of the male social spectrum, the same values were not consistently applied to Jewish women, and the position of seamstress generally had few of the negative stigmas associated with tailoring.

In a comment revealing of the difference between male and female occupational status, Rose Cohen, who grew up in a small shtetl in Russia, related the contrasting images of the seamstress and the tailor. When Cohen's aunt left home at the age of sixteen and traveled to Minsk to become a nursemaid, it precipitated a minor family crisis. "As grandmother expected her to be a seamstress, this choice of occupation caused grandmother as many tears as father's becoming a tailor instead of a rabbi. For a nurse girl was thought to be as much below a seamstress as a tailor below a rabbi."[58] In the Reznikoff family, Sarah wanted very much to pursue her education but was urged by her father to become a seamstress because the family needed her earnings. However, when her brother, who had been singled out for a religious education, apprenticed himself to a tailor against their wishes they reprimanded him for disgracing the family. While they criticized Sarah for being too intellectually ambitious, they accused her brother of being "unambitious" and "low," saying that tailoring was not good enough for their educated son.

> Father answered, "I should not like a child of mine to be a shoemaker or a tailor. The ignorant people of the town have done this work for generations. When a family has a stupid or a bad child, they apprentice him to one of these trades." . . . Then Father turned to me and said, "Little girl, you were born into the wrong family with your ideas." I became red. "You were born the eldest girl and this family needs your help badly. . . . You can read and write. Many Jewish girls of the well-to-do families cannot do that. You are also handy with the needle. Now you must make plans to suit your circumstances."[59]

Most eastern European Jews considered the needle trades a respectable occupation for a woman. Only among the social elites of the shtetl, the so-called *sheyne yidn* (beautiful or fine Jews) who felt that manual labor was beneath them, was there any doubt about the propriety of this work. Fear of downward mobility encouraged these families to try to keep their children out of the manual trades. Although they made special efforts for sons, the more socially prominent families evinced similar concerns about daughters' occupations. As Elizabeth Hasanovitz, the daughter of a Hebrew teacher, recalled, "The tradition of a respectable family in our town, no matter how poor, was to keep their daughters at home." The very idea that Elizabeth might become a "working girl" was intolerable to her mother.[60] Leon Kobrin, who grew up in a Lithuanian shtetl, explained that it was only the "ill-favored" girls—presumably those difficult to marry off—who were sent away to a large city to apprentice to a dressmaker or, in the worst case, to become a servant.[61] One Jewish woman who emigrated to the United States from the Bessarabian region of Russia in 1914 had come from a family that had achieved sheyne status because there were educated people on both her father's and mother's side. But they were poor. Her father's tobacco business failed, and her parents concluded they must either apprentice their daughter to a trade or migrate as a family to America to try to earn a living. As she remembered, her parents "would have preferred starvation" to the prospect of her learning a trade, and she was sent to America where her family would follow.[62]

Especially as economic conditions worsened for Jewish families toward the end of the nineteenth century, concerns about social "pedigree" gave way to more immediate financial imperatives.[63] One woman who grew up in a middle-class household in a small shtetl in Russia recalled how her parents had to compromise their social status when they found themselves in increasingly difficult economic circumstances. Her father had once held a good job as a construction foreman, which at the time was an engineering post. But with changing conditions in the Jewish economy, he was no longer able to find enough work. As a result, she and her sister were sent to another city to learn the dressmaking trade, and her brothers also went away at a young age to learn trades. Later, some manufacturers built a glass factory in her home town, and her sister returned to work there until she married.[64]

For Sarah Rozner, becoming a dressmaker's apprentice was at first a source of humiliation. Her father, a poverty-stricken but highly respected Hungarian-Jewish religious scholar, had little choice but to send her to learn a trade. "My people, my parents came from the elite; . . . they were all educated; even my grandmother knew how to read and write." They were also landowners, "big shots in the town. . . . But by the time I was born, they were down to nothing. We were starving; there wasn't even enough bread to go around." Unable to continue her education, Sarah dropped out of school and went to learn dressmaking. "I used to take the finished garments and deliver them to the customers. They would try to give me tips, but I was so God-damned proud that I refused to take the tips or to kiss their hands as was the custom—even though I was starving." But she added, "I finally got wise to myself and one day I took the tips." When her family later decided to emigrate to America to improve their economic circumstances, Rozner had acquired a knowledge of machine sewing. "I finally got it, and believe me it helped a lot when I came to this country," she explained.[65]

Learning a Trade

The children of artisans regularly followed in their parents' footsteps and learned a trade such as tailoring. The occupational patterns in Swislocz, a shtetl in the Grodno province of Russia where Abraham Ain grew up, were typical.

> The years between twelve and fourteen were years of decision for the boys. Most of them entered at that age in the leather factories, or were apprenticed to artisans. A small number . . . left for the Yeshivas. Boys from the wealthier homes helped their parents in their factories or stores and simultaneously continued their education with a private tutor.
>
> As for girls, their education was delayed to the age of seven or eight. . . . At the age of thirteen or fourteen girls were usually apprenticed to a seamstress. The poorest became domestics. Some girls worked as saleswomen in their parents' stores part of the time and continued their education.[66]

In other towns and cities Jewish girls from artisan families followed a similar course: they were packed off to the local dressmaker, seamstress, or tailor to learn a trade or to work as an assistant. Mollie Wexler, one of nine children born to a Jewish family in Brest-Litovsk, was taught that in a household with many mouths to feed, "the stronger ones had to go and help make a living." For Mollie this meant learning how to use a needle. "I was one of the healthy ones," she later recalled. "My mother took in dressmaking in the house. . . . I must have been about six years old and she began to show me how to sew . . . and by eight years I was working on a machine." Later her mother apprenticed her to a dressmaker who lived several miles away. "She told me I'd better go away and learn something to do, because I'm capable."[67] Further south in the Ukraine, tailor's daughter Rose Kaplan went to work in a small factory when she was twelve years old, making fur coats for the local peasants.[68]

When parents decided that their daughter should learn a skill, they made arrangements for her apprenticeship, which required a sacrifice of time and money. Since many families could not afford to pay for the instruction their children were to receive, apprenticeship agreements commonly stipulated that the young person was to work under the mistress or master for a set period of time (usually a year or more) without compensation. In exchange for learning the trade, the child would perform various household duties for her teacher. The experience of one young Jewish girl in Russia was typical of many others who apprenticed in the needle trades: "It was decided that I am already a big girl and it's about time to teach me a trade. The stipulation was three years' work without pay. Otherwise they would have to pay for the teaching. When my grandmother brought me to the tailor, I was barely eight years old."[69]

During her term of apprenticeship, a young girl lived with the seamstress or tailor, going home only for the Saturday Sabbath rest period and for holidays. Frequently, apprentices learned very little of the trade during the first year, as much of their time was devoted to numerous household tasks required by their employer.[70] Brucha Gutrajman, who was apprenticed to a dressmaker as a teenager, recalled the routine she followed while she was learning the trade and the resentment it stirred in her.

> Naturally, the first year I wouldn't get paid. My employer promised to make me a dress for the holidays. . . . The main point: she will teach me the trade. I begin my apprenticeship by doing all the various house-chores, including taking care of a baby, and running all the errands. As for [the] trade proper, I had two functions. One was to rip old clothes. . . . The other function was to prepare the iron.[71]

"One day," Gutrajman explained, "I noticed that, as soon as my employer's husband came home from work, he turned the clock back . . . to make me stay longer, in order to wash the dishes and clean up the shop."[72]

In the clothing trade, as in other industries that operated primarily out of the artisan's home, relations between worker and master were usually intimate if not always friendly. "In such a setting," Brucha Gutrajman recalled, "the worker inevitably became part of the family life, giving and receiving advice on strictly private matters, sometimes even participating in family disputes." That kind of closeness yielded both joys and abuses. Employers often took the liberty of disciplining apprentices as they would their own children. Both male and female apprentices in the clothing trade recalled that their "bread givers," as employers were called, beat them on occasion.[73]

Working hours, especially in the artisans' shops, were rarely less than ten per day. During rush periods when special holiday orders had to be sewn, some seamstresses and tailors worked as many as sixteen hours a day, six days a week. At times, recalled Mollie Wexler, "there was no stop, just work," often late into the night.[74] Few artisans' shops established set working hours. "You stopped when your boss told you to stop," recalled one former tailor's apprentice. This schedule could be quite arbitrary: when the master decided it was time to quit, the rest of the workers laid down their needles and shears.[75]

These conditions created resentments and unrest, including spontaneous strikes aimed at gaining shorter hours. Among the more common demands were the institution of a twelve-hour day and an end to arbitrary treatment by employers.[76] In some shops, apprentices and assistants resorted to sabotage in order to shorten their hours, bursting the glass over the kerosene lamps to cut off the source of light in the shops and in some instances breaking windows as well.[77]

The work songs of the Jewish seamstresses in late nineteenth- and early twentieth-century Russia reflect the unregulated hours of work in this trade. Such songs as "Tog Azoy Vi Nacht" (Day the same as night) told of the endless days and nights of toil and exhaustion that young women endured in the garment workshops.

> Sewing and sewing, sewing on and on,
> Stitch and hem, stitch and hem again,
> Oh, sweet God, you know the bitter truth,
> How my eyes do ache and my fingers pain.

Another song complained:

> No sooner in my bed
> Then I must up again
> To drag my weary limbs
> Off to work again.
>   * * *
> Why was I born to be a seamstress, why?[78]

A poem by the Yiddish writer I. L. Peretz dramatized the concerns of seamstresses in Poland: the grueling labor in the workshops, the poverty and exhaustion, and the nagging fear that in spite of their hard work they might remain old maids.

> The eyes red, the lips blue,
> No drop of blood in the cheek shows through

On the pale faces the sweat beads lie,
The breath is hot, the tongue is dry,
Three girls sit sewing.

The needle gleams, the linen snow,
One thinks to herself, I sew and sew,
I sew by day and at night I sew,
But no wedding dress for me, ah no, ah no!
What is the use of my sewing?

There is no food, no sleep for me
I would give my few pence to charity,
That God in recompense maybe
Might send an old widower for me,
Even with a host of children.[79]

In spite of long hours, physical exhaustion, and exploitation by mistresses and masters, some apprentices, especially those who showed a talent for the trade, suffered less than others. That was Mollie Wexler's experience. She described her employer, Mme. Aptheker, a Russian gentile, as "a bright woman, very intelligent, [who] treated us fairly well." Wexler recalled that "as long as you were capable of doing the work," Mme. Aptheker was "respectful." Yet even in the relatively dignified surroundings of this shop, young employees worked extremely hard. Mollie's parents did not have to pay for her training; instead she lived with Mme. Aptheker and had to do "things she wants you to do besides dressmaking." Like most apprentices Mollie had to help with the dishes and care for her teacher's children. Fortunately, her skill saved her from the more odious household chores. "There were other apprentices that weren't as capable of the work, so she let them do most of the housework, and me most of the dressmaking. I became a specialist at a very early age."[80] Gradually, she and the other apprentices received some remuneration for their work, "and naturally I gave it away to my mother because they were very much in need." By the end of her apprenticeship she had "advanced" considerably in the dressmaking trade. "I began to realize what it really means to learn the better things, you earn better, and you have a profession."[81] As one of four apprentices in Mme. Aptheker's shop, she learned hand and machine sewing from the older, more experienced girls while the mistress waited on customers and oversaw the routine of the shop. Girls and boys who apprenticed in the needle trades commonly began by learning simple and then more complicated hand operations, and finally graduated to the sewing machine.[82] An expert machine operator commanded a great deal of status in the clothing shops of early twentieth-century Russia, but many apprentices learned only the "fundamentals" of machine sewing.[83]

Some aspiring seamstresses could learn the same skills without ever enduring apprenticeship. Especially toward the end of the nineteenth century, industrial training schools emerged in the cities and larger towns. In Minsk, for example, girls could learn to sew at an industrial training school that also provided room and board. But serious shortages of equipment in these schools hampered the education of seamstresses. The Minsk school, with seventy-five pupils in 1891, had only two sewing machines.[84]

Whether a girl learned to sew through private apprenticeship, as most did, or went to a special trade school, if she succeeded she could either set up her own shop in her parent's home or continue to work for an established seamstress or tailor. When Mollie Wexler completed her apprenticeship in Brest-Litovsk, she left for Warsaw to go to work for another dressmaker: "There was a woman that lived not far from us that was also a dressmaker. She took in a little work and she didn't have any help at all. She decided to move to Warsaw and she asked my mother if she could take me along. She took me with her, and two more of my friends that I worked with went, and she took us in the house."[85]

A World in Transition

By the end of the nineteenth century, the economy in which these women helped earn a living for their families was in a state of upheaval, as was the whole way of life in the Jewish Pale of Settlement. In contrast to the frozen-in-time portrait that Elizabeth Herzog and Mark Zbrowski give us in their sentimentalized study *Life Is with People*, this was a world battered by the winds of change and dislocation. The deepening economic and political crisis wrought by these changes would encourage nearly two million Jews to leave for the United States.

The changes that were taking place had several interrelated aspects. Industrialization began to transform the economy at the same time that Czarist edicts were constricting Jewish liberties and opportunities. Both contributed to the gradual decomposition of the artisanal and petty entrepreneurial economy of the Pale, creating labor and population surpluses and widespread misery. Along with these changes came new ideologies and social movements that sought to explain and rectify the oppressive conditions of Jewish life. The tumult of these movements challenged traditional ideas and practices and eventually loosened the grip of theocratic control in the Jewish communities of eastern Europe.

In the 1880s and 1890s a series of government edicts restricting Jewish residence in the Russian Empire forced Jews into urban centers of the Pale. The May Laws of 1882 prohibited Jews from settling in rural areas, including villages where they might hope to earn a livelihood by trading in grain, timber, and other agricultural products traditionally handled by Jewish merchants.[86] The government also expelled Jews from Moscow, St. Petersburg, Kiev, and other cities of the Russian "interior" where they had resided both legally and illegally as artisans and merchants. In 1891 approximately 30,000 Jews had been driven from Moscow, and a year later 70,000 others returned to the cities and towns of the Pale from other parts of the Russian Empire. Forced to resettle in the urban areas of the Pale, they exacerbated the fierce competition for business and employment in a region already overcrowded with unskilled laborers, artisans, and petty merchants.[87] Residence restrictions not only made it difficult for Jews to trade in agricultural products but also cut them off from the large industrial centers outside the Pale. Sugar mills, mines, metal and glass works were located in areas off-limits to Jews.[88]

At the same time that legal restrictions were causing new problems, the process of commercial growth and consolidation also adversely affected some sectors of the Jewish population. The distillation and sale of liquor, for example, which had provided an income for tens of thousands of Jews, came under state monopoly by the turn of the century. Similarly the growth of the railroads threatened the thousands of independent teamsters and draymen. Furthermore, discriminatory policies of the Czarist government in letting contracts for construction projects in the Pale kept many Jewish builders and carpenters from finding employment.[89] Industrialization also threatened the livelihoods of thousands of artisans whose methods could not compete with factory production. Larger manufacturers who relied upon machinery and more sophisticated marketing techniques increasingly cut into the profits of independent Jewish producers, not only in the needle trades but also in shoemaking, weaving, and other crafts.[90]

Many craftsmen and women eventually gave up their attempt to subsist independently and began to produce for middlemen and larger stores. Others sought jobs in factories. Yet as a rule, the only factories willing to hire them were those owned by other Jews, and these tended to be small, undercapitalized, unmechanized, and poorly regulated compared to gentile-owned enterprises. Moreover, the few modern factories under Jewish ownership tended to favor gentile workers.[91] Both Jewish and gentile manufacturers discriminated against Jewish workers. Factory owners assumed that Jews would not work on the Saturday Sabbath. Russian law required employers to close their businesses on Sunday, and few manufactures could afford to shut down their factories on Saturday as well.[92] Many employers also considered Jewish artisans too backward and too attached to older methods to adapt to modern production methods. Finally, some feared Jewish radicalism and labor unrest and believed that gentile workers were more docile and less prone to strikes. Thus the masses of Russian peasants who had flocked to the cities since 1861 when the serfs received their freedom stood a better chance of finding factory employment than did Jews.[93]

These prejudices made for a difficult transition to industrial life. Craftsmen and women in the small towns held onto independent trades longer than those who worked in big cities where mass production industry was growing. But especially in urban centers, artisans could neither compete with new industries nor hope to better their lot by taking a factory job. Even in Bialystok, a boomtown of the textile industry, Jewish weavers rarely found work in the larger and better-regulated factories.[94] Economic conditions for Austro-Hungarian Jews were little better. The Galician economy was especially depressed, and a growing population of impoverished Jewish artisans haunted the land.[95]

By the 1890s overcrowding of the labor markets both for skilled and for unskilled workers resulted in widespread unemployment.[96] In every Jewish workshop and factory visited by American Immigration Commissioners in 1891, employers and workers alike exhibited an attitude of despair. In Bialystok they complained of "paralyzed trade," shrinking profits, fierce competition, and irregular employment, and they were generally pessimistic about the future.[97] These conditions prevailed into the next century. For even as industrialization created jobs, Jews lost ground because of prejudice. Squeezed out of old forms of employment, they often found themselves unwelcome in the new workshops and factories.

Anti-Semitic violence, both random and organized, further threatened the prospects for Jewish survival. Pogroms, some of them sanctioned by the government, terrorized eastern European Jews, underscoring their social and political marginality. The most famous pogrom, the bloody Kishinev massacre of 1903, served as a watershed for Jews, erasing any doubts that they stood unwanted and unprotected in their homelands.[98]

These political and economic crises were accompanied by the development of organized movements for Jewish self-defense and for the radical restructuring of the traditional way of life. The two most important were revolutionary socialism and Zionism, both of them partially rooted in a much earlier Jewish intellectual and literary movement known by its Hebrew name *Haskalah*. The Haskalah, or movement for secular enlightenment, originated in Germany. Beginning in the 1820s it spread eastward into the Russian Empire, where over the decades it underwent various transformations, finally culminating in the rise of secular Yiddish literature in the 1870s. Followers of the movement, called *maskilim*, many of them educated, middle-class, but still deeply religious Jews, believed that the key to Jewish "emancipation" and equality was the reconciliation of Judaism with modern western ideas and practices.[99]

The maskilim criticized the backwardness and provinciality of Jewish life in the Pale. They called upon eastern European Jews to "productivize" themselves and move into more practical and "dignified" (i.e., middle-class) occupations. They attributed the poverty of the Pale to entrenched economic traditions and laid the blame upon the social practices that led men to marry without adequate preparation to support a wife and a family. And they criticized the tendency of shtetl men to pursue "impractical" forms of petty mercantilism such as hawking and peddling or, in the case of scholars, "self-indulgent" study and prayer.[100]

In the manner of the European Enlightenment, the Haskalah movement saw education as the key to lifting the cloud of backwardness from Jewish life in eastern Europe and advocated secular education for both sexes. Insisting that religious teachings were insufficient to solve the practical dilemmas of Jews and, in any case, not an accurate measure of the social worth of individuals, the maskilim stressed the need for literacy and exposure to the secular teachings of modern, western society. Only through the new learning, the maskilim argued, would Jews in eastern Europe gain the tools that would enable them to become middle-class and thus win the acceptance of their gentile neighbors.[101]

This was a radical proposal, and the implications were particularly significant for women. In Russia the quota on Jewish attendance in government schools, the distrust of outside influences by Orthodox rabbis, and the Jewish bias against prolonged education for females had frustrated the ambitions of many young people but were especially hard on girls. The result, Miriam Shomer Zunser recalled, was a "sadly neglected" and abbreviated education.

> According to the custom of the time, all the education a girl needed was enough Hebrew to enable her to stumble through her prayers; enough Yiddish to enable her to write a letter and to somehow read the Ze'enah-U-Re'enah [the Yiddish Bible for women]; a rudimentary idea of arithmetic; and instruction in the special duties of a Jewish woman.[102]

The Haskalah call for extended education made a significant impact in some circles. Girls and boys growing up in *maskil* families benefited most directly from the movement's efforts. Some of them were educated by private tutors, others sought entrance into Russian schools and universities where Jews were still admitted or, failing that, went to study in Switzerland, Germany, or France.[103] But for many other Russian Jews, the idea of secular education became an aspiration rather than an immediate accomplishment.

Beyond the question of education, the Haskalah directly addressed the issue of women's place and responsibility in eastern European Jewish society. If the central concern of Haskalah literature of the 1860s, 1870s, and 1880s was the plight of the exploited, illiterate shtetl Jew, another major theme, Celia Adler points out, was the "woman as underdog," the female as "prime repository of social injustice." As the oppressed of the oppressed, women performed endless labor in the home and the marketplace but continued to suffer from patriarchal exclusion from Jewish communal life.[104]

The solution to women's individual and collective victimization, the maskilim believed, was almost an inversion of what modern feminists view as liberation: the enshrinement of domesticity as a female vocation. Influenced by western bourgeois standards, Haskalah writers such as Peretz saw domesticity as emancipation and women's economic responsibilities as exploitation and degradation. Modernization of Jewish life required shtetl women's "release" from the marketplace, redemption in the "tranquil" world of noneconomic home life, and the transfer to men of all breadwinning responsibility.[105] Such ideas won a limited acceptance in Russia but would take on a compelling new importance for those Jews who emigrated to America.

The Haskalah thrived primarily among the middle classes but paved the way for the development of far more influential movements that swept the Pale in the last decades of the nineteenth century. Out of this middle-class movement would come some of the ideas and much of the early leadership of the Zionist and socialist movements.[106]

A Jewish socialist movement had first appeared in the 1880s. With the founding in 1897 of the "General Jewish Workers' Union in Lithuania, Poland, and Russia"—better known as the Bund—the socialist movement became a significant force in Jewish political and industrial life, organizing thousands of workers in small artisans' shops and larger factories, rivaling traditional communal leaders in influence, and providing an organized basis for discontent within the Pale of Settlement. The Bund significantly broadened the Haskalah critique of traditional cultural patterns and aimed it at the religious authorities who dominated Jewish life. This critique was linked to a still-wider agenda that called simultaneously for the Jewish working classes to better their economic condition, for the Jews in Russia to improve their legal position, and for the replacement of the Czar with a socialist form of government. If the Haskalah had initiated an ideological confrontation with traditional culture, the socialist intellectuals who founded the Bund challenged the old order with new ideas and a much bolder program for social and political change.[107]

The Bundists differed greatly from, but also had much in common with, their political rivals, the Zionists. Both movements rejected the fatalistic Messianism of Orthodox Judaism, insisting that Jews should militantly defend their political, social, and ethnoreligious rights, thus providing their followers with what historian Gerald Sorin calls "new forms of Jewishness."[108] The Zionists, some of whom were socialists, claimed that the only solution to Jewish problems lay in mass emigration to Palestine and the building of a Jewish state. The Bundists rejected this agenda, criticizing Zionism as a narrow, escapist form of "bourgeois utopianism." The only acceptable program for Jewish emancipation and redemption, the Bundists insisted, was to struggle for socialist revolution on Russian soil.[109] Originally allied with the Marxist-led Russian Social Democratic Workers' party (RSDWP), by 1903 the Bund, especially in its nationalism and its claim to hold authority over the Jewish working classes, was creating serious tensions within the larger Russian revolutionary movement. Eventually the Bundists were ostracized from the Marxist mainstream.[110]

Mixing socialism and Jewish nationalism, the Bund spread its message among artisans and laborers, adopting a program of revolutionary agitation and building a secret, underground Jewish workers' movement that culminated in massive strikes in the industrial centers of the Pale. The sound of revolution could be heard in the workshops of the

Pale, as economic and political discontent spread among the Jewish laboring classes. Bessie Udin, a merchant's daughter who later went to work in America's garment industry, learned about the workers' movement from the dressmakers who rented a room in her parents' house. "I used to hear them report that 'Oh, we had such a wonderful meeting in the woods.'" Even their work songs expressed the revolutionary mood of the times.

> We're weaving, we're weaving
> We're weaving a shroud for the Czar.[111]

The Bund promised to redress the collective social and economic injuries of the Jewish masses, calling for an end to the caste structure and promising an equitable redistribution of power and authority not only in Jewish society but throughout the Russian Empire. Thus the Bund had a double agenda, aimed at both internal and external subjugation—agitation against the Czarist regime on the one hand and against the theocratic and bourgeois oppressors within the Jewish community on the other.

For Jewish seamstresses, tailors, shoemakers, weavers, domestic servants, and others who lived in the hard-pressed economic conditions of turn-of-the-century Russia, the Bund's Marxist ideology with its stress on social equality and the historic mission of the working class provided a new and welcome sense of dignity. Socialism gave them a reason for pride, a basis for denying the degradation associated with the status of manual labor in traditional Jewish society.[112]

Bundist ideology addressed the wounds and resentments of class discrimination that ran deep in shtetl society. Manual workers such as tailors and shoemakers were stigmatized as *proste yidn*, inferior Jews. Rabbis and religious scholars, no matter how poor, were always considered *sheyne yidn*. Well-to-do persons, if they assumed philanthropic and charitable obligations to the community, were also highly respected. The combination of religious education and wealth assured high social status, though money by itself did not confer respectability.[113]

Many aspects of shtetl life reflected the wide gulf between the social elites and the masses of Jews. The sheyne yidn felt superior to the artisans and common workers and avoided social contact with them. Some towns had separate synagogues for artisans; in other cases, although the two classes worshiped together, the sheyne occupied the front rows of the synagogue and the proste sat in back. "Life in a *klain shtetl* [little village] is full of class differences," the son of a tailor from the Podolia region of Russia recalled. "I couldn't play with certain children because my father was an ordinary tailor."[114] Conversely, May Horowitz, the daughter of a Minsk store owner, remembered, "I couldn't even mingle or be friends with a worker."[115] Lottie Spitzer, whose parents owned a jewelry business in Russia, was also forbidden to socialize with workers because her mother came from a wealthy and educated family. Lottie explained that "to her, it was a disgrace that I talked to a . . . tailor. . . . And a maid, that was for sure I couldn't talk to a maid."[116]

The same considerations affected the marriage arrangements parents made for their daughters and sons. Marriage might lead to upward or downward mobility in the shtetl. Depending upon circumstances, a family could improve its class position by marrying a daughter to a learned man or face humiliation if she ran off with an ordinary worker. The desire to maintain or acquire social status through marriage forced parents to protect their children from liaisons with people of a lower social station. As Miriam Shomer Zunser recalled:

> In those days seeking a wife did not mean looking for a girl. It meant searching for a family, for *yiches*—pedigree, or caste, if you will. The girl was really the last thing to be considered. Of prime importance were not only her immediate forebears, but those of generations back. . . . Although affluence and influence were considerations of importance, *yiches* usually involved learning and scholarship.[117]

Another woman explained that in her family, "We couldn't marry just anybody. I remember there was a *bocher* [young man] courting my sister. He came from Odessa and was a tailor. He also came from a tailor family. . . . He was rich, and he was good looking, and he wanted to marry my eldest sister." Despite the young man's wealth, the family intervened to prevent the match. The girl's uncles were astounded that her mother could "even think of marrying her first daughter to a *shnaider* [tailor] from a '*prosteh*' family."[118]

Although the Bund could not do away with these prejudices, it did provide a framework and a language for addressing them. As a challenge to the entrenched values and leadership of Orthodox Jewish society, the movement provided a lightning rod for dissent and unrest of all kinds and symbolized the growing struggles between the forces of tradition and the winds of modernity. As several historians have noted, the Bund itself understood socialism not only as a program for a new political and economic order but as a blueprint for a new secular civilization.[119]

That blueprint significantly challenged the traditional place of workers. And in a manner different from the Haskalah, it also addressed the
predicaments of women in Jewish society. Thousands of Jewish girls
were drawn into the movement. Something like one-third of the Bund's
membership consisted of unmarried women from both middle- and
working-class homes. In a sense they became the new folk heroines of
the younger generation of women. Transporting arms, ammunition,
and illegal literature, working in underground printing shops turning
out contraband leaflets and manifestos, serving as labor organizers and
agitators, making speeches, and sitting on both local and central committees of the Bund, Jewish women played a considerable part in the
successes of the radical movement in the Pale.[120]

Women derived from the socialist movement a sense of personal
dignity and importance available nowhere else in Jewish society. With
their commitment to the principle of social equality, Jewish socialists
moved tentatively toward the idea of gender equality. The notion was
rarely elevated to the level of an articulated party position, but in
practice the Bund afforded women a new kind of public authority and
responsibility that clearly implied a greater, though not a perfect, sense
of equality.[121] Women and men would together make the revolution as
comrades in the struggle. A popular song of the radical movement
captured this ethos:

> *Genug shoyn tsu sholfn, ir shvester un brider. Vacht oyf! Fareynigt aych!*
> *Zet as ale zoln zayn glaych.* Cease your slumbering, sisters and brothers.
> Awake! Unite! See to it that all . . . are equal.[122]

Even the Bund's hymn, the *Shvue* ("Oath") sung at meetings and demonstrations, proclaimed that the class struggle would be carried out by
"brider un shvester fun arbet un noyt"—brothers and sisters of work
and need.[123] Thus the socialists not only gave workers a new dignity but
promised women a legitimate political role as well. Women would now
be partners in the class struggle just as they had been partners in the
struggle to earn a living. For growing numbers of young women who
resented the inferior status of females, this idea proved extremely compelling.

Teenage dressmaker Mollie Wexler was just one of thousands of
young women who were drawn into the radical movement. She recalled
in detail her initiation into revolutionary politics in Warsaw:

> We found out from other people that there's going to be a meeting in the
> park. Students are coming to tell us how to improve the conditions of the

2. Members of the Jewish Workers' Bund, Gabin, Poland, 1908. YIVO Institute for Jewish Research.

workers. The fact was that they wanted to acquaint us with the idea that there was going to be an overthrow of the Czar, but they couldn't talk about it freely. We found out that workers must be together to demand something. I'll never forget, I thought it was so sensible!

When the leaders asked for volunteer organizers, Mollie stepped forward. "They looked at me, I would probably be too young, but it was all right." To be taken seriously by the leadership of the movement filled her with pride. "It was a joy to think that they [girls] were called upon. Imagine, my mother couldn't get over it, she couldn't believe it."[124] Yet for Mollie Wexler, as for most young people in the movement, gender equality was never as important as working-class equality. Whatever social equality women gained was usually a consequence of their radical activities, not the result of agitation on behalf of women's needs.

In many respects the Bund was a generational phenomenon, a rebellion of laboring- and middle-class young people against what they considered the archaic principles and restrictions of Orthodox Jewish society. Above all, affiliation with the revolutionary movement gave

Jewish youth of both sexes a feeling of belonging, a sense that as *"brider un shvester"* they were part of a larger-than-life struggle for the liberation of mankind. Young women and men who joined the movement viewed themselves as a kind of revolutionary "family." They addressed each other as *"chaver"* (comrade, friend) or *"bekante"* (known ones) and found in the movement what historian Ezra Mendelsohn called "a new framework of conventions within which to live and work." Complete with its own holidays, terminology, songs, literature, secret meeting places, and revolutionary institutions, the Bundist movement gave Jewish youth a new identity, purpose, and program for righting the wrongs of Jewish and Russian society.[125]

Radicalism, with its modern orientation, became a new faith for some of the young. Dressmaker Brucha Gutrajman, who joined the Bund as a teenager, insisted that "we opened wide the generation gap." Though she still paid lip-service to the traditions of her parents and tried to minimize their concern, she along with many of her socialist peers increasingly distanced themselves from the strict Orthodoxy of their upbringing and threw themselves into the secular struggles of the movement.[126] Michael Charnofsky, who grew up in a small town in the Ukraine, recalled that in his shtetl, "the dawn of the twentieth century was talked about by young and old." But the generations frequently disagreed on what shape the future would take. The old people, he said, "predicted that in this century the messiah would come and liberate the whole world. . . . The Jews, God's children, would be back in their homeland." The Orthodox elders quoted from the great Jewish philosophers to make their point and "demanded that the people start getting ready." But many among the shtetl youth were "amused" rather than inspired by these Orthodox prophesies. Young intellectuals offered their own predictions: "They talked about social and economic changes in the twentieth century, great scientific advances and a free society."[127]

Every summer radical students from the cities returned home to the shtetlekh talking of revolution, of freedom and equality. To the Orthodox Jewish community leaders this activity seemed dangerous and threatening, but young people of all classes often perceived the radicals as romantic figures. One Jewish immigrant from Russia remembered that radical students home for the holidays "talked a different language, dressed differently, and everybody in the shtetl regarded them as outlaws. The religious Jews in the shtetl said that they brought trouble to the village, but I used to envy them."[128] Rose Pesotta, who would later become an organizer in America's garment shops, recalled that the evening meetings of the revolutionary reading circles attended by seamstresses, tailors, shoemakers, and itinerant workers provided an "escape from the monotony of everyday existence."[129] Living in what she called the "sleepy backwater" of the Pale of Settlement, Eva Broido, daughter of a Torah scholar and a working mother, was introduced to revolutionary politics in that way. With their radical ideas and their bright hopes for the future, these students brought "fresh vigor to our stagnant life," she recalled.[130] Rebelling against parental concerns about social respectability and religious Orthodoxy, some middle-class daughters and sons went off to the cities to join in the activities of the radical movement and, as a final act of defiance, to take a job in a factory or to learn a trade.[131] A Russian Jewish boy who "wanted to learn a trade" but knew that his father would "never agree to this . . . as he was of high 'yiches' [status]" remembered how much of an impact the Bundists had upon him. "A friend took me for the first time to a gathering of a small group of the Bund, and I was surprised to hear their respect for the proletariat, and that gave me the courage to speak to father."[132]

Working-class daughters and sons also risked arrest, internment, and of course parental opprobrium by joining the movement. Esther Frumkin, who helped spread the revolutionary message among Jewish wage earners, recalled the sense of danger and excitement that political involvement created and "how many tragedies young workers would suffer at home if it became known that they were running around with the *Akhdusnikes*, with the 'brothers and sisters'" of the Bund.[133]

"All this had to be done secretly of course," a former Bundist explained, "because it was against the law." His house in Russia was always filled with "yugent"—young people, friends of his brother and sister. "They would have all kinds of cultural and political meetings." The group kept a "gelatine board for hectographing pamphlets," and "we even kept ammunition in the house." Although "mamma never liked what went on in the house . . . there was nothing she could do about it." When the Jews of his village suspected there might be a police raid, his mother would protect her children and their friends by carrying their ammunition and hectograph board out into the fields behind the house.[134]

The Bund grew rapidly within the Jewish communities of the Pale of Settlement. By the opening of this century it boasted some 30,000 members, but its influence stretched far beyond its actual numbers. Establishing itself as a potent political force not only in Jewish life but in the broader revolutionary movement of the Russian Empire, the organization reached its peak of strength in 1905 as Jewish workers and intellectuals alike rallied to its calls for revolution.

On the heels of the bloody St. Petersburg workers' uprising of January 9, 1905, revolutionary agitation quickly spread to other cities and towns. Local committees of the Bund played a major part in the uprising, especially in the western provinces. Working alone or in conjunction with gentile revolutionaries, they published and distributed revolutionary propaganda, organized meetings, strikes, and demonstrations, captured government offices, and battled Czarist troops.[135] But because of its major role in the failed revolution, the Bund suffered seriously from the Czarist repression that followed. Anti-Semitism reached a fever pitch at the end of 1905 as Jews were blamed for the revolutionary uprisings, and a renewed wave of pogroms quickly followed. As revolutionary leaders were arrested or killed, many Bundists avoided the Czarist police by fleeing to America.[136]

The experiences of Dora Bayrack's household must have been familiar to thousands. She tells of the escalating fear of arrest and the subsequent emigration of her sisters. In the aftermath of the 1905 revolution, she recalled:

> Things became more strict than even before, and for any little thing they arrested young people. My father was afraid, so my oldest sister went to America. She was mixed up with the movement. And they came to arrest her, and we sent her away to America. And then the second sister was the same thing, was mixed up with the working movement. And the third sister they also sent away, because they were afraid that she's going to get mixed up. I was not involved in anything because my father was very strict at that time. To get rid of three daughters was not so easy for him. But he was afraid for me too, so they sent me away. I was fifteen and a half.[137]

Emigration

By 1905 much had changed for Jews in eastern Europe. Not only had secular and revolutionary movements challenged traditional patterns of thought and behavior, but changing economic and political restrictions had increased the sense of Jewish vulnerability and marginality. Although the response of many was to stay and persevere, millions of others reasoned that the prospects for family and communal survival were dim. Between 1880 and 1910 over a million Jews left Czarist Russia to settle in the United States, and over the next decade another million followed. This outflow began slowly in the 1880s and 1890s, as economic dislocation forced many people to look abroad for another source of income. The migration peaked in the years 1905 and 1906, amid political repression and the pogroms that followed the 1905 revolution. Emigrants continued to leave the Pale in substantial numbers until the 1920s when American immigration restrictions finally cut off the exodus.

The emigrants came largely from the most overcrowded regions of the Pale of Settlement, the northwest provinces of Lithuania and White Russia—areas where economic competition between struggling artisans and newer industries was most intense, and where the socialist labor organizers of the Bund had their greatest successes. Yet large numbers also came from southern and southwestern Russia and Galicia. Romania, where anti-Semitic activity was particularly virulent, also sent many Jews to America. Among the emigrants were substantial numbers of skilled artisans as well as laborers and so-called *luftmentchen*—those with no regular occupation. It was, like most large population movements, a migration of young people. Of those Jews who arrived in the United States between 1880 and 1914, 70 percent were in the "working ages" between fourteen and forty-four years.[138]

Every migrant family had its own compelling reasons for seeking a new life in the United States. For many, the desperate need to earn a living and the gnawing fear of pogroms were sufficient inducements to leave. Mollie Linker recalled how mounting uncertainties, both political and economic, encroached upon her family in Moghilev, Russia. Her father left for the United States in 1910, and the rest of the family followed over the next four years.

> I remember sitting by the window . . . and looking out. When it got dark, you close the shutters, you were afraid. You were actually always in fear because of big *pogroms*. In that town wasn't much, but there was the fear. I remember that scare . . . was in us all the time. Then my father left for America to better himself. He was a scholar. He did work for a while as a bookkeeper in another town, but children were born, you know. He had a sister here [in America], and she thought maybe here he can do a little better; so she sent him a ticket.[139]

When asked why she wanted to leave for America, Sarah Deborah Fodiman explained that, try as she might, she could find no work. At the age of thirty-eight, this mother of nine went looking for a job making artificial flowers, work she had done before she married. Her husband had left his bakery business in Minsk the year before and had emigrated to America, where he thought it would be easier to earn a living. Hearing of opportunities for flowermakers in the United States, she hoped to join him soon.[140] For Myer Abrahamson, a watchmaker who had been forced by residence restrictions to leave Moscow, emigration to America seemed like a better prospect than returning to the Pale where there were already too many in his trade.[141] One housewife living on the outskirts of Minsk expressed the feelings of many economically hard-pressed Jews when she said: "Our lives are lost, but we want to alleviate the condition of our children."[142] For millions like her, America promised to fulfill this hope.

Mary Antin summarized part of the dilemma that led millions to view America as a final destination. Growing up in the town of Polotzk, she experienced the atmosphere of physical confinement and the over-crowding of occupations typical of many places within the Pale during the last years of the nineteenth century.

> It was not easy to live, with such bitter competition as the congestion of the population made inevitable. There were ten times as many stores as there should have been, ten times as many tailors, cobblers, barbers, tinsmiths. A Gentile, if he failed in Polotzk, could go elsewhere, where there was less competition. A Jew could make the circle of the Pale, only to find the same conditions as at home.[143]

These conditions, along with political repression, made emigrating Jews feel that once they left for America, there was nothing worth returning to.

News about American opportunities reached prospective emigrants through letters from relatives and *landsleit* (countrymen and women). By the turn of the century, glowing stories about the successes of earlier immigrants circulated among the residents of shtetl and city alike. In the midst of economic and political crisis, such stories provided a new basis of faith. Countless young people read the letters that arrived from America and, like one woman, believed that "everyone in America was a friend to strangers and . . . it was an easy country to make money in."[144] Even children's lullabies sang the praises of America and conjured up images of a land of plenty.

> In America, they say
> There is never any dearth.
> It's a paradise for all
> A real heaven on earth.[145]

Jacob Doroshkin, an immigrant from Russia, explained that Jewish workers in early twentieth-century Russia put much faith in the notion that great prosperity awaited immigrants who went to the United States.

"It was a well-known fact," he recalled, "that as soon as one came to America, one earned money."[146] Similarly, Jewish girls at the sewing school in Minsk heard about opportunities for seamstresses in New York from former classmates who had already emigrated. Their letters reported that garment workers were paid three or four dollars a week to begin with—as much as many seamstresses in Russia might expect to earn in a month. Not realizing that the cost of living in America was twice as high as in Russia, the girls could not help but be impressed.[147]

Migration was not a new economic strategy for Jews. They had long moved from shtetl to larger towns and big cities searching for a means to earn a living. This inter- and intraregional migration had primarily involved individuals—daughters, sons, husbands—who left home on a temporary basis. The pattern of overseas migration differed dramatically; it was a movement of families determined to make a permanent home in America.

Economic motivations provided major push and pull factors. But a range of other concerns also fueled the Jewish exodus. Some of the men wanted to escape the military draft; others feared arrest for illegal political activities; and still more hoped to find in the United States more fertile soil for the growth of a newer and freer social order, particularly after the failure of the 1905 revolution in Russia.

Some migrants simply longed for a vague but powerful state of mind they called "freedom."[148] The intellectual and radical movements of Haskalah and socialism had unleashed disquieting challenges to the traditions of Jewish life, and many imagined that the promises of those movements could be better fulfilled elsewhere.

Jewish youths whose values had been influenced by the socialist movement looked forward to the prospect of a more democratic society, free from the stigmas of class and social status. As Joseph Morgenstern, an immigrant from Lithuania, recalled, "the the idea of going to America was based on the certainty that a worker there was a respected human being, that no one in the United States was ashamed of hard work."[149] Rose Pesotta said she emigrated in part because she wanted to live in a society where ordinary workers commanded respect. In America, Pesotta thought, "a decent middle-class girl can work without disgrace." Had she remained in Russia her only choice, given her upbringing, would be to marry and become a housewife, a future that had little appeal to her.[150]

For others, "freedom" had a more transcendent meaning. A son of Russian Jews who went to Paris in the early part of this century described his parents' reasons for emigrating in terms that also applied to those who went to America: "I can write without falsehood that my parents fled the police repression of 1905. This, however, was only incidental; they fled from their families, from nineteenth-century morality, from fanaticism and bigotry, and to a certain extent, they fled from themselves."[151]

Young people were especially likely to view their journey as one that would bring the personal freedom they could never attain in the Old World. Like other teenagers, Fannie Edelman wanted to leave the restrictive boundaries of shtetl and home life. She explained that emigration was the only means of escaping the marriage her father planned to arrange for her. Only in America, she thought, could she "fall in love and marry." If she stayed in Russia her father would have his own way. "I was fourteen years old when I heard that people were leaving for the United States," recollected Edelman. "I used to think of running away from our little town and from my severe father and coming to a free world called America."[152]

Prior to their migration, many young Jews took trips to larger towns and cities and were filled with a longing for change and excitement. Mary Antin recalled how the periodic visits she made to her relatives in the city of Vitebsk, where there were "magnificent avenues and . . . splendid shops and houses," opened her eyes to the possibilities of life outside the small town of Polotzk. "Vitebsk was a metropolis beside provincial Polotzk," she remembered thinking.[153] This fascination with the world beyond the shtetl came in time to be focused upon America. "All my life I have wanted to come to this country [America]," one seventeen-year-old Jewish immigrant woman explained in 1915; "I had friends here and I heard so much about it . . . I was not at all afraid. I was just excited. I didn't like to leave my mother, but she wouldn't come, and I just had to."[154]

Still another young immigrant said she left her home in Lithuania in 1909 because "the house was like a Gehenna" (a hell). "Besides me, my parents had five more unmarried daughters. My father was a Hebrew teacher. We used to help out by plucking chickens, making cigarettes, washing clothes for people, and we lived in poverty. . . . There was always yelling, cursing, and beating of each other. It was bitter for me until a cousin of mine took pity on me. He sent a steamship ticket and money. He wrote that I should come to America and he would marry me."[155]

Others emigrated hoping to further their education. Jewish prejudices against women's education were strong, and anti-Semitism in Russia further blocked chances for schooling. Girls like Mollie Wexler lived with the constant reminder that school was a luxury for Jews in Russia. Mollie was seven years old when she began to wonder about her chances for education. "I began to see children go to school with books, and I told my mother that I'd like to go. . . . And she said, [you] can't do it, you have to pay for it [because of] the Czar." When she tried to enter a government school she and several other Jewish children were turned away. "Because the law under the Czar was that only three Jewish children could get into a class of one hundred gentile children. And these three children had to be children of merchants of the city, wealthy people, the others no."[156] Dora Bayrack was luckier: her father had "pull" with the local authorities and succeeded in getting her into school. "Up to that time I used to look through the window and see children go to school and my heart used to go out." Even so, family responsibilities interfered. When her mother fell sick, Dora left school to take care of her. "I was considered the oldest because the other daughters were away." On the eve of her migration to America, she still "craved for education."[157] The dream of schooling in America was a powerful attraction for many girls. "My whole hope was coming to this country to get an education," Fannie Shapiro explained. "I heard so much about America a free country for the Jews and you . . . didn't have to pay for schooling, so I came."[158]

The economic, political, and social oppression of eastern European Jews shaped the nature of their emigration, giving it several distinctive qualities. Nearly half (an estimated 43 percent) of the Jewish emigrants were women, compared to only 21 percent of southern Italians. Among all the immigrant groups who left for America in the nineteenth and twentieth centuries, only the Irish sent a greater proportion of women (52.9 percent). The presence of so many women reflected the special urgency of Jewish emigration. Unlike many other European emigrants, few Jews from eastern Europe intended to return. Political repression, anti-Semitism, and economic distress created a feeling of desperation and hopelessness, and the vast majority of Jews who left Russia did so for good. Italians, Poles, Bohemians, and many other emigrants from eastern and southern Europe often aimed to earn enough money to make a better life for themselves when they eventually returned to their land of origin. For non-Jews from eastern and southern Europe, the estimated rates of return ranged from 25 to 60 percent. Return rates for Magyars ran as high as 64 percent, for Slovaks 59 percent. Approximately 56 percent of central and southern Italians returned to their homelands. In contrast, the estimated return rate for eastern European Jews was a mere 2 to 3 percent.[159]

The permanence of Jewish resettlement was not the only distinctive aspect of their migration experience. More than any group except the Irish, Jews considered women as appropriate participants in the avant-garde of the overseas movement. Rarely was it possible for the entire family to emigrate at one time, and many years often elapsed before its members could be reunited. For most ethnic groups, males led the migration, and in the first decade of Jewish migration Jews followed the same course. Before the turn of the century the husband usually made the journey first, sent for the working-age children, and eventually arranged for his wife and the youngest family members to emigrate.

But after a network of relatives and countrymen and countrywomen upon whom they could depend was established in American cities, Jewish families adopted a new, more dramatic strategy for resolving their economic predicament. In growing numbers, Jewish families were willing and found it practicable to send one or more children including their working-age daughters, in advance. Artisans, factory workers, merchants, and others who found it difficult to make a living in Russia began to allow their daughters to travel to America ahead of the rest of the immediate family.

Daughters who might have otherwise entered the sewing trades or tried to find factory work in Russia left for the United States, where it was hoped they could earn a better living. Although the trades in Russia were overcrowded, the clothing industry in New York, Chicago, Philadelphia, and other cities was rapidly expanding. Families hoped their daughters would find employment and earn enough money to bring over the rest of the household. The experiences of one Russian Jewish family suggest the pattern. The husband's grain business had fallen on hard times, and a relative in America offered to look after their daughter until she had "worked herself up" and could send for her parents. "So we sent our sixteen-year-old daughter to America and we remained at home," the mother explained.[160] In another family the father could not support his household on the money he earned working in a match factory. With five children to feed he concluded that the only solution was to borrow the money to send his sixteen-year-old daughter to New York, so that she could find a job in a garment factory.[161]

The full extent of this practice is difficult to determine. Certainly it was uncommon among most immigrant groups. The major exception was the Irish, among whom the migration of single women, either alone or in the company of other females, was the rule in the nineteenth century.[162] For eastern European Jews, the practice, though not typical, was frequent enough to come to the attention of philanthropic agencies.

In one single year, 1909 to 1910, the Council of Jewish Women met with nearly 5,000 unmarried Jewish women who arrived at the Ellis Island immigration station in New York harbor. Some were joining relatives, others were the first of their families to arrive. Significantly, two-thirds of them reported they had been clothing workers, predominantly seam-stresses, prior to emigration.[163] Even the memoirs and autobiographies of immigrants commented on the practice of sending an avant-garde of daughters to the United States. In the towns and cities of Russia and Poland, nearly every Jew knew of some family with a daughter in the United States. Elizabeth Hasanovitz, who migrated shortly after the Triangle Shirtwaist factory fire in 1911, recalled how news of the disas-ter had reverberated throughout her small shtetl in Russia: "I still remember what a panic that news caused in our town when it first came. Many a family had their young daughters in all parts of the United States who worked in shops. And as most of these old parents had an idea of America as one big town, each of them was almost sure that their daughter was a victim of that terrible catastrophe."[164]

The consequences of this mass migration for young people were cultural as well as personal. As children and teenagers moving to a new country, they would constitute a transitional generation, a generation steeped in the ways of the shtetl but young and malleable enough to move easily between two cultural worlds. These young women, and the thousands who emigrated with parents and relatives, had come from a world where patriarchy and theocracy had been mediated by a wage-earning partnership between women and men, where the position of workers and of women had been challenged by the critical ideology of secular movements, and where a traditional society of artisans and independent producers was decomposing under the impact of economic and political change. The new American world they were entering was itself in the throes of a major transformation. Daughters of the shtetl would become important participants in that process, witnessing as well as shaping its outcome.

2 Mothers and Daughters

Remaking the Jewish Family Economy
in America

At sixteen she came to America. As a skilled dressmaker she easily
found work, but was never paid her worth.... Living on three dollars a
week, doing her own washing and ironing and mending, she saved the
rest of the money in order to bring her people over here.[1]

"Without passports or anything," Mollie Wexler and several
friends from her town in Russia left for New York in 1913. "We went to
Poland by train from Brest-Litovsk. It took eight hours, and from
Poland we went over the German borderline, and on to Antwerp. And
we took a boat, a big beautiful boat. And off we went, five of us girls. It
took about ten days. We went third class, with the poverty-stricken, but
it was lively, everybody talking and looking forward to God knows
what kind of future it was going to be."[2]

Two years earlier, another Jewish immigrant woman had traveled
alone from her small shtetl in the Ukraine to join her father in New
York. As Rose Kaplan neared the end of the journey, her thoughts
turned more and more to the prospective family reunion. But when the
ship finally pulled into New York harbor, it encountered delays caused
by the Labor Day holiday, and the immigrants could not land for several
days. Growing impatient, the families and friends of many other pas-
sengers hired special boats to take the new arrivals ashore, but Rose
Kaplan's father did not appear until the second day. "My father didn't
come. That was my first disappointment in America. Then there were a
lot more."[3]

Rose Kaplan and Mollie Wexler had much in common with other

Jewish daughters who came to the United States in the early part of this century. Saying goodbye to relatives and friends, they embarked upon a journey into an uncertain future. Rose went to join her father and sister, but Mollie, having no relatives in the new country, went to live in a "home" for Jewish immigrant girls. Though their immediate circumstances differed, as newcomers they faced the challenges of adjusting to unfamiliar conditions of daily life; and as young people they were not spared the burdens of responsibility for daily economic survival.

The presence of relatives and *landsleit* (countrymen and countrywomen) eased the process of resettlement, but with or without a network of support the process of adjustment frequently proved difficult and frustrating. Entering the United States for the first time, Jewish immigrants from eastern Europe confronted not only a new physical setting but a whole range of personal challenges. Immigration officials tested their patience, the urban landscape bombarded their senses and taught them new survival skills, and a variety of decisions about where and how they would begin their new lives in America enabled some and forced others to reconsider the customs and beliefs of the Old World.

First Encounters

For all new arrivals, the first contact with American institutions took place in the cold, inhospitable atmosphere of the immigrant-processing centers. Coming to "the promised land" from her home in Russia in 1885, young Emma Goldman described her first day on American soil as "a violent shock." The scenes at Castle Garden immigration station in New York appalled her. Nowhere, Goldman recalled, could she find a "sympathetic official face," and nowhere could new arrivals, least of all the pregnant women and young children, find provisions for their comfort.[4]

By the turn of the century Ellis Island had replaced Castle Garden as the immigration station for New York, and it quickly came to be known in a variety of languages as "the Isle of Tears."[5] Although Ellis Island had more amenities for the new arrivals, an elaborate bureaucratic apparatus continued to exclude immigrants thought to be medically or socially undesirable. Did they carry a contagious disease? Did they have a criminal record? What kind of work had they done in the Old Country? And what kind of job did they expect to hold in America? To whom and to what address were they going? Wrong answers could mean delays of hours or days or even result in deportation. On a typical day close to half of the Jewish immigrants processed at Ellis Island might be detained by government agents.[6] All that one Jewish woman recalled of her experience at the immigration station was the "crowds of waiting people."[7]

Young women traveling alone underwent a special kind of scrutiny at Ellis Island. Every year after 1900 several thousand young single Jewish women emigrated to the United States by themselves. Although girls under sixteen were not supposed to be admitted without an accompanying parent, many lied about their age to avoid deportation or detention.[8] Most young women traveling alone planned to join relatives and friends who had sent them steamship tickets. But some financed their own passage and came to the United States to seek out distant relatives or friends from the Old Country.[9] In either case, women who came to the United States on their own often shared concerns different from those of women who arrived in the company of their parents.

Even before they had left their homes in Russia and other parts of eastern Europe, Jewish girls had been frightened by stories of prostitution rings that preyed upon unaccompanied females on the ships and at the seaports. Their fears were not unfounded. The Jewish underworld made a steady profit by supplying the brothels of eastern Europe, Latin America, and the Near East with "white slaves." One study has estimated that in 1909 half of the prostitutes in Buenos Aires were Jewish women, presumably transported from the poverty-stricken regions of eastern Europe.[10] The Jewish press in Russia carried lurid reports of abductions and sales of girls into brothels, and parents often warned their daughters not to speak to men while en route to America.

Lottie Spitzer, recalling preparations to leave her home in Russia in 1910, remembered how worried parents, including her own, "attached" their daughters to other families in order to protect them for the duration of the journey.[11] But often such arrangements proved impossible, and many young women made the trip in the company of young friends or traveled by themselves. In 1906 Fannie Shapiro arrived by herself at Ellis Island. Like so many of her contemporaries she had heard stories of "nice-looking" girls snatched from ships and transported to Argentina or some other exotic place to become prostitutes. Convinced of her own vulnerability, she panicked when her uncle showed up to take her home from the immigration station. Without his old-country beard and side-locks he looked like a total stranger. "I didn't recognize him. And he comes to the gate, and they open the gate and call his name and mine, and I wouldn't go." Eventually he persuaded her not to be afraid. "I was shivering," she remembered, "but I went."[12]

Fearful and alone, Jewish girls sometimes took special precautions to avoid contact with strange men. Arriving at Ellis Island, they were relieved to find that immigration agents were also concerned about their safety. Most important, the agents took steps to ensure that women on their own were released only into the custody of friends or relatives who could prove they were suitable guardians.[13] When Sylvia Bernstein came to New York in 1914, she and the other women traveling alone felt "constantly watched" by the agents at Ellis Island. "They were very nice," she insisted, but also "very strict. . . . But it was of comfort," she admitted. "They watch you. If you go out, there's a woman go after you," she recalled. "You are going to a brother?" they asked her. "Would you recognize your brother, if you'd see him?"[14]

Other assistance came from representatives and agents of philanthropic groups such as the Council of Jewish Women, who stationed themselves at Ellis Island. They acted as interpreters for women and children, contacted their relatives and friends, and arranged transportation to the city and provided other services for female arrivals. If no one showed up to take a woman off the island, or if relatives could not be contacted by telegram or letter, the council and other Jewish welfare agencies provided temporary guardianship. For the unattached woman stranded at the immigration station, such agencies eliminated the possibility of indefinite detainment. During Mollie Wexler's first weeks in New York, she stayed at a home for Jewish girls on Delancey Street. "They took us off [Ellis Island] and we stayed there. I wasn't married and I didn't have any family." Without the agency "there would have been a problem," she explained.[15]

Having endured the examinations, the questioning, and the waiting, Jewish arrivals set out to find their new homes. An estimated 64 percent of all Jewish immigrants arriving in the period between 1899 and 1910 headed for New York's Lower East Side; others made their way to Philadelphia, Boston, Chicago, and other cities, attracted by the presence of relatives and landsleit or by job opportunities. By 1905 an estimated 600,000 Russian Jews had settled in New York, 60,000 in Chicago, and 55,000 in Philadelphia.[16] Wherever they settled, Jews congregated in their own neighborhoods and ghettos. When Jewish immigrants from eastern Europe began arriving in American cities in the 1880s, relatively few had friends and countrymen to greet them. But by the turn of the century, as writer Abraham Cahan would observe, America no longer seemed "a land of mystery."[17] In the following decades the migration of hundreds of thousands of Jewish immigrants from Russia, Poland, Romania, Galicia, and other parts of Austria-

Hungary transformed once-isolated pockets of settlement in American cities into thriving ethnic communities.

The noise, the bustle, the congestion and confusion of American cities invariably impressed the new arrivals. Some Jewish immigrants had lived in eastern European cities, others had visited a big city, perhaps in transit to America, and many had known only the life of the small shtetl. But whatever their previous urban experience, immigrants expressed amazement at the scale and pace of big-city life in America.

Immigrants unfamiliar with city life found the atmosphere of the Lower East Side of New York particularly disorienting. Especially where the vast majority of Jewish immigrants settled, the density of population matched or exceeded that of any city in the world. By the early twentieth century as many as a thousand people were crammed into each acre of the Lower East Side neighborhood between Broadway and the East River.[18] The streets, one immigrant remembered, sent forth "a symphony of discordant noises" as men, women and children carried out their business by screaming and yelling at one another.[19] New arrivals from the shtetl felt strange, uneasy, "out of place."[20] Pauline Newman, who arrived in New York from a small shetel in Lithuania in 1901 and would spend many years of her youth in New York's garment factories, could hardly believe her eyes when she first walked down Hester and Essex streets on the East Side. "I never saw so many people on the streets, shouting, going in all directions. Having come from a little bit of a village with a few houses, it was to say the least disturbing."[21]

If the streets proved unsettling to some new arrivals, others found them full of excitement. A sense of wonder, even elation, at the unfamiliar, the bizarre, the unimaginable commotion and landscape of the city reaffirmed their hopes for a new and better future. The human energy of the streets, the displays in shop windows, the height of the buildings, the glow of the street lamps, the modern fashions, all provided a feast for the eyes of immigrants from small and relatively primitive towns in eastern Europe. Before she went to work with her father in a New York clothing factory, Rose Cohen spent her first week getting accustomed to New York. At first she felt "dazed" by her surroundings. "As I had never seen a large city and only had a glimpse of a small one, I thought these things [were] only true of America."[22] When Jennie Matyas arrived from her small village in Hungary in 1905, she could scarcely contain her amazement at her first sight of children on the streets of New York. Like other young people in her native village, she was accustomed to going barefoot. "It must have been about

3. Orchard Street, 1898, the heart of the Lower East Side ghetto. Some immigrant daughters took comfort in this environment; others found it too confusing. Byron Collection, Museum of the City of New York.

three o'clock in the afternoon when we were taken out of Ellis Island and we came on one of these open horse-drawn cars in New York City, and I looked around to see the terrifically tall buildings. I saw all these children and they were dressed with *shoes and stockings on!*" Having seen such a display only on holidays, Matyas reasoned that there must have been some special celebration. Why else would children be dressed so well? It took some minutes before her father could convince her that American children regularly wore shoes and stockings.[23]

Even as immigrants found much that was new and jarring in American city life, they also discovered many reminders of the Old World. On the Lower East Side of New York, as in the Jewish neighborhoods of Chicago, Boston, and other large cities with substantial immigrant populations, Jews settled down among thousands of their coreligionists from eastern Europe in a neighborhood far removed from the "uptown" world of gentile Americans. Though much about this new existence seemed foreign, life in an immigrant enclave such as the Lower East Side offered a large measure of comfortable familiarity. The homey "sing-song" of Yiddish-speaking pushcart peddlers and vendors, the traditional Old Country garb worn by Orthodox men and women, and the myriad of shops hung with Yiddish and Hebrew signs recalled remnants of the life they had left behind, providing newcomers with an initial sense of security.[24] "Only the heavy shadows of elevated trains thundering above . . . spoke of another world," remembered one immigrant; everything else was reminiscent of home.[25]

But the Lower East Side of New York, like other immigrant ghettos, did not belong to east European Jews alone. The neighborhood housed a mixture of immigrant groups. Jews from eastern Europe shared the streets with Italians, Syrians, Slovaks, Germans, Irish, and Poles. By the turn of the century these neighborhoods burst with a host of cultures, each with its own institutions and language. Sharing neighborhoods but usually not other aspects of social life, each group established its own religious and benevolent organizations, its own newspapers, cafes, restaurants, theaters, and business establishments. And although immigrants of many nationalities did business with one another and often worked side by side in the same factories, ethnic groups kept a comfortable social distance from each other.[26]

Jewish immigrants themselves lent cultural diversity to urban neighborhoods. Although east European Jews from various nations had much in common culturally, they did not constitute a homogeneous social community. A vast array of social types and a multitude of backgrounds and dispositions characterized the population. They came from different regions of eastern Europe, spoke different Yiddish dialects, and practiced different customs. The Jewish ghetto in New York constituted what journalist Abraham Cahan called "a human hodge-podge with its component parts changed but not yet fused into one homogeneous whole."[27]

The heterogeneity of Jewish immigrants was reflected in their organizational life. Immigrants created institutions that maintained regional and local ties from the Old Country, the *landsmanschaftn*—societies of immigrants from the same towns in Europe. Immigrants from Bialystok, Bobruisk, Dobromil, Tarnopol, Odessa, Kaminitz-Podolia, Kielce, and hundreds of other towns established separate synagogues, burial grounds, and funds for mutual aid and charity. Whereas the religious and social life in the shtetl had often been based upon class or occupation, in America regional ties provided a basis for worship and became an important feature of economic life. Frequently a clothing manufacturer or contractor would seek out workers from his home town in Europe. Certain shops in the garment trades were populated almost entirely by workers from the same town.[28]

Apart from all these east European subgroups stood the German Jews, who had largely arrived during an earlier wave of immigration that began in the mid-nineteenth century. Disclaiming any cultural or social affinity to their east European coreligionists, many German Jews preferred to think of themselves as assimilated Americans with a duty to educate, modernize, and "uplift" the newcomers from eastern Europe. German Jews who could afford it fled the residential district on the Lower East Side but maintained steady contact with the newer immigrants both as philanthropists and as major employers in the garment trades.[29] For their part eastern European Jews regarded the Germans with a mixture of envy and disdain. They admired the material progress of the Germans but resented their snobbery and their patronizing concern for their social "inferiors."[30]

Having cut themselves loose from the moorings of their older communities in eastern Europe, the new immigrants felt for a time very much adrift in a sea of unfamiliar faces and a babble of strange new tongues. The persistence of ethnic and subethnic enclaves was an important expression of their longing for security, and they tended to create social forms and institutions that would provide a sense of belonging in an unfamiliar environment.

Housing and Living Conditions

Arriving with bundles and trunks or with most of their worldly belongings on their backs, newcomers first faced the task of finding a place to live. Very often, relatives and landsleit helped with the initial arrangements, but many families and individuals had no one to assist them. In either case, Jewish immigrants usually arrived in America with little money, and frequently they could afford nothing but the cheapest kind of housing.[31]

The typical tenement in late nineteenth-century New York was a monument to urban congestion. Rising between five and seven stories, with each floor consisting of four sets of apartments divided by a long and often perpetually dark hallway, tenement buildings were usually poorly lit, poorly ventilated, overcrowded, and unsanitary. Only a few rooms enjoyed the luxury of direct sunlight and fresh air from the street; the rest depended for light and ventilation on an "air shaft" that merely recirculated foul air from within the building. Dark and airless rooms and corridors, toilets down the hall or outdoors, and the ever-present sounds of too many people crowded into too little space completed the dreary portrait of tenement life.[32]

The response of Jewish immigrants to their new homes reflected both the range of their expectations and the conditions they had left behind. Most immigrants imagined that living conditions in the United States would be an improvement over what they had been accustomed to. Thus many of the new arrivals were surprised by the material poverty of immigrant life in American urban ghettos, especially when they first set eyes upon their new living quarters. "I had all sorts of visions of this *wonderful* America to which we were going," Jennie Matyas confessed. Accustomed in her native Hungary to hauling heavy buckets of water up a steep road, young Matyas could imagine nothing more thrilling than the prospect of having "*the water right inside your house.*" But in the end she found that housing for immigrants in New York did not measure up to her dreams. Even as the novelty of the tall buildings and the well-dressed children on the streets of the city helped reinforce her visions of a wonderful America, so the sight of the "tiny, tiny three-room apartment" on New York's Lower East Side considerably dampened her optimism. Flinging open the door to the tenement apartment, Matyas immediately sensed the discrepancy between the excitement of the streets and the depressing living conditions. Compared even to the one-room house she had known in Hungary, the tenement apartment in New York seemed "dark and dingy," with "a feeling of austerity and poverty about it." But she made up her mind immediately to accept "the fact that we were very poor and that was that."[33]

One young Jewish woman arriving in Chicago also discovered that living conditions bore little resemblance to the fantasies she had brought from Russia. All she knew about her cousin's house in Chicago was that it stood on Liberty Street, but she "imagined that she was coming to live on an avenue which would symbolize all that one bearing that precious name should." Instead, she was horrified to find her cousin residing in a rear tenement house on a narrow, unpaved, dirty street in the poorest section of the city.[34]

Immigrants who had grown up in the open-air atmosphere of the shtetl were apt to have a particularly difficult time adjusting to tenement life. Marie Ganz, who would later become a garment worker and an East Side activist, described the disillusionment her mother experienced when she entered her first American apartment. Ganz's father, who had come to the United States two years ahead of the rest of the family, could hardly wait to show Marie and her mother the home he had struggled to prepare for them. But his wife, having known only the "comfortable farmhouse" in Galicia, reacted to the heat and stuffiness of "the two miserable rooms" with immediate dismay. "But father ushered us in with a great show of joy and enthusiasm. Suddenly his smile gave way to an expression that reflected . . . injured pride as he became aware of disgust which my mother could not conceal." Ganz would vividly remember her mother's words: "So we have crossed half the world for this!"[35]

If some immigrants had overly optimistic visions of conditions in their new home, others had seen too much poverty in eastern Europe to be shocked or disappointed by anything America had to offer. Despite its austerity, Rose Schneiderman had few initial complaints about the Ludlow Street tenement apartment the family rented on the Lower East Side. The apartment, located at the top of four flights of stairs, had no gas, electricity, or running water, and the only toilet was in the backyard. Still, to Rose the arrangement and look of the apartment seemed "quite advanced" compared to their old home in Khelm.[36]

Even if living conditions failed to meet immigrant expectations, the tenements on the Lower East Side and in other neighborhoods where immigrants settled were in many respects no worse than the cramped and primitive housing frequently occupied by Jews in the shtetlekh and cities of eastern Europe. Most shtetl dwellings consisted of two or three rooms in a house or hut built of logs or constructed of mud or straw. Only the wealthiest members of the community lived in brick houses.[37] In the cities, artisans could seldom afford more than dimly lit "cellars" and "hovels" where wet walls and floors added to their misery.[38] In Vilna the apartment houses had stinking courtyards and outdoor plumbing.[39] In Kiev, where Zena Druckman spent her childhood, families of ten crowded into three-room houses. In her home one of these rooms also served as her father's workshop. "We slept everywhere," she recalled, and poverty forced them to make their beds out of chairs.[40]

Jewish daughters sometimes experienced their first encounter with material poverty differently from their mothers. Immigrant mothers viewed living conditions in the context of their household duties and obligations; daughters often had other plans for themselves and imagined that much of their day would be spent outside the home. Thus some young people viewed their new living conditions with more tolerance than their elders did. Their idealism about prospects for education in

America and their hopefulness about greater social and political freedom sustained their optimism and allowed them to overlook, at least
temporarily, the squalor of tenement life. When Mary Antin first entered the sparsely furnished rooms her father had rented for the family
in the Jewish ghetto of Boston, her excitement about the opportunities
that awaited a school-age girl in the new country mitigated the poverty
of her surroundings. The ordinary objects that furnished the tiny, drab
tenement apartment suddenly took on a "glorious" quality. Antin took
comfort in the powerful notion that "these wooden chairs and tin pans
were *American* chairs and pans." Antin's mother, on the other hand,
took a dimmer view: "Perhaps my mother alone, of us newcomers,
appreciated the shabbiness of the little apartment, and realized that for
her there was as yet no laying down of the burden of poverty."[41]

What mattered to Ella Wolff when she first arrived in New York from
her home in Vilna in 1891 was not so much the comfort of her new
living quarters as her childhood longings for personal autonomy and for
education. She recalled that the apartment into which the family moved
seemed "at the time" like a relatively "nice home" compared with the
overcrowded buildings inhabited by other East Side Jews. But at that
moment her major preoccupation was not where she lived, or even how
the apartment compared to her home in Europe, but the overwhelming
feeling that she "was young and . . . free here."[42] Another young
garment worker, who could afford only a badly kept room in an apartment belonging to another Jewish family living on the Lower East Side,
told an interviewer, "I don't like the place I live in very much, but it is
great to be free to do what I want. There are so many new things to see
and so much happening on the streets. I can be happy for hours, leaning
out the window watching it."[43]

Young Women Alone

The thousands of Jewish women who emigrated alone to the
United States faced a set of adjustments different from those of immigrants living in a family setting. Single travelers, female or male, usually
found a room as a boarder in a private home or, less frequently, in a
lodging house. Whenever possible, young women tried to recreate a
homelike environment by living with relatives or close landsleit. Sometimes their hosts accepted them into the household like a welcome part
of the family, but in other cases boarders felt like intruders and outsiders.

To many Jewish daughters the experience of boarding, whether with relatives, friends, or strangers, was less than pleasant. Squeezing into already crowded apartments, boarders frequently could claim little more than makeshift beds, couches, and floors as their living space. Only the most fortunate boarders had a bedroom to themselves, and even a bedroom shared with others proved a rarity. More often their quarters doubled as kitchens, parlors, or hallways. Sometimes their beds consisted of no more than a mattress on the floor or a board placed across two kitchen chairs.[44] In the language of the day this was referred to as "renting a sheet." For three dollars a month, female boarders could rent a mattress, perhaps to share with another boarder or a member of the household in a crowded tenement apartment.[45] With little chance for privacy, tensions and emotional strains easily flared up between boarders and their hosts.

The bonds of kinship did not necessarily ease the lot of the boarder. One sixteen-year-old Jewish garment worker from Russia boarded with her cousin's family in New York. Although they allowed her to stay with them out of a feeling of obligation, they clearly resented her presence in their already cramped quarters. Frequently they criticized her for consuming too much of their food, and their hostility increased when slack season in the garment trades left her unemployed. As relations with her cousin's family further deteriorated, she threatened to leave and "find her own spot."[46]

Even when no specific tensions arose in the household where they boarded, young women on their own rarely found it easy to adjust to life in a new country far away from parents. For Lottie Spitzer, the most painful aspect of the early period of resettlement in America was the loneliness. Before she landed in a Chicago clothing factory, Lottie moved from relative to relative hoping to recreate the family life she longed for. The aunt and uncle she originally stayed with in Fall River, Massachusetts, did not provide the closeness she had known with her own parents in Poland. "I didn't have a home atmosphere," Lottie complained. "I had girlfriends, but . . . my cousins were busy with their families, with their children . . . And I was lonely. I didn't have a family. . . . So every time I wrote to my aunt [in Chicago] she said, 'Come to us!' "[47]

Even some young female boarders who felt emotionally integrated into the family life of the household found that in exchange for the closeness and trust of their hosts, they were expected to tolerate an unusually heavy set of household chores and responsibilities. Women who boarded with strangers frequently felt oppressed by the demands of their hosts for housework or baby-sitting. In addition to paying for a place to sleep and for their weekly meals, female boarders, unlike their male counterparts, sometimes helped with cooking, cleaning, mending, washing, ironing, and other duties, often after a long day at the factory or shop.[48]

Raised with scornful attitudes toward domestic "service," many Jewish women from eastern Europe felt humiliated by the household tasks assigned to them. Seamstress Sarah Reznikoff at first resented the suggestion that she perform certain chores in the home where she boarded. "I did not mind washing the clothes of my own family, but I did not like to do it for others. I had helped with the dishes and about the house but this was hard for me to stomach," she recalled. "But I thought I ought not to feel that way about it—I was [now] one of the family—and I washed their clothes."[49]

Middle-class observers of urban immigrant life stressed that in the absence of a "real" home, boarding with a private family, even if they were strangers, was still the "nearest approach."[50] And most young women on their own in a strange city probably agreed that a private family offered more emotional security than institutional boarding houses could. In the best of circumstances, boarders in private apartments developed some degree of closeness with the "missus" and her family, and at times they derived a measure of protection against economic hardship. When slack periods in the clothing industry temporarily put young women out of work, many families allowed boarders to live on credit until the next busy season.[51] The relationship between boarders and landladies, however, was primarily an economic one, and in the absence of bonds of kinship there was no assurance that the missus would extend special favors to her boarders. One Jewish garment worker who had a good relationship with her missus still received periodic threats of eviction when she could not get enough work to pay her rent. The landlady admitted that her need for the rent money outweighed her commitment to the young boarder.[52]

Immigrant women understood that living alone was considered scandalous. The only alternatives to boarding with a family were to share a small apartment or room with other female friends or to find a furnished room in a public lodging house. Neither arrangement seemed completely respectable in the immigrant community, because they had little in common with a homelike environment. In an attempt to provide a "better" set of circumstances for the Jewish immigrant girl on her own in the city, middle-class philanthropists established residences for working girls. The Clara de Hirsch Home in New York, the Home for Jewish

Working Girls, the Josephine Club, the Ruth and the Miriam clubs in Chicago, and the Rebecca Gratz House in Philadelphia offered room and board to hundreds of young women who for one reason or another could not board with a private family. These philanthropic homes tried to provide an "uplifting" environment for their residents, giving "needy" female immigrants an inexpensive place to live and at the same time attempting to improve their "mental, moral, and physical condition." For a modest weekly fee, women received room and board and access to various edifying activities, including in-house lectures, concerts, and industrial training classes. Some Jewish homes had small libraries, and others tried to assist girls in finding employment. Before 1920, however, few of these establishments existed, and they could accommodate only small numbers of working girls.[53]

Women and the Reconstruction of Family Life

Most Jewish immigrant daughters did not board with relatives or strangers but lived with their parents and siblings. Yet even within the relative security of the nuclear family, they were hardly immune from strain. The process of adjusting Old World family life to New World conditions posed significant dilemmas for each member of the immigrant household.

As they settled into their new homes, immigrant families had to calculate how they would support themselves in the new country, to decide which members of the household would work, who would take care of the children and the house, who would be able to go to school, and for how long. At first these questions could be answered only provisionally. It took time to understand how much money they needed to sustain themselves, which family members could most effectively "earn the living," and what kind of work the women in the family could do without seriously violating cultural norms.

The degree to which immigrants could maintain their traditional family values in face of unfamiliar circumstances has been the subject of debate among several generations of social historians. One school stressed the destabilizing impact of migration and resettlement, especially on family life. More recent historians, particularly those who have studied the Italian experience, instead emphasize family resiliency, focusing upon the ways in which immigrants used traditional values to help the family survive and adjust to changing circumstances.[54] Through what Virginia Yans describes as "a dynamic process of give and take between new conditions and old social forms," immigrant families rebuilt their lives in America. Immigrants accepted changes, Dino Cinel has argued, "but only those changes least disruptive of their traditions or those that allowed them to recreate the old way of life in the new."[55]

This give and take also characterized the adaptation of eastern European Jewish families to American urban conditions. Immigration did not totally destabilize family traditions even if it created enormous pressures and strains. Nevertheless, for eastern European Jewish women and their families, the purposes and the process of adapting to American conditions were somewhat different than they were for Italians and other groups. Of all the immigrants who came in massive numbers after 1880, Jews alone planned to stay on a permanent basis. That fact shaped the psychology of their adaptation. Like Italian families, Jews relied upon Old World traditions to make the transition to a new way of life, but to a greater degree than Italians they consciously attempted to interpret their behavior as conforming to the social standards of their newly adopted country.

For eastern European Jews, as for other newcomers, the most significant expression of tradition in the service of adaptation was the persistence of what Judith Smith has aptly called "a family culture of work." Here, as in Europe, families assumed that each member of the household had an obligation to help sustain the whole.[56] Irregular employment frequently precluded the possibility of earning more than a bare subsistence. At a time when economists estimated that a worker's family needed a minimum of $800 a year in order to maintain "a normal standard of living"—food, housing, fuel, and transportation—most male heads of immigrant households earned considerably less.[57] The United States Immigration Commission's 1911 study (based on data collected in 1907–8) of earnings among Russian Jewish men revealed an average annual income in seven cities of only $463. In New York City earnings were somewhat higher, $520 a year, whereas men in Jewish households in Boston earned only $378 during the year.[58]

Regardless of their former training and backgrounds, the vast majority of Jewish immigrants who worked for wages found jobs in some type of industrial setting. In 1890 a private census of Jewish residents on New York's Lower East Side showed that the majority of employed Jewish men and women worked in some branch of the clothing industry. More than 57 percent of gainfully employed Jews in that sample of over 20,000 households earned a living in the needle trades, a seasonal industry characterized by periodic layoffs and underemployment. Ex-

4. A tailor from Bialystok and his family, not long after their arrival in New York City. New, American-style clothing has replaced their Old World garb. Courtesy of the Haberman family.

panding at an unprecedented rate, industry's need for unskilled and semiskilled workers attracted immigrants of both sexes. Another 15 percent were manual workers in other industries, artisans, and craftsmen of various sorts—including blacksmiths, mechanics, tobacco workers, printers, shoemakers, and carpenters. The remainder of the working population engaged in some form of petty commerce as butchers, bakers, grocers, and storekeepers. With the exception of a tiny group who were teachers, musicians, and rabbis, few people could be considered part of a professional class.[59] By the first decade of the twentieth century the occupational pattern of east European Jews had changed somewhat. Most immigrant male heads of household still worked in the garment industry or in some other form of wage labor, but a growing number of husbands were self-employed. Depending upon the city, an estimated 26 to 48 percent of Russian Jewish male heads of household were in business for profit, usually as peddlers, storekeepers, and petty contractors.[60] A few made substantial incomes as real estate speculators or as garment manufacturers.[61]

As a practical matter, most Jewish immigrant men found it impossible to support their families on their own. This was true for many engaged in small business and peddling as well as for the majority of wage workers.[62] In New York City the Immigration Commission found that only about 20 percent of Jewish husbands were financially able to support an entire household without the help of other family members, compared to 64 percent of native-born American husbands.[63] After observing the living conditions of Jewish immigrants on the Lower East Side, one settlement-house worker described the complex earning patterns of a typical family in 1907:

> A Russian Jewish family . . . consists of six persons. The head is 49 years of age, a tailor earning about $200 a year, with a wife and four children. The oldest girl, 19 years of age, works at tailoring and earns $200 a year, the next eldest, a girl, had been working six months at neckwear at $2.50 a week, which makes $87.50 for the six months period; the two younger children were at school. The rent of the three rooms is $16 a month. . . . The total family income will be $575, which approximates the average family income for the block.[64]

As in eastern Europe, where cultural traditions as well as economic circumstances encouraged Jewish females to work, conditions in the United States required women's economic contribution to the household. To a great extent, this requirement involved a continuation of work roles already established before Jews left the Old World. However, new requirements, new opportunities, and new ideas altered some of the ways in which Jewish women would contribute to the family income.

Immigration led to a significant redistribution of female work roles. Whereas in Russia Jewish wives and mothers had often borne the main burdens of female breadwinning, Jewish families in the United States increasingly turned to daughters and sons to supplement the earnings of husbands. While married women's economic participation had been an openly acknowledged part of Jewish family life in the Old World, over time immigrants came to think of it as a source of embarrassment.

Rarely did immigrant wives accept industrial wage work in the United States, even though industrial homework had been a common source of income for married women in the Russian Pale. Generally, only dire economic circumstances—illness, death, or desertion of a husband—or the absence of children of working age would push Jewish immigrant wives into this type of employment.

The scarcity of Jewish immigrant wives in the labor force was revealed in several surveys. Jewish immigrant wives had a lower rate of labor force participation than all other groups of married women, immigrant or nonimmigrant. In an 1880 survey only 2 percent of immigrant Jewish households in New York reported wives who worked for wages, and in 1905 still fewer listed wives in paid employment.[65] A few years later the United States Immigration Commission conducted a large survey of female work patterns, sampling households in seven cities. The study revealed that an average of only 8 percent of Russian Jewish wives were working, compared with 11 percent of Poles, 17 percent of southern Italians, 20 percent of Germans, 35 percent of Bohemians, and 68 percent of Blacks.[66]

Jewish and Italian Immigrant Family Economies

The Immigration Commission survey of families in seven cities shows the distinctiveness of the Jewish family economy. Compared to southern Italian immigrants, with whom they shared a pattern of employment in the garment trades, Jewish immigrant families had somewhat fewer husbands making a contribution to household income and dramatically fewer wives who were contributing. Because of a higher rate of desertion, Jewish husbands were present and employed in 85 percent of families surveyed, compared to 94 percent among Italians.[67] Jewish husbands, when present, tended to earn more than their Italian counterparts, reflecting the heavy representation of Italian men in unskilled day labor. Jewish men more often held skilled or semiskilled industrial jobs or engaged in some sort of commercial activity. Yet in both cases the majority of families also depended on other sources of income, different sources depending upon the group (see Table 1). Among the Italians 17 percent of wives contributed wages, mainly from industrial homework. In another 27 percent of Italian households, wives contributed by taking in boarders or lodgers, and 22 percent of households benefited from the contributions of working children. The Jewish family economy depended to a greater degree on income from boarders and lodgers as well as the earnings of children. Although married women worked for wages only in exceptional cases, in 43 percent of households they cared for boarders and lodgers, a higher rate than for any other immigrant group. They did so especially in families with children too young to be sent to work; the pattern changed as children reached the legal working age of sixteen. Then the income-producing burdens shifted away from mothers toward the outside wage work of daughters and sons. In all, 36 percent of Jewish families depended upon the earnings of children.[68]

A more detailed portrait of immigrant family economies is presented in the Bureau of Labor's five-city survey of families with at least one woman employed in the men's clothing industry. The survey, published in 1911 but based on data gathered in 1907—8, shows that of the sample of 1,900 employed Jewish females, only 128 (7 percent) were married. The rest were single females between the ages of sixteen and twenty-two years. The Italian case stands in stark contrast. Of 3,445 employed Italian females surveyed, 1,404 or 41 percent were married. This group of married Italian wage earners spanned the ages between twenty and forty-four, but most were women in their twenties and thirties who worked at home as garment finishers and also cared for young children. Italian daughters in the sixteen to twenty-one age group made up the other 59 percent of the sample.[69]

Both surveys show that the most significant difference between Jewish and Italian households lay in the patterns of married women's employment. In both groups daughters worked for wages, with Jewish girls represented somewhat more frequently than Italians. But among Italian families, mothers in their child-bearing years show up with greater frequency in the paid labor force than do their Jewish counterparts. Italian wives usually took jobs finishing garments at home, whereas Jewish wives typically took in boarders and lodgers to supplement the husband's income.

Change and Continuity in
the Jewish Family Economy

This portrait of the Jewish family economy presents some important ironies and bears further exploration. Russian Jews, who had long validated the role of married women as breadwinners, became the group whose wives were most conspicuously absent from the labor force. Even native-born American women of native-born fathers were more likely to work for wages. In trying to understand what appears to be a paradigm shift, we need to consider a number of factors, some structural, others attitudinal. The dramatic change in behavior that shows up in the statistics turns out to be a less fundamental transforma-

Table 1. Income sources in Jewish and Italian family economies

Households	Russian Jews	Southern Italians
Husbands contribute to family income	85%	94%
Wives contribute to family income	8	17
Children contribute to family income	36	22
Income from boarders or lodgers	43	27
Income from other sources	9	5

Sample size: 721 Jewish families, 1,261 Italian families.
Source: United States Immigration Commission, *Immigrants in Cities*, vol. 1 (Washington, D.C., 1911), Table 79, p. 139; Table 401, pp. 546–547.

tion than it appears. Some patterns of married women's activity had altered by the first decade of this century, but for the most part the alterations were a consequence less of changing values than of changing circumstances.

In reconstructing a statistical overview of married women's economic behavior, consider the possibility that the available data are not altogether accurate because of underreporting of women's wage earning.[70] Jews, as we will see, contrived a particular language for describing a wife's economic activities, and certain forms of work were not likely to be acknowledged as such. Caring for boarders was not counted as work, nor, curiously, was the frequent participation of Jewish wives in commercial activities. In point of fact Jewish wives were "working," but the structure of economic opportunity in the United States helped to make their economic activity invisible. The nature of economic life in American cities limited the choices open to wives who needed to add to the household income and permitted immigrants to describe those choices as something other than work.[71]

In eastern Europe married women rarely took factory jobs or paid work that demanded long hours away from the home. They were more likely to participate in the system of home-based artisanal or outwork production. Factory production in late nineteenth- and early twentieth-century Russia and Poland was in its infant stage, and most industrial jobs were still off-limits to Jews. Such was not the case in the United States, where production had in large part moved from the home into factories and workshops. This was the primary reason for the changing nature of married women's work patterns. Cultural values about the proper activities of Jewish wives now conflicted with the prevailing direction of industrial opportunities.

Several considerations militated against paid employment for married women in a factory or shop. It had long been customary for Jewish husbands to worry about contacts their wives might have with other men. For a wife to come under the authority of a male employer or to come into intimate association with strange men in a workroom threatened the husband's domain even though the idea of women's work itself did not. The issue was laden with sexual jealousy and male pride. One daughter of Jewish immigrant garment workers recalled how her father became "very nervous" whenever her mother, a highly skilled seamstress, would let him know how much she felt appreciated by the manager of a raincoat shop where she worked. "My dad would try to tell her that she was being used. . . . He was threatened by the fact that she was going out, and also thinking all kinds of thoughts of her working together with other men."[72] Italians too worried that outside wage work would threaten traditional patriarchal control of husbands over wives. Consequently Italian wives took jobs away from home only when husbands could be assured that such work would not disrupt the patriarchal family system.[73]

The practical problems of child-rearing also played an important part in keeping mothers out of factories and workshops. The task of caring for children proved much more complicated in the United States than it had been in the Old Country, where the prevalence of home-based cottage and artisanal industry had closely linked economic and domestic functions and strongly reinforced dual roles for married women. In Russia, when Jewish wives did leave home to earn a living—usually by selling in the marketplace or running a family business—they relied upon grandparents, older siblings, relatives, servants, or young apprentices to care for their children. Mothers who had to leave the house sometimes followed the tradition of trusting the care of younger children to their eldest daughter. Rose Pesotta recalled how she raised the younger children in the house while her mother went out to run a family business in their tiny Ukrainian shtetl. "Two of the children in our family I considered my very own, for I had much more to do with their upbringing than my mother who was occupied with the store and other household chores."[74] Sibling care was also less feasible in the United States because of the new opportunities open to young girls. Leaving the care of children and home to an older daughter might interfere with her schooling or, if she was of legal working age, keep her away from a more lucrative form of outside industrial employment.

Some immigrant mothers who had no choice but to leave the house to help earn a living relied upon day nurseries to care for their children. But in American cities, institutional forms of childcare never met the needs of immigrant women. In 1904 only three Jewish day nurseries operated on the Lower East Side, and by 1917 only 1,400 children could be accommodated in the fourteen Jewish nurseries spread throughout Manhattan, Brooklyn, and the Bronx.[75] Without recourse to organized childcare and lacking reliable alternatives such as older children or relatives, some mothers simply coped the best they could. Occasionally, as settlement worker Mary Kingsbury Simkhovitch observed, "children are locked up alone at home to await the mother's return."[76]

Other domestic duties besides child-rearing made it difficult for married women to work away from home. Meals had to be cooked, apartments cleaned, and washing, mending, and marketing needed to be done. What is more, tenement life made the daily battle against what immigrant novelist Anzia Yezierska described as "the deadening dirt" a never-ending task. The run-down condition of many tenement buildings, the soot and grime of the city itself, and the cramped quarters inhabited by so many immigrant families created serious sanitation problems and increased the burdens of housework. The American school teacher's rule "a place for everything and everything in its place" seemed ridiculous in the face of tenement realities. "So much junk we had in our house," Yezierska wrote, that middle-class prescriptions about housekeeping were "no good for us."[77]

The customary household tasks of Old World wives and mothers proved much more complicated in the United States. As Elizabeth Ewen points out, America introduced immigrants to more rigorous standards of cleanliness, more complicated household technologies, and dwellings that had a more complex design than the simple shelters of the Old World. Women in small European towns and villages went in groups once a month to wash their clothing in the river; new immigrant women in American cities faced the more lonely and difficult task of doing laundry by themselves inside a cramped tenement apartment.[78] Even shopping for household necessities took countless hours of a woman's day. The need to pinch pennies, to be constantly on the lookout for bargains such as cheap food, made shopping in the big city a time-consuming task for most women. In order to cover her own household expenses and put aside money to repay her ship's passage, Jennie Matyas's mother scoured the neighborhood to find affordable prices. Matyas recalled how she and her mother "walked blocks to where we could get milk for a penny a quart cheaper than we could get it in the immediate vicinity."[79]

Just as important as these obstacles to married women's wage work outside the home were alternative income strategies that more easily met domestic needs and fulfilled cultural expectations about proper wifely conduct. Reluctant to become factory workers and bound to their homes by time-consuming domestic duties, Jewish wives followed a course common among other immigrant women—they did piecework at home and took in boarders to help pay the rent.

Industrial production in the home required no break with tradition. It had provided Jewish families in late nineteenth- and early twentieth-century Russia with an important source of income. Contractors had distributed raw materials and goods to Jewish homes in eastern European shtetlekh and cities, and women and their families assembled the finished product. In America clothing manufacturers and other producers of consumer goods employed thousands of immigrant women willing to work in their own homes for wages invariably below those paid to factory workers.[80]

In the 1880s and 1890s Jewish women and men had played an important role in the homework sector of the American garment industry. Ephraim Wagner, a Jewish immigrant who came to New York from a small town in Galicia in 1888, boasted in his memoir of the first years in America: "As soon as I was able to earn six to seven dollars a week, I did not let my wife go into a shop, but stay at home and prepare our meals." Yet as Wagner admitted, his "industrious" wife, not content to live on his wages alone, took in work from a nearby clothing factory to earn a few extra dollars a week.[81]

"Finishing" clothing and making neckwear, artificial flowers, and other items at home allowed married immigrant women who were willing to work for very meager piecewages to combine economic and domestic tasks. With no one to care for her children, Elizabeth Stern's mother depended upon homework to earn money. Looking back upon her immigrant childhood, Elizabeth could recall her mother occupied in only two positions, either "standing at the stove" or "her hands stitching, stitching." Stern's mother "eked out the family living" by making aprons, which were peddled on the streets by her neighbor. On the "rare occasions" when her mother had to leave the house, she tied the children to the legs of the kitchen table.[82] Rose Cohen also remembered how her landlady would sit all day in the tenement apartment "finishing" clothing and rocking the baby cradle with her foot.[83]

By the early twentieth century, as the locus of production in the United States shifted to the factory, opportunities for homework were declining. In 1911 the Immigration Commission concluded that with the exception of Black, Bohemian, and Moravian women who took in laundry work, "the proportion of apartments in which homework is carried out is nowhere large." Among Jewish households the number of homeworkers was particularly small. Except in family "sweatshops" where the tenement apartment doubled as workroom and the husband, his wife, and paid helpers sewed clothing for a small profit, the Immigration Commission found little in the way of homework among Jews— only 3 percent of the Jewish households it visited.[84]

The presence of other nationalities in the steadily shrinking homework market may have set limits on the opportunities available to Jewish wives. By 1910 tailoring, especially "finishing" men's clothing, in New York was the preserve of southern Italian women. The Bureau of Labor's 1911 study of women and children in the men's clothing industry found that Italian women "practically have a monopoly" on the home finishing market in every city but Rochester, New York, where German women did most of the homework.[85]

Other homework industries were similarly monopolized. One study of tenement homeworkers in New York in 1911 revealed that Italian women not only "finished" most of the clothing but also controlled the making of artificial flowers and the willowing (cleaning) of ostrich plumes. Syrians made most of the kimonos, lace, crocheting, and embroidery, and Germans sewed custom vests. Irish and native-born homeworkers made neckties, as well as clothing for the Navy. For their part, Jewish women concentrated in the home production of straw hats, women's neckwear, and fancy bows.[86]

Nevertheless, this pattern raises more questions than it answers. Particular immigrant groups may have come to dominate areas of the homework market through their ability to underbid competitors or as a result of their connections to powerful labor contracting networks such as the Italian *padrone* system.[87] But there is every reason to believe that Jewish women could have been effective competitors had they chosen to be. The fact that many employers of homeworkers in the garment trades were fellow Jews would have given them an advantage over other groups.

The steady evacuation of Jews from the homework market was at least partially voluntary. Among immigrants who had been in this country for several years, in all likelihood, homework lost its earlier respectability and came to be seen as a "greenhorn" occupation. More important, however, was the availability of a more attractive source of income. Taking in boarders had fewer of the stigmas associated with paid employment either inside or outside the home. Industrial homework might be perceived as an extension of paid factory work, whereas taking care of boarders or lodgers was a purely domestic enterprise. Since the tasks associated with caring for boarders were indistinguishable from other domestic duties, a wife's role as "missus" tended to mask the fact that she received a wage payment for her labors. Eventually such work would offend the dignity of some immigrant women. But in the period of mass migration from eastern Europe, caring for boarders remained a vital source of income in Jewish households.

The thousands of homeless immigrant women and men who arrived in American cities from eastern Europe each year provided a steady stream of boarders willing to pay the missus for a place to sleep and often for meals as well. And the majority of Jewish immigrant wives at some point took advantage of this opportunity to commercialize their domestic talents. More than any other immigrant group in New York, Russian Jewish families kept boarders. The Immigration Commission's 1911 study reported that 43 percent of the Russian Jewish households surveyed in seven cities had boarders living with them. But in New York the number jumped to 56 percent, compared with only 20 percent of southern Italian and 17 percent of Bohemian and Moravian families in the city.[88]

Although Jews in Russia and Poland had added to their incomes by taking in boarders, the practice grew dramatically in the United States and became by far the most important economic activity for Jewish immigrant wives.[89] If Old World traditions influenced this development, one of the most important precedents was the large number of young male and female apprentices in the Pale of Settlement who lived or ate with master artisans. One Jewish woman who emigrated from Russia in 1913 described how her mother cooked and cleaned up after the workers in her father's house. "At home in Lida, my father had a factory in the house, so they would come to eat by us. Our family was not small, and with the workers we had almost a dozen people eating and working in the house." After the family emigrated to New York, they had as many as five boarders at a time.[90] In addition, Jewish traveling peddlers, Yeshiva students living away from home, and young factory workers had also boarded with relatives and friends in the cities and towns of Russia. In the United States immigrant women from a variety of backgrounds took in boarders. It helped pay the rent, the woman was her own boss, she maintained authority over the household, and she did not have to leave the house to earn money. Even if taking in boarders meant more cooking and cleaning for the wife, and greater overcrowding for the family, many women no doubt considered the sacrifice worthwhile.

Both homework and taking in boarders enabled wives to carry on traditional income-earning roles in the United States. One other activity also allowed wives to duplicate familiar patterns: Jews considered "business" the preferable occupation for a married woman. To manage or simply to "help out" in a family business, or to peddle goods out on the streets, had vastly different connotations from working for wages. If wage work outside the home was questionable, earning a living in one's own or in a family business had always seemed perfectly respectable.

Even as most Jews in Russia acknowledged that a wife's participation in commerce and trade was "work," immigrants in America often sought to understand it as something else. Nothing sums up Jewish immigrants' need to fit married women's commercial activities into a noneconomic framework better than a statement by a woman from a small town near Vilna. "At that time when girls were married it was terrible to go to work," she insisted. "[But] if they worked in their own business, they could have worked day and night, that didn't matter. But to go out to work, that was forbidden."[91]

The assumptions underlying the distinction between "work" and "business" revolved around issues of authority, independence, and the concern over a woman's domestic duties.[92] Jews in Europe and immigrants in the United States believed that in a family business a wife retained some control over the work situation: she did not have to take orders from a man other than her husband; she helped define the relations between herself and the customers; and, equally important, she could, if need be, combine economic, household, and child-rearing tasks.

In a family-owned business the married woman escaped the problems associated with working for a strange employer. "In the store, that's your own business, you haven't got any bosses to run you," explained an immigrant woman from a small shtetl near Warsaw.[93] Mollie Millman, whose mother had run the family's flour business in Russia, underscored the important distinction between that kind of occupation and the alternative of going out to work for wages. "My mother worked for herself, the customers came to her, she didn't go out."[94]

Not only did the wife who helped in a business maintain the independence so important to her respectability, but she could also see the store as an extension of the home. In many cases, in fact, store and home were physically connected, with family living quarters above or in back of the commercial area. Under these circumstances, a wife could reasonably expect to combine economic and domestic responsibilities. As one immigrant woman put it, "If you had to help out in the store, you were still home."[95] May Horowitz, whose own mother had managed a small business in Russia, explained that for a married woman to work in the store was "not a shame like when the wife goes out to work." In a business, she emphasized, "you have your kids together in the back of the store."[96]

Not all businesses, however, allowed married women the same benefits. Some stores and stalls were located away from the family residence,
and women peddlers obviously could not attend to household duties
while selling their wares on the streets. Still, these commercial endeavors
had far more legitimacy for a Jewish married woman than did wage
work, since they still gave her more independence and a greater degree
of flexibility regarding child-rearing and domestic tasks. Yet in some
cases the distinction was more symbolic than actual. "Business" in the
minds of many Jewish immigrants, even when it tended to interfere with
a wife's other responsibilities, still conferred a traditional mark of social
acceptance, whereas wage work for married women did not.

Because Jewish women and their husbands did not consider a wife's
participation in a family business as work, the census and other investigations do not accurately portray the extent to which immigrant
married women participated in American commerce and trade.[97] But
many Jewish wives assisted or assumed major responsibility in the
operation of grocery stores and other small businesses. In households in
New York, Philadelphia, and Chicago, between a quarter and nearly a
half of married men were in business for themselves, and thus there is a
strong possibility that their wives performed a statistically hidden economic function—the traditional breadwinning partnership in a family
business.[98]

Women pushcart peddlers and street vendors were a common sight in
New York and Chicago. "Upon visiting Jefferson Street, Maxwell Street,
and many other streets," a reporter for Chicago's *Jewish Daily Courier*
observed in 1912, "you will witness how many women run stands of
fruit, clothing, fish and other products, and several manage complete
stores. In other localities you can meet Jewish women running candy
stores, groceries, butcher shops, cleaning and dying stores and so
forth."[99] Louis Wirth, in his classic study of Jewish immigrant life in
Chicago, noted that Russian Jewish women "monopolized" both the
fish and poultry stalls on Chicago's Maxwell Street. And in New York,
"armies" of pushcart women hawked goods or helped their husbands in
"the selling."[100]

The Rise of the Breadwinner Ethic

All of these breadwinning activities—industrial homework, taking in boarders, and laboring in family-owned commerce and trade—
enabled married women to contribute to the family economy in ways

that separated them physically and psychologically from the ranks of outside wage earners. Because such labor entwined itself with daily domestic tasks, it was possible for immigrants to deny that wives were actually working.

As Virginia Yans points out, "the actual fact that women worked is perhaps less important than the immigrants' interpretation of the situation." When Italians chose to interpret women's economic contribution as something other than work, Yans has argued, they were attempting to fit immigrant wives' activities into an Old World framework to preserve traditional family patterns.[101] The same was true for some Jewish families, but certainly not for all. Growing numbers of Jewish immigrants chose to underplay or deny women's economic contributions because they wished to conform to modern, not traditional, understandings about women's proper roles.

The reluctance of Jewish wives to go out to work for wages and their eagerness to explain their economic contribution as something other than work was in part related to the rise of what might be called a breadwinner ethic. Over time Jewish immigrants became increasingly sensitive to bourgeois notions of respectability. Those who sought to identify themselves with upwardly mobile, assimilated Americans insisted that a wife should devote herself exclusively to her domestic obligations and leave the task of breadwinning to the husband and other family members. That was clearly the advice of *Sholem Aleykhem tsu Immigranten*, a Yiddish-language guidebook issued in 1903 by the reform-minded German Jews of the Educational Alliance in New York to acquaint newcomers from eastern Europe with "life in America." Stressing that Americans treated women with respect, the guidebook instructed the immigrants that in the United States a family man could not "throw the burden and worry of work upon his wife." If Russian Jewish husbands in America chose to remain "idle" while their wives earned the living, American courts of law would compel these men to find jobs. In America, the booklet warned, a husband had a "duty" to support his family.[102] Although for the western, bourgeois world this notion was quite traditional, for poor Jews from eastern Europe it represented a concept that was still somewhat new.

The attack upon the Old World stereotype of the "idle" Torah scholar and his industrious wife, and the insistence that such an arrangement was unacceptable in the United States, came both from German Jewish reformers and from within the eastern European Jewish immigrant community itself. In Russia, Haskalah writers had already criticized traditional practices, calling upon men to support their households without the help of women. Yet that critique never resonated as fully in the Old World as it did in America. In the United States the growing secularization of immigrant life and the declining prestige of the religious scholar meant that success would be measured less in terms of religious learning and more on the basis of wealth and material gain. This changing ethos had important implications for ideas about the proper role of married women. Abraham Cahan, the socialist author and newspaper editor, captures the changing ethos in *The Rise of David Levinsky*, his 1917 novel about immigrants striving for success on the Lower East Side. In one episode Levinsky, fresh off the boat from Russia, meets a countryman who complains that in America his wife "had changed for the worse. . . . When we were at home" in Russia, she was

> "a different woman. She did not make life a burden to me as she does here.". . . For, lo and behold! instead of supporting him while he read Talmud, as she used to do at home, she persisted in sending him out to peddle. "America is not Russia," she said. "A man must make a living here." . . . His wife . . . would take no excuse. He must peddle or be nagged to death.[103]

Anzia Yezierska's novels also characterize the conflict between Old World cultural patterns and changing immigrant values. In her 1925 novel *Bread Givers*, Reb Smolinsky, a Talmudic scholar whose way of life has lost its relevance in the worldly clamor of New York, attempts to maintain his calling while his daughters support the family. When one daughter becomes engaged to marry, Smolinsky makes it clear that he expects his prospective son-in-law to go on supporting him. "I'm marrying your daughter—not the whole family," the future bridegroom protests. "In America they got no use for Torah learning. In America everybody got to earn a living."[104]

What began as a critique of the old Orthodox scholarly class of men who depended upon their wives to earn the living soon grew into a more general criticism of any husband who allowed his wife to work and thus did not assume full responsibility for his household. May Horowitz, who emigrated from Minsk and worked in New York's garment industry, explained that although many times in Russia "the women made a living for the man," in the United States the roles got turned "upside down." Among immigrant Jews in New York, Horowitz added, it was widely acknowledged that "a man of character never let his wife work."[105]

From within the framework of a Jewish immigrant culture in transition came the idea that even religious scholars had to support their wives in America. From outside the traditional culture came other influences, most important the new and appealing image of the American middle-class "lady" whose husband earned enough to support her comfortably. The ideal of the lady did not have a universal acceptance among first-generation Jewish immigrants but had a special appeal to those upwardly mobile families who put on middle-class pretensions and to nouveau-riche immigrants, both sometimes referred to as "all-rightnicks" because of their uncritical affection for American ways.[106]

The concept of the lady had several levels of attraction. Symbolizing upward economic mobility, it also embodied an exalted notion of femininity that broke with the traditional Jewish notion of female inferiority. The American lady seemed to have gained the respect, honor, and dignity that many immigrant women wanted for themselves.

The growth of a breadwinner ethic and the growing tendency to describe married women's breadwinning activities in noneconomic terms represented an important step in the rethinking of eastern European Jewish family roles. Partly the changes in married women's roles reflected a shift in attitudes, partly they were a consequence of the differences between Old and New World economic opportunities. Although married women continued to participate in breadwinning responsibilities, their contribution often remained hidden and unacknowledged. The very opposite was true for immigrant daughters.

The New Importance of Breadwinning Daughters

Jewish immigrants questioned whether a married woman should work outside the home, and some came to doubt that a wife should work at all; but few families held similar reservations about their daughters. The labor of daughters had been necessary to their families before migration to America, and it became even more important after immigrants arrived. Unlike their mothers, daughters saw their economic role expand in the United States. As immigrants deemphasized the labor of Jewish wives, they foisted greater responsibility upon the shoulders of daughters. While married women went out to the factory infrequently, their daughters did so overwhelmingly. In most families the work of daughters made it possible for mothers to remain at home.

Economic realities in America reinforced the occupational patterns followed by Jewish daughters in eastern Europe. As seamstresses, tailors, tobacco workers, and wage earners in the developing factory systems of Russia and Poland, daughters played an increasingly important part in the premigration economic life of the Jewish family. Financial need had driven many of them to seek employment, but prevailing economic conditions severely limited opportunities for wage work. Unskilled factory jobs had been relatively hard to find, and most young Jewish women in eastern Europe had to undergo a long apprenticeship with a seamstress or tailor in order to learn a trade. Otherwise they would engage in some form of home production or, as a last resort, become domestic servants. In the United States, by contrast, the doors of the factory were open to Jewish labor. With industrial opportunities plentiful, large numbers of Jewish daughters entered the workplace.

Since the early nineteenth century, American factory owners had sought the labor of inexperienced girls and women willing to work cheaply. In the clothing industry, where most immigrant Jews went to work, unskilled hands could learn one of the many subdivisions of production in a short time. This was especially true in the manufacture of blouses and women's undergarments. Even in the less modernized branches of the industry, in the smaller shops that demanded some skill, there were often openings for untrained "learners."

The vast majority of unmarried Jewish immigrant women living in American cities worked for wages by the time they were sixteen years old. The Immigration Commission's 1911 study of Russian Jewish families in seven cities includes data on the wage-earning activities of American-born daughters of Jewish immigrants. Of those daughters age sixteen or older, 6 percent were going to school, 21 percent were "at home," and 74 percent were working for wages. Foreign-born Jewish daughters were even more likely to be found in the labor force. While precise data on daughters in this age group were not available for all cities, the Commission study reveals that in Boston 89 percent of the foreign-born single Jewish women age sixteen and older contributed to the family's income by working outside the home.[107] Even among younger daughters between the ages of fourteen and fifteen, the Immigration Commission found, nearly 40 percent of foreign-born Jewish girls in all the cities surveyed worked outside the home.[108] To examine the occupational patterns of Jewish families living on Cherry Street, on New York's Lower East Side in 1905, is to underscore the economic participation of young Jewish girls. In more than a hundred Cherry Street families sampled from the New York State census of that year, all of the children under the age of fifteen were going to school; yet almost every child above that age was working.[109] Although the majority of other ethnic groups in the United States followed the same pattern—sending daughters rather than mothers out to work in factories—this division of labor was especially striking for Jewish immigrants.

Jewish immigrant daughters entered the labor force in greater numbers than their mothers not only because they were given fewer domestic responsibilities but also because fewer social taboos and conventions stood in their way. Jews from eastern Europe made important distinctions about proper behavior for married and unmarried women. In traditional Jewish culture, marriage symbolized the only rite of passage for a woman. Whereas boys, at the age of thirteen, attained a formal membership in the community through the religious ceremony known as *Bar Mitzvah*, girls did not acquire any socially acknowledged status until marriage.[110] Only when a girl married was her social standing in the community confirmed. Unlike her mother, she did not even have a place in the synagogue.[111] But after marriage, when she had attained a social position in the community, she also had to conform to a new set of religious customs and laws designed to regulate her behavior and demeanor.

The rules governing the married woman related to issues of piety, modesty, and the protection of the family. Social distinctions between married and unmarried women were recognized in two important rituals. Judaism required that a married woman undergo a monthly purification rite after her menstrual period. A visit to the *mikveh* (bath) for ritual immersion was one of the important deeds expected of a married woman. Until she had gone to the mikveh a woman could not resume sexual contact with her husband. Adherence to this custom demonstrated her faith and piety. Unmarried females, even those who had begun to menstruate, were not to have sexual relations and thus did not have to undergo ritual purification. As anthropologists studying Jewish life in the shtetl have noted, menstruation was considered "a physiological fact for the girl, but a social fact for the matron."[112] Moreover, only after a woman married was she required, for the sake of modesty and to prevent her from being "too attractive" to other men, to cover her hair or her shaved head with a wig (*shaitl*) or a kerchief. Orthodox Jews regarded a married woman's hair as a highly provocative sexual symbol, to be seen only by her own husband. In contrast, unmarried women went about freely with their hair exposed.[113] The shaitl and the mikveh distinguished a married woman's special status and defined her sexuality in social and religious terms. Even when young unmarried girls and women were aware of the erotic and procreative functions of their sexuality, there were no religious rituals aimed at sanctifying their modesty. After the second decade of the twentieth century, Orthodox customs regarding married women were observed with decreasing frequency; nevertheless, they symbolized important distinctions between married and single women that did not quickly disappear.[114]

Daughters were also expected to be modest, pure, and virtuous, but their sexuality was not as fully recognized (in a social sense) as their mothers'. This difference partially explains why daughters had greater freedom to accept employment in factories and other jobs that took them away from the home. And it also suggests some of the reasons why many Jewish daughters were allowed to make the journey alone to America. By working in factories or shops where they had contact with male employers and employees, they were not compromising the sanctity of a marriage or threatening a husband's domain. When they married new definitions and rules of propriety would apply to them and thus make their presence at work with other men more controversial, more of a threat to their social status as wives. Unmarried women, who in theory had not yet discovered sex, were seen as more socially neutral and thus more flexible than their mothers when it came to outside employment.

In the Old World, however, middle-class and prestigious families still maintained an interest in sheltering daughters from contact with strange men in the workplace. Parents feared that such contact might lead to undesirable marriages. But by the early twentieth century, as the economic crisis in the Pale worsened, older class restrictions began to break down and more and more daughters from both middle- and working-class families went off to the big cities and towns to seek employment. Once in the cities, daughters began to form new kinds of relationships with men, not only as a result of their work but also through their participation in socialist reading circles, clubs, and trade unions.[115]

This is not to suggest that single Jewish women in Russia or in America felt free to engage in premarital sexual relations; they clearly did not. Even friendships with the opposite sex were a very modern innovation. With fewer concerns about her social image than her mother, however, a single woman could move with greater ease into new social and economic settings. And that was especially true in America. Parents did worry about the virtue of their daughters, yet families felt they were making fewer social compromises if daughters rather than mothers entered the industrial environment. Without the social concerns of their mothers, without the same kinds of domestic responsibilities, without the burdens of child-rearing, daughters along with sons could more easily take advantage of the wages paid to factory and shop workers.

Immigrant daughters occasionally became more than supplementary wage earners, earning most or all of the family income. Nothing illustrates more dramatically the importance of an immigrant daughter's ability to help earn "the living" than the family budgets of the victims of the Triangle Shirtwaist factory fire in 1911. Following the catastrophe, which claimed the lives of 146 young workers, most of them Jewish and Italian immigrants, the Joint Relief Committee of the Waistmakers' Union, the Red Cross, and the Women's Trade Union League called upon the families of fire victims. As they talked to grieving parents, they discovered the enormous economic responsibility young immigrant women had borne.[116] Even Elizabeth Dutcher, a member of the Women's Trade Union League and no stranger to the plight of working women, was struck by the degree to which many families had relied upon their daughters for support. "To all of us," Dutcher admitted, "these budgets come as a shock and bring a revelation. . . . There are many people who secretly believe that women come into industry in a very casual way; that they are not earnest about it; that their chief desire is to obtain through it extra spending money; and that men are their natural protectors." But the family budgets of the Triangle fire victims revealed instead that Jewish and Italian immigrant girls "were supporting old fathers and mothers, both in this country and abroad; mothering and supporting younger brothers and sisters, sending brothers to high school, to art school, to dental college, to engineering courses."[117]

The personal experiences of several of the Triangle factory workers underscores the critical role they played in the economic life of the family. With the help of her sister, a seventeen-year-old woman from Russia had supported her family on her earnings at Triangle. Her father, a shoemaker, had been unable to provide for his family on the $7 a week he earned. Her brother, a house painter, was unemployed, and two young children remained in school. The major burden of earning the living thus fell on the two daughters. When work in the shirtwaist industry was plentiful, the two girls had managed to bring home $16 to $17 a week between them—twice the amount their father could earn.[118] In another family the daughter was earning about $12 a week at Triangle, while her brother worked as a cloakmaker in another factory. The father earned very little as an insurance agent, so the brother and sister were the main support of a family that included six brothers and sisters under school age.[119] In still another family the daughter worked not only to support her parents but to keep her brother in high school. Although her father tried to help out by teaching Hebrew, he could make very little money, and his eldest son, who was about to marry, paid only for his board.[120]

The young women who worked at Triangle were by no means unique. In clothing factories throughout the country, countless other Jewish immigrant women worked to supplement the earnings of parents and, in many cases, to support themselves while their families remained in Europe. The same year as the Triangle fire, the Bureau of Labor published a massive investigation of the wages, hours, and economic conditions of women and children in selected industries, including the men's clothing industry. This study also revealed the importance of the Jewish daughter's earnings to the family budget. In New York and Philadelphia, in nearly a third of the households where at least one daughter worked, the father provided no income at all because he was unemployed, dead, or no longer living at home. These working daughters acted as primary breadwinners, contributing on the average about 63 percent of family funds during the year. In families where the father had employment, working daughters provided approximately a third of the family income, roughly the same as the father's average contribution.[121] Overall, in the Jewish families surveyed, working daughters brought in nearly 40 percent of the family's total yearly earnings, slightly more than Italian daughters in the same situation.[122]

So important were a daughter's wages to the family that in some instances her marriage would be postponed until another child could earn enough to replace her. Mollie Wechter, who came to the United States from Poland when she was eleven, went to work soon after her arrival. She did not marry, she explained, "until she could be spared at home."[123]

Few Jewish daughters considered their wages their own; rather, they understood them to be part of the family fund. "They were waiting for my check, I was the oldest child," garment worker Mollie Millman explained.[124] And Nettie Licht, who began working as a milliner in 1910, faithfully gave her pay envelope to her parents without even bothering to open it.[125] Many other Jewish daughters apparently did the same: as one 1916 report noted, the majority of women in the New York shirtwaist factories gave their "untouched and unopened" pay envelopes to their parents.[126] Most Jewish working daughters then received a small allowance to cover their weekly expenses. Both Mollie Millman and Nettie Licht recalled that their mothers gave them "whatever they needed" in the way of clothing and money.[127] Definitions of "need" varied from one family to the next, but one survey suggests that Jewish daughters were allowed to retain a greater proportion of their earnings for personal use than were their southern Italian sisters—11 percent compared to the latter's 1 percent.[128]

Jewish women who came to the United States by themselves were often no less tied to their family's economic needs. Some of them had emigrated in order to send a portion of their wages to parents caught in the troubled economy of the Jewish Pale. One young woman, sent to America in 1909 at the age of fifteen so that she might find a job in the garment industry, had no illusions about why she was working. "I had to support, besides myself, the rest of my family in Russia," she insisted. "My sister had preceded me to this country by one year. She worked in a dress shop, and the Monday following my arrival I entered the shop where everything was ready to receive me."[129]

Even when they had not come to America for the specific purpose of sending part of their earnings to parents in Russia, many women continued to feel a deep sense of responsibility for family members on the other side of the Atlantic. When Dora Bayrack was sixteen years old, she received a steamship ticket and a letter from her sister asking her to come to Boston. Dora said goodbye to her mother and father and left her home in Bobruisk, Russia. When she arrived in Boston, she went to work in a clothing factory in order to support herself and pay her sister for the ticket. Although her parents had sent her away for political rather than economic reasons, Dora took it upon herself to help her parents in any way she could. "I lived with my sister, and I went to work right away, I assumed responsibility right away," she explained. "The money that I earned, I had it to pay for my own upkeep and I saved a little bit to send back to Russia. They didn't wait for it, but I knew they needed it very badly."[130]

Other daughters tried to put aside part of their earnings in order to help family members emigrate to America. Although the process of reuniting the family might take years, the dream provided another compelling reason for Jewish girls to work and heightened the already formidable responsibilities of self-support or household contribution. A week after young Rose Cohen arrived in New York to join her father, she went to work in a coat shop to help earn the money needed to bring over the rest of the family. Father "told me he would take me to his shop and teach me part of his own trade. . . . He made me understand that if we worked steadily and lived economically we should have money to send for those at home." Cohen recalled that as the meaning of his words registered, she resolved to work very hard.[131]

Another young immigrant woman, the second in her family to arrive from Poland, also worked for years in the garment factories to save enough to purchase ship passage for other family members. "I was not quite sixteen when I came over here. Then I sent my sister a ticket. . . . I took the ticket on an installment plan through a peddler." Her brother had been the first in the family to emigrate, and he eventually saved enough to bring over two other sisters. Finally, these two sisters enabled the parents to make the journey. "They started working . . . and brought my mother and father over." After the parents arrived, in 1918, "we three girls helped support them till they got themselves established," she recalled. Then, she added, "my father supported my mother."[132]

Most daughters willingly assumed these breadwinning responsibilities, understanding what was required of them and never questioning the need to help their families or to pay for their own upkeep if they had come by themselves. But some did so with regret. Going to work might mean compromising personal ambitions. Having been excluded from schools in Russia, many Jewish daughters had come to America hoping to acquire an education. Instead, they found that school was a luxury, a dream they would have to pursue in the little free time they had left after work. Fannie Shapiro recalled the great disappointment she felt when she discovered how unrealistic her expectations had been.

> I was so naive . . . I didn't realize—I didn't understand how things are. . . . I didn't think, I didn't know . . . so I thought that I'll stay with the family. I'll help probably in the house, with the children, wash the dishes, and I'll go to school. But it didn't work out that way. I came in on a Saturday, and Monday I had to go and look for a job.[133]

One Jewish immigrant from Galicia had planned to stay with relatives in Philadelphia while she completed her education. But her aunt and uncle had different ideas. There was "no need to go to school," they told her; in America, "everyone works," even "American" girls. Several days later she found a job as a sewing machine operator on women's dresses.[134]

The economic needs and priorities of immigrant families frequently required daughters to drop out of school in order to become wage earners. In New York (and in other states) before 1903, only four years of schooling were required before a child could legally go to work, and working papers were relatively easy to obtain. When stricter compulsory education laws went into effect, however, children were supposed to remain in school until the age of fourteen. But little effort was made to enforce "Progressive" education laws, and children routinely obtained false working papers.[135]

When Ella Wolff came to New York with her parents in 1891, it was still possible to send underage children to work without incurring the suspicion of local authorities. The absence of strict laws, she bitterly recalled, allowed her father, an Orthodox artisan from Vilna, to sacrifice her education. Soon after they arrived in New York, her father brought her to work in the factory where he trimmed women's clothing. "We landed on a Thursday, and on Monday he took me to the shop where he worked. I was eleven years old. You see, his son was going to be saved for the rabbinic field." Her father held on to the traditional belief that schooling for girls had little value. Like many other Jewish girls, Ella Wolff tried to compensate by attending evening school after work, but her father did not approve and she quit after several months.[136]

Tradition dictated that sons rather than daughters should be educated; nonetheless, in the United States that pattern was changing. Here most Jewish immigrant families encouraged education for both sexes. There is evidence that when it came time to decide which child should go to work, Jewish girls under the age of sixteen had as much chance of remaining in school as their brothers did. The variation in schooling patterns of Jewish children was based not upon sex but upon age. The Immigration Commission reported that while most Jewish immigrant girls and boys age sixteen or older worked, the majority of fourteen- and fifteen-year-olds were in school.[137] The eldest child, regardless of sex, rarely had a choice in the matter, but younger siblings might remain in school if finances permitted. Mary Antin's family made the decision even before they emigrated. "It was understood," Antin recalled, "that she [Antin's sister] would go to work and I to school." Her father "divided the world between his children in accordance with the laws of the country and the compulsion of his circumstances." Frieda was of legal working age, Mary was not. Frieda had made "excellent progress" learning dressmaking in Russia, but Mary had "failed" as a milliner's apprentice. "Then there was the family tradition that Mary was the quicker, the brighter of the two, and that hers could be no common lot." In the end, she explained, "there was no choosing possible. . . . Frieda was the oldest, the strongest, the best prepared, and the only one who was of legal age to be put to work."[138]

Practical considerations most often dictated when a child would go to work. Despite the efforts of parents to keep their children in elementary school as long as possible, girls from poor families often left at the legal age of fourteen in order to help support the family. Mollie Linker's brief school experience in Chicago ended abruptly halfway through the first year. It had not been an easy sacrifice to make: "Right after Passover, I entered school. When school was out in June, I knew I couldn't go back any more, so coming home I cried all the way. . . . My father had a job for me. I couldn't do any thing—at that age, you know, you couldn't work till you were sixteen, but kids worked at fourteen and thirteen."[139]

Jennie Matyas recalled similar feelings of remorse at having to leave the schoolroom for the factory. "When I had to quit school in the fifth grade, I felt terribly abused though I accepted it as part of life for a girl of a poor family."[140] Other daughters were much less accepting. When Sara Abrams reached her thirteenth birthday, her parents started to talk to her about making a living. "I began to hear such things as 'job', 'work', 'salary'. I thought they were crazy. I was going to study all of my life."[141]

If some daughters went off to work reluctantly, others met their responsibilities with a spirit of selflessness, a willingness to sacrifice personal happiness for the good of the family. In 1907 a fourteen-year-old immigrant girl wrote to the advice column of the *Jewish Daily Forward* asking for help on how to decide whether to go to work or remain in school. She told the editor that education was a luxury her family could ill afford.

> There are seven people in our family—parents and five children. I am the oldest child . . . and my father, who is a frail man, is the only one working to support the whole family.
>
> I go to school where I do very well. But since times are hard now and my father earned only five dollars this week, I began to talk about giving up my studies and going to work in order to help my father as much as possible. But my mother didn't even want to hear of it. She wants me to continue my education. She even went out and spent ten dollars on winter clothes for me. But I didn't enjoy the clothes, because I think I am doing the wrong thing. . . .
>
> I have a lot of compassion for my parents. My mother is now pregnant, but she still has to take care of the three boarders we have in the house. Mother and Father work very hard and they want to keep me in school. I beg you to tell me how to act.[142]

The Tannenbaum family had come to Philadelphia from Kiev in 1910, and thirteen years later the father developed a kidney condition that kept him from earning enough to support the family. Bertha, his wife, who had never worked for wages, secured a job in a men's clothing factory to help support their four children. This event provoked a crisis for their sixteen-year-old daughter, Rebecca. To stay in school while her mother went off to the factory did not seem right. Hoping that her mother would be able to stay at home, Rebecca left school and found a job. "You see," she explained, "I had to go out. I saw my mother go out and I couldn't bear the suffering."[143]

As immigrants struggled to balance economic needs and cultural beliefs, daughters emerged as the primary female breadwinners in the Jewish family. While their mothers labored at home and confined themselves largely to domestic tasks, daughters along with their brothers entered the industrial work force and took on the major burden of supplementing their fathers' earnings. In the process of resettlement and adaptation to American conditions, this pattern was a shift from the traditional way that east European Jews had defined the economic role of women. In eastern Europe both mothers and daughters had helped earn the living; married women especially had been charged with a major portion of that task. Although wives continued to make a contribution to the family economy in the United States, immigrants increasingly stressed their domestic over their economic role. By contrast, daughters were expected as a matter of course to go out and earn a living. That, one young worker recalled, "was . . . as inevitable as eating and breathing and finally dying. It was just part of the scheme of life."[144]

This redistribution of economic responsibility was a behavioral shift more than a shift in values, but it represented the first in a series of changes that would redefine the nature of Jewish womanhood. The increasing emphasis on daughters as the main female breadwinners in the Jewish family and the prevalence of unmarried women in the factory workforce had important implications for the identities of young immigrant women. Immigrant daughters would find their sense of self shaped as much by the experience of the workplace and world outside the home as by the anticipation of married life.

3 Unwritten Laws

Work and Opportunity in the Garment Industry

So there was great alarm among the tailors when they heard that at the Lithuanian Meklash's shop on Cherry Street, women had started working at the machines. The news evoked a bitter debate. One faction proposed that the women be dragged out of there by the hair. The other faction said that the guilty ones were really the men who had agreed to work with these women and that such men "should have their bones broken."[1]

By the turn of the century over two hundred thousand women and men, most of them immigrants from eastern and southern Europe, earned their living in the American garment industry. For immigrant Jews, this one industry had become the single most important source of urban employment and would remain so for at least two decades.[2] The search for familiar forms of work decisively influenced the movement of Jewish women and men into the garment industry, but other factors, including the state of the industry itself, proved equally important in pulling immigrants into the shops and factories.

Unlike many other industries which employed young female wage earners but confined them to sex-segregated, low-skill, dead-end jobs, the labor market in the garment industry was fluid enough to encourage, and then as a consequence often to frustrate, women's ambitions for better jobs. Though opportunities were circumscribed because of occupational stereotyping, Jewish daughters in the industry labored at a remarkable range of occupations, from the most menial jobs to positions requiring a high degree of skill.[3] Because garment making in Jewish Old World communities and in the United States was traditionally a female as well as a male trade, occupational boundaries remained somewhat permeable. The kinds of tasks performed by females in one branch of the industry were in other branches performed by men. Definitions of men's and women's work were inconsistent and contradictory, varying from one branch of clothing manufacture to the next, from city to city, and across ethnic groups.

The entrance of eastern European Jewish immigrants into the American garment industry had important consequences for its evolving labor market. Well before the arrival of masses of eastern European Jews, the ready-made clothing industry had entered a period of unprecedented expansion, stimulated by the rise in consumer demand, the growth of new markets, the development of new technology, and the available labor that an earlier wave of immigrants had provided. Before the middle of the nineteenth century, most Americans wore homemade clothing, purchased secondhand garments, or patronized custom tailors and dressmakers. A so-called slop trade, consisting mainly of cheap ready-made garments, sold primarily to sailors, grew up in many early nineteenth-century port cities. But with the commercial revolution of the Jacksonian Era a significant consumer demand for mass-produced apparel began to emerge among other sectors of the population. By the outbreak of the Civil War the production of ready-made garments consisted mainly of men's coats, pants, vests, and shirts. A more limited but growing industry also developed around the production of women's cloaks and hoop skirts. The women's ready-made industry slowly expanded during the 1870s. By the 1880s and 1890s, when masses of Jewish immigrants from eastern Europe began to arrive, the women's clothing industry had branched out to include shirtwaists (blouses), skirts, undergarments, dresses, suits, cloaks, coats, and every other type of garment worn by females.[4]

Underlying the rapidly growing demand for ready-made clothing in the second half of the nineteenth century were technological developments that drastically reduced the price of garments and enhanced the appeal of ready-mades for working- and middle-class consumers. The availability of the Singer and other models of sewing machines after 1850, the introduction of cutting knives in the 1870s to replace traditional shears, and the use of such innovations as buttonhole machines and steam-powered "sponging" machines for the preparation of cloth reduced production time, lowered costs, and stimulated the market for ready-made clothing. A skilled worker could sew by hand at an estimated rate of thirty-five stitches per minute, whereas the most efficient machines could make approximately three thousand stitches in the same time. To sew the seams of one hundred coats formerly took a thousand hours; by machine a worker could accomplish the same task in about sixty hours. Similarly, new cutting machines, which could handle sixteen thicknesses of cloth at one time, allowed workers to accomplish in a little over four hours what had previously taken more than thirty-three hours.[5]

As technology stimulated productivity, the market for ready-made clothing increased, and so did the demand for both skilled and semi-skilled workers. In the men's clothing industry, which in 1849 had employed approximately 96,000 workers, the labor force grew steadily decade after decade, and by 1909 it numbered more than 190,000. But a more dramatic expansion occurred in the women's and children's garment industry, which as late as 1859 had employed fewer than 6,000 workers. Fifty years later, in 1909, more than 150,000 people labored in those branches of the clothing trade.[6]

This rapidly increasing demand for labor, much of it coinciding with the years of heaviest migration from eastern Europe, opened the door to widespread Jewish employment. Before the 1880s much of the labor force in the garment industry had come from an earlier wave of immigrants, mainly Irish, English, German, and Swedish women and men. These immigrant groups remained important in the industry well into the early twentieth century, but in the 1880s and 1890s, eastern European Jews and southern Italians began to displace them.

By the beginning of the twentieth century nearly 40 percent of New York City's garment workers were foreign-born Jews, mainly from Russia. Another 27 percent of the work force, the next-highest aggregation of immigrants, came from southern Italy. In other cities the pattern was much the same. Even in Chicago, where the work force in the garment industry remained far more heterogeneous than in New York, Jews were the largest group of immigrant employees. There they worked alongside southern Italians, Bohemians, Poles, Lithuanians, Moravians, and second-generation German immigrants.[7]

Jewish employment was partially stimulated by the important entrepreneurial role that Jews had played in the American ready-made clothing industry since the mid-nineteenth century. Jewish entrepreneurship increased the access of immigrants to jobs, creating over time a growing ethnic enclave of manufacturers, contractors, and workers, an enclave that attracted—through a network of kin and landsleit connections—more and more Jewish newcomers to the shops and factories.

The first Jewish immigrant entrepreneurs had come from Germany, not Russia. The "Yahudim," as their Russian and Polish coreligionists dubbed these German Jews of an earlier wave of Jewish settlement in America, pioneered the women's cloak industry during the 1870s and 1880s. And even before that, German Jewish merchants and second-hand clothing dealers, seeing possible profits in the expanding men's clothing industry, had turned from retailing to manufacturing. Large German Jewish manufacturing firms such as Blumenthal Brothers, Hart, Schaffner & Marx, Joseph Beifeld & Co., Blum Brothers, and Kuppenheimers, as well as a host of medium- and small-sized firms, emerged in New York, Chicago, and other major garment-making cities in the late nineteenth century, facilitating the entrance of eastern European newcomers into the wage-earning and petty entrepreneurial ranks of the industry. By the 1890s Russian and Polish Jews, many of them skilled tailors, entered the fray, opening small manufacturing shops and working as clothing contractors.[8]

The peculiar industrial structure of garment manufacturing encouraged immigrant entrepreneurship. Garment production contradicted the anticipated trajectory of modern industrial development. Unlike heavy industry, which tended toward centralization and consolidation, the garment industry's "uneven" development resulted in a highly decentralized crazy quilt of small- and medium-sized firms with varying degrees of labor specialization. As Benjamin Schlesinger of the Women's Cloak and Suit Makers' Union put it in 1913, "we must never forget that the cloak and suit trade, in comparison with other big trades, is a 'beggary one.'" Only one manufacturer in the entire industry, Reuben Sadowsky, had a capital investment of a million dollars. Most of the other prosperous firms were worth $25,000 to $50,000. But the brunt of production and the source of much of the competitive fever, according to Schlesinger, were the "hundreds of small 'insects' of manufacturers" who yearly entered the trade.[9]

As late as 1914 the garment industry claimed only a handful of giant firms, the best-known of which was Hart, Schaffner & Marx, a multifactory complex employing six thousand Chicago workers. A much larger proportion of "inside" factories employed anywhere from thirty to several hundred workers. But by far the largest number of firms—at least 60 percent according to the federal census of 1914—were tiny shops employing fewer than thirty workers.[10] A low-capital, labor-intensive enterprise, garment making provided a relatively accessible avenue to both petty and large-scale entrepreneurship. It took only a small capital investment to turn a tenement dwelling or a rented loft space into a workshop. Purchasing or renting sewing machines or, cheaper still, hiring workers who furnished their own machines, "outside" contractors arranged with the "inside" manufacturing firms or factories to produce a line of garments.[11]

A contracting system had been integral to the garment industry from its very beginnings. Inside manufacturing firms, which cut, sewed, and shipped garments from one central factory, regularly farmed out precut "bundles" of certain styles to outside clothing contractors, who produced them with the help of sweatshop labor. In the antebellum period most contractors distributed the sewing to homeworkers, but in the late nineteenth and early twentieth centuries Jewish immigrant contractors set up their own outside shops. Although the majority of garment workers was to be found in the inside factories and shops, the contracting sector represented a vigorous component of this highly competitive industry. Especially in branches of the clothing industry where styles changed frequently and demand was difficult to predict, many of the inside firms, both large and small, relied upon contractors to handle overflow orders and other aspects of production.[12] For ambitious immigrants of all nationalities, this kind of industrial decentralization meant economic opportunity, opportunity that Jews were particularly quick to seize upon.

In the decades after 1880, as more and more eastern European Jews became contractors or small-scale manufacturers, scores of tiny neighborhood shops sprang up on New York's Lower East Side and in other immigrant ghettos. Employing family members, landsleit, and neighbors, contractors set up workrooms that often consisted of no more than a few tables, chairs, and sewing machines squeezed into a tenement apartment. The struggle for economic survival bred an atmosphere of cutthroat competition among contractors. Competing for bundles from the manufacturers, none could be assured of a decent living. The only way for a contractor to remain in business was to underbid the others, a condition that drove wages down and also drove many petty employers out of business after a few difficult seasons. As Abraham Bisno recalled from his family's experience contracting in Chicago: "Normally there was not enough work to go around, so each of the tailors would bid rock-bottom in order to get the work at all. In a number of cases, the bidding was done away with altogether. The employer simply offered bundles and paid [the contractor] for them after they were completed, just as little as he saw fit."[13]

From tiny beginnings as contractors, some eastern European Jewish immigrants expanded their businesses into larger operations and became all but indistinguishable from the inside firms that supplied them with bundles. Moving into a modern downtown loft building in Brooklyn around the time of World War I and paying "big rent" for the factory, the contracting firm of Pilatsky & Cohen kept its work force occupied as much of the year as possible, for the owners could not afford to let their machines sit idle. Saddled with high fixed operating costs, they had to diversify production. When they could not obtain contracts for shirts, Mr. Pilatsky told an investigator, they worked on children's blouses, middy blouses, and any other related article readily available from the inside factories.[14]

The most successful Jewish immigrant contractors established inside firms of their own, taking orders directly from retailers or using "jobbers" to market their styles. Like the older German Jewish firms, they hired their own designers and cutters. Often these newcomers produced cheap lines of apparel or attempted to compete with more prestigious clothing firms by turning out the same fancy designs for a fraction of the price. On the Lower East Side of New York these immigrant parvenus, known in the women's cloak trade as "the moths of Division Street," ate into the profits of the "giants of Broadway," the larger and older German Jewish firms.[15] In the early years of this century, "newfangled manufacturers of this kind were . . . springing up like mushrooms," journalist Abraham Cahan observed.[16] And as older cloak factories and Division Street "moths" jockeyed for position, some of the Broadway giants succumbed to the competition of small shops. The battle, as Jacob Riis characterized it in 1890, "ended in a victory for the [immigrant] East Side."[17]

The growing representation of Jewish employers in the garment industry attracted increasing numbers of Jewish workers. So too a web of personal ties that extended from the shop throughout the immigrant community beckoned Jewish wage earners. Contractors usually hired their landsleit and neighbors, and these workers brought still others into the trade. From the contractors' shops, immigrant women and men often gravitated to the inside factories, establishing there, as well, a network influential in pulling newcomers into the workrooms.

Even before migrants landed in America, relatives were busy negotiating the terms of the newcomers' employment. Goldie Share recalled that "arrangements had been previously made, with the management" of a shirt factory in Philadelphia, that she would become a sewing-machine operator.[18] Shortly after her arrival in Chicago, Sarah Rozner was "taken in" to a corset-making factory by one of her landsleit.[19] Mollie Steinholtz went to work at Hart, Schaffner & Marx in Chicago because her sister worked there.[20] Anna Gold got a job in a necktie factory through a friend in Philadelphia and later brought her sister,

Lena, to work in the factory with her.[21] And Anna Doskow, a Jewish teenager from Romania, found her first job in America working on men's vests in a shop where "the boss" was a friend of the family.[22] Reminiscent of the larger processes of chain migration from Europe, these patterns accounted for the placement of countless immigrant women and men in America's garment industry.

Family and social connections drew into the garment shops immigrants of all occupational backgrounds—skilled needleworkers, those without previous work experience, and even women and men who had practiced different trades or crafts before coming to America. Lottie Spitzer, trained as a watch repairer in her native Russia, was only one of many Jewish immigrants to abandon her former trade and turn to the garment industry. "My aunt had a friend that was married to a foreman in a tailor shop. And she took me over there to that man in the tailor shop," she explained.[23]

Various immigrant institutions also encouraged the flow of newcomers into the garment industry. In the heart of the immigrant marketplace on New York's Lower East Side, the *chazer mark* ("pig market") served simultaneously as the place where housewives gathered to buy fruits, vegetables, and all kinds of consumer goods, which overflowed pushcarts and stalls, and as the site of an open-air labor exchange where clothing contractors went to recruit new workers. According to journalist Jacob Riis, the pig market at Hester and Essex streets was so named because pork was practically the only commodity that could not be purchased there.[24] In addition to the main labor exchange on Hester Street, more specialized labor markets dotted the Lower East Side. A second "tailors' market" stood at the corner of Ridge and Delancey streets, and a "pressers' market" operated at the intersection of Ludlow and Grand. Similar to the *birzhe* or open-air labor exchanges frequented by unemployed urban workers in the Jewish Pale, pig markets in American cities served as informal hiring halls and places where gossip and political ideas could also be traded.[25] Although none of the descriptions of these outdoor labor exchanges refers to them as exclusively male institutions, they are conspicuously silent about the presence of female job-seekers. To sell one's labor on the street may have carried unseemly associations, and it is likely that the majority of women sought employment by going directly to the shop or factory.

In a somewhat different way Jewish charities reinforced wage earners' ties to the needle trades. Active in finding work for unemployed immigrant women and men, charities frequently directed job seekers to garment shops, in part because many of the large German Jewish firms who underwrote these philanthropic efforts encouraged them to do so.[26] Moreover, many Jewish-owned garment firms used the local Yiddish press to advertise job openings in their shops. Typical advertisements in the classified pages of the *Jewish Daily Forward* announced openings for button sewers, operators, pressers, and finishers, promising "steady work" and good pay.[27]

Religious and cultural concerns also encouraged immigrants to enter the garment industry. Sabbath-keeping Orthodox Jews placed a high value upon employers who closed their doors on Saturdays and who made allowances for workroom prayer. Many newcomers preferred to work in neighborhood shops alongside others who shared their religious beliefs and practices and who spoke the same language.

Especially for newly arrived immigrants who neither spoke nor understood English, the desire to find employment where they could communicate in Yiddish or even Russian was often the determining factor that led them to the clothing shops. Rebecca Gealt, a Jewish widow from Romania, was typical in that regard. Arriving in Philadelphia, she began her search for work by going to Jewish shops where she could "talk to the foreman."[28] After visiting a number of workrooms, she finally found a job in a neighborhood dress factory. A Jewish shoemaker from Russia who had intended to return to his former trade instead ended up in a tailoring factory because of the language problem. "I could not go to a shoe factory," Philip Armon insisted. "They were located in DeKalb Avenue, and I did not know any English so I worked one block from my cousin."[29] Like many other young immigrants who initially felt uneasy about venturing beyond the safe confines of the Jewish neighborhood, Esther Carroll reported to an investigator in Philadelphia that she selected her job in garment making because the shop was close to where she was living.[30]

By the turn of the century the influx of Jewish capital and labor had created such an important presence in the industry that Jews were drawn into the trade almost as a matter of course. Because of the whole weight of community expectation and personal relationships, and regardless of previous skill, training, or inclination, women and men in search of employment often perceived the garment industry as the most accessible and practical place to begin their working lives in the new country. Men and women alike, skilled tailors and seamstresses as well as totally "green" hands who knew nothing about operating a sewing machine or stitching with a needle, and immigrants skilled in very different occupations, followed the path of opportunity that led to the garment shops.

5. A New York sweatshop at the turn of the century. YIVO Institute for Jewish Research.

From Seamstress to Operator

The opportunities open to Jewish immigrant daughters who entered the garment industry in the first two decades of this century were shaped by the uneven nature of industrial development and the variety of production methods in various industrial branches, locales, and individual shops in the trade; by the skills they could transfer from Old to New World trades; by the peculiar ethnic customs and unwritten rules that shaped work and business cultures; and not least by prevailing assumptions about masculinity and femininity.[31]

Immigrants who brought tailoring and dressmaking skills to the United States could not always apply them directly to the production methods in American shops and factories. Although skilled workers remained an integral element in the workforce in the early twentieth-century American garment industry, in most workrooms the responsibility of an individual worker for the finished product had been reduced considerably since 1860 as specialization of labor and cheaper, more efficient production methods undermined older craft techniques. In most shops and factories garment making had departed from the older artisanal system in which one skilled worker, perhaps with the assistance of apprentices or family members, sewed the entire coat or dress from start to finish.[32]

Nevertheless, the adoption of mass-production techniques occurred unevenly in the American garment industry. During the first two decades of the twentieth century production methods in the United States varied according to the nature of the garments, the type of shops where they were made up, and the individual preferences of manufacturers and employers. A 1913 survey of the New York shirtwaist and dress industry showed that at least a quarter of the workers still sewed the entire garment.[33] In this branch of garment manufacture, as in other sectors of the trade, the routines of shopworkers ranged dramatically. In some factories a limited division of labor prevailed, with the basic tasks divided between a cutter, a sewing-machine operator, a baster, a finisher, and a presser. Elsewhere the work was further subdivided, with machine- and hand-sewing operations shared among as many as ten or twelve workers. Other types of garment factories adopted the most extreme form of labor subdivision, known in the trade as "section work," where a single shirtwaist or coat passed through the hands of forty or fifty workers before it was completed.

Industrialization had also transformed the needle trades in Russia, but the emphasis upon speed and the degree of labor subdivision in Russia had not been nearly as extreme as newcomers would encounter in American factories. In the larger shops in Odessa and Warsaw Jewish employers were experimenting with modern mass-production techniques. In these firms factory workers specialized in vests, jackets, trousers, or overcoats, and each part of a man's suit might pass through the hands of ten workers before its completion.[34] Yet compared to what was happening in America's factories, innovation in work processes remained rather limited. In Russia, most clothing workers still labored in small shops where artisanal or semi-artisanal methods prevailed. Even in shops that used sewing machines, skilled hand sewing remained an important part of the work process. When work was subdivided, it was usually between skilled handworkers and skilled machine operators.

Once they arrived in the United States, Jewish immigrants found that division of labor was not the only innovation clothing manufacturers had devised. To increase productivity, whatever the system of production, employers demanded that work proceed at high speed. In many shops immigrants discovered that speed counted as much as, and sometimes more than, quality. Indeed, speed was considered "a skill in itself."[35]

During the late nineteenth century contractors perfected a system of labor that immigrant Abraham Bisno claimed was "about the most stimulating for the purposes of speeding up that has so far been invented by man."[36] The "task" or "team" system to which he referred was a common feature of the small Jewish-run coat shops that sprang up on New York's Lower East Side. Working together as a production unit, a sewing-machine operator, a baster, a presser, and a finisher (usually the only woman) completed the various operations associated with making a coat. What distinguished the task system from other methods of production was that each team worked on a *collective* piecework basis, with wages determined not by what an individual operator or presser accomplished but by the number of coats the group turned out.[37]

Each team member received a percentage of the group wage. Since remuneration was tied to the collective efforts of the team, each person had "an interest in the production of his fellow workmen and in speeding him up," Bisno explained. "The highest speed of one was in substance made the minimum speed of the others, since no man could get ahead in his work without his fellow workman keeping up the same speed in the productive formation."[38]

The task system proved extraordinarily effective in stimulating productivity. A Bureau of Labor report suggested that even using foot-powered (as opposed to steam- or electric-powered) sewing machines, a task shop could produce a coat nearly as fast as a modern factory. "In the factory with five times the number of employees, with a far more minute subdivision of labor, and with mechanical power, the time occupied on a coat is only 14 minutes less."[39]

Shops using the task system achieved speed through the use of a collective wage but only a minimal subdivision of the labor process. It still required each member of the team to have considerable knowledge of the tailoring trade. However, the trend in many early twentieth-century workrooms was toward a dilution of skill and a more extensive subdivision of labor. Inside manufacturers and even many of the larger contracting shops saved time and money by restructuring the labor process to make each worker a specialist on one small part of the garment.

By the beginning of the twentieth century the "section" system represented the epitome of manufacturing efficiency and permitted the greatest speed. By breaking the production of a man's coat or a woman's shirtwaist into as many different steps as possible, and by narrowing the responsibility of each worker to only one operation, the pace of work could be intensified. Equally important, instead of hiring fully skilled needle workers, employers found it cheaper and more efficient to use a workforce of unskilled "learners" whom they trained to repeat one task over and over.[40]

Immigrant women and men who became section workers in New York's dress and shirtwaist industries might be hired to perform one of dozens of minute sewing tasks. In many work rooms the pattern of specialization included the following jobs:

> sleeve makers
> body makers
> closers (side seams and hems)
> sleeve setters
> skirt makers
> belt makers
> joiners (join skirt and waist)
> hemstitchers
> tuckers
> hemmers
> lace runners
> trimmers
> binders
> button hole makers
> button hole markers
> button setters
> collar makers
> cuff makers
> collar setters
> machine embroiderers.[41]

In some workrooms each of these operations was further subdivided so that as many as four or five women made a single sleeve.

Marie Ganz, who worked for a time in a dress factory where a minute division of labor was the key to what she called the "speed-up system," described the long rows of workers who sat with "bodies bent over the machines." After each worker completed her special portion of the garment, she passed it on to the next girl in her row while the foreman paced back and forth relentlessly "urging us on." Should anyone in the row lag behind in her work, the foreman would "prod her," sometimes "pulling on the garment to hurry it along to another worker."[42]

Jewish and other immigrant women who had earned their living in the Old Country as seamstresses, dressmakers, and tailors frequently had trouble adjusting to the work regimes in American industry. One Jewish girl, who had taken up hatmaking in Russia because her father had written from New York that "it was a good trade" in America, experienced what she described as "bitter disappointment" when she started working in an Orchard Street millinery shop. Milliners in Russia might spend an entire day making a hat, but on Orchard Street "everything must be done in a hurry," she told an investigator.[43] "Methods and speed are so different on the other side, that it often happens that the more skilled [women] are unable to earn a living here," one representative from the New York Council of Jewish Women reported.[44] "Here whatever skill the girl may have acquired at home counts for little, because she . . . is given the kind of . . . work for which speed rather than skill is essential," an investigator from the Immigrants Protective League concluded after interviewing thousands of Jewish women tailors and dressmakers in Chicago.[45]

The heightened pace and increased subdivision of work threatened the craft identities and status of skilled artisans who arrived in America to confront a new system of production. Although labor history is often written as if this crisis of identity was limited to male artisans, in this case it involved women as well. In Old World clothing shops women had usually learned how to make the whole garment. To become a full-fledged dressmaker or tailor in Russia or a *sarta* (seamstress) in southern Italy had once been a source of pride.[46] To accept the more limited status of "operator" or "finisher" and to encounter a new work regime that emphasized quantity over artistry proved frustrating and humiliating for some women.

A proud and independent young dressmaker from Brest-Litovsk, Mollie Wexler had to make the psychological transition from dressmaker to operator. In Poland and in Russia she had known only the slower, more traditional methods of the small dressmakers' shops, where fussy customers demanded expert workmanship and where each employee was trained in the intricacies of her craft. Arriving in New York, she first found work in a French dressmaker's shop but soon took the advice of friends and got a job in a dress factory where she hoped to earn more money. In the factory she labored among twenty-five other women and men, at a pace she had never before experienced and under a production system that rendered her traditional dressmaking skills obsolete.

They began to teach me how to become an operator. See, a dressmaker is one thing and an operator is another. A dressmaker you fit on the person and then you adjust it. But an operator, they give you a bundle, and the bundle may be six garments, and you have to know how to run it, to make first the cuffs, and the collars, and give them to the baster, and it goes to the presser, and then it comes back to you. This is factory work, and I wasn't used to it. It took quite a little while . . . [but] they trained me. And see it's a certain rush, but they paid a little bit better.[47]

Despite her early misgivings about these new industrial routines, she determined to learn the ways of the factory. But lingering craft pride continued to inform her response to American industrial conditions. Surveying the situation of her fellow immigrants who labored in clothing factories that used section work, she felt fortunate to have found an employer who relied upon a relatively modest subdivision of labor. To adjust to that routine was difficult enough for a trained dressmaker; to make the transition to section work was out of the question for Mollie Wexler. She vowed never to work under what she considered a dehumanizing form of labor. "It took me a long time to understand how they could do it. You don't have to think, and pin together and put together . . . they just sit and shoot like the machine itself."[48]

Whatever the feelings of skilled needleworkers about the factory routines in America, immigrant women who came to their jobs from artisanal backgrounds or who managed to acquire "all-around" sewing skills were often in a relatively advantageous position within the industry. Once a woman had adjusted to the pace of work and learned to accept the fragmentation of production, she could often move into one of the more skilled jobs open to females in the factory hierarchy. Frequently she was better situated and thus more economically secure than the untrained worker who entered the shop as a "learner."

Unskilled workers of both sexes were in a paradoxical position in this industry. On the one hand, the extensive subdivision of work eliminated the need for long training periods and opened the door to employment for people from many different backgrounds, making it possible, say, for Talmudic scholars to become sewing-machine operators. On the other hand, it increased the vulnerability of those who were relatively easy to replace.

At the outset, at least, many Jewish immigrant women who began their working lives as learners must have viewed their situation with considerable optimism. The same extensive division of labor that so bothered their skilled sisters often appeared a source of important

6. Jewish seamstresses pose for a photograph in a turn-of-the-century sweatshop in New York City. YIVO Institute for Jewish Research.

opportunities to untrained workers. For in America, one could enter the garment shops and become an operator without undergoing the tedious apprenticeship still common in the Old World. By contrast, the minute division of work in the new country allowed a learner to master her job in a short period of time and thus to start to earn what must have initially impressed her as a respectable income, at least compared to what young women were earning back home in Russia. Lottie Spitzer remembered her first day at work in a large Chicago tailoring factory. "The foreman asked me what I could do. And I said 'I don't know anything.' In fact, I couldn't even handle a needle. But he taught me and [soon] I was basting sleeve linings."[49]

For immigrant women who couldn't even handle a needle or operate a machine when they entered the shop, performing one task over and over made it possible to gain proficiency and speed in a relatively short period of time. But the system imposed severe limitations on their opportunities for "working themselves up" within the garment trades.

Chief among the obstacles to advancement of unskilled immigrants was the pervasive use of "inside subcontracting," an arrangement that allowed skilled workers in the factories to exploit the labor of untrained learners. Employers in nearly every branch of the ready-made clothing industry would hire a few skilled all-around workers who knew how to make the whole garment, assign each of them five or ten sewing machines or pressing irons, and encourage them to take on their own helpers or learners. The subcontractor took responsibility for overseeing the work of the learners and paid them out of his or her own wages what was deemed necessary. The philosophy, according to one investigation, was simply to "get as much work out of a young girl for as little money as he [the subcontractor] could."[50] The subcontractors were paid by the piece and profited from the number of garments their learners could help turn out; the learners themselves received a fixed weekly wage from the contractor, usually no more than $3 or $4, regardless of how much work they produced.[51]

Because learners in the factory had no direct contractual arrangement with the firm itself and received their wage directly from the subcontractor, the arrangement represented what one observer called "a shop within a shop."[52] It eliminated the need for foremen, foreladies, and supervisors, since the subcontractors took responsibility for hiring, firing, disciplining, and paying their learners.[53]

Inside subcontracting benefited everyone but the learners. Aside from the speeding that was endemic to this system, the worst feature of inside subcontracting was that it deprived newcomers of any real opportunity to acquire more than the most elementary level of skill. In fact, the system made a mockery of the very notion of apprenticeship, for at every turn it conspired to undermine an immigrant's prospects for occupational mobility. Jennie Matyas, who worked as a learner in a dress factory in New York, experienced the treatment that was typical throughout the garment industry. "This operator would keep a learner on one operation because it became profitable to him. . . . The learner would become very proficient in one operation and would stay there."[54] Elizabeth Hasanovitz, who at one time had a group of beginners working under her, explained that "the poor learners were never given a chance to learn to make a complete garment, because the work went much quicker when each girl worked on one part continuously." And because she lacked skills, the learner "would be afraid to look for other jobs, and she was thus dependent upon the man for whom she worked, being obliged to accept any salary paid to her."[55]

The Gendered Division of Work

Women who came to this country without prior training confronted the most serious barriers to advancement in the garment industry, but the opportunities for all women, regardless of prior training and level of skill, were limited in other ways. Informal shop rules and gender stereotypes in various sectors of the industry categorized some jobs as masculine, some as feminine. This gender differentiation of tasks, like the subdivision of work itself, helped define the place of women within the industrial system, widening their prospects for mobility in some sectors of the trade and restricting them elsewhere. Some immigrant women found themselves excluded from jobs for which Old World training had prepared them. Conversely, immigrant men were able to transfer Old World skills to new branches of American manufacture, gaining an upper hand in areas formerly dominated by native-born American women.

Garment production was not the only industry that became an arena of gender contest in this period. In traditionally "male" trades such as cigar making and printing, turn-of-the century employers hoping to cut costs and to exercise greater control over the production process encouraged an "invasion" of unskilled women wage earners onto the customary terrain of skilled male workers.[56]

The situation in the garment trades was somewhat more complicated. On both sides of the Atlantic the sewing trades had been the province of skilled Jewish workers of both sexes. Although the garment industry in the United States developed into two main branches—men's and women's clothing, both of them with various subspecialties—at no point after 1880 was either branch sex-segregated. Because of this shared occupational turf, and because of wide variations in the production process, the gendered division of labor in the early twentieth century evolved unevenly across and within various branches of the garment industry.

A sexual division of labor had characterized the American garment industry from its very beginnings. As early as the 1830s and 1840s journeymen tailors began to sew men's ready-made clothing along with their custom trade, and they generally agreed to work only on the better-quality men's apparel, leaving the "slops" (the cheaply made and less finely tailored garments) to women. Only during the slow seasons, when higher grades of work were unavailable, did tailors turn to "inferior" garments such as shirts, vests, and pantaloons to earn a living.[57] From the outset, then, in the making of ready-made clothing for men, males took over the production of garments made of finer fabrics and requiring more extensive tailoring, preferring work on high-quality coats and jackets and shunning cheaper, lightweight, loosely constructed garments as "women's work." In the making of apparel for women the situation was more complex. Eighteenth-century tailors' account books and early nineteenth-century tailoring manuals show that in the custom trade, before the growth of a ready-made industry, male tailors were making finer grades of feminine attire: everything from gowns to equestrienne garments for women.[58] This practice had changed by the middle of the nineteenth century, when male tailors in the United States were inclined to leave the sewing of female attire to women themselves. And so, along with inferior garments made for men, feminine apparel eventually became the province of seamstresses and dressmakers.[59]

Until the late 1850s, then, the sexual division of labor had been dictated by the types of garments sewn by either men or women. In subsequent decades the gender differentiation of work was also defined by the kinds of tasks that men and women performed on the same garment. This later development occurred at a time when the work process in the ready-made industry was becoming increasingly subdivided and when women and men were moving into sectors of the garment trades formerly monopolized by the opposite sex.

In the years following the invention of the sewing machine the fragmentation of the labor process opened the door to the employment of women in sectors of the men's clothing industry previously closed to them.[60] In fine coatmaking, for example, manufacturers took on women as poorly paid finishers, leaving the major sewing tasks and the cutting to male workers. Conversely, by the 1870s a new generation of male tailors, many of them immigrants, began to move into skilled and semiskilled positions in the manufacture of garments that earlier nineteenth-century journeymen tailors in America had shunned, including certain types of women's clothing.[61]

The arrival of eastern European Jewish immigrants at the end of the nineteenth century hastened the movement of male needleworkers into areas of women's garment manufacture that had once been female domains during the antebellum decades. The garment trades in eastern Europe had been less rigorously gender-divided than their counterparts in the United States. Unlike most native-born American tailors, male

Jewish tailors had no objection to working on feminine apparel. Jewish tailors had worked as either ladies' or gentlemen's tailors in Russia and Austria-Hungary, and they easily transfered their skills to the burgeoning women's cloak and suit industry in New York.[62]

This development had important implications for women in the industry. With the movement of immigrant men into such areas of garment production as women's cloaks and suits, females were crowded not only out of the cutting and pressing departments but out of machine operating as well. By the early twentieth century female work in cloak-and-suit making shops was limited mainly to hand sewing. Jewish immigrant entrepreneurship facilitated this male invasion. As immigrant manufacturers and contractors were inclined to hire members of their own kin and ethnic groups, and to give preference to the hiring of male breadwinners in certain occupations, so native-born women, who had once formed the core of the work force, were pushed to the margins of the trade.[63]

By 1910 Jewish men had established their dominance in the women's cloak and suit industry. Although women comprised about 20 percent of the work force in New York, where the trade was centered, their labor was limited to such auxiliary tasks as finishing, making and inserting linings, and certain types of basting.[64] Thus a formerly small industry whose work force had been largely female had become by the early twentieth century a large enterprise dominated by males. Even women who had learned ladies' tailoring in Russia or Poland were usually forced to occupy inferior positions in the American cloak industry and were not given much individual authority over the work they performed, a situation that some of them clearly resented. "At that time," Rose Kaplan recalled, "the women were not full-fledged workers, they were helpers. Most of the girls worked not for themselves, but they had to have somebody responsible for the work, and some of them knew the work just as good as the men."[65]

The Men's Tailored Clothing Industry

Immigrant women who knew the skills of tailoring "just as good as the men" usually found a greater range of opportunities working on men's tailored garments than on women's cloaks and suits. For while opportunities for women workers were contracting in the ladies' cloak and suit industry after 1900, the division of labor in the men's tailored clothing industry remained fluid. Indeed, the range of women's opportunities in the manufacture of men's tailored clothing such as vests, trousers, and coats varied dramatically from one city to another, from one ethnic group to the next.

New York had the smallest range of opportunities for women in the making of men's apparel, Chicago the largest. In New York, where women comprised 36 percent of shopworkers in the men's clothing industry, Jewish tailors managed to assert control over the most important jobs and practically had a stranglehold on operating sewing machines.[66] In New York tailoring shops, Sam Liptzin recalled, "there was an unwritten law" that women could not become machine operators. "In the men's clothing field, they did only certain operations—making buttonholes, sewing on buttons, basting linings and other handwork— but machine operation was reserved for the men."[67]

But this "law" varied according to the immigrant group in control of a particular shop. The Bureau of Labor reported in 1911 that "race influence" played a role in determining the extent to which women worked as sewing-machine operators. In shops owned, managed by, and employing Jews, Italians, and Lithuanians, "the machine operators are almost always men." By contrast, German, Bohemian, and Scandinavian shops gave machine work "almost exclusively" to women.[68]

In Chicago women found substantially better prospects for more skilled and better-paying jobs on men's tailored apparel than they did in New York or Philadelphia. This was partly because immigrant men in Chicago enjoyed a wider range of opportunities, which drew many out of the garment industry and so left the field open to women. But the pattern of women's employment was also a result of the structure of Chicago's garment industry. There the industry was slower to develop than it was in New York, in part because of a smaller influx of skilled immigrant tailors. To compensate, Chicago garment manufacturers undertook a more extensive program of training new workers, a program that gave women an entrée into a considerable range of hand-sewing and machine-operating positions.[69] Shop size may also have influenced the structure of opportunities. Chicago's large clothing factories, though they still relied upon skilled tailors, also used a more highly developed system of section work than was common in the smaller shops of New York. In Chicago's factories an extended subdivision of labor enabled unskilled women to move easily into different types of machine- and hand-sewing jobs, which in smaller workrooms, such as those common to New York, would have been monopolized by a handful of skilled and semiskilled men.

Chicago's workrooms offered women a wider range of positions. An estimated 33 percent of female garment workers in Chicago operated sewing machines—a job with more status and higher pay than finishing—compared to only 15 percent of women working in New York's industry.[70] But in Chicago, as elsewhere, the structure of female opportunity varied from one sector of the industry to another. Coat making remained a bastion of male privilege. Coats, considered "more important" than either pants or vests, still required the work of skilled tailors, even in factories that employed an extensive subdivision of tasks. Skilled male tailors, many of them former European artisans, not only commanded the most skilled machine jobs but also monopolized the expert handwork.[71]

Lottie Spitzer, who went to work in a Chicago coat factory in 1914, recalled the special place of skilled tailors in her shop. "There was the nicest handwork done by men on stitching lapels." "So they were doin' the finer work. . . . That's the way it was, men sitting by the big jobs and women by the little jobs."[72] But though circumscribed, the range of women's jobs in Chicago coat shops was still greater than in New York. Female operators in Chicago tailoring factories often started out as canvas stitchers. Many of them moved into pocket facing, pocket making, lining making, and, if exceptionally skilled, trained to be sleeve makers.[73] Women found an even broader spectrum of job opportunities in Chicago's pants and vest shops. One immigrant woman described the breakdown of occupations in the pants shop of a large Chicago tailoring factory: "We had a lot of men operators. But the men mostly were in the cutting room or pressing." As a result many skilled jobs in hand and machine sewing went to women.[74]

The "Women's Industries"

Unwritten laws about male and female jobs affected the working life of immigrants in the garment industry as a whole, but they did not foreclose all opportunities for women to step up the occupational ladder.[75] Moreover, though women workers in the tailored branches of both men's and women's clothing manufacture faced serious limitations on their access to certain types of jobs, opportunity was much greater in other sectors of the garment industry. The production of shirtwaists, women's and children's dresses, undergarments, kimonos, and wrappers (robes) came to be known as "women's industries."[76]

Dressmaking and related kinds of sewing on untailored garments worn by females had traditionally been women's occupations on both sides of the Atlantic. In the United States in the first decades of this century women comprised between 85 and 95 percent of the workforce in these industries and monopolized not only the machine-operating jobs but every other task except for cutting.[77] In these industries women were able to rise to positions of authority and prestige, opportunities hard to find in other branches of the garment industry. The division of labor at Weisman and Son's in the spring of 1914 was not unlike the situation in other New York dress and waist factories: out of a total of sixteen sewing-machine operators, eleven were women and five were men. Two women worked as sample makers, a job requiring the highest degree of skill and knowledge of how to make the whole garment, and another woman headed the pressing department.[78] In other branches of garment production (on both men's and women's apparel) these jobs were usually monopolized by men.

Women in the shirtwaist, dress, and undergarment factories worked as designers, sample makers, and drapers and even assisted the cutters as slopers and markers.[79] Although men also worked as operators, their presence in the shops did not serve to block female mobility as it did in other branches of garment manufacture, making employment in the "women's" industries much less gender-stratified. A detailed view of employment patterns in New York's dress and shirtwaist industry appears in Table 2. In 1913 garment cutting was still dominated by men, and women predominated in the lower skill occupations such as garment cleaning and finishing. But women and men shared the other positions of high to medium skill, including sloping and marking, sleeve setting, dressmaking, and special machine operations such as tucking.

More revealing still are the few surviving payroll records of individual New York shirtwaist factories.[80] These records indicate that the sexual division of labor in the garment industry did not sort all males into the category of highly paid skilled labor or consign all females into the ranks of the low-paid and unskilled. For example, in the spring of 1914 Weisman and Son's shirtwaist factory listed twenty-one workers on its payroll. The highest-paid male worker, M. Zuger, an operator, had worked for the firm for seven years and earned a weekly wage of $17. Abie Rothenberg, the lowest-paid male, also an operator, had worked at the firm two weeks and made only $3 a week. The highest-paid woman was samplemaker Beckie Lieberman. Employed at Weisman's for two and a half years, she earned $15 a week. Dora Weisman's earnings as an operator were only slightly better than Abie Rothenberg's; she had one month's experience and made $4 a week (see Table 3).

Table 2. Occupations of male and female workers in the dress and shirtwaist industry, New York, 1913

Occupation	Number		Percentage	
	Females	Males	Females	Males
Cutting	—	1,701	—	100
Buttonhole making*	66	79	45	55
Pressing	582	537	52	48
Sloping and marking	21	16	57	43
Skirt operating*	228	171	57	43
Sleeve setting*	86	53	62	38
Tucking*	627	248	72	28
Closing and hemming*	104	30	78	22
Dressmaking*	350	90	80	20
Sleeve making*	300	44	87	13
Waist operating*	5,061	764	87	13
Button sewing*	136	19	88	12
Lace running*	103	10	91	9
Hemstitching*	170	10	94	6
Joining	196	11	95	5
Sample operating*	559	21	96	4
Trimming	612	22	97	3
Assorting	147	4	97	3
Examining	842	10	99	1
Embroidering	183	1	99	1
Draping	1,315	6	99.5	0.5
Garment cleaning	2,086	—	100	—
Finishing	5,363	—	100	—
Unclassified	5,591	864	87	13
TOTAL	24,726	4,711	84	16

*Indicates a sewing-machine operation.
Source: United States Bureau of Labor Statistics, Bulletin no. 145, April 10, 1914, p. 145.

The Language of Occupational Sex-typing

By the end of the century, then, the occupational structure in the garment industry was a complex of skills and tasks that, depending upon locale, ethnic group, and type of production, were often labeled either men's or women's work. Although the gender divisions of labor were variable and inconsistently applied throughout the garment industry, certain general patterns shaped the labor market for women. The tailored branches of both the men's and the women's clothing industry, which produced garments such as coats, cloaks, and suits, tended to give men the more skilled and better-paying positions, leaving women to do many of the menial tasks. In the sewing of less tailored women's

Table 3. Employees and wages at Weisman and Son's Factory, March 19, 1914

Name	Occupation	Weekly wage	Starting wage	Time at firm (months)	Time in trade (months)
Males					
M. Zuger	Operator	$17.00	$15.00	15	84
Louis Summer	Operator	16.00	12.00	30	60
E. Summer	Operator	16.00	11.00	30	42
Joe Meiser	Operator	5.00	3.00	1	6
Abie Rothenberg	Operator	3.00	3.00	0.5	6
Females					
Beckie Lieberman	Sample mkr.	$15.00	$11.00	30	48
Sadie Boort	Sample mkr.	12.00	11.00	5	84
Sarah Ornich	Presser	9.50	9.00	15	36
Julia Tans	Operator	13.00	7.00	30	30
Stella Rosen	Operator	11.00	10.00	13	36
Mollie Seigel	Operator	10.50	10.00	13	36
Celia Turetzky	Operator	9.50	6.50	6	36
Dora Freedlender	Operator	9.00	6.50	13	13
Sarah Sprerigan	Operator	9.00	7.00	15	24
Jennie Panich	Operator	8.00	3.00	18	18
Rose Schwartzman	Operator	6.00	4.50	5	5
Ida Berger	Operator	6.00	5.00	2	8
Beckie Cohen	Operator	5.00	4.00	3	4
Dora Weisman	Operator	4.00	3.00	1	1
Rose Schein	New employee	—	—	first day	
Fannie Kaplan	New employee	—	—	first day	

Source: Minutes of the Joint Board of Grievances in the Dress and Waist Industry, Chief Clerk's Investigation, March 19, 1914, Weisman and Son's. Unpublished typescript, ILGWU Research Dept., New York.

clothing such as dresses and shirtwaists, on the other hand, female labor predominated in all positions except garment cutting.

Contributing to the shape of the labor market were the expectations that employers and workers held about gender. Two distinct but reinforcing cultural frameworks—American and immigrant—came into play. Turn-of-the-century Americans were still trying to order their world in terms of distinct gender categories. Female wage labor, a source of controversy for Victorian America, became an especially urgent concern as more young women went out to work in factories and offices. Middle-class literature increasingly focused on the kinds of work a "lady" might perform without forsaking her femininity.[81] These concerns emerged in the various government- and industry-sponsored reports that tried to argue that men and women in the garment industry labored at distinct occupations that befitted the social and physical characteristics of masculinity and femininity. The tendency to justify the allocation of certain tasks to men or to women on the basis of what were understood to be the innate capabilities of each sex was common throughout American industry. But in the garment industry, where many jobs labeled "men's work" had formerly been performed by women and where most tasks could clearly be undertaken by either sex, gender stereotyping sometimes bore no relationship to the requirements of the job and even contradicted actual patterns of employment.[82]

Despite the tremendous variation in work opportunities from city to city, and from one ethnic group to another, Progressive Era social investigators, anxious to understand the world in clear-cut categories of masculine and feminine, wrote about garment-industry work patterns in ways that made them appear more orderly than in fact they were.

Stretching hard to find a physiological relationship between the sex of the worker and the job that he or she performed, factory investigators and industry observers often created what Ruth Milkman has called "idioms" of occupational sex-typing.[83] Using biological and sexual metaphors to describe the labor market, industrial investigators claimed that only men were strong enough to handle the "heavy" and "masculine" woolen fabrics used in the production of suits, coats, and cloaks; women's more delicate touch suited them for the sewing of "lighter" fabrics used in the manufacture of dresses, shirtwaists, and undergarments. As one investigator reported, the New York women's suit and skirt industry "created conditions favorable" to employment of male sewing-machine operators since those garments and the fabrics used in making them were "heavy," "dark" and "made up upon lines unusually simple and severe," qualities identified with masculinity. To handle such fabrics, it was argued, required a degree of "mechanical skill" and physical strength women were thought not to possess. [84] So too a representative of the Bureau of Labor reported in 1911 that tasks requiring the handling of the whole coat of a man's suit were, by definition, "too strenuous" for a woman's delicate constitution.[85] On the other hand, this investigator reasoned, since men's vests and trousers were "lighter" in weight and thus by definition "more agreeable" to women, a biological relationship explained why females performed machine operations on these garments.[86]

The lexicon of symbols used to differentiate men's and women's jobs in the tailored branches of garment making also applied to the so-called women's industries: dresses and shirtwaists, undergarments and kimonos. The cottons, silks, and other "glossy" and lightweight fabrics used in making such garments seemed to correspond perfectly with prevailing middle-class American images of the female character. Using the language of high Victorian sensibility, one investigation of employment patterns insisted that "light colored" and "easily soiled" materials necessitated the careful handling that women could best provide.[87] The importance of the feminine touch even applied to the pressing department in the shirtwaist and dress industry, "owing to the lightness of most of the materials used."[88] Thus it seemed almost axiomatic that woman was the "natural prototype of the worker in the dress and waist trades."[89]

This attempt to find a gendered order in a messy and chaotic industry often ignored the facts of work distribution. Investigators took pains to point out that "wherever the nature of the work calls for patience, delicate touch, and nimble fingers, women are found holding the field." But "where speed and quantity of output count for most, men, on account of their greater strength and endurance, are preferred."[90] In fact, the very same operations allegedly requiring men's superior strength, speed, and endurance were frequently performed by women. Describing the preferred qualities in sewing-machine operators on women's skirts, for example, the same writer insisted that "speed is the chief requirement" but neglected to reconcile that assumption with the fact that over half of the skirt operators in the dress and waist industry were women.[91] On the other hand, another report stressed that females were exceptionally qualified to insert the lightweight linings into women's tailored cloaks and suits. Women's "quickness" and "deftness" enabled them to line a garment "in perhaps half the time that would by required by a tailor."[92] The report declined to explain how, in view of the requirement for quickness and deftness, the work of liners was also performed by "superannuated tailors" and other men "who are not skilled enough to secure employment as tailors."[93]

American investigators rooted complex labor-market patterns in simple, biologically determined frameworks. Far from offering a logical explanation for the structuring of work, or even an accurate portrait of the work performed by men and women, the gendered language of middle-class investigators reveals a preoccupation with defining, locating, and limiting women's place within an emerging and still chaotic industrial society.

How much these perspectives influenced opportunities for women cannot be determined. But there is some evidence that larger manufacturers who considered themselves assimilated into the American culture tried to live up to a formula for gender divisions. They may have helped perpetuate the limits of opportunity in various branches of the industry.

Certainly such ideology was potentially a powerful weapon in the hands of those who wished to justify or occasion the exclusion of women from various occupations. The pervasive understanding in America that women's primary function was (or should be) domestic rather than economic gave credence to the notion that as temporary wage earners, females should content themselves with menial, less remunerative tasks, allowing men to occupy the most skilled and best-paying jobs.

Eastern European Jewish men may have taken advantage of this rhetorical mode of protecting their occupational turf, but these idioms did not originate in their culture. Most Jewish men and women understood the labor market in terms of social and kin connections or "unwritten laws" that had more to do with patriarchal dominance than with biological determinism. Coming from a culture that did not romanticize or glorify female "delicacy" but rather emphasized the close relationship of women with the marketplace, eastern European Jewish workers and bosses were latecomers to this kind of cultural conditioning. And there is little evidence that neighborhood shops used sex-typed idioms as a basis for their hiring decisions.

Jewish immigrants entered the garment industry with their own kinds of expectations. The unwritten laws that kept women out of certain jobs were in part a product of the status anxieties of immigrant men. Jewish men who in Russia had practiced other, more prestigious occupations (or perhaps had come from a scholarly background) now faced the humiliation of becoming tailors to earn a living in America. The anxieties associated with this downward social mobility led some individuals to compensate for their own loss of status by erecting a pecking order that gave all male shopworkers more privileges and opportunities than women or, perhaps, excluded women altogether from the workroom. Sam Liptzin recalled working in one shop where "a woman could not even get a job as a finisher." An elderly man in the finishing department had managed to keep women from getting work by claiming: "With me the shop is like my synagogue. I don't sit together with women."[94] Thus women became the victims of men's efforts to assert, or perhaps reclaim, their masculine dignity.[95]

Closely tied to this status anxiety was the mounting pressure on immigrant men to assume a larger responsibility for the family's economic welfare. The rise of the breadwinner ethic, and the accompanying shift away from the traditional economic partnership between husband and wife in the Jewish family, placed a greater pressure than ever before on men to enhance their earning power. Even as daughters assumed a greater burden of family economic welfare, the male breadwinner as the model for Americanized masculinity encouraged Jewish men to identify an occupational turf for themselves and protect it even from their own daughters and sisters. Thus, ironically, outward social pressures upon men contradicted internal family need for young women's wages and may have limited women's access to certain types of jobs. And male garment workers, continually fearful of the possibility of feminine encroachment into their occupational territory, employed various strategies to protect their favored positions. Though they grew out of different cultural frameworks, immigrant Jewish and American reformers' concerns about gendering the labor market became mutually reinforcing influences.

Where trade unions had the power, they cooperated to keep women out of skilled male preserves. But more important, male workers used informal mechanisms to protect their jobs, refusing to train women in the requisite skills and instead training other men. Although some employers felt a degree of ambivalence about this issue, and occasionally hired women as a means to undercut men's wages, they generally supported the social logic of gender divisions.[96]

Gendered Earnings

This labor market, with its complex gender distribution, was also built upon a pattern of wage inequality. Identical tasks were often performed by men and women, and gender differentiation was expressed in unequal earnings. Nevertheless, fluidity rather than rigidity characterized women's earning power. The fairly wide range of female occupations within the various branches of the clothing industry was reflected in women's earnings.

Almost without exception, men earned more money. Census data on average annual earnings for selected years between 1899 and 1914 reveal that women employed in the men's clothing industry earned slightly less than half as much as men. In the women's clothing industry women fared somewhat better, earning approximately 52 percent of men's annual income.[97]

This disparity in earnings reflected the exclusion of women from the highest-paying occupations, most notably the cutter's trade. But even when the earnings of cutters are disregarded, a substantial gap remains. A Bureau of Labor study of the payroll records of production workers (operators, hand sewers, and pressers) in the men's clothing industry in five cities shows that in representative weeks during 1907 and 1908, the median earnings of women were two-thirds those of men, though with considerable variation among cities. In Chicago, for example, women's median weekly earnings were 70 percent of men's (roughly $7 compared to $10), whereas in New York women made about 60 percent of male garment workers' wages (just under $6 compared to $10).[98]

Since many women entered the industry as teenagers and remained only five or six years until they married, it might be expected that age played a role in the unequal earnings of male and female garment workers, and to some extent it did. Because women tended to "marry out" of the industry, usually by their mid-twenties, many left work before they could reap the economic benefits that time spent on the job often brought. Yet comparisons of men's and women's earnings at different age levels suggest that the longer industrial experience of fathers and husbands was not the main source of economic inequality.

Teenage girls and boys entering the world of work as learners in Chicago's men's clothing factories started out on a fairly equal basis, both earning slightly over $3 a week. Payroll records compiled by the Bureau of Labor show that during their first years in the industry, girls between the ages of fourteen and eighteen kept pace with the earnings of boys of the same age, falling no more than 10 percent behind them (see Table 4). After age eighteen however, the earnings of men tended to move ahead. And from age twenty-two on, women's median weekly earnings fell to between two-thirds and three-quarters of what men earned. Apparently the five or six years of on-the-job training that brought garment workers to the peak of their earning power left men and women at different income levels: women's average earnings would hover between $7 and $9 for the rest of their careers, while the average male earned between $11 and $14 a week.[99]

Even when women and men performed identical tasks, men frequently earned more money. Wage statistics broken down for various occupations show that men's earnings for the same tasks and skills almost always exceeded women's. In Chicago, during representative weeks in 1907 and 1908, male sewing-machine operators on men's pants earned an average of $9.87 a week, women operators only $8.56. And in New York skilled male hand sewers on men's coats averaged $10.23 a week, compared to $7.20 earned by women for the same kind of work.[100]

Several factors may have accounted for this inequality. Social investigators who looked at the factory through the lens of biology most commonly pointed to innate differences in the speed and endurance of the sexes, insisting that men's superior ability to perform on the job

Table 4. Average weekly earnings of Chicago shopworkers (men's clothing), by age and sex, 1907–1908

Age	Males	Females	Ratio of female to male earnings
14 years	$3.34	$3.16	91.6%
15 years	4.30	3.81	88.6
16 years	5.52	5.60	101.4
17 years	6.88	6.30	91.6
18 years	7.22	6.86	95.0
19 years	8.59	7.32	85.2
20 years	9.49	7.46	78.6
21 years	9.46	8.17	86.4
22 years	11.55	8.16	70.6
23 years	10.70	8.47	79.2
24 years	13.00	8.35	64.2
25–29 years	11.34	8.02	70.7
30–34 years	12.69	8.47	66.7
35–39 years	13.20	8.85	67.0
40–44 years	10.99	8.48	77.2
45–49 years	14.61	6.95	47.8
50–54 years	10.55	8.01	75.9

The size of each age cohort was not reported.
Source: U.S. Congress, Senate, *Report on Condition of Woman and Child Wage Earners in the United States*, II, Men's Ready Made Clothing Industry (Washington, D.C., 1911), p. 155.

boosted their wages.[101] And in certain capacities there was some truth to that argument. Women workers themselves sometimes commented on the ability of men to work faster and keep up a stronger pace throughout the working day. As one woman employed at Kuppenheimer's tailoring factory in Chicago admitted, "the most a man can make at 'backing' is 175 vests a day but that is because he is so strong and a girl can make . . . 150 to 160 vests in a day and the average girl only 100. She has not the strength in her hands."[102]

Nevertheless, it was not unheard of for women to outspeed their male coworkers and thus to earn considerably more money. In a Chicago factory Rose Soskin operated a serging machine to seam men's sack coats. "I used to be very fast," she boasted. "And even those men that used to work in the shop . . . used to come around" to compare pay envelopes. "And they used to say, 'Roseleh how much?' I was ashamed to show them because they were jealous."[103]

In shops where women and men performed the same jobs and received the same piecerates, ability and speed accounted for most of the differences in their earnings. Yet many employers paid variable piecerates, compensating each worker at a different rate per dozen cuffs, seams, buttonholes, or whole shirtwaists they turned out. Moreover, not all workers were paid by the piece; perhaps as many as half labored as "week workers," earning a set salary regardless of how much their production exceeded the minimum required by the employer. In that situation women often found themselves at a special disadvantage.

Table 5 shows the disparity in bargaining power between men and women working at a fixed week wage as sewing-machine operators in the New York shirtwaist and dress industry in 1912. Although a remarkable 55 percent of the women earned at least $10 a week, and some earned considerably more, as a group men commanded a much higher price for similar work. Half of the male operators earned at least $14 a week compared to only 17 percent of the females in the same occupation.

Prior to the unionization of the garment industry, wage rates, whether for week work or piecework, were almost never standardized. Reformer Mary Van Kleeck described the great variety of wage rates in the men's clothing industry in terms that could easily have been applied to other branches of garment production: "Marked differences are found in the earnings of individuals in the same occupation in the same locality. Equally marked is the diversity in different cities, in different races, between men and women in the same division of work, and between homeworkers and shop workers."[104] In many shops it was common to find groups of workers sitting side by side, each laboring at the same kind of operation and at the same pace but earning different amounts because of the variation in the "bargains" they had made with the employer. One young woman complained during a strike in 1910 that her employer, B. Kuppenheimer, one of the largest men's clothing factories in Chicago, paid every worker in her section a different piece rate. "For one hundred linings they paid one girl 1.75, and the next girl sitting [across] from me she gets 1.50 and the third 1.25 and they never pay the same wages . . . never!"[105]

Wage rates were based upon individual wage bargains separately negotiated between each worker and the boss or foreman; fixed, said the Bureau of Labor, "either according to the efficiency or capacity for bargaining of the worker, or by an arbitrary determination."[106] Usually newcomers would work in a shop for as long as a week before any wage determination was made. After the trial period in which a new worker's skills were evaluated, the employer decided how much he thought she was "worth." She could disagree, press for more money, and of course refuse to work for the offered wage, but in reality the wage bargain

Table 5. Week-rate earnings of male and female operators in the New York dress and shirtwaist industry, 1912

Weekly rate	Females		Males	
	Number	Percent	Number	Percent
Under $7	997	17	40	5
$7–$9	1,720	28	85	12
$10–$14	2,296	38	230	31
$14 and above	997	17	378	52
TOTAL	6,010	100	733	100

Source: U.S. Dept. of Labor, Bureau of Labor Statistics, Bulletin no. 146 (April 28, 1914), p. 45.

tended to be a one-sided affair. Only those workers whose skills were much in demand could assert any degree of effective pressure upon a recalcitrant employer.[107]

Elizabeth Hasanovitz was one immigrant who actually could bargain for the wage she wanted. A highly skilled all-around worker who knew how to make the whole shirtwaist, she had more leverage than the countless semiskilled women and men who filled America's garment shops. Although she did not always get the wage she wanted, she recalled one particular incident in which circumstances proved especially favorable.

> When the week was over, I asked the foreman for a price. He nearly fainted when I told him I wanted fourteen dollars a week. It was fortunate for me that . . . two girls had left in the middle of the week, for the foreman, being very busy and having few skilled workers, was afraid to lose me too. So after two hours' bargaining, I remained there for thirteen dollars a week, but was strongly forbidden to tell anybody in the shop of the 'extravagant amount' I was getting. I was the highest paid worker in that shop.[108]

More typically the boss or foreman unilaterally decided how much a worker deserved to be paid, and the woman (or man) either acquiesced or sought a better bargain elsewhere. In rare instances the employer erred on the side of generosity, offering a bargain that exceeded what a worker had expected to receive. Jennie Matyas recalled the tension she experienced while waiting to discover how much she would be paid by her new employer.

> I got the job and I was frightened day after day; I thought I'd lose my job. . . . I thought "Oh if only I could make as much as $8 a week, wouldn't

that be wonderful." And my mother kept asking me day after day how much I would get. I said, "Mother, you know they never tell you until the end of the week." . . . Well finally the week was up and I went to my employer, praying I would get $8 a week, and I asked him how much I would get and he said, "Well, what do you think you're worth?" I said "I really don't know, but what do you think I'm worth?" He said, "Well, I tell you, you're not too bad, I'll start you on $11 a week and see what happens." I had to control my excitement so he wouldn't see that I didn't really expect that much.[109]

This highly individualized method of wage bargaining worked to the disadvantage of women, many of whom were not as skilled as Elizabeth Hasanovitz and Jennie Matyas. Not only did some women find it more difficult than men to negotiate with an employer, but the expectation that women would (and should) work for less money often resulted in bargains inferior to those received by men hired to do the same jobs.[110] In fact, the whole weight of expectation that women were only temporary workers seriously weakened their bargaining position.

Thus even as Jewish immigrant women found that jobs in the garment industry were plentiful, and easily obtainable through a network of relatives, landsleit, and neighborhood connections, the specific opportunities open to them within a given workroom were defined and shaped by factors beyond their control: the organization of work, the often inadequate methods of training new workers, the problem of inside subcontracting, the sexual division of labor, and women's inferior bargaining power in the settlement of wages.

Stretching the Limits of Opportunity

How did Jewish women perceive and respond to such limitations? Did they accept their second-class status in the industry, knowing that a paid job represented only a temporary interlude before marriage? Did they feel fortunate simply to have a job? Or did they press for greater opportunities? Leslie Tentler's study of wage-earning women in early twentieth-century America argues that "the routine nature of most women's work inhibited the development of personal interest in the job," channeling feminine energies into workroom social relations that undermined "the development of ambition, aggressiveness, [and] competitiveness." If that characterization accurately describes the lives of some women, it nonetheless overlooks the very different attitudes and experiences common among Jewish immigrant women in the garment industry.[111]

Although Jewish women found personal relations at work an important source of support, the pleasure derived from social life in the shop did not blunt all other ambitions, expectations, and goals. And while usually not challenging the logic of social norms that placed females in inferior occupational and wage strata, many women struggled to better their position within the industry by taking advantage of those opportunities open to them. For most women the important consideration was not how men got the most skilled and best-paying jobs or why they earned more money for the same type of work. Rather, they were concerned with the accessible means by which females could "work themselves up" within available channels for mobility.

Pressing economic need, an image of America as a land of opportunity, and Old World cultural values that included a long tradition of women's work in the needle trades provided the necessary incentives for female job-related ambitions. Incentive also came from evidence that some women did rise to relatively well-paid and prestigious positions in the industry, and from the fact that women at the bottom of the occupational and wage hierarchy were never isolated from men and women who were relatively skilled and better-paid. Working and living in close contact with other, more experienced Jewish garment workers provided examples of better circumstances.

Old World artisan traditions served as a reminder that women could legitimately aspire to become skilled needleworkers. In the shtetl women had been expected to maneuver in the marketplace as well as to gain competence in such crafts as dressmaking and tailoring. And many shtetl-reared daughters, whether they had learned a sewing trade or not, had grown up in towns where the local dressmakers, seamstresses, and tailors were important figures in the urban economy. Southern Italian women brought with them similar artisan traditions, emigrating from villages where the independent *sarta* was a highly respected figure in the community. Immigrant women in America, then, could remember when young people like themselves excelled in the crafts of garment making and even ran their own shops.[112]

Although most wage-earning immigrant daughters had more limited ambitions, the past provided a model of women's work that differed from the circumscribed role of female wage-earners in contemporary American industry. Here we see the conflict between Old and New World definitions of the female sphere generating something novel. An immigrant daughter might aspire to marry out of the labor force and be supported by her husband, but during her work career she wanted to make the most of the job she had. One Jewish immigrant woman who arrived in New York as a twelve-year-old and went to work in an East Side garment shop put it in more personal terms: "When I came here I *just* wanted to be a dressmaker. And a good dressmaker. I worked for two dollars a week [initially] and I wanted to make something of myself."[113]

Older traditions aside, economic imperatives alone would have been sufficiently compelling to fuel the work-related ambitions of Jewish immigrant daughters. Most immigrant daughters viewed their work in the garment industry as a temporary interval between adolescence and marriage; they nevertheless took their economic responsibilities seriously. The financial imperatives of their daily lives, which might include helping support households on either side of the Atlantic and paying for their own upkeep if alone in the new country, meant that for substantial numbers of young women the job was an essential source of income.[114] Beyond the problem of subsistence and daily survival, many immigrants had come to America hopeful about prospects for economic improvement and anxious to leave behind the poverty of the shtetl. Once in America, they were further tempted by the material rewards that an advancing industrial society had to offer—a better apartment, store-bought clothing, pianos, and other luxuries that money could buy.[115]

None of this—not craft traditions, nor economic imperatives, nor desire for material well-being—was unique to Jewish daughters. Other immigrant women, most notably southern Italian garment workers, expressed some of the same sentiments and shared some of the same aspirations.[116] Yet Jewish daughters appear to have been particularly aggressive in their pursuit of self-promotion.

This tendency among Jewish women raises an important question for historians who have studied Jewish immigrant mobility. If, as Thomas Kessner has argued, "Russian Jews were driven by a demon, seeking security that had constantly eluded them in Europe," was women's ambition driven by the same demon as men's?[117] The answer is yes and no. Women's search for security equaled that of men, but gender socialization shaped women's identities in particular ways. Male ambition had strong extrinsic benefits: success was measured in terms of wealth and social status. For women, these issues were less significant. Women wanted to get ahead financially, yet to a greater degree they viewed that goal through the prism of household responsibility rather than as a symbol of individual career success. Jewish daughters expected to work for wages only until they married, and thus, to a greater extent than their male counterparts, their economic drive was rooted in familial rather than strictly personal ends. Yet female ambition involved another element, one that *was* deeply personal but not necessarily recognized socially. Lacking the social rewards of male success, theirs was a more private search for self-improvement. Women's aggressiveness on the job reflected, in much the same way as their quest for education, a drive for accomplishment for its own sake.

Ambitious young women faced many obstacles. The unwritten laws that structured job divisions, the ideology of occupational sex-typing, and the limited provisions for formal training worked against the aspirations of female breadwinners. As long as women were seen as temporary workers, moreover, employers could justify limiting them to dead-end, low-wage positions. Under such circumstances, striving for occupational mobility required great motivation and ingenuity.

Of all the branches of garment production, the shirtwaist and dress industry held out the greatest promise of upward occupational and wage mobility. These "women's trades" offered females the possibility of becoming highly skilled and relatively well-paid drapers, sample-makers, or even, for the fortunate few, designers. And in those shops which produced expensive or elaborate garments or used a minimal subdivision of labor, women with all-around sewing skills had a reasonable chance to exercise their talents either by making the whole garment or by handling the more difficult operations.

Immigrant women seized the opportunity. Industrial investigators found "considerable evidence that a strong desire for real craftsmanship" existed among women workers in the dress and shirtwaist industry, an industry that was predominantly Jewish. Investigator Cleo Murtland wrote in a 1914 study of New York City workers that "whether the motive be for immediate returns to meet pressing economic need or a response to talent and inclination," dress and waist workers, most of whom were immigrant women, expressed ambition for "jobs higher up."[118]

But the key to "jobs higher up" was acquiring the requisite skills. Few factories and shops in American cities made any provision for the training of all-around workers, depending instead upon small numbers of skilled women and men who had learned their trades elsewhere (in an Old Country apprenticeship or in a trade school). Others had learned various skills from a coworker. It was not uncommon for women to work as "partners" in a particular shop or factory. Sometimes a friend or relative who was more experienced was willing to pass along his or her knowledge to a less-skilled partner.[119] Less fortunate women labored for inside subcontractors who had little incentive to teach learners more than a few simple operations. Occasionally a sympathetic skilled worker tried to teach learners the kinds of tasks that would help them advance in the trade. But as Elizabeth Hasanovitz well knew, such efforts antagonized bosses and foremen. "I had two girls, helpers, under my direction," she recalled. "I was forbidden to bother much with them, but I could not help instructing them in the work. My teacher's temperament was aroused unconsciously. I would give them every day a new part of the garment to make up so that they could learn how to make a complete waist." When the foreman discovered her activity, however, he warned her that she was not being paid for "teaching the girls how to work."[120]

Unskilled women were not the only ones to face the problems of working in an industry that subdivided the labor process and preyed upon the vulnerability of "greenhorns." Their male counterparts labored under similar conditions. But unlike those women who came unprepared for a sewing career, a number of men found the privileges of apprenticeship open to them. Such practices were informal. A greenhorn convinced a skilled tailor to initiate him into the mysteries of the craft: paying $5 to learn the presser's trade, $10 to become a collar maker, and as much as $50 to learn the art of garment cutting. Often the arrangement required the apprentice to work for his teacher without pay for a set time period. Exploitation was rampant, for it was not uncommon for male learners to be deliberately kept at a low level of skill and then to be charged an additional fee to complete their training.[121] Eventually, however, such training enabled many immigrant men to move up into the ranks of skilled labor.

This method of apprenticeship seems to have been less common for women. Ambitious females usually learned their skills in a more circuitous manner, resorting to what a Bureau of Labor Statistics investigator called "piratical methods."[122] To avoid confinement to dead-end, low-skill positions, they created do-it-yourself apprenticeship systems, jumping from one learner's job to the next and slowly acquiring all the different skills needed to complete a whole garment. "I learned the trade the hard way, changing jobs often, for in those days there were not training classes," recalled Rose Pesotta of her first years in the women's garment industry. Jennie Matyas similarly remembered the discrepancy between her own "ambition . . . to be a good worker" and the inadequate instruction she and other learners received under subcontractors working in the dress and shirtwaist factories. Determined to acquire the level of training that would make her a skilled garment worker, she embarked upon a self-styled apprenticeship. "I'd be very eager to learn more and more and as soon as I got so I knew one operation, I'd quit my job. He'd give me a raise. Maybe he'd bring me up to $4 or even up to $5. I'd quit my job and look for another job as a learner again so that I'd learn another operation, though I had to start at $3.50 again."[123] Eventually, she explained, "I got to the point where I really knew how to work and I could hold a job on my own," making the whole garment.[124] Finding a job that paid her $11 a week, she worked until "I got so I thought I would like to learn a little more." So once again she quit her job "and went to work somewhere where they made a better-quality garment." In that factory she was promoted to sample maker and worked closely with the designer. "I arrived at the point where I was treated magnificently and where I got a nice wage because my work was so topnotch."[125] Thus a woman who was willing to pursue more extensive sewing skills the hard way had a reasonable chance to move up the occupational ladder.

Even within branches of the garment industry that tended to perpetuate male dominance in the most skilled and better-paying jobs, many women evinced a determination to take advantage of those limited opportunities for advancement which were open to them. Rather than learn how to make the entire garment—a skill that usually benefited female labor only in one of the "women's" industries—ambitious women in the men's clothing trades more typically sought to learn the operations and tasks that paid the most money. "We have had girls make eight or ten dollars on their work and then they will willingly stop . . . and start again in another position in which they can advance themselves further on . . . something which will promise . . . more money in the future," the foreman at Rosenfeld and Weil, a men's clothing factory in Chicago, testified in 1913.[126] "I was ambitious," Sarah Rozner insisted, "I didn't stay on one job, I promoted myself."[127] Motivated by a mixture of craft consciousness and economic interest, Rozner, a former dressmaker's apprentice from Hungary, moved from one task to the next in the men's clothing factory, seeking work that was more satisfying and more remunerative. "I always wanted to do something else [on a garment]. It was very monotonous to do the same thing. I wasn't satisfied just to baste a collar. I liked to get ahold of something and create it."[128] Although Rozner spoke of wanting an outlet for her craft talents, for her as for other Jewish immigrants trying to earn a living, a primary concern was money. She admitted that part of her ambition stemmed from the desire to "earn enough . . . to go back [to

Hungary] . . . to save for a dowry . . . and marry a Yeshiva-bocher . . . and have a dozen children"—goals she eventually abandoned.[129]

In contrast to Sarah Rozner's more complex motivations, Mollie Steinholtz, another Jewish immigrant who had served as a dressmaker's apprentice in Russia before she went to work on men's coats at Hart, Schaffner & Marx in Chicago, had only one concern when she tried to get her foreman to move her from skilled hand sewing to better-paying sewing-machine work: higher wages. She explained:

> My other sister was working on special machines and was making more and more. I begged him, I said, "Mr. Sepkin, I wish you would learn me how to sew on the special machines," because I could have made more money. He said, "No Mollie, you're too good of a hand girl . . . I think I can make a tailor out of you, if you'll give me time." So he showed me first how to make armholes, and then how to baste the collars and everything else.[130]

While some Jewish immigrant women changed jobs within the same factory, willingly giving up current earnings to learn other tasks that would in time pay them more, such tactics were usually most effective in the larger shops and factories, which allowed that kind of flexibility. In smaller workrooms, where new openings occurred less frequently, the opportunities for in-house mobility were fewer, and women who were frustrated and dissatisfied were forced to quit their jobs and find work in another shop if they were to learn different skills or earn a higher wage for work they already knew.

Job-changing was thus a favorite tactic for self-promotion, a "trick of the trade" as one observer noted.[131] The recollections of individual women reveal the continual scramble for better positions. Fannie Shapiro first found work in a clothing shop in Harlem. Toiling six days a week, she barely earned $2. Dissatisfied, she determined to seek more remunerative work. "I thought to myself, I'm gonna work another while and I'm gonna go out look for a job, and see what I can accomplish. So I met up with a girl. We went to look for a job together. We went up and found a job. We worked as partners, and we made each six dollars a week."[132] Ruth Katz got a job working on fancy bows and collars in a shop owned by a German Jew, "a very nice guy." Trying to support herself and pay the hospital bill for her sister's operation, she needed more than the $5 a week her employer paid, even though "that was good [because] . . . some people got three or four dollars." Nevertheless, she decided to look for other work. "I thought maybe if I'll change jobs, I'll make a little bit more. I went in and applied to work by machines and that was by the dozen . . . garters and suspenders. Seven cents a dozen. I worked and made ten . . or twelve dollars a week."[133] Leah Smith, a Jewish immigrant from Romania, had been a clothing finisher in her father's shop. In the New Country she got a job in a men's tailoring shop. After two years she asked for a raise; the boss refused, so she quit to find another job.[134]

But as writer Cornelia Stratton Parker discovered while working in a New York dress factory in the early part of this century, quitting a job to seek better wages did have its risks, particularly because of the uncertainties of making a new wage bargain. Even if a dress worker left one job with the hopes of receiving better pay in another shop, she usually had to wait a week before she found out if her new employer's bargain was better than her previous wage. Thus to protect themselves, women usually did not formally quit their jobs but simply took an unannounced leave of absence while they negotiated the terms of the next bargain. "If after one week it was found they were getting less than they had at the old place," wrote Parker, "they would go back and say they had been sick for a week. Otherwise they planned to stay on at this factory."[135]

Such stories could be repeated endlessly. Job-changing by women seeking higher wages was commonplace in an industry noted for a high rate of labor turnover. Between 1907 and 1908 payroll investigations revealed that an estimated 28 percent of women employed in the men's clothing industry in five major cities worked less than five weeks in the same shop.[136] And there is no reason to believe the turnover rate was any lower in other branches of the garment trade.[137]

Of course many factors accounted for the huge labor turnover, the most important being the seasonal layoffs that were endemic to the needle trades. And although most investigations of employment irregularity in the clothing shops do not indicate what proportion of labor turnover was due to women's dissatisfaction with working conditions, a few studies do offer important insights. Caroline Manning's survey of immigrant women living in and around Philadelphia in 1925 provides detailed work histories, showing that 52 percent of clothing workers interviewed left their jobs because work was slack, the plant closed down, or they were laid off or fired. But Manning and her staff also found that low wages and an interest in finding better work were given as reasons for quitting a job by 29 percent of the clothing workers they surveyed.[138] Louise Odencrantz, who interviewed young laboring women in New York City in 1909, many of them clothing workers, reported that 12 percent quit their previous positions either because the pay was "too small" or because they wanted "to advance."[139] No doubt many Jewish immigrant women shared the sentiments of a young hat maker in New York who told investigator Mary Van Kleeck that changing jobs was the only means by which working women could expect to improve their economic position: "If you stay too long in a place . . . you begin to think more of the shop than you do of yourself, and they will let you stay at wages lower than they know you could get somewhere else."[140]

This young woman, and many others, developed a strong work identity. Often women sensed their labor was worth more than the boss was willing to pay. They knew or had heard about other women garment workers who made more money for the same work, and this knowledge created a strong sense of personal entitlement. Yet that entitlement was sometimes tempered by the internal dynamics of the immigrant family economy. In some households the earnings of fathers were large enough to enable daughters to follow self-styled apprenticeships that would eventually pay off. But in other families vulnerable economic circumstances militated against risk-taking. As one Russian Jewish woman put it, "I know I am a good operator and should be earning $9" a week. At the time she was unable to assert her claims to a better wage because she and her sister were the only employed members of the family, but she told an investigator that "just as soon as times are better" she planned to change employers.[141]

The peculiar features of the garment industry's labor market, mediated as it was by ethnic group cultures, local conditions, and variations in shop size and production methods, created a situation of fluidity and ambiguity rather than a fixed, dead-end place for female wage earners. In an industry where gender boundaries remained somewhat permeable, where the deskilling process was uneven and incomplete, and where Jews of both sexes had traditional ties to the needle trades, "women's" work defied easy categorization.

Encouraged by the ambiguities of the labor market, many immigrant daughters continued to seek ways of bettering their situation. Job-changing, either by moving to other positions in the same factory or by quitting one employer for another, was an important expression of immigrant women's work-related identity and a means for individuals to assert some control over their labor.

While not directly challenging the gendered structure of the labor market, Jewish women were prepared to push to the outer limits of female opportunity. For even as most young women looked forward to marriage and motherhood as the ultimate resolution of a life of toil, and as a means of womanly fulfillment, few immigrant Jews were willing to settle in the short run for working conditions that undermined their economic needs and aspirations and assaulted their sense of self-worth.

But the search for better opportunities to satisfy their ambition symbolized only one means of resolving the tension between Jewish women's expectations and the realities of the industrial system. The workroom alliances that women formed and the mass strike movement in the garment industry would also become critical vehicles for articulating women's concerns, not only about wages and limited opportunities for advancement but also about a variety of problems they would encounter in the course of their working lives.

4 "All of Us Young People"
The Social and Cultural Dimensions of Work

The working lives of Jewish immigrant daughters profoundly affected their social and cultural understandings. Going to work meant confronting a world of conflicting messages and sensibilities, a world that both assaulted women's dignity and introduced them to the liberating potential of new ideas and social patterns. In its negative as well as its positive associations, working life served as a powerful incubator for young women's emerging identities.

Even before Jewish daughters left their homes in eastern Europe, many of them shared an orientation toward social and cultural change. Although they did not necessarily eschew traditional customs and values, growing numbers of Jewish women (and many men as well) were striving to make a place for themselves in the modern world. In their longing for new and better educational opportunities, in their appreciation for modern conceptions of womanhood and marriage, in their growing faith in the redeeming power of socialism, Jewish women looked to the possibilities of the future while still respecting and practicing traditions of the past. "While we did miss the *shtetl*," one immigrant woman insisted, "it was not in the sense to go back" to an earlier way of life.[1]

The attitudes of these women toward the workroom environment were no exception. In contrast to the attitudes historians have often associated with new immigrant workers—namely a tendency to cling stubbornly to older patterns of work and social relations—many Jewish women disdained the traditional workroom environment common to small neighborhood shops run by immigrant contractors, preferring instead to labor in larger, more modern factories.[2] Even as these women sought to preserve some features of traditional shop life and work customs, they also displayed a range of social concerns about the workplace that reflected their curiosity about, and interest in, change. In the shops and factories where they spent most of their waking hours young, first-generation immigrant women expected to find more than the means of earning a living. They also sought a social environment that would open up new possibilities for personal growth and learning.

The garment factory, with its strict rules, arbitrary discipline, and sometimes extensive subdivisions of labor, hardly seems an inviting place for recently arrived immigrants. But many daughters preferred it over the small neighborhood shop. In order to understand this preference, we need to explore the differing social contexts of these two types of work environments.

A Family-Like Environment

As late as the 1920s the garment industry exhibited a complex mixture of modern industrialism and artisanal practices and habits.[3] As Steve Fraser points out, the contracting and inside-manufacturing sectors produced two fairly distinctive but symbiotic "business cultures," varying in degree of capitalization, technological sophistication, and division of labor.[4] Within this dichotomous but interdependent business world, Jewish garment workers also encountered and helped shape two relatively distinctive shop-floor cultures. With some qualification, the cultural and social world of the small neighborhood shop could be described as traditional, whereas factory life exposed workers to a greater range of modern influences.

Even though factories in the garment industry were usually quite small (averaging fewer than fifty workers) compared to manufacturing plants in some American industries, next to the contractors' shops, which frequently relied upon only a handful of workers, they seemed large. However, more than size separated these two types of workroom. The "inside" factories, which by 1914 employed between half and three-quarters of the garment industry's work force, shared some features associated with the modern American industrial establishment. By contrast, contractors' shops preserved many features of work associated with the traditional artisan's shop and bore a strong resemblance to what tailors had known in the shtetlekh of Russia.[5] And though some immigrant daughters clearly felt more comfortable in the traditional workroom environment of the contractor's shop, most did not share that attitude.

Immigrant novelist Sholem Asch captured the essence of the social environment and the interactions between workers and bosses in the tiny neighborhood garment shops in New York when he described the dynamics as "not purely industrial, but rather personal—almost in the nature of a family relationship."[6] Describing the differences in 1913 between the contractors' shops scattered through the congested parts of the West and Northwest sides of Chicago and the large downtown factories of the city, one investigator observed that although the physical conditions of the factories were superior to the "dirty and untidy" state of the small shops, the "relation" between the employer and employees in the small shops "is more personal." In those tiny, cramped, poorly ventilated quarters run by Jewish immigrant contractors, "the girl . . . knows whether her 'boss' is making or losing money, and she realizes how her interests are regulated by his; so that her work is perhaps less mechanical" than in the factories.[7]

Two important factors contributed to the familial tone of workroom life in these ghetto shops: the economic position of the contractor, and the Old Country ties he shared with the workers in his shop. Like the artisans who ran the small tailoring and dressmaking establishments in the Jewish Pale in Russia, many contractors worked alongside their employees. "Contractors, working as hard as their employees, would often argue that their interests were the same as those of the workers, for the real exploiter was the rich manufacturer," one immigrant explained.[8] Sitting at a sewing machine or a basting table, the contractor was often indistinguishable from the rest of the work force, putting in the same long hours, undergoing the same backbreaking labor. "The sweater," as one Jewish trade unionist called the contractor, was a recent immigrant himself. He came from the ranks of the very people he was "bleeding white in his shop." They "may have been playmates together in the old country and perhaps attended the same Hebrew school."[9] Because of that special relationship, the social barriers that separated bosses from workers in the inside factories were not always clear in the neighborhood shops.

This situation contributed to an atmosphere of informality, even intimacy, in the shops. Here everyone, including the boss, addressed others on a first-name basis, knew most of the details of one another's personal lives, and labored together almost as if they were a family. The familial atmosphere was especially pronounced before the turn of the century, when many contractors set up their shops at home in the tenements. In this environment the lines between living and working often blurred. Meals were cooked on the same stoves where pressers heated their heavy irons. Sometimes the contractor's wife cooked supper for the working men and women. At other times workers brought meat and other foods to prepare for themselves on the shop stove.[10]

The ethnic and geographic ties that many contractors shared with their employees also contributed to the familial atmosphere. Coming from the same town or region of Russia, Poland, or Galicia as his workers, a contractor could effectively manipulate the emotional ties that workers held to the people and places of the Old Country even as he exploited their labor. As a *landsman*, the contractor knew all about his workers' personal and social circumstances. Often he had known their parents and relatives in Russia, and he made it his business to know who still had family members and loved ones in Europe. He knew who was struggling to procure a *shiftscarte* (steamship ticket) for a relative. He knew about the pogroms and the poverty. In short, he shared a past as well as a present with his immigrant laborers. And he knew how to encourage their loyalty by expressing a fatherly concern for their welfare: lending money to impoverished greenhorns, helping underwrite ship passage for a relative, and otherwise offering advice and consolation and, of course, providing a job.[11] One immigrant who had worked for a Jewish contractor in New York described his landsman employer as "a regular department store" who assisted his employees by selling them tickets "to bring over the wives."[12] For some young immigrant women, especially those on their own in America, the contractor and his wife occasionally took on the role of surrogate parents, offering guidance and direction and sometimes even a meal. Rose Cohen, who worked alongside her father earning money to bring her mother over from Russia, recalled how the wife of her first boss freely counseled her on such mysterious matters as Americanizing her name.[13]

The informal authority of the boss, the small size of the shop, and the shared ethnic background of the work force created a relatively unstructured work environment. Few rules governed shop life. Hard work was expected, but any form of social behavior that encouraged it was usually tolerated. As a result, singing, talking, smoking, drinking, eating, and other "merry makings" were a regular part of the routine in these shops. "Most of them [the workers] smoke cigarettes while they work; beer and cheap whiskey are brought in several times a day by a peddler. Some sing Yiddish songs while they race. The women chat and laugh sometimes—while they race," one observer noted.[14] Rose Cohen's memories evoked a similar image of the casual, homey atmosphere of the small ghetto workroom:

> When we had been in the shop about an hour a grey-bearded little old man used to come in lugging a big basket of food covered with black oil cloth. He was the shop peddlar. . . . The men looked at him with pity and Atta [the finisher] at the sight of him sometimes began to sing "The Song of the Peddlar." If the boss was not in the shop or the men were not very busy, one of them would take the basket from the peddlar and place it on a chair in the middle of the room. Then each shop hand picked out a roll and the little old man poured him a tiny glass of brandy for two cents. Father used to buy me an apple and a sweetened roll. We ate while we worked. . . . At noon we had our big meal. Then father would send me out for a half a pound of steak or a slice of beef liver and a pint of beer which he sometimes bought in partnership with two or three other men. He used to broil the steak in the open coal fireplace where the presser heated his irons.[15]

Without strict rules of conduct, the shop often generated a lively and socially congenial atmosphere, where workers felt free to indulge in an easy conviviality. Morris Hillquit insisted that "the operator in the stuffy little workshop spent at least as much time in discussing social and literary topics as in turning out shirts." And the whir of the sewing machines "was often accompanied by the loud and hearty sound of revolutionary songs."[16]

Among the most valued customs of working life in the contractor's shop was the absence of workroom discipline that enabled immigrants to smoke, eat, and even send out for a pint of beer.[17] By contrast the larger inside factories often forbade or eliminated such customs and demanded regularity and promptness from the workers.[18]

While they appreciated some of the freedoms associated with the traditional artisan work culture of these tiny neighborhood shops, young immigrant workers found other aspects of the environment less attractive, even oppressive. The cramped and unsanitary quarters of these sweatshops posed a health threat to employers and laborers alike. Conviviality and informality did not mask these conditions, nor did they mitigate the grueling pace of work in a sweatshop or the downward pressure on wages. As every immigrant who labored in this type of setting knew, "to squeeze his own profit out the contractor must squeeze his workmen's wages down."[19] Moreover, the familial intimacy of the immigrant sweatshop sometimes had a dark underside, as the boss overstepped the bounds of patriarchal authority and, like some of the master tailors in the Pale, used verbal or physical violence to intimidate his workers.[20]

The Lure of the New

Young people had their own special reasons for disdaining the landsleit shops and preferring to work in the larger factories. These reasons were as much cultural as economic. Although immigrant women found the factories inhospitable in some respects, they knew that factories offered important opportunities absent in the shops. Often work was steadier in the factories, and larger manufacturers often paid better wages than what one Jewish writer referred to as "the small boss with his 'one-cent' soul."[21] Moreover, inside factories such as those in New York's shirtwaist and dress industries and Chicago's modern tailoring establishments tended to provide women with a greater range of jobs and more potential for occupational and wage mobility than the contractors could.

Beyond the chance to make more money, always a priority of young wage earners, other considerations made the factory an enticing place. Women discovered in the factory the social benefits of a young female work group, a peer culture that offered opportunities for social and cultural experimentation. For many foreign-born women, working in a factory also signified a kind of cultural mobility: they were moving out of the ghetto and into a more Americanized environment.

Social scientists and reformers insisted that industrial wage work provided immigrant women with an important vehicle for learning the "ways and spirit" of their adopted country; most Jewish workers would certainly have agreed that the contractor's shop offered few opportunities in that regard.[22] Instead, the contractor's shop actually appeared, as one study claimed, to retard assimilation.[23] Rather than come into contact with American ways, another observer remarked, Jews working in the shops of immigrant contractors "live just as though they were . . . in Russia. . . . They live and work within that small compass, meeting only people of their own nationality."[24]

Reflecting on her experience in the tiny clothing workrooms of New York's Lower East Side, Rose Cohen wrote: "Though I was in America, I had lived in practically the same environment which we brought from home. Of course there were differences in our joys, in our sorrows, in our hardships, for after all this was a different country; but on the whole we were still in our village in Russia." Having gone directly into the shop upon her arrival in New York, without the benefit of American school-ing, Cohen, like other young girls, said she felt trapped by "the old environment," "the old people," and the "old traditions."[25]

This is not to suggest that first-generation Jewish immigrant daugh-ters rejected the ethnic community. On the contrary, they felt more at home with women of east European Jewish heritage than with other immigrant groups or with native-born women. Rather, it is to argue that young Jewish immigrant wage earners wanted to open themselves, and their ethnic community, to new ideas and opportunities. This attitude was certainly not unique to women. As Irving Howe reminds us, an affinity for "new tastes" and "new styles" and a desire to divest them-selves of greenhorn ways were prevalent among younger, European-born immigrants of both sexes.[26]

To many immigrant Jews, the factory setting offered a respectability absent in contractors' shops. The factory was modern: it stood for progress and new ways. The contractor's shop connoted the opposite. "No matter how good conditions might be" in the contractors' shops, an editorial in the *Jewish Daily Forward* stressed in 1913, "we must take into consideration a psychological fact," that certain workers "de-spise" them. The small shop, "in the old-fashioned building in the dark and narrow streets, is too narrow for their spirit." In the "big factory," they feel "somewhat dignified, somewhat higher spiritually."[27] One Chicago garment worker was considering the economic as well as the cultural issues when she said: "I thought I have to better myself," and for that purpose, "there's nothing like a big place to work."[28]

Although factories were often cleaner, lighter, more spacious, and had better machinery than the small contracting shops, not every fac-tory was superior. Differences between the physical conditions of work in the factories and shops were at times more apparent than real. In some factories, posh front offices and beautiful showrooms concealed behind-the-scenes working conditions that rivaled tenement shops: lit-tered floors, dark and dangerous stairways and halls, filthy and broken-down toilets, an absence of drinking water and dressing rooms, blocked exits, inaccessible fire escapes, stifling heat in the summer and chilly drafts during winter. The disastrous fire that took so many lives at the Triangle Shirtwaist Company in New York exposed the terrible over-crowding and dangerous conditions that plagued even the most modern garment factories. One worker in a New York dress factory employing two hundred fifty women told the Women's Trade Union League: "We are so crowded together that there is not an inch of space."[29] A worker at the Bijou Shirtwaist Company, one of Manhattan's largest garment factories, complained that "the machines are so close together that there is no way to escape in case of immergansie [*sic*]."[30] One neckwear worker in a factory employing a hundred women reported that "when a girl has to get up to get work all the other girls have to get up and let her pass, so close together girls sit."[31]

Still, the idea of working in a modern factory rather than a small shop seemed to have an intangible appeal for many immigrants. The threadbare contractor's shop reminded them of the material deprivation of the shtetl, whereas the inside factory suggested the prosperity of America. It was partly because the factories were often owned by more assimilated German Jews who, for all their pretensions to social superiority, had a closer association with the prosperity of the New Country.[32]

Like the young button sewer in Anzia Yezierska's story "America and I," many Jewish daughters who worked in small ghetto shops were asking themselves, "Where is America? Is there an America? What is this wilderness in which I am lost?"[33] For a good many women, that wilderness was the ghetto itself, its poverty, its family pressures, its restrictive traditions. Denied the opportunity to continue or even to begin full-time schooling, strapped to their family's economic needs and their own dilemmas of self-support, often living and breathing a social and cultural environment distressingly reminiscent of what they had known in the Russian Pale, many women longed for the chance to break away, if only nominally, from the past. Even at the workplace immigrants were seeking opportunities to learn more about and become a part of that elusive place called America. Most of their waking hours were spent at work. And the realization that the workroom environment could either bind them more closely to the Old World culture or introduce them to new ways had an important impact on their attitudes toward their jobs. For many daughters of the shtetl, factories stood for a modern world they were anxious to enter.

Religious Dilemmas

To disdain the Old World work environment of the contractors' shops and go to work in a modern garment factory did not, however, mean to forsake all connection to traditional Jewish culture. Many young immigrants who wished to take advantage of factory jobs did so at some emotional cost. The factory environment that women were entering left little room for religious Orthodoxy. To work in a factory

7. Men and women share the daily round of toil. A small neighborhood tailoring shop at 132 Maxwell Street, in the heart of Chicago's Jewish ghetto, in 1905. Chicago Historical Society.

usually required that Jews abdicate a central component of their religion—keeping the Saturday Sabbath. Rarely did the factories accommodate immigrants' religious needs. Contractors rather than factory bosses were more likely to share a concern for the Sabbath and close their doors on Saturdays. By 1912 the estimated 25 percent of Jewish workers living on New York's Lower East Side who continued to observe the Sabbath probably worked in contracting shops run by their landsleit. In growing numbers contractors also remained open on Saturdays, but nearly all factories operated on that day.[34]

The attitudes of immigrant women toward the Sabbath issue suggests the diversity among them. For some it posed little conflict, for others it created a moral dilemma, and for still others it represented a full-fledged crisis. Ella Wolff was among the many immigrants who felt very keenly the conflict between opportunity and religious commitment. She re-

8. The female work force in a large, modern Chicago undergarments factory, c. 1915. The conspicuous absence of men in the workroom presents a sharp contrast to other types of garment shops. Chicago Historical Society.

mained in the same neighborhood shop throughout her working life because of her strict Orthodox upbringing. "I had to stop [work] Friday at four because of my father's religion," she explained. Although she periodically sought employment elsewhere in the garment industry, once hired she would soon be fired for absenteeism on Saturday. "Nobody else would have me," she said. "If I stopped Friday at four o'clock and didn't come in Saturday.... I was given notice that I'm not wanted."[35] Another immigrant told a New York factory inspector in 1915 that the issue of work on the Sabbath had reached such a state of crisis in her life that she contemplated suicide. She had "lost every job she secured simply because she would not work on Saturday." Her Orthodox father commended her as "an example of martyrdom to religious conviction." But this parental approval still left her in a "terrible quandary."[36]

Not everyone shared this young woman's quandary. By the first decade of this century strict Orthodoxy was declining in Jewish immigrant communities, especially among the younger generation. In premigration Russia and Poland young people, especially those in sympathy with radical political movements, had already begun to question and sometimes reject the religious Orthodoxy of their parents and grandparents. As a former Bundist admitted, young radicals who had grown up in Orthodox households later became "anti-ists, anti-everything" that related to their religious upbringing.[37] Many newcomers must have shared the feelings of one immigrant woman from Russia who recalled that in her youth her sense of being Jewish in terms of nationality was very real to her because of the pogroms in her shtetl. But as far as religion per se was concerned, there was much she willingly abandoned. "I discarded plenty, I discarded *shabbes* [Sabbath], kosher meant nothing to me, even before I left [Russia]."[38]

Immigration, with its new challenges and opportunities and the ethos of modernity that many Jews associated with becoming American, eroded Orthodoxy still further. The vast majority of Jewish immigrants were not openly defiant about "discarding" the Sabbath, yet feelings of doubt and even indifference toward strict Orthodox practices were growing. Sarah Rozner recalled that the cynicism of young immigrant women made it terribly difficult for a deeply religious person such as herself to function in the industrial setting. Rozner, who arranged with her employer to scrub toilets on Sunday instead of sewing on Saturday, described her own feelings of isolation in a factory where most of her coworkers had already ceased to follow strict Orthodox customs. "I disregarded all the fun they poked at me. Before I opened my lunch, I went to wash my hands and made all the prayers, and after I ate, I prayed. I paid no attention to them. I used to say, 'Dear God, don't punish them in my behalf.' "[39]

The anti-ists and the strict Orthodox women represented only two extremes among the diverse attitudes held by young Jewish wage earners. The majority stood somewhere in-between, respectful of tradition yet willing to make adjustments and compromises as desire or necessity required. In a larger sense, however, individual beliefs and preferences counted less than the cultural context of everyday life. As one wage-earning daughter explained, although she personally was "never too religious," as a Jew living within the ethnic community on the Lower East Side she was never really outside what she called "that atmosphere of religion."[40] Thus many Jewish clothing workers struggled for a time to honor the Sabbath out of "respect for their stern father's memories, or a devotion to his wishes now, if he is still alive," one Boston investigator observed.[41]

Overall, however, circumstances and necessity contributed to a pattern of religious neglect, if not a decline in faith. Even those who felt committed to keeping the Sabbath often resigned themselves to working because they had little choice in the matter and because the need to earn a living took precedence over all else. As one New York garment worker recalled: "It was either you take it or leave it and you wouldn't leave it because in those years it wasn't easy to get a job, the industry was a seasonal thing."[42] In the Chicago men's clothing industry, according to Sarah Rozner, working on Saturday was "a forced situation, it was either do or die."[43] Lottie Spitzer, who lived with her aunt and uncle in Chicago, recalled the constant friction in her household over the problem of Saturday work. Her uncle, a deeply religious man, refused to work at tailoring on the Sabbath and, consequently, found it difficult to get a job. "So he worked very little," eking out a shadow of a living by making men's suits at home. But Lottie worked on Saturdays. "He used to go mad. But if I wouldn't have worked on Saturday, I couldn't have gotten a job."[44]

Even as they grappled with the religious dilemmas of factory work, many daughters agreed that the larger, more up-to-date establishments had greater attractions than the small contractors' shops. "You cannot get a job if you don't work Saturdays and if you do get anything it is in some awful place down here [the Lower East Side], and I want to work uptown," one Russian-born daughter of Orthodox parents told an investigator.[45] For her, and for others, "uptown" meant the district above 14th Street in Manhattan—the area where many of the larger dress and shirtwaist factories were located and the cultural and geographic boundary between the immigrant Lower East Side and what many believed was the "real" America that lay beyond. Uptown thus represented more than the physical distance between place of residence and place of work; it vaguely but powerfully referred to the social and cultural associations of the workroom itself. Uptown conjured up an image of modernity, America, and the inside factory that symbolized both. The image of downtown was inextricably tied to the residential ghetto, the old-fashioned shops of the immigrant contractor, and the greenhorn ways of older immigrants.[46]

The Female Community at Work

Young immigrant women, especially those who longed to broaden their social and cultural horizons, viewed the factory environment as more conducive to their goals than the tiny neighborhood shop.[47]

Women found that factory work, in addition to providing a living, exposed them to new sources of sociability and new kinds of information. The demographics of the inside factory were an essential element of its appeal. In contrast to the small contractors' shops, where the work force was usually dominated by men, the factories in the shirtwaist, dress, and undergarment industries employed large numbers not only of young Jewish women but of female workers of other nationalities as well. In these industries women vastly outnumbered men, comprising between 80 and 90 percent of the work force. Even in the men's clothing industry, in cities like Chicago, women made up as much as 50 percent of the workers in the inside factories. Here, then, was an opportunity to participate in a female world, a world of young people that provided an array of possibilities for socializing, informal education, emotional and moral support, and challenging the more degrading aspects of industrial wage work.

Even in Russia young women had displayed a certain excitement about going off to work in urban factories. In Europe the large factory had a mysterious, almost forbidden quality, in part because industrial jobs had been restricted mainly to gentiles. Despite the long hours and low wages characteristic of industrial wage work in the Russian Pale, Jewish teenagers flocked to the cities to seek employment in the factories. At the turn of the century Zionist writer Shmarya Levin observed that "every girl in Grodno who had to work for her living preferred the factory," even though domestic service provided greater economic security. As he watched "half-grown girls" pouring out of the city's factories, "their lungs filled with tobacco dust," he marveled at their attraction to this kind of work but did not speculate why jobs with poor conditions and low pay proved so popular among Jewish girls.[48] Yet to read those girls' memoirs is to gain some understanding of their youthful concerns as well as the concerns of immigrant daughters in the United States. Factory work in Russia, as in the United States, offered a certain amount of freedom from familial authority and gave Jewish girls novel opportunities for social life. Growing up in small shtetlekh, Jewish daughters never had enough time for friendship or play, burdened as most were by household chores. Factory life provided a youthful society and a community of peer interest.

Etta Byer had quit her job in her sister's tobacco store, preferring to join the female community of the local tobacco factory: "My sister's partner was . . . the owner of a big cigarette factory, and I was often sent there for goods. As I watched the girls working and singing, I wanted to work there too. The foreman was a cousin of my father's, and I begged him to let me work in the place, so he took me in."[49] Emma Goldman also recalled how the social environment of the factory attracted her more than the isolation of home-based production. She had helped support her family by knitting shawls at home, but when her father's cousin opened a glove factory in St. Petersburg, she eagerly accepted the position he offered her. "The factory was far from our place. . . . The rooms were stuffy, unventilated, and dark. Oil lamps gave the light; the sun never penetrated the workroom. There were six hundred of us, of all ages, working on costly and beautiful gloves, day in, day out, for very small pay. But. . . . [w]e could talk and sing while at work."[50]

So too, in big cities of the United States, many Jewish immigrants viewed the factory setting as an important source of social life. "I confess, that I go to work with much pleasure," a recent immigrant wrote to the *Jewish Daily Forward* in 1906. "Often I can hardly await the minute" when work begins. "Do not think, that boys play a part here. At our place only girls are working, not a single boy. . . . I very much love to sit with the other girls at work and I work with much zeal."[51]

Few immigrant women found this degree of exhilaration in the male-dominated workrooms of the contractors' shops. The masculine work environment of the small shops instead left young women feeling insecure and socially isolated. Though social dynamics obviously varied from one shop to another, it was not unusual for young immigrant women to complain that their older male coworkers displayed little interest in or sensitivity to their needs and concerns.

Working in a contractor's shop, a young woman frequently found herself alone among a group of Jewish men. As the only female or perhaps as one of two female garment finishers in the work group, she often had great difficulty adapting herself to the male-dominated world that surrounded her during the long working day. Young immigrant women, many just becoming accustomed to close social contact with strange men, felt intimidated and embarrassed by the behavior of the masculine work group. Rose Cohen recalled how out of place she felt in one tenement shop: "The machines going at full speed drowned everything in their noise. . . . Sometimes the machines stopped for a whole minute. Then the men looked about and talked. I was always glad when the machines started off again. I felt safer in their noise."[52]

From the standpoint of such young women, the most humiliating aspect of this male work group was its vulgarity. Some men found release in joking, storytelling, and casual banter, which might be heavily spiced with sexual innuendo and outright obscenity. Young women, preoccupied with their own self-respect, felt repulsed and humiliated by the behavior of their male coworkers in these tiny shops. Rebecca Holland described her brief experience in a small cloak and suit shop in Chicago in ways that help illuminate the range of Jewish women's concerns:

> A Brother-in-law of mine who worked on skirts took me into his shop. And I worked there, and I couldn't stand the language of the men. They used to tell dirty sex stories, and I didn't understand anything about that. This was a "men's" shop, cloaks and suits, and I was the only girl, and I couldn't stand it. I used to come home and cry at night because they always talked about sex relations and sex stuff.[53]

In one East Side contractor's shop where Rose Cohen worked, the situation was much the same. Try as they might, the few women employed there could not shield themselves from the men's behavior. Each passing day brought them a growing sense of humiliation:

> There was one man in the shop, the designer and sample maker of the cloaks, to whom the other men looked up. . . . Whenever he was not busy he would come and amuse himself by telling obscene stories and jokes. He did not like me, for when I had first come I had managed to gather the courage to ask the boss whether we girls could not sit at a separate table. The news of this unusual request soon spread and I began to be looked at as one who put on airs. . . . He talked of the most intimate relations of married people in a way that made even the men exclaim and curse him while they laughed. We girls as usual sat with our heads hanging.[54]

Such incidents bespoke the growing sexual tension that attended the many personal and social transformations experienced by immigrants as they adjusted to new circumstances. A male garment worker ascribed the harassment to the loneliness of many of his coworkers. "Many of the immigrant men were without their wives. And even those who had already brought their families over seldom had time to spend in their company. The result was that many of the men became coarsened and their language inside the shop verged on the pornographic."[55] For a young woman unaccustomed to such language, he insisted, "there was no greater torment than to work in the midst of this vulgarity."[56] Another immigrant was less charitable about the causes of Jewish men's insulting behavior. "Gentile workingmen talk about the weather and their work," he wrote to the *Jewish Daily Forward*, "Jewish workingmen usually talk about work affairs, about people and especially about women. The lower classes of people regard women as towels, they permit themselves to say anything about women, even in the presence of women."[57]

Whatever grievances they shared with men in the shops and factories, women lived with the added fear of unwanted physical attention.[58] Not uncommonly, young immigrant women were pinched, fondled, patted, or grabbed by a boss or foreman, either in full sight of the other workers or in a hall, corridor, or office. In rare cases a woman might even be forced to sleep with the boss in order to keep her job. Most often, sexual harassment took the form of more superficial but no less infuriating acts of physical aggression.[59] Fannie Shapiro had to quit one job "on account of the boss pinched me. . . . One day the machines—these old machines—broke; I had to get up on the table to reach [the power belt] and the boss, an old man, he went and he pinched me. So I gave him a crack and he fell. He was very embarrassed, so the whole shop went roaring. He thought I would keep quiet."[60]

One study labeled this problem "the Americanization of sexual attitudes." In the shtetl, Orthodox Jews had insisted upon separation of the sexes outside the domestic setting and had viewed women as potential seductresses who were likely to distract men from religion. In America's garment shops the old restrictions on social contact between men and women broke down, producing new sources of tension between the sexes. The new environment of permissiveness afforded men the license to take advantage of women and to behave in cruel and insulting ways.[61]

Yet it is just as likely that such behavior on the part of men also reflected the persistence of traditional Jewish notions of female inferiority, especially among older workers. In America the more frequent contact between men and women exposed females to conversations that previously had taken place privately among men but now became part of the public language of the shops. Whatever its causes, men's behavior proved a source of irritation and anxiety for women.

Jewish women's distress over the crude behavior of men at work reflected their changing expectations about gender relations and the proper treatment of women in the New Country. They had learned that American "ladies" were held in high regard by their menfolk and, no doubt, wanted the same for themselves.

Sexual harassment was a fact of life in factories and in small shops. In contrast to the male-dominated environment of the small shop, however, the factory, though not a female-controlled world, often allowed women to exert a mediating social influence. Men were still present and invariably in charge of the workroom; verbal and physical harassment continued to be a problem. But female work groups provided a degree of emotional and psychological support less available to those who worked in small contractors' shops.

Factory supervisors might tell "dirty" stories to other men as part of their social exchange, but mainly they used their position and authority to tease, taunt, and even physically harass women workers. Rather than social manifestations of the male work group found in the contractors' shops, the sexual aggression of factory supervisors was men's way of asserting their power in what in some workrooms amounted to a largely feminine environment.

Although women had only marginal success in curtailing offensive behavior, the existence of the female work group in the factories provided emotional buffers against verbal and sexual abuse. When a foreman came in and called Chicago dressworkers "vile nicknames," the women might at least gain some degree of satisfaction in criticizing him among themselves. A raised eyebrow as a signal of disgust and camaraderie as a foreman or a boss made a pass at one of the workers must have provided an important and reassuring gesture of sympathy. And the moral support of a predominantly female work group occasionally enabled women to fend off an aggressor. At the very least the surrounding presence of other sympathetic workers might deter a potential seducer or embarrass a boss or foreman who was caught in the act.

Sarah Rozner must have taken comfort in the presence of the other women in her group at Hart, Schaffner & Marx, where the foremen were reported to be particularly "mean to the girls."[62] There workers were apparently expected to listen to the supervisor's dirty jokes and to put up with their pinches, pats, and tickles. [63] But when one foreman at Hart's grabbed Sarah Rozner "by the bust," she threatened to stab him with her scissors. "I said, 'you son of a bitch, I'll run this through your nostrils.'"[64]

Although the outcome of women's resistance was often uncertain—Fannie Shapiro was fired, Rozner was fired but immediately reinstated—it is likely that some women had the courage to respond aggressively because the presence of many other females in the shop provided moral support for their actions. Even when a woman would not or could not challenge the verbal and physical insults of the boss or foreman, she could take comfort in knowing that she was not alone in her outrage. Whatever power men possessed to insult or harass her, at least she knew the female work group was on her side.

Discipline, Competition, and Cooperation

Factory life provided women with important social resources, but as in any work situation these were partly shaped by the structure of their jobs. Sewing, especially at a machine, required intense concentration and attention to speed. Unlike workers in industries such as textiles, who moved about freely on the shop floor as they tended their machines, garment workers had little physical mobility, spending the workday seated at their machines or sewing tables.[65] Thus conversations were usually limited to women who sat nearby or else took place during the lunch break. Moreover, the method of payment—by the piece or by the week—affected the degree to which a worker might socialize on the job.

Immigrant daughters' need to maximize their earnings put constraints upon their willingness to socialize, but pieceworkers were generally allowed a greater degree of personal autonomy at work than were immigrants who received a weekly wage. Many pieceworkers in the factories enjoyed the privilege of coming and going at their own discretion. Not only did pieceworkers make their own hours, but bosses and foreman felt little compulsion to impose standards of workroom demeanor on them.[66] One Jewish immigrant woman working in a Philadelphia shirtwaist factory displayed an attitude typical of pieceworkers in this industry. Insisting that she was not subject to any set work schedule, she boasted, "I work piecework so its nobody's business."[67] Describing the liberties afforded pieceworkers in the neckwear factories, Anna Weinstock explained: "If they ever got tired and wanted to go home, they could, . . . that has been the custom."[68]

Some bosses believed that pieceworkers were self-motivated and required neither rigid work schedules nor constant discipline.[69] The notion that "in piecework you can socialize because its your own time" shaped the dynamics of factory life for many immigrants. "I always admired the operators because they were pieceworkers. They were sitting and talking and jolly, having fun, which I didn't have. So I became an operator as soon as I could," one Russian Jewish dressmaker recalled.[70]

Of course, pieceworkers always felt some tension between the desire to socialize and the compulsion to maintain a high level of production. Annie Marion MacLean, who observed women workers in New York's garment factories, noted that many girls "talked as freely as they could above the noise of the machines," but "on the whole the work was too serious to be coupled with much conversation."[71] And Mollie Millman, a former neckwear worker, stressed that she and her female coworkers were painfully aware of the necessity for intense concentration; they limited their workroom conversation accordingly. "We had a long table, and if you had anything to say you did," she recalled. Yet she and the other pieceworkers could not afford to lose time by talking too much. "I was a very conscientious worker. You don't fool the boss, you fool yourself," she insisted.[72] Similarly, Lottie Spitzer recalled that in the men's clothing factories where she worked, the women "exchanged words" while they sewed, "but we never put our heads up. Because I had to watch my work. It was very particular work to do."[73] Mollie Linker, one of hundreds of women who worked at Hart, Schaffner & Marx during the early part of the century, also shared that attitude:

> On big overcoats, I had to do a certain stitch. Piecework. Each one does something else on the overcoat. I was very fast. The machines were all in a row. And it was so hot. . . . And you had these big heavy winter coats on your lap, and you worked, and you sweated. . . . You had a little half hour for lunch (we worked close to ten hours). And you talked. But you kept so busy and the machines were roaring but you talked. You had to be careful not to stitch your fingers in.[74]

The system of payment affected the social dynamics of the factories in other ways as well. The incentive of higher wages fostered a spirit of competition among pieceworkers. Not uncommonly women fought over who should get the biggest or best bundles of garments to sew. Before the advent of unionization work was unequally distributed, and the most profitable bundles often went to the foreman's or forelady's "favorite" worker.[75] As Lottie Spitzer explained, if a garment cutter "liked a girl, so he gave her a big bundle." The cutters "knew already what was good work, and what was bad work, what was a big bundle, a small bundle. And they had made up with the people to tip them off."[76] Thus when the women who worked at Hart, Schaffner & Marx went up to the distribution counter to pick up a bundle, some of them already knew which one to grab first.[77] Not infrequently competition between women for the best work erupted into the kind of yelling and screaming matches described by one young garment worker: "Suddenly voices are raised above the machinery. Red, the girl on the machine next to me, is fighting with a smaller girl for taking all the easy work. Immediately the boss comes over and yells at both of them and divides the work. After he goes the girls continue to insult each other. Some take sides; others remain neutral."[78]

This competitive spirit among pieceworkers did not preclude the possibility of work-group cooperation among immigrant women. Even as individual economic interest encouraged them to grab the best bundles, an awareness that as workers and as women they shared many common problems created countervailing sentiments of sisterliness and sympathy.[79] More experienced women, whether they worked by the piece or were paid by the week, taught newcomers in the factories time-saving techniques and tried to disguise mistakes that learners made in their sewing. "My neighbors [in the factory] were very kind," wrote Elizabeth Hasanovitz, "each one would help the other out of difficulties in the work."[80] Rose Pesotta similarly recalled that on her first job at the large Bloom and Millman shirtwaist factory in Manhattan, "some of my coworkers showed me tricks that enabled me to attain facility." By the end of that year, she wrote, "I could keep pace in any shop."[81]

The pressures faced by week workers in garment factories were somewhat different. In the absence of the self-imposed discipline of pieceworkers, week workers were more heavily subjected to the watchful eye of the boss or supervisor. Week workers, though paid at different rates according to the bargains they struck with employers, received a weekly sum that did not vary with the hours they worked or the amount they produced. Although most had to meet a production quota they had little incentive to exert themselves beyond the minimum required by the employer. Consequently, bosses and supervisors took pains to speed their work and to insure their time on the job was well spent.

Through a system of fines and the threat of dismissal, supervisors and bosses attempted to shape the habits of week workers. While pieceworkers "were glad of the opportunity to earn an extra dollar by working longer hours," according to Pauline Newman, week workers like herself had no choice.[82] They were told when to be at work and when they could leave, and the bosses used stern measures to enforce their rules. Requirements for working overtime were among the most hated features of the factory regimen for week workers who, unlike pieceworkers, had no financial motivation for extending their hours. Thus every Saturday during the busy season at the Triangle Shirtwaist Company, where Newman worked as a child, the supervisor put up a sign near the elevator that read: "If You Don't Come In On Sunday, Don't Come In On Monday."[83]

Not only did week workers have little choice about the time they worked, they were continually subjected to what Rose Pesotta called "the whip of the foreman."[84] Foremen, foreladies, and bosses felt compelled to oversee the demeanor and behavior of week workers in the factory. Too much talking, singing, or visiting the restroom or the drinking fountain cut into production time and thus had to be controlled. One former week worker described the discipline in her factory as a kind of bondage. "We were like slaves," she said. "You couldn't pick your head up. You couldn't talk. We used to go to the bathroom. The forelady used to go after us, we shouldn't stay too long."[85]

In general both pieceworkers and week workers faced a good deal more in the way of rules and regulation than their sisters in the small contractors' shops. Walter Reubens, whose Chicago undergarment factory employed 186 women in 1916, established a regular fifty-four-hour workweek—a vast improvement over the unlimited hours that many garment workers were required to labor. But at the same time the rules of his factory specified that each employee be at her machine promptly at 8:00 A.M. Any woman who arrived fifteen minutes late received a hefty fine.[86] B. Schnall, a New York cloak manufacturer, attempted to instill order in his factory through a system of punishments based on withholding work. Pieceworkers who arrived late were forced to sit idle at their machines while workers who came on time were given bundles to sew. Anyone who did not sit down at their machine "promptly" at 8 A.M. had to wait until one o'clock in the afternoon before being allowed to sew.[87]

By the end of World War I the movement to modernize factory management began to further erode customary distinctions between the privileges of piecework and the treatment of week workers. Some larger manufacturers began to impose new forms of work discipline upon all of their employees, regardless of how those workers were paid. Such changes incorporated some of the tenets of the modern management movement, whose main thrust was to bring efficiency and rational organization to the workplace in order to increase productivity. But before World War I the vast majority of factories never actually followed the blueprints of "scientific management." Instead of replacing the arbitrary power of the foreman with management experts who would standardize work rules and apply them universally, they merely increased the foreman's authority.[88] With that increased authority, foremen and foreladies enforced new rules and regulations to control the time, behavior, and efficiency of both piece- and week workers. The Bureau of Labor reported in 1913 that a growing list of clothing manufactures found it a "necessity" to keep records of the "units" of work performed by each employee and to impose "strict" rules "as to the time of beginning and ending work" even for pieceworkers.[89]

In some factories the erosion of the customary practices of pieceworkers may have coincided with growing anxiety about unionization and the fear that too much shopfloor socializing would create an atmosphere conducive to labor organization. But whatever the source of the concern, garment workers like Lottie Spitzer viewed it as an assault upon their freedom. "The foreman didn't like it if you talked too much," she recalled. "You couldn't talk to each other . . . the foreman came over and said, 'Shut up!' You couldn't open your mouth you had to be sittin' just like a straight jacket. Not to be moving around." The only time she and her coworkers could really talk was in the restroom. "And then you couldn't go to the toilet. They wouldn't let you go . . . all the time." If a worker went to the restroom too often, she would be fired. "Although you were on your own, piecework . . . they wanted you to be always down at the table."[90] At the Triangle Shirtwaist Company, "no conversation and no singing were allowed," Pauline Newman remembered. Discussion, even among workers sitting next to each other, was strictly forbidden. "If the girls felt like singing, they were told to be quiet."[91]

Discipline—whether applied in the form of well-established rules or arbitrarily imposed at the whim of the boss or supervisor—generated feelings of hostility and indignation toward the employer. "He was a monster. He was so bad," a Jewish immigrant said of her first employer. "When you work at the machines you couldn't take a look over there, you have to keep your eyes *right there*. And he never went away, he was just walking back and forth, back and forth. I hated that fellow."[92]

Factory discipline was part of a common set of grievances that bound women together in opposition to their employers and supervisors. To argue, as one historian has, that industrial discipline served only to exacerbate women's feelings of impotence and inferiority as workers is to oversimplify its impact. Jewish women probably did feel powerless as individuals to redefine their relationship with their employers, but the frustration that resulted ultimately intensified their commitment to industrial reform and their tendency toward labor militance. Not only did the oppressive behavior of bosses and supervisors threaten to interfere with the social pleasures of their jobs, but it also clashed with Jewish immigrants' image of America as a land of freedom. Those who imposed the excessive discipline and rules became the enemy against whom women could unite.[93]

On a daily basis, however, immigrant women found ways of compensating for the limitations of their work environment. When the factory imposed rules against singing and conversing on the job, women communicated in more subtle ways. Sometimes their interaction consisted of little more than an exchange of friendly glances and smiles to the girl at the next machine or a word or two spoken in haste after the forelady left the room or turned her back. At other times women would talk and sing quietly "when the boss didn't see."[94] But even in the best of circumstances most shopfloor interaction took place during the lunch period, usually thirty to forty minutes.[95] Lunch time constituted the most important arena for social life. Whether a woman sat at her machine or work table, or gathered with others in a special lunch area or cheap restaurant, that time gave women an opportunity to converse freely, joke, sing, and even dance with their coworkers.[96]

The Factory as School

The factory work group served as an important source of emotional support for young immigrant women. It also provided a new kind of social life and functioned as an informal school—indeed, that was part of its attraction to women who were interested in cultural experimentation. Like the classroom, the work group provided information and an exchange of ideas about a range of topics and problems of interest to young immigrants.[97] The whole idea of broadening their cultural horizons was centrally important to Jewish immigrant daughters and had been even before they left their homes in eastern Europe. Hungry for new forms of knowledge, they had viewed the journey to America as an avenue not only for formal schooling but for learning in general.

Something of that hunger is revealed in their conflicts about dropping out of school to go to work. It also shows clearly in their commitment to evening-school attendance, even after a long day on the job. More than one observer noted that "Jewish girls come expecting to make America their permanent home, and they attend night school more regularly than the girls of any other nationality."[98] Garment workers, most of them Russian Jews, made up the largest proportion of working girls attending public evening schools in New York City.[99]

Young women who had dropped out of day school to go to work, and those who had gone directly to the factory upon their arrival, continued to cherish the possibility of an education. Of particular concern to Jewish women was their ability to converse in English, because it represented their progress toward Americanization. Even the young people who attended the evening classes at the socialist Rand School of Social Science in Manhattan in 1918 demanded that the course of study should really be a night school for English and that other subjects should be secondary.[100] But hardworking immigrants did not always have the energy to attend or keep up in evening school and, like Pauline Newman and her coworkers, tried to educate themselves in more informal ways: "I recall on Saturday nights we'd gather in each other's apartments and try to read English. We were limited, naturally enough, because none of us went to school. We tried to go to school and then overtime would interfere. Evening classes, when they were available, were useless because it was a question of attending school or keeping a job."[101]

Frustration about insufficient time not only for schooling but also for other kinds of learning and exploring remained a powerful force in the lives of Jewish immigrant daughters. "Here in this country," Lottie Spitzer explained, "I had different ideas all the time. I liked music, I liked lectures. I wanted to learn things. I wanted to learn everything . . . everything was open for me. The only thing is, the time; I needed time."[102] In Russia, Elizabeth Hasanovitz insisted, "I had time, but no freedom; here I had freedom, but no opportunity to enjoy it."[103]

Given these concerns, it is not surprising that Jewish daughters sought new kinds of knowledge wherever they could. The female work group partly served that function. If individual women lacked the time for evening school or other forms of outside education, they might try to learn from more worldly and enlightened coworkers. Socializing at work with their contemporaries—some of whom had the benefit of American schooling, spoke some English, and knew more about American culture than greenhorns—provided immigrant women with important sources of information about life outside the shop. Sometimes newcomers practiced speaking English with each other at work, struggling with conversation, or rehearsing the latest American songs. Dora Bayrack explained that very few of the women in the Boston shirtwaist factory where she worked in 1912 spoke English. Many were Jews and Poles, a few were Armenians, and even fewer were native-born. "They used to teach me English in the shop," she said. "We used to sing and talk to each other. We used to sing Russian songs and Yiddish songs, and the American songs, I liked very much the American songs, the 1912 songs. I loved it and I learned there."[104] Just the opportunity to spend time with other young people of the same age and sex allowed immigrants, whatever their background, the freedom to explore new ideas and values in an atmosphere of comfortable feminine sociability. Although much of the informal education that young Jewish women acquired as a result of working in this factory setting was also available outside, on the streets, the workroom provided an important cultural space into which new influences and habits filtered and grew.

The garment-factory work force was a font of much-coveted knowledge about the ways and possibilities of the new country. With coworkers in the shop, immigrant women mused over the excitement of
modern urban culture, sharing with one another the details of their
experiences and understandings.

No subject was more important than men and the intriguing business
of dating and courtship. Given the attraction of the female work group,
this was something of an irony. Immigrant daughters valued the sisterhood they found among young women at work, but not because they
sought out an exclusively "homosocial" or same-sex environment so
valued by many middle-class American women. For working-class
daughters, the female gang at work served as a mediating force to funnel
them into the still somewhat unfamiliar territory of mixed-sex socializing. As Kathy Peiss has argued, the workroom served as an arena in
which young female wage earners "articulated their sexual feelings and
shared their acquired wisdom about negotiating the attentions of men,
both on the job and in their leisure time."[105] Just as female work groups
might serve as a buffer against the unwanted attentions of bosses and
supervisors, so they provided a safe harbor for rehearsing one's entrance
into the world of dating and courtship.

During the lunch period or, if permitted, while sewing at their machines, and even on the way home from work, women explored the
world of boyfriends, romance, popular music, fiction, fashion, movies,
and plays. They discussed almost anything, one Jewish garment worker
admitted, "but the work itself."[106] Fannie Edelman was one of countless Jewish immigrants who acquired her knowledge of "the facts of
life" from other women at work. She arrived in America at age sixteen
and went immediately to work in a factory making men's shirts. "Here I
became acquainted with a girl who was a little older than I. She told me
she was going out with boys and having a good time." Having been
taught by her mother that even sitting near a man could make her
pregnant, Edelman was shocked to discover that dating was a respectable American pastime. "The girl opened my eyes. From that time on I
began to look at life differently—I started to make the acquaintance of
young men."[107]

The social education that began in workroom conversation spilled
out of the factory when the workday ended. Ruth Hirsh, who came by
herself from Russia to live with an aunt in Pittsburgh, recalled how
friends from the factory provided her with a rich social life after working hours. "I worked sewing pants for a factory, and all the girls who
worked there were immigrants like me. So, I had friends and we met in

the street . . . that's how I met my husband, just on the street where all the immigrant people walked."[108] This was part of an important transformation in courtship practices. Ruth Katz maintained that in Europe, young women like herself were "not supposed to talk to a young man, or take a walk, God forbid." Socializing took place at the girl's home, with her parents in supervision. But all that changed in America. "I met my husband after I was a year here. . . . We used to go out, the four of us, My sister and I, and his brother and him. . . . Who was chaperoned? Not in this country."[109]

The work group provided a forum for debate about romance, marriage, and gender roles, a debate that reflected the need to reconcile Old and New World values. The social environment in the garment factories helped introduce Jewish immigrant women to American mores and modern conceptions of romance and marriage, reinforcing attitudes that had already begun to emerge before they had left the Old Country. Even in the conservative atmosphere of small Russian towns and villages, some Jewish girls and boys had become aware of, and aspired to, western notions of romantic love and had, in some cases, rebelled against the prospect of a match arranged by their parents. But it was in the American setting that these ideas took on new urgency. The work group in the factory provided an important vehicle for their dissemination.

Conversations with other young women at work strengthened the emerging belief that what mattered in marriage was love, not whether the groom brought *yichus* (prestige) to her family. Ruth Katz maintained that "in this country . . . all my generation got married for love."[110] Although she exaggerated the uniformity of this practice, her claim captured a growing ethos among Jewish immigrant daughters and sons.

The converted worried that some of their coworkers still cared more about marital status than about romance. Early marriage had been important in traditional Jewish society, and fear of being left an old maid undoubtedly led many to place practicality above idealism. Too, many young garment workers probably married simply to get out of their parents' house and out from under wage work as well. Especially for women who feared they were past their youthful prime, it must have seemed risky to wait for true romance and more sensible to marry out of the factory before it was too late. As Mary Antin explained, using her sister Frieda as an example, "a long girlhood, a free choice in marriage, and a brimful womanhood that are the precious rights of an American woman" were wonderful goals but frequently out of reach even for the most idealistic workers. Some felt they could not wait until the perfect marriage partner came along, and like Frieda wanted to wed "while the roses were still in her cheeks." For Frieda, as for others, marriage, even "premature" marriage to a less-than-ideal mate, at least promised "escape from the workshop."[111]

Jewish daughters debated whether marriage, romantic or pragmatic, promised economic salvation. A good many immigrant wage earners fantasized that being married would solve all of their problems, whereas others took a more realistic approach, insisting that matrimony, though desirable, would not put an end to either poverty or drudgery. Familiarity with the American assumption that married woman's primary role should be domestic rather than economic led to flights of fantasy about being rescued from the factory by an economically secure mate. As Ida Richter recalled, her fellow workers in the dress factory loved to gossip about marriage as an escape from the burdens of wage-earning:

> The girls used to talk about this one got married and this one got rich; even if she wasn't rich, she pretended she was. And we used to sit in the sweatshop and work and we used to think: "Oh, look at this one; she's much better off than I am." Another one says, "What, so what! She's got a husband; she has to scrub and clean and [wash] diapers and have the babies."[112]

Another Jewish immigrant garment worker expressed these conflicting sentiments when she admitted: "I have been to the fortune teller's three or four times, and she always tells me that though I have had such a lot of trouble I am to be very rich and happy. . . . So I keep working in the factory for a time. Of course it is hard, but I would have to work hard even if I was married."[113]

The chorus of Jewish women's voices on the topic of marriage was also joined by socialist women in the factories, who contributed to the evolving pool of ideas about modern Jewish femininity. Both here and in Russia, socialists stressed the importance of greater equality between the sexes and emphasized that only through freely chosen marital union could that ideal be attained. Critical of the growing assumption that marriage was "the remedy of the working girl," socialist women in the factories tried to convince others that they should marry for love, not convenience.[114] Marriage could not be the working woman's "remedy," Elizabeth Hasanovitz told her friends at work, because "the kind of man I shall marry is likely to be a poor wage-earner, also exploited as we all are, and our lives would be miserable under the present conditions. As for marrying money—you know what I think of marriage without love."[115] Change the working conditions, the socialists argued, and women would not have to be "driven from the shop" either to a life of prostitution or, equally tragic, to a loveless and confining marriage.[116] The unsettled debate about the goals of marriage suggests the complex process by which Old World daughters were redefining the meanings of Jewish womanhood. But whether they married for romantic love or opted for less idealistic unions, most immigrant daughters made marriage a central social preoccupation.

Fantasies and Pleasures

At the same time that young garment workers were learning more about romance and modern marriage from others at work, they were also exploring the related world of leisure and consumption. During the long working day women shared with each other the details of last night's fancy dress ball, the plot of the movie or play they had seen, or the expensive hat they had spied while walking down Grand Street after work. New tastes in dress and adornment, along with the seductive lure of new commercial amusements, were cultivated in the social world of the work group. Encouraged by the interests of fellow workers and enticed by the bright lights of the street and the seduction of the music or matinee, immigrant girls both talked about and participated in the excitement of modern American urban culture.[117]

After work immigrants were surrounded by an array of new urban "amusements." New York City "is dance mad," wrote reformer Belle Lindner Israels in 1909. Walk along Grand Street, Delancey, Stanton, Allen, or Houston Street any night during the winter months, Israels observed, and the "glare of lights and the blare of music strike you on every side."[118] Not only dancehalls of every description but movie houses dotted the neighborhood streets in most major cities. "There are now about a hundred movie houses in New York, many of them in the Jewish quarter," the *Jewish Daily Forward* reported in 1908. "Hundreds of people wait in line. . . . Five cents is little to pay. A movie show lasts half an hour. If it's not too busy, you can see it several times."[119]

Movies, dances, rides at the amusement park, the Yiddish theater, the ice-cream parlor, the downtown cafés, even the shop windows on big city streets gave young working women new outlets for pleasure and fantasy. The Lower East Side of New York was a haven for amusement seekers. In the area bounded by Grand, Christie, East Houston, and

Suffolk streets (less than one-third of a square mile), immigrants could patronize seventy-three soda fountains, nine dancing academies and dance halls, eight movie houses, two recreation centers, and a Yiddish theater.[120] Those women who indulged in American amusements enthusiastically reported their activities to others at work, and the less fortunate women listened to their stories in awe and anticipation.[121]

Commercial amusements made up an important but not the only source of young peoples' leisure. Young Jewish wage earners also participated in mixed-sex recreational activities that took place largely within an ethnic, working-class context. Single Jewish working girls went to dancehalls, as one immigrant daughter put it, "to meet fellows" but also attended at-home social gatherings of boys and girls who had formed social or dramatic clubs. These clubs became a potential medium for romance and courtship among working-class immigrant youths, some of whom had met at work or at school.[122]

Even more central to the factory social world was an interest in American styles of dress and personal attire. For new immigrants, buying American clothing was the first symbolic step in the long, complex process of adaptation. By the 1890s the terms "ladies" and "gents" appeared in the clothing advertisements of the Yiddish press, promising immigrants "instant gentility" through the purchase of fashionable clothing. Through these ads immigrants imbibed the message that one had only to "put on style" to become a respectable "lady" or "gentleman."[123] "Almost immediately upon the girl's arrival her relatives buy her American clothes," observed one Chicago social worker. The shopping ritual aimed to outfit newcomers in clothing that would not betray their greenhorn status. One Jewish woman she interviewed said quite proudly: "Yes, I'm almost like an American, I have a rat [puff] for my hair."[124] Another immigrant humorously recalled how her efforts to become fashionably American complicated her morning routine and consequently made her late for her job.

> [At] that time they [working girls] wore the big puffs on the hair, like wigs. Until I put on the girdle, my brother and my cousin used to pull the laces for me. Until I fixed my hair, until I walked to the place to work, so I was ten minutes late, five minutes late, I had to punch a clock. I didn't know in Russia from that. You know every minute counts, on four dollars a week, I never had full pay.[125]

And Ida Richter remembered the fascination she and other Jewish working women had for American styles. "We used to love the Ameri-

9. Immigrant daughters at the beach. Courtesy of the Haberman family.

can people, to copy them. I wanted to be American very much. I saw
people who looked better and dressed better and I wanted to be like that
kind."[126] For these women, and for countless others, clothing remained
a powerful cultural symbol—a signal to others that one was no longer a
"greener"; a way of communicating one's identification with America
and Americans; and even more, an attempt to appear more prosperous
or middle-class than one's living conditions or working life would have
suggested.[127]

The meaning of these preoccupations with leisure, consumption, and
romantic fantasy for working daughters' identity was multifold. Historians have discussed these issues in terms of generational conflict, noting
the tensions that arose between financially and socially conservative
parents and adventurous working-class youth.[128] Leslie Tentler has

gone further, arguing that this generational conflict over romance and consumerism diverted women's attention away from the problem of low wages and poor conditions, channeling the potential for labor protest into resentment toward parents who denied working daughters sufficient funds and freedom to enjoy modern city life.[129] For Jewish daughters, the issues were more complex. Although generational conflict was one source of tension in the lives of young workers, resentment toward employers who underpaid and robbed them of the energy to pursue leisure activities was another.

At times the interest of working daughters in dress and consumption created serious tensions with parents at home. But historians disagree on the extent to which immigrant mothers and daughters were at odds over issues of leisure and consumption. It is generally agreed that Jewish mothers allowed their daughters greater latitude in the pursuit of social activities than their Italian counterparts, who tended to be somewhat more restrictive and more fearful of nonfamily-oriented leisure. Jewish girls were still chaperoned to some social events, but parents allowed them to attend dances and go walking with men as long as permission was given beforehand.[130]

Less frequently discussed is the evidence that leisure and consumption were not the exclusive preoccupations of immigrant daughters. Mothers also shared an interest in the world of urban products and pleasures. The movies are a good example. An especially potent medium for introducing new attitudes about dress and sex roles as well as a vehicle for exploring generational and cultural tensions over these issues, movies were a family entertainment in the immigrant ghettos, a cultural and consumer experience shared by parents and children alike. Some Jewish immigrant mothers also shared their daughters' fascination with consumer goods, including store-bought clothing. The difference between mothers and daughters may have been a matter of degree rather than kind, and also a function of generational styles of consumption. Andrew Heinze, writing about Jewish immigrant consumerism in this period, suggests that Jewish wives and mothers participated as fully as daughters in the rituals of urban consumerism. What distinguished mothers from daughters was that immigrant mothers had well-honed commercial skills that made them expert "bargain hunters."[131] Daughters, on the other hand, may have been more impatient and less skilled at buying. In any case the lines between mothers and daughters over issues of leisure and consumption cannot be rigidly drawn, expecially since many wage-earning daughters would soon drop out of the work force to become wives and mothers themselves and were bound to take their own fascination with consumerism into the world of domestic life.

Many Jewish immigrant mothers tended, then, to sympathize with their daughters' interest in consumption and personal adornment. Nevertheless, as household managers mothers had to carefully scrutinize children's spending habits. The meager household budgets of most immigrant families limited the amount of money daughters could squander on dances and personal adornment. Given the serious financial constraints in most immigrant households, young female garment workers had to struggle to keep up appearances among their friends in the shop and on the streets. Most could afford only the cheapest mass-produced clothing but took great pains to make it look stylish and clean. One Jewish garment worker told an investigator how important it was to have a new suit given to her by a charitable friend. "You see, I have always had my suits from a pushcart or sometimes from a little store in Hester Street. It is wonderful to have one from Wanamakers. I wish I could wear the label on the front."[132]

Most Jewish daughters continued to turn their pay envelopes over to their parents in exchange for a weekly allowance averaging about 11 percent of their wage. But occasionally there were disagreements over how large that allowance should be. One Jewish garment worker recalled the argument she had with her mother over the purchase of a new blouse. She and her girlfriends spent many an hour strolling down Grand Street, "the Fifth Avenue of the Lower East Side." In one store "there were very beautiful blouses, and I always wanted to buy one, but I always turned my pay envelope over to my mother. I wanted that blouse and my mother did not see where I needed such a fancy blouse."[133] Lillian Wald remembered how similar disagreements produced strains between mothers and daughters who lived near the Henry Street Settlement on the Lower East Side. In one family Mollie, who normally gave her wages to her mother, had taken "the accumulated pay for many weeks' overtime, amounting to twenty-five dollars, and 'blew it in' on a hat with a marvelous plume." The hat itself quickly became "a white elephant, a source of endless embarrassment, but buying it had been an orgy," Wald explained. Recognizing that the "harmless gaiety of attire" afforded poor working girls a "sense of self-respect and self-importance," Wald finally succeeded in convincing Mollie's mother "to refrain from nagging and too often reminding the girl of the many uses to which the money might have been put."[134]

The popularity of new Americanized forms of consumption and leisure may have heightened tensions between parents and children, but there is little evidence to suggest that such conflict threatened the basic understandings which sustained the immigrant family economy in the decades before 1920. Jewish daughters in the labor force probably desired a greater degree of social and economic freedom than their parents would allow, but most of them did not openly rebel against their family responsibilities and continued to view their earnings as an essential part of the welfare of the household. Most recognized that even if their parents had agreed to give them a larger say in the disposition of household funds, wages were often barely sufficient to pay the rent and put food on the table, let alone spend on dress and leisure.

Working daughters in pursuit of consumer pleasures found ways of getting around tight household budgets. Young wage earners learned to use the American installment system to pay for clothing they could not afford to purchase in one lump payment. And once a girl began "keeping company" with a boyfriend, she could sometimes persuade him to help her with the payments.[135] Moreover, much of the time dating meant treating. "I want a good time," one Russian-born clothing operator who was helping to support her family told an investigator. "And there is no . . . way a girl can get it on $8 a week. I guess if anyone wants to take me to a dance he won't have to ask me twice."[136] Thus like other working girls in American cities, many immigrant daughters relied upon young men to treat them to movies, dances, and other city pleasures.[137]

All of these topics—dating, treating, romance, and clothing—which immigrant daughters discussed with one another and pursued during their free time, were not exclusive preoccupations of the work group. But they did represent an important focus of working women's fantasy life. The work group functioned as an outlet for these fantasies, as well as a peer society for venting frustrations and disappointments over insufficient income or opportunity for clothing and social life. Within the work group the problem of parental restraints represented one symbol of young women's frustrations, but the work group also functioned to turn resentments in other directions.

The interest in consumerism had dual implications. It offered an escape from working-class drudgery. Paradoxically, however, it also added an incentive to work-related ambitions and ultimately helped fuel workplace militance. Not surprisingly, the rising interest in consumer goods and the more general aspiration for a better standard of living heightened Jewish women's concerns about low wages and added complicating expectations to the relationship between immigrants and their employers. Although wages were usually better in the inside factories than in the contractors' shops, they were still insufficient to satisfy appetites for new clothing and commercial amusements. Moreover, the dirt, the overcrowding, and the absence of the most basic amenities in many factories were hardly conducive to workers' efforts to look and feel like respectable young ladies. It was not unusual, then, for young

10. Striking shirtwaist workers in 1909. This photograph reveals the several dimensions of immigrant New Womanhood. The fashionable attire of immigrant daughters indicates their attraction to new forms of urban consumerism, an attraction that did not divert them from the serious purposes of the strike movement. International Ladies' Garment Workers' Union Records, Labor-Management Documentation Center, Cornell University.

women who took such pains to look presentable to be angered not only by low wages but by employers' failure to provide decent dressing rooms to protect the cheap clothing they *could* afford to purchase. As Russian-born Clara Lemlich, a leader in the 1909 shirtwaist strike, told a reporter, shirtwaist workers "have to hang up their hats and coats—such as they are—on hooks along the walls. Sometimes a girl has a new hat. It is never much to look at because it never costs more than fifty cents, but it's pretty sure spoiled after it's been at the shop." Protested Lemlich, "we're human, all of us girls, and we're young. We like new hats as well as any other young women. Why shouldn't we?" To buy a new hat, "even if it hasn't cost more than fifty cents, means that we have gone for weeks on two cent lunches—dry cake and nothing else," she added.[138]

The female work group in the garment factories cultivated new patterns of social life and contributed to rising expectations about consumption and leisure. Yet this was only one aspect of the "education" that immigrant daughters received at work. Peer-group sociability did not turn attention away from the problems of low wages, long hours, unsafe conditions, fines, discipline, insults, and the general insecurity and poverty in which most immigrants lived.[139] The fantasy world that many women created as they discussed the latest style in hats, swooned over movie or stage actors, or dreamed of leaving the factory for the arms of a rich suitor provided comfort from the pressures of their jobs. But that escapist interest did not define women's lives: it was merely one of several influences that shaped their identities as females, as workers, and as Jewish immigrants. For along with their fantasies about romance, marriage, or clothing, eastern European Jewish women shared with one another their dreams about the possibilities for social justice and economic equality—possibilities that many had imagined would be fulfilled in America. Women's dreams, one garment worker eloquently recalled, were broad and varied enough to embrace romantic images of marriage and equally romantic visions of class struggle:

> All of us young people were sitting and dreaming in the shops. "Well it's only for a season or two. I'll be doing this, I'll be doing that, I'll marry a man that will be able to take care of me." And we used to even sing the songs from Edelstadt, Bovshover, all these writers, the Yiddish naturally. Singing the dream songs, the love songs, and this is how we dreamed away our youth, and go out gay and happy.[140]

But, she quickly added, the very same women who "dreamed away their youth" were also committed to the struggle for working-class dignity and union organization. Many young people like herself "were already class-minded" when they came to America, she said. "The boys and girls that came were young: fourteen, fifteen, sixteen. They didn't have anything" except the memory of poverty and pogroms in the Old Country and consequently felt they had to "seek out places of bettering our lives."[141] As we shall see, many of those women who were not yet class-minded when they arrived in America would later become so as a result of the blend of industrial experience and the cultural and political influences in which they worked and lived.

Female work groups would prove to be extremely elastic in their preoccupations and concerns, focusing sometimes on the latest fashion in hats or petticoats but in other instances on the problem of labor organization. Depending on the influences they absorbed, and on the force of circumstance, work groups could either function as an outlet for romantic fantasy or become a vital mechanism for focused and purposeful labor protest.

5 Uprisings

Women and the Mass Strike Movement

"When," said the teacher to one of the pupils, a little working-girl from an Essex Street sweater's shop, "the Americans could no longer put up with the abuse of the English who governed the colonies, what occurred then?" "A Strike!," responded the girl promptly. She had found it here on coming and evidently thought it a national institution upon which the whole scheme of government was founded.[1]

All through the winter months from late November 1909 to mid-February 1910, young shirtwaist workers braved the wind and the cold as they kept up their picketing outside the factories of lower Manhattan. Week after week, despite freezing temperatures and police harassment, the strikers persevered. Teenage firebrand and strike organizer Clara Lemlich, hailed by union organizers as "a pint of trouble for the bosses," was a regular, appearing at the factory doors to encourage the other girls to stand fast against the hired thugs who regularly charged their picket lines. Pickets marched in twos up and down in front of factory doors, singing working-class songs in Yiddish and Italian to keep up their spirits and help the time pass.

The 1909 "uprising," a general strike involving more than 20,000 shirtwaist workers, began a cycle of labor organization that helped build the garment industry unions. The uprising began with separate, spontaneous strikes in three different factories: in July at Rosen Brothers and in September at Leiserson's factory and the infamous Triangle Shirtwaist Company, scene of the terrible fire that would claim the lives of 146 young people just two years later. The strike at Rosen Brothers was settled after five weeks with a union agreement; the other two factories refused to settle with the workers. Employers at Leiserson's and Triangle met striking workers with brutal resistance, hiring thugs and prostitutes to verbally and physically harass the young strikers.

For weeks on end, the pickets, most of them young women, held their ground. In each of these strikes workers had appealed to the Ladies' Waist Makers' Union Local 25 for help. By October 1909 the Executive Board of Waist Makers' Local 25, which consisted of Clara Lemlich, a striker at Leiserson's, five other Jewish immigrant women, and nine Jewish men, pressured the International Ladies' Garment Workers' Union (ILGWU) to call a general strike of the entire New York shirtwaist industry. Chartered four years earlier, Local 25 was a fledgling organization with only a hundred dues-paying members and a depleted treasury of $4.00. Skeptical of the wisdom of Local 25's general strike request, the ILGWU assumed a wait-and-see posture.

In early November, as the Triangle strike wore on, the arrest of Mary Dreier, an upper-class society woman who had joined the pickets on behalf of the Women's Trade Union League, turned the spotlight of the press on the brutal treatment of strikers by local police and brought the plight of the shirtwaist workers to the attention of the entire city. In mid-November, anxious to gauge the sentiments of New York's shirtwaist workers, Lemlich and the other leaders of Local 25 had distributed leaflets throughout the factory district calling for a general strike in the shirtwaist industry and announcing plans for a mass meeting to be held at Cooper Union on the evening of November 22. In the weeks before the Cooper Union meeting several thousand workers had joined Local 25, but this was hardly the number needed to sustain a strike of the entire industry.

On the night of the mass meeting the overcrowded hall was filled to capacity, and several other meeting places were needed to accommodate an overflow crowd that spilled out into the streets. At Cooper Union various speakers, including AFL president Samuel Gompers, addressed the restless gathering, urging the workers to have patience and use restraint. Not until Clara Lemlich made her way through the crowd was the uncontrollable enthusiasm for a general strike revealed. In her native Yiddish, Lemlich told the packed meeting hall, "I am a working girl, one of those who are on strike against intolerable working conditions. I am tired of listening to speakers who talk in general terms." When Lemlich moved that a general strike be declared, the crowd leapt to its feet and cheered wildly. No one, not the ILGWU nor Lemlich nor the other officers of Local 25, anticipated the emotional outpouring of support for the general strike that began the next morning. Fifteen thousand shirtwaist workers walked off the job, and their numbers nearly doubled in the weeks that followed.

Striking workers demanded a 52-hour workweek, paid overtime, the abolition of fines and inside subcontracting, and union recognition; the last item proved a major stumbling block in union negotiations with many employers. Enthusiatic strikers faced daunting conditions on the picket lines. During the first month of the general strike more than seven hundred women were arrested, and many more were clubbed or verbally abused by police, thugs, and employers. With the onset of winter the strike was still unsettled in many shops, and the effort began to lose much of its early momentum. By mid-February settlements or partial settlements had been reached with more than 300 of the estimated 450 firms in the New York industry. In most of the settled shops hours of work were reduced and inside subcontracting was abolished, but some of the largest shops refused to recognize the union. With more than a thousand workers still out on strike, the union called an end to the strike on February 15. Many workers returned to their shops without any concession from employers, but others succeeded in winning all or some of their demands.[2]

Although the shirtwaist workers' uprising was not entirely successful, it touched off a decade of labor unrest in the garment trades. Between 1909 and 1920 a wave of strikes and mass organizational campaigns swept through the garment trades, changing a largely unorganized industry into a union stronghold. Although unionization came only slowly, and with major setbacks along the way, by the end of World War I clothing workers were among the best-organized members of the American labor force.

Jewish immigrant women played a major role in this process, helping transform their shops and factories and, equally significant, being transformed themselves in the course of the struggle. Politicized in the ongoing workroom debates and mass strikes, immigrant women who participated in the organizational campaigns gained a new visibility in the political arena of the immigrant community. Strikes linked shopfloor grievances with larger communal concerns for economic and social justice, reflecting a complex mixture of individual ambition and collective consciousness. They also revealed women's evolving awareness of the power of their public voice and political agency.

Following the 1909 "uprising" of New York shirtwaist and dress workers, strikes paralyzed the clothing industry in major cities across the country, bringing unprecedented numbers of previously unorganized workers into the union fold. In 1910 nearly 50,000 cloak and suit workers went out on strike in New York, and some 40,000 struck against men's clothing manufactures in Chicago. In subsequent years white goods, kimono, and house dress workers in New York, dress-

11. An enthusiastic gathering of striking shirtwaist workers, New York, 1909. International Ladies' Garment Workers' Union Records, Labor-Management Documentation Center, Cornell University.

makers in Boston, and once again workers in the men's clothing trades in Chicago staged massive organizational strikes. These were only the best-known of many bitter confrontations that marked the era.

Two unions benefited from the labor unrest. Founded in 1900, the International Ladies' Garment Workers' Union (ILGWU) had limped along with only a few thousand members before the 1909 shirtwaist strike. By 1920 the ILGWU boasted 102,000 dues-paying members, making it the sixth-largest union in the American Federation of Labor. In the men's clothing industry the only significant union before 1914 was the craft-oriented United Garment Workers (UGW). But in that year, just as the strike movement reached its peak, the UGW was pushed to the background by a breakaway union led by Jewish immigrant socialists who rejected the UGW's craft orientation. The new union, the Amalgamated Clothing Workers of America (ACW), set out to organize the semiskilled immigrants who numerically dominated the industry. By

12. Striking shirtwaist workers and their supporters line the streets of lower Manhattan in 1909. International Ladies' Garment Workers' Union Records, Labor-Management Documentation Center, Cornell University.

1920 the Amalgamated had enrolled nearly 170,000 members, the majority of the work force in the men's clothing industry.[3]

Although none of the major garment industry unions was completely victorious in bargaining efforts with manufacturers, they did win important concessions that gave rank-and-file members a greater sense of control over the conditions of their labor. In the women's garment industry the ILGWU signed various "Protocols of Peace" that increased wages, reduced working hours, abolished such abuses as inside subcontracting, and provided for the establishment of impartial arbitration committees and boards of sanitary inspection. In the men's garment industry union agreements with such industrial giants as Hart, Schaffner & Marx brought similar gains.

Women were at the forefront of this union movement, accounting for nearly two-thirds of the membership of the ILGWU and one-third of Amalgamated members.[4] Equally important, females spearheaded several of the initial mass strikes of the unionization campaign, leading walkouts involving an estimated 165,000 previously unorganized workers in New York, Philadelphia, and Chicago in 1910 and 1911.[5] In the "great revolt" of New York's cloakmakers in 1910 women, who made up only 20 percent of the labor force in that industry, were frequently the first in their shops to observe the strike order.[6] Some women strikers demonstrated a greater militance than their male counterparts. During the waistmakers' strike in 1909 union officials noted that the women held out for the union's demands long after the men were ready to give up the struggle. "Neither the police, nor the hooligan hirelings of the bosses nor the biting frost and chilling snow of December and January damped their willingness to picket the shops from early morn till late at night," one observer claimed.[7] "If any shops did go to work without settlement," another insisted, "it was because a majority in that shop were men."[8]

Before the 1909 shirtwaist workers' strike female wage earners had played only a minor role in American labor unions. The explosion of female militance in the garment industry appeared, by all accounts, an exceptional development. Nowhere else on the industrial landscape did women workers display the same commitment to labor organization. During the first two decades of the twentieth century women in the garment industries were the single most important bastion of female unionization, far outnumbering unionized women in other industries. In 1920 female garment workers represented 42 percent of all unionized women in the United States. In the industry as a whole 169,000 women, 46 percent of the female labor force, belonged to unions, compared to 10.2 percent of women in all other manufacturing industries.[9]

In the other major center of female industrial employment, textiles, only 11.5 percent of women workers belonged to unions. In the cigar and tobacco industries, other important sources of jobs for women, 13.5 percent of females were organized, as were only 7 percent of female telephone and telegraph workers. Even in traditional union strongholds, such as the printing and publishing trades and the boot and shoe industries, the percentages of female union members lagged behind those in the garment industry.[10]

At a time when female wage earners were perceived as passive and indifferent workers, poor material for unionization, the perseverance and dedication of immigrant women in the garment industry was an unexpected development. Most contemporary observers, along with the conservative leadership of the American Federation of Labor, had long reasoned that there was little to be gained by trying to organize women workers, whose major goal in life was marriage and motherhood. Indeed, even in the garment industry, where females figured so prominently, some union officials had initially been reluctant to devote time and resources to the task of organizing women. After women took the initiative and proved themselves willing candidates for unionization, however, the garment unions could no longer afford to ignore their demands for organization.[11]

The Shopfloor Context of Female Activism

What accounted for this upsurge in female activism? Why did women, most of whom planned to marry out of the industry, join in the struggle to improve conditions that they expected to leave behind? Interrelated factors brought women together on the picket lines and drew them into the unions. A complex of immediate industrial abuses, women's evolving concerns about their dignity as females and as workers, the influence of a cadre of Jewish radicals within and outside the workplace, and a sentiment within the Jewish immigrant community sympathetic to the right and necessity of labor organization contributed to the rising tide of militance.

Much of the discontent that fueled the upsurge in female unionism originated on the shop floor and reflected the on-going struggle between employers and workers over power, control, and economy. In the larger factories fines, wage deductions, speed-ups, and changes in production that increased profits and undercut workers' earnings and autonomy clashed headlong with the struggle for daily survival and for dignity on the job. Young working women with serious financial responsibilities to their households bitterly resented these economizing efforts; they also chafed under shopfloor rules that attempted to regulate nearly every aspect of their behavior. Periodic economic downturns, such as the devastating depression of 1907–1908, heightened tensions, exacerbating workers' insecurities. Throughout the garment industry shopfloor grievances over wages, conditions of work, and treatment by employers and supervisors created the precondition for militant strikes.

Two protests, both initiated by women workers at Hart, Schaffner & Marx tailoring factories in Chicago, illustrate the shopfloor origins of militance in the garment industry. Each suggests how women's consciousness of their obligations and responsibilities as breadwinners, combined with moral outrage against employers who denied them the right to the fruits of their labor, contributed to collective action. Rebecca August led a revolt among buttonhole makers at one of Hart, Schaffner & Marx's big Chicago factories in 1907. "I was a hand button-hole maker. They paid 3 ½ cents for a button hole. I was very fast because there was an urge behind it. The more money I made, the sooner we could send for my mother and the six children." When the head foreman ("who used to see to it that the workers didn't make too much money") realized that a woman in the buttonhole department was earning $25 a week, he decided to cut the piecerates for the entire group, ignoring the fact that most women earned substantially less. "He said it was an *outrage* for a *girl* to make $25 a week." That, Rebecca August insisted, "was my first realization of injustice, of being an underdog." Every woman in her work group received a notice that the price had been cut a half-cent a buttonhole. "My ire was aroused," she recalled. "I said to the girls, 'Are we going to take it?' At that time I knew nothing of unionism but it was that . . . injustice towards the workers that awakened [rebellion] in me." The women left their work tables and went to the restroom, where they agreed to protest the wage cut, but their effort failed, and Rebecca August lost her job.[12]

Three years later, in 1910, Annie (Hannah) Shapiro and a handful of female pants seamers at Hart, Schaffner & Marx succeeded where Rebecca August and her group had failed. When the firm issued a half-cent wage cut, they walked out in protest. The revolt quickly spread to workers in other parts of the factory and eventually touched off a general strike affecting more than 40,000 unorganized Chicago garment workers. The issues prompting this walkout were little different from those which had concerned Rebecca August and her work mates three years earlier. The strikers complained about fines for violating factory rules and for errors in the work; they resented the time lost by pieceworkers who were forced to wait twenty or thirty minutes for the assistant foreman to distribute work; they demanded that the firm build more restrooms for the women and insisted that the foremen be prohibited from insulting them with "improper language." Finally, they asked for an increase in wages.[13]

Typical of grievances and demands in garment workers' uprisings in this period, the issues in these Chicago strikes reflected more than a concern over bread-and-butter issues of wages and hours. At the heart of these strikes also lay fundamental demands for what eastern European Jews called *mentshlekhe bahandlung* (humane treatment).[14] Such demands had also motivated Jewish strikes in Russia and in the new immigrant ghettos on the European continent, but they took on a special intensity among immigrant Jews in the United States, where images of

America as the "goldene medine"—the golden land of freedom—were difficult to reconcile with daily realities on the shop floor. More than any other group of new immigrants to America, Jews had come to make a permanent home. Having traveled half-way across the world in the hope of finding a better life, Jewish immigrants of both sexes responded with a special sensitivity to the degrading and dehumanizing conditions they found at work. Unlike other groups who still dreamed of a return to the homeland, for Jews there was no turning back.

Women had their own special concerns about dignified treatment. Though workers of both sexes complained about disrespectful employers, women felt particularly sensitive to certain kinds of abuses, especially to sexual harassment and innuendo from bosses and foremen. Living in America, where it was presumed "ladies" received respectful treatment, immigrant women insisted that this respect be applied to them as well. "The bosses in the shops are hardly what you would call educated men," strike leader Clara Lemlich told reporters during the 1909 shirtwaist workers' uprising. "They yell at the girls and they 'call them down' even worse than I imagine slaves were in the South. They don't use very nice language. They swear at us and sometimes they do worse—call us names that are not pretty to hear."[15] As Sarah Schwartz, a seventeen-year-old Chicago dress worker, testified, abusive language not only contained sexual vulgarities but at times was mixed with anti-Semitic slurs. "We are all Jewish, he [the foreman] used to call us 'Lousy Jews.'" In addition, she said, each girl received a "vile" nickname from the foreman. "I don't think it is nice for me to pronounce it."[16]

Given immigrants' concerns about female respectability and their sensitivities to anti-Semitism, it is hardly surprising that such violations of workers' dignity contributed to the rising tide of militance. In 1913 striking Jewish white goods workers made that clear when they said they had gone on strike for numerous reasons, including the fact that they "wanted to be treated like ladies." "With the union behind us," one of them announced, the bosses "wouldn't dare use the same language to us."[17]

Issues of worker dignity, wages, hours, sanitation, and shopfloor practices fueled worker militance in the garment trades and provided proximate causes for the massive wave of strikes that brought so many unorganized immigrants into the union fold. Yet neither workplace grievances nor industrial unrest were new to the garment shops and factories in 1909 and 1910. Shopfloor grievances had often triggered protests and walkouts. Jewish girls, Rose Schneiderman reminded the Women's Trade Union League in 1908, were "always ready to strike" over wage cuts, working conditions, and the "tyranny" of employers.[18]

Well before the masses of immigrant garment workers were union-ized, informal workgroups in the shops and factories periodically joined together to revolt against the actions of employers and supervisors, but they had not succeeded in establishing stable organizations. The pat-tern, as one historian of Jewish labor has put it, was "dissatisfaction, union, strike, disorganization, apathy, reorganization," a sequence that led contemporary observers to describe Jewish immigrants as "good strikers" but "bad unionists."[19]

This pattern of labor organization and disorganization had its coun-terpart in the informal, community-based protests of Jewish immigrant housewives. In 1902 immigrant mothers on the Lower East Side of New York, many of them wives of garment workers, staged a militant kosher meat boycott to protest price-gouging on the part of the "beef trust." Their language and tactics were radical and extremely violent, and their cause was supported by the leaders of the garment workers' union and both the socialist and the Orthodox Jewish press. In 1904 and 1907–8 Jewish housewives repeated the patterns of the 1902 boycott, this time staging rent strikes. Like early garment industry strikes, these incidents were spontaneous and shortlived. They generated neither an ongoing leadership nor a permanant organization. But like the pre-1909 gar-ment industry strikes, the communal protests of immigrant wives and mothers served as what Paula Hyman calls a "prelude" to the explosion of female activism, an activism that became institutionalized within the union movement in the wake of the great shirtwaist workers' uprising of 1909.[20]

What had changed by 1909 was not so much the specific nature of workroom grievances as the ability of immigrant women and men to channel grievances into a mass movement with the potential for con-tinuity and stability. A temporary economic upturn between July 1909 and the summer of 1910 encouraged garment workers to press for unionization. Moreover, in the period following the 1909 shirtwaist industry uprising some of the larger manufacturers of both men's and women's clothing—giants like Hart, Schaffner & Marx and several of the more "progressive" shirtwaist and cloak firms—concluded that the rational needs of production might be solved if workers could be effi-ciently managed by unions.[21] While these structural changes created new possibilities, they provide a backdrop rather than an explanation for the organizational thrust among garment workers. Efforts to union-ize continued despite economic ups and downs in the industry and went forward even in the face of the most brutal resistance by employers.

Even more vital to garment workers' efforts to unionize was support from urban reform leaders, who gave legitimacy to the cause of labor organization and, most important, brought the special plight of women workers to public attention. Progressive-era reformers, including settlement-house workers, consumer organizations, and "uptown" figures like New York's reform rabbi Stephen S. Wise, abhorred working conditions in the garment industry and endorsed the drive for unionization. Often seeking to mediate between Jewish unions and Jewish employers, they helped create a political climate sympathetic to working peoples' rights.[22]

Of all the reform groups that rallied to the cause of labor, none was more central to the process of female organization than the Women's Trade Union League (WTUL). Composed of both middle-class allies and working women, this women's organization provided funds, meeting space, and guidance to female workers struggling to unionize. WTUL members, some of them the daughters and wives of prominent or wealthy individuals, walked the picket lines with young immigrant strikers, risking arrest or even the violent assaults of the police. The League also held mass meetings at various society gathering places to publicize the plight of the strikers and to win support for their cause. "People had respect for them," Jewish garment worker Rebecca Holland recalled of the middle- and upper-class allies in the WTUL. They lent prestige to working women's struggles. The Chicago League, she said, was "our link" between the working girl and the city at large. Wealthy women in the League had access to the press; "that was important to us," she explained.[23] The League was particularly adept at calling public attention to "female" issues in the garment strikes. Portraying working girls and women as hapless victims of industrial abuse, they publicized employers' violations of womanly virtue. Attempting to rouse the public conscience, they stressed how poor sanitation, sexual harassment, and overwork threatened the "future motherhood" of young female workers.[24]

The Radical Subculture

As important as these external factors were in advancing the union movement in the garment trades, they do not in themselves explain the enormous groundswell of labor militance among immigrant women workers, nor do they fully account for the growth of labor organization. For it was within the immigrant working-class community that the roots of labor militance took hold and spread. Only by looking at the community context of labor militance can we understand the social and cultural forces that brought discontented workers into a labor movement.

That investigation must begin with the radical political subculture that emerged among eastern European Jews in the first decade of the twentieth century. In Jewish immigrant communities in cities such as New York and Chicago the growth of a socialist movement helped create momentum behind the new union movement in the garment industry and the basis for a permanent working-class organization. Jewish immigrant socialism had roots in the historical circumstances of the European past and also reflected the search for new sources of dignity and fulfillment in America. More than simply a means of alleviating the economic insecurities of the Jewish working class, both in Russia and in America the twin causes of socialism and union organization became a critical vehicle for articulating the frustrations and longings of Jewish women and men.

During the late nineteenth and early twentieth centuries the Jewish Pale in Russia was torn by class strife and labor unrest, much of it attributable to the growth of revolutionary socialism. The Russian Jewish socialist movement, its major strength concentrated in the Bund, was first composed primarily of intellectuals and students, but by the turn of the century the movement was beginning to spread beyond its early educational "circles," reaching out to the Jewish working classes.[25] Between 1897 and 1904 Jewish workers in Russia and Poland staged more than two thousand strikes, many of them with the support of the Bund. Most of those strikes involved employees in tiny workshops who were seeking higher wages and uniform, regulated conditions: a twelve-hour day, regular paydays, and an end to the chaotic state of relations between workers and employers. The crux of the struggle revolved around what Ezra Mendelsohn has described as the desire of workers to institute "modern" relations based upon contract rather than habit or whim. Other strikes involved urban factory workers in the textile and tobacco industries, where the work force included girls who would later enter the garment trades in America.[26]

The Bund, in loose confederation with the Russian Social Democratic Workers' Party and the Polish socialist movement, carried on a program of revolutionary agitation in addition to the strike movement. In big cities such as Vilna, Minsk, Bialystok, Grodno, Warsaw, and Odessa, and in scores of small shtetlekh, the men and women of the Bund spread the message of socialism and revolution, printing or smuggling contraband literature, holding clandestine meetings, and organizing demonstrations.[27]

Several historians have sought to explain the compelling attraction of socialist ideals for Russian and Polish Jews. Some have focused upon the status of Jews, as an oppressed minority and socialism's ideology of equality, with its promise of economic equity and political inclusion, as important motivating factors in the rise of the radical movement. Others have pointed to the growing economic misery and political repression in the Pale of Settlement during the late nineteenth and early twentieth centuries, suggesting that these developments undermined the position of Jewish artisans and created serious class tensions.[28] Still others have suggested that socialist ideology appealed to Jewish workers in part because it helped strip away the pretensions of the Orthodox leadership, challenging a harsh system of social stratification that stigmatized workers as *proste yidn* (lowly Jews) and focusing resentments upon the religious scholars and merchants who dominated Jewish society. For tailors, shoemakers, and other workers, socialism held the promise of equality (even superiority), since the working classes would be the vanguard of the coming order. Related was the movement's special appeal to women and the new role it gave them in remaking the political and economic foundations of industrializing society.[29] Finally, some scholars have argued that socialism filled an emotional and philosophical void for the increasing numbers of Jews who had abandoned traditional religious orthodoxy. Socialism, like the Judaic faith itself, had a messianic quality and can be seen, says Moses Rischin, as "Judaism secularized."[30]

Whatever the precise combination of influences, it is clear the movement struck a responsive chord among Jewish immigrant workers in the United States. Young women and men brought their radical orientation with them to America, helping to spread the message of socialism within the immigrant population and playing a critical role in the struggle to unionize the garment industry. Jewish radicals had been coming to the United States since the 1880s, and by the opening decade of the new century the Lower East Side of New York was brimming with excitement about socialism. Settlement worker Mary Kingsbury Simkhovitch observed that on the Lower East Side of New York the press, the clubs, and the theater were all "centered in the thought of a changed order."[31] In other cities as well the socialist message reverberated through the immigrant community. "The air was tinged with movements," one immigrant woman said, describing the mood among Chicago Jews in the early part of this century.[32] There, as in New York City's Jewish quarter, socialists speaking on street corners, in the parks, and in front of shops and factories held forth about the need for a new social, economic, and political order and about the importance of the union movement to the cause. Immigrants had only to pick up a copy of the socialist *Jewish Daily Forward* or walk past the ever-present array of soap-box speakers and street meetings to absorb the radical ideology.[33]

If anything, the influence of socialism among Jews grew stronger in America than it had been in the Old World. In part it was strengthened because so many radicals fled to America after the failure of the 1905 Russian revolution. Pouring into American ghettos, they stoked the flames of immigrant Jewish radicalism and gave the movement the critical momentum that built the ILGWU and the Amalgamated. But socialism thrived in the American setting for other reasons, too. Many Jews had come to the United States with inflated, sometimes extraordinary expectations. America, some had thought, would be the land of perfect freedom, opportunity, and equality that the socialists envisioned in their utopian plans. "Being in Russia and living in constant danger, I always fancied that when I shall come to America, I would almost find here the true socialist world," one immigrant confessed in a letter to the *Forward* in 1906.[34] For some, socialist dreams and American images were tightly intertwined. Yet capitalist America was no utopia, and disillusionment fed radical discontent. "I was always humanistic," a striking white goods operator told an investigator in 1913. Having come to America in search of liberty, she discovered that as a worker "you would have to strike for it."[35] Fannia Cohn put it somewhat differently: "Many girls came here from a revolutionary background. They were struck by the atmosphere of freedom here. But then they were plunged into the sweatshop. The sweatshop was not only a physical condition, but moral and anti-spiritual. They found there was no Bill of Rights off the street, in the shop. They were thrown out if they mentioned the Bill of Rights in the shop."[36]

The political and cultural milieu that Jews encountered in America also accounted for the growing strength of socialism in the immigrant communities. America, unlike Czarist Russia, offered widespread opportunities for legal political activity. And it was the socialists who had political experience and were most adept at organization. Years of clandestine activity in Russia and Poland had prepared them for what would become a very public political culture in America.

Moreover, Jewish immigrant socialists would gain increasing strength from the power of the indigenous American socialist movement, which reached its peak between 1912 and 1916. Although the mass movement of Jewish socialists on New York's Lower East Side arose independently, Jews proudly conceived their own struggle as part of a larger American movement.[37]

13. New York shirtwaist workers sell a special "strike edition" of the Socialist *Call*, 1909. From *Munsey's Magazine*, April 1910. International Ladies' Garment Workers' Union Records, Labor-Management Documentation Center, Cornell University.

The success of the socialists in America also reflected the waning power of the rabbinical elites. The theocratic structure that had dominated shtetl life could never be fully reestablished in the secularized atmosphere of the United States, and the socialists filled the vacuum with an ideological orientation that became almost a religion for many followers. As one historian of the movement has suggested, the ideological flexibility of Jewish socialism enabled the movement to attract a mass following in a culturally diverse immigrant community.[38]

Jewish socialists in America, as in Russia, articulated a version of Jewish nationalism, combining calls for worldwide socialist revolution with programs for the defense and protection of the Jewish working classes. This concession to the special concerns of group survival enabled the movement to speak to elements in the community that might have been alienated by a strictly internationalist ideology. In the face of pogroms in Russia and an increasingly vocal American nativist movement bent on restricting immigration, Jewish socialists came to embody a synthesis of nationalism and socialism dedicated not only to class struggle but to the protection and preservation of Jewish life.[39]

Voting patterns do not always provide the best guide to political culture, especially when the community contains large numbers of non-voting members such as women and newly arrived immigrants. But some sense of the attraction of socialism for eastern European Jews can be gleaned from election results on New York's Lower East Side. From 1910 on, as Melvyn Dubofsky has shown, Socialist political strength on the Jewish East Side grew year by year. Initially competing with Tammany Democrats and the newly formed Progressive party, in 1912 Jewish Socialist Congressional candidate Meyer London collected 31 percent of the vote on the Lower East Side. Two years later he outdid his rivals, gaining 49 percent of the vote, thus becoming the first elected New York City Socialist. By 1917 Lower East Side districts routinely gave as many as 50 percent of their votes to Socialist candidates for various city and state offices.[40]

Despite the increasing success of Socialist candidates in Jewish districts, the Socialists as a party and socialism as a subculture never fully dominated the political life of the Jewish immigrant community. Always they competed with more traditional political parties and with the still-powerful forces of religious Orthodoxy. Nor should it be assumed that those who supported Socialist candidates were fully committed to radical ideology. As Dubofsky points out, New York Socialists had to temper their rhetoric to compete with "reform" candidates. Depending upon issues, personalities, alternative office seekers, and whether or not the Socialist candidate (as in London's case) was a fellow Jew, Socialists might win or lose the East Side vote.[41] Yet if the socialists never represented more than a minority voice in the immigrant community, as Irving Howe and others have stressed, they were nonetheless a "vital minority" whose concepts of social justice and equality articulated the concerns and longings of the wider community of newcomers.[42]

Significantly, the movement found its most enthusiastic adherents among garment workers. The socialist movement and the garment unions grew hand in hand. Whereas the party organizations in Russia and Poland had represented the core of Jewish socialist strength, in America economic organizations, most important the socialist-led garment unions, personified the spirit and locus of movement culture. In the years of its greatest success the New York Socialist Party drew much of its strength from the established union locals of the ILGWU.[43] Yet well before this, the Jewish labor movement had learned to depend upon and was closely connected with socialist radicalism. The first broad-based Jewish labor organization in the United States, the Farey-nikte Yiddishe Gverkshaftn (United Hebrew Trades), had been founded by socialists in 1888. An umbrella organization that emphasized direct action and gender equality, the UHT helped charter various Yiddish-speaking unions and paved the way for the founding of the ILGWU by moderate Jewish socialists in 1900.[44]

Radicals at Work

The 1905 revolution in Russia marked a turning point for the labor and radical movements among immigrant Jews in America. The migration of thousands of Jewish Bundists and radical activists invigo-rated and expanded the earlier movement, turning weak and unstable garment unions into viable organizations.[45] The arrival of this radical cadre made an immediate impact within the shops and factories of the garment industry. Already legendary for their heroism and bravery, veterans of the radical movement in Russia had a special aura for their less politically experienced coworkers. The presence of radical and socially conscious women and men in the shops helped to inject a new political awareness into the work group, turning the conversations away from the usual talk of romance and dances to the need for strikes and union organization. One Jewish immigrant woman recalled the receptiveness of coworkers when she and several other female socialist "intellectuals" in her New York shirtwaist factory proselytized about the union. "When I came into a shop, I'd start to carry on," she ex-plained. Seeking out "a few girls who were also socialists," she and her sympathizers tried to spread the message of unionism to the other women in the shirtwaist factory. "I used to go into the ladies' room, and a few would follow me, and I was talking to them [about the] union."[46]

For Jewish women, such political discussion might easily be seen as part of the secular education they were so eager to imbibe. Radical women in the work group served as teachers, spelling out lessons of political economy and trade unionism, describing to their coworkers how society functioned and how it might be transformed. Eager to learn about the world around them and awed by both the knowledge and the conviction of their radical instructors, many Jewish women listened closely. As a result, in some workrooms radical women gained consider-able authority. One immigrant who worked in a New York underwear factory recounted the influence of an older coworker on her evolving political consciousness:

I admired her because I was quiet and mousy and she was so outspoken. I used to follow her around because she was a very educated girl from Europe. She was a radical. She had two brothers and two other sisters, they were all radical socialists. And they had a very religious mother and father. I knew right from wrong but I did not have the courage to say it, she did. So I sort of followed her around, and following her around I always got into trouble because she got into trouble. And during the strike she was marching up and down in front of the picket line to give us courage to stay there.[47]

In Boston shirtwaist worker Bessie Udin had also been drawn into the ILGWU by a radical activist in her factory. Her coworker had recently emigrated from the big city of Vilna, where she had been involved with the workers' movement, and she proceeded to enlighten Bessie about the mysteries of unionism. "This girl came from Vilna. First thing she's asking me, 'there is going to be a mass meeting, are you going?' So I said, 'what is a mass meeting?' She says, 'they're going to propose a union.' So in that way I got acquainted with what was going on," Udin recalled.[48]

Working in a New York cap factory in 1903, Rose Schneiderman met a young woman named Bessie Braut, an outspoken activist who "wasted no time in giving us the facts of life." The male cap makers already belonged to the union, and Bessie urged the women to organize themselves. "My mind was ready for Bessie's lessons," Schneiderman recalled. "As her words began to sink in, we formed a committee composed of my friend Bessie Mannes, who worked with me, myself, and a third girl. Bravely we ventured into the office of the United Cloth Hat and Cap Makers Union and told the man in charge that we would like to be organized."[49] Often the militant leaders of the work group only reinforced political messages that women heard on the streets or from relatives and landsleit. Rose Schneiderman's mind had been "prepared" for Bessie's lessons by the socialist landsleit with whom she stayed not long after she arrived from the Old Country. "My entire point of view was changed by the conversations I heard at their house," she admitted. Previously she had known nothing about strikes or trade unionism "and . . . was inclined to look upon strike-breakers as heroic figures because they wanted to work."[50]

The authority of radical women in the factories derived from their ability to articulate in clear and sympathetic ways ideological tenets that were part of the cultural milieu of the immigrant communities. If many young workers knew little about politics themselves, they were inclined to pay attention to those who seemed more knowledgeable. Noting the pattern in the 1909 shirtwaist workers' uprising, one observer wrote that in each factory there were "a few girls in the lead" who were able to carry "their sisters along with them by force of their own determination."[51]

It was no accident that many radical women were also highly skilled workers; some of them had perfected their craft in eastern Europe, and others, like Jennie Matyas and Clara Lemlich, had "worked themselves up" in the trade after they arrived in America. Their role in the organizational drive illuminates one of the paradoxical qualities of Jewish immigrants at this time: their ability to combine individual ambition with a spirit of collective consciousness and labor radicalism. Their drive for self-improvement, their quest for dignity as women and as workers, and their sense of moral outrage at the treatment of working people fueled their ambition for better treatment of working people and turned their energies toward the radical labor movement.

This conjunction of radical consciousness and skill gave certain women a special prominence in the work group, enabling them to play a leading role in the strike movement. As was common in other industries, skilled workers frequently held the keys to any effective work action. Semiskilled workers who initiated some of the more dramatic uprisings of the period were often too vulnerable, too easily replaced, to be successful by themselves. Aware of overall trade conditions, skilled workers were often in the best position to gauge the efficacy of a strike, could exert pressure on employers once a walkout had begun, and could afford to act on behalf of the more easily replaceable members of the workgroup.[52]

The "girl leaders" of the 1909 shirtwaist strike numbered among the best-paid in their shops, helping to organize their more vulnerable and less fortunate sisters.[53] Knowledge of the trade, the benefit of a certain number of years in the industry, and long-held resentments toward exploitative employers gave these women a special effectiveness in the organizational struggles. Numerous women interviewed on the picket line told investigators that they themselves earned between $12 and $15 a week—a wage paid to the most skilled of female workers—but "struck in behalf of those poor girls under the sub-contractors" who sweated away for only $5 a week.[54] Clara Lemlich, whose impassioned speech on the eve of the 1909 shirtwaist strike served as a call to action for thousands of young immigrant workers, earned three times as much as most of the women in her trade, and that was true for other female strike leaders as well. A well-paid draper who could have her pick of jobs told a newspaper reporter that "she had no personal grievances" but "struck because all the others should get enough."[55] So too Jennie

Matyas, who joined the strike movement several years later, admitted that as a highly skilled sample maker she had been "treated magnificently," but she committed herself to unionism because, as she put it, "I was very disturbed by how the other people were being treated."[56]

Gender, Ethnicity, and Activism

Skilled women workers played a critical role in bringing other women into the mass strike movement. Yet women did not act alone. Although the organizational strikes in the garment industry have been portrayed as a "united front" of women, that image of homogeneity masks rather than clarifies the nature of labor activism.[57] Far from being a "united front" or a sexually or culturally homogeneous mass movement of "women's strikes" orchestrated by immigrant women radicals and their female reformer "allies," strikes by garment workers brought to the fore the diversity and complexity of the industry's labor force and the many cross-cutting influences that shaped immigrant women's consciousness. Organizing garment workers required complex linkages and negotiations between the different subgroups within the industry and among workers in individual shops. As in other labor movements, so here success hinged on particular configurations of support within the work force and the ability of immigrants to bridge divisions based on ethnicity, skill, and gender.

To use the term "women's strikes" is first of all to obscure the cooperation and mutual support between rank-and-file women and men. Gender divisions of work and tensions between men and women had the potential to undermine labor organization, and cooperation was not always easily attained. The American Federation of Labor (AFL) had an uneven policy toward women, often opposing female wage work as destructive to family life and as threatening to the economic position of men. Only reluctantly did the Federation take on the task of organizing women, motivated in large part by the desire to protect male wages.[58] Although generally more favorable to the idea of organizing women, the socialist leaders of the major garment unions periodically expressed their own misgivings and cynicism about the efficacy of spending precious resources to unionize females. Jewish women frequently found themselves, as Alice Kessler-Harris puts it, "court[ing] the unions that should have been courting them."[59]

If Jewish women had to court the male leadership of the garment unions, they often had less to do to convince their male coworkers and ethnic community members of the righteousness of their strikes. Jewish women and men, refugees from Czarist oppression and outsiders struggling to make their way in a new country as underpaid wage earners, shared not only mutual antagonism toward employers but a conviction that going out on strike meant defending communal interests. Thus while the demographics of industrial life put women at the forefront of the strike movement in some branches of the garment trade, even their "women's strikes" were mixed-sex, ethnic working-class community events.

The broader, communal context of women's strike activity was symbolized in the Cooper Union meeting that initiated the 1909 shirtwaist workers' uprising. When Russian Jewish garment worker Clara Lemlich issued her now legendary general strike call, the plea and the pledge were delivered not to women alone but to the larger Jewish working-class community. When the crowd rose to cheer at Lemlich's speech, the chairman of the meeting, Benjamin Feigenbaum, came to the platform and, raising Lemlich's arm along with his own, connected her strike call to the cause of Jewish working-class survival. "Do you mean faith?" he asked in Yiddish. "Will you take the old Jewish Oath?" Raising their right hands, the crowd joined in the oath: "If I turn traitor to the cause I now pledge, may this hand wither from the arm I now raise."[60]

The class and ethnic context of the mass strike movement encouraged cooperation between male and female workers. A closer look at the dynamics of garment strikes in this period reveals a good deal of cooperation between rank-and-file women and men. In fact, male workers, some of them highly skilled cutters and inside subcontractors, often played an essential role in the women's strike movement. "It came as something of a surprise," one observer wrote of the 1909 shirtwaist industry uprising in New York, "that from twenty to forty percent . . . of the shirtwaist 'girls' were men," most of them highly paid workers serving as inside subcontractors.[61] "Curiously enough," one account of the strike noted, "it was a sub-contractor who started the strike." Eighteen months before the great uprising he had led a protest at the Triangle Shirtwaist Company. Complaining he was "sick of slave-driving," he threatened to take his charges out on strike, only to be dragged out of the shop by the employer. Four hundred female operators promptly "walked out" on his behalf.[62]

Sometimes skilled male workers led the actions; in other instances they played a supporting role. Frequently that part was played by highly paid male cutters, the so-called aristocrats of the industry, who had long enjoyed the benefits of unionization. Generally more conservative than other occupational groups, they held critical control over the flow of materials and could hold up the entire production process. Even in the so-called women's trades, such as housedresses and kimonos, where a huge strike paralyzed the industry in 1913, the cutters were, according to one account, "very largely responsible for the strength of the fight."[63] In Chicago, the 1910 men's clothing workers strike, which began with a walkout by semiskilled women in one department at Hart, Schaffner & Marx, gained strength because male cutters and trimmers—at that point the only formally organized sectors of the work force—supported their actions.[64]

Ethnic rather than sex divisions were far more likely to complicate the task of labor organization during strikes. Relations between workers of different nationalities varied from factory to factory and from one work group to the next. At times there were serious tensions, particularly when employers and supervisors manipulated underlying ethnic suspicions in order to lower wages and undermine class cooperation. Not infrequently employers tried to undercut the piecerates of Jewish workers by giving, or threatening to give, the work to Italians who might have made the garments for less money. The Women's Trade Union League received numerous complaints that manufacturers deliberately attempted to "stir up race antagonism between Jewish and Italian girls for the purpose of retaining the cheaper labor of Italians."[65] Among other tactics, employers would seat Italian and Jewish women side by side so that they were constantly "at daggers' points."[66]

In spite of such incidents, most women made an effort to be friendly toward workers of other nationalities. Language and cultural differences made communication difficult at times, but immigrant women usually found ways of overcoming the barriers, speaking to one another in broken English, using hand gestures, entertaining one another with songs from the Old Country, exchanging food at lunch time.[67] Nor was it unusual for women of different nationalities to help each other with problems in their work or even with personal matters. Lottie Spitzer, for instance, wrote letters home for an illiterate Polish woman at her factory.[68] As a result of these interactions, deep and lasting friendships sometimes formed between Jewish and gentile women. More typically, however, relations between various ethnic groups in the factories were cordial but not close, characterized by what garment worker Rebecca August called "a certain clannishness," perhaps the inevitable result of cultural and language barriers.[69]

Ethnic differences were often exacerbated as the issues of unionization surfaced. Jewish women and men usually took the lead in union

14. The union movement in the garment industry brought women and men to-gether, as at this meeting of striking New York shirtwaist workers in 1909. Interna-tional Ladies' Garment Workers' Union Records, Labor-Management Documenta-tion Center, Cornell University.

activity, and the garment unions themselves came to be closely identified with the Jewish immigrant community. That dynamic posed problems for organizers. Although Jewish women set out to organize fellow workers of other nationalities, non-Jews did not always display the same eagerness for the struggle. Different cultural priorities may have been one factor; reluctance to follow the lead of the Jewish group was another.

Only the exceptional group of Jewish women could secure the un-qualified cooperation of the entire work force in an ethnically mixed factory. The Jewish women in the Boston shirtwaist factory where Dora Bayrack worked in 1912 managed to persuade their Polish, Armenian, and "American" (probably including second- and third-generation Irish) coworkers to go out on strike, but at the outset the success of their effort was not at all predictable. Two representatives from the ILGWU

had called the workers in Bayrack's factory to an organizational meeting. "I went, a few other girls went—all Jewish. The Jews were the first
ones that felt like they had to go," Dora recalled. She and another
Jewish woman volunteered to approach the boss about the workers'
demands. And when the employer stood fast against the union, Dora in
her "broken English" managed to convince this mixed work group to
strike.[70]

But that kind of solidarity was unusual. More often Jewish women
who took the lead in organizing their shops found at least some degree
of resistance among women of other nationalities. Organizing an ethnically mixed work group, as Lottie Spitzer well knew, could be accomplished only if one or more workers of each nationality stood firmly
behind the union cause. Otherwise communication broke down, and
ethnic suspicions and misunderstandings prevented cooperation. At the
C. B. Shane factory in Chicago where most of her fellow workers were
Italians and Poles, Lottie Spitzer turned to "one fella Louie, an Italian,
[who] had ideas about union shops already. He was the only one that I
could talk [to], and he conversed with the rest of the Italian girls and
men," she explained. "I talked to Louie and I told him I was in the
union, and I had talked to the boys [the cutters in the Amalgamated].
And 'they're goin' to whistle tomorrow from across the street, we
should all get up and walk out.' " Fluent in Polish as well as Yiddish, she
also won the confidence of several Polish women who proved critical in
gathering support for the walkout. One of the women, Anna, identified
those Poles likely to be receptive to the union and pointed out those to
avoid. "I was told not to talk to some of them. . . . Be careful for this
one." In the end, Spitzer recalled, "some of the workers were with us
and some were not."[71]

Ethnic rivalries and antagonisms nearly always hampered organization to one degree or another. And not uncommonly Jews became
impatient with what they considered the backwardness of other workers. As an editorial in the Women's Trade Union League journal, *Life
and Labor*, noted in the aftermath of the 1909 shirt-waist strike: "The
Russian Jewish girl . . . is accounted as being by far the readiest to get a
hold of the idea of solidarity and the most reliable in standing by
principle . . . at any self sacrifice. This Russian Jewish girl thinks that the
American working girl is as hopeless as the Italian."[72]

Jews were particularly disparaging of American women, an ethnocentric attitude that contained some ironies. Although many Jewish
women aspired to look and behave like American "ladies," they did not
wholly approve of this model of womanhood, frequently considering

native women flighty and frivolous. "It is no use trying to organize American women," a Jewish millinery worker told Mary Van Kleeck. "They don't care about anything but making dates. It's all men and dances."[73] A similar observation came from another Jewish daughter who wrote to *Life and Labor* complaining about the overly "pleasant" tone of that publication, implying that though it might appeal to American girls, Jews needed something different:

> I am a Jewish girl, and I like *Life and Labor* but the girls in our factory are not interested. . . . What they need is stories that will stir them. . . . The stories of *Life and Labor* do not mean much to Jewish girls. You see, they are all *pleasant* stories, and we Jewish people have suffered too much to like just "pleasant stories." We want stories that tell of struggle, and that tell of people who want justice passionately.[74]

"Americans" may not have been as frivolous as some Jewish workers thought, but many clearly wanted little to do with a union that was led by people whose customs and values they neither respected nor understood. American women in her factory, Elizabeth Hasanovitz wrote, "considered it beneath their dignity to belong to a 'labor organization,' especially to a 'Yiddish Union,' as they called the Waist and Dressmakers' Union."[75] Garment worker Bessie Mintz, commenting on organizational problems during the 1913 dressmakers' strike in New York, observed that very few Jewish workers "refused the union," but large numbers of American women proved intractable. "They used to say it's only for greenhorns, but not for Americans to belong to a union."[76] And Bessie Udin similarly recalled that native women working with her in a Boston dress factory identified the ILGWU as a union of foreigners. Americans would willingly ask for higher wages, she said, but would not become involved in an immigrant organization.[77]

Jewish and Italian Women

Southern Italian women, the other major immigrant constituency in the garment trades, also appeared, from the perspective of Jewish immigrant organizers, to be less than reliable strikers and unionists. Of the more than 20,000 workers who responded to the strike call in 1909, only about 6 percent (2,000) were Italian women, even though they were approximately 34 percent of the labor force in the shirtwaist industry. While Italian women's rate of strike participation was disproportionately low, the rate for Jewish women was disproportiontely high. Although they made up about 55 percent of the industry's work force, they comprised somewhere between 66 and 70 percent (20,000 to 21,000) of the strikers.[78]

Unaware of the cultural and communal obstacles faced by Italian women, Jews often mistook their coworkers' reticence about unionism as an irrational willingness to be exploited by the employer. One Russian Jewish woman who characterized her Italian shop mates as "dumb" was exasperated by their unwillingness to go out on strike. Describing her failure to organize the predominantly Italian work force in a New York shirt factory, she said: "They worked for cheap. They didn't like me because I was no good for them, because I wanted a union shop. I didn't like how they worked there, they were slaves."[79]

Such comments reveal deep misunderstandings and ethnocentric prejudices. Typically, Jewish women stressed their own militance and class consciousness in contradistinction to the values and behavior of other groups of women. This was a powerful ethnic myth Jews constructed about themselves and outsiders believed about them. Part fact, part a product of rhetorical romanticism, the idea of the special claims of working-class Jews to militance was an essential aspect of group self-definition.[80] But was there something truly exceptional about Jewish women's response to the union movement? How are we to understand what, on the surface, appears to be a substantial ethnic difference in women's attitudes toward labor activism?

Jewish women garment workers provide the preeminent example of a successful effort at female unionization. But success is not the only criterion for understanding women's attitudes, and Jews were not the only group of women to struggle for unionization. History provides numerous examples of female labor militance among different occupational and ethnic groups. Measured against the activism of striking Irish collar workers in 1869 in Troy, New York; Irish, German, and native women who struck the carpet factories in upstate New York in 1885; Polish immigrant women who staged a massive strike against Detroit's cigar manufactures in 1916; or the Italian, Polish, Lithuanian, Greek, Syrian, Armenian, Portuguese, and other foreign-born daughters and wives who participated in the famous Lawrence textile strike of 1912, the militance of Jewish women may not be exceptional.[81] Many other groups of women organized to improve their wages and working conditions, a pattern that contradicts what one historian has claimed was women workers' inability to engage in "disciplined or self-interested activity."[82]

Measuring Jewish women's activism against these other episodes of female militance provides little in the way of direct contextual comparison. We can learn more by examining Jewish women and their southern Italian counterparts in the garment industry. Such an examination offers some degree of specificity with regard to time, place, structural variables, and the role of culture.

Italian women did join the union movement in the garment industry and in some situations proved even more militant than their Jewish sisters.[83] Yet in many of these early twentieth-century strikes their participation was uneven and unreliable. In the 1909 New York shirtwaist strike many young Italian workers refused to leave their sewing tables and served as scab labor. By 1913, however, Italian women in New York's garment trades took a more militant stand, turning out in record numbers for the white goods and other garment workers' strikes of that year. As time went on, the willingness of Italian women to participate in the city's organizing campaigns grew, so that in 1919, while some continued to cross picket lines, most Italian women working in the New York women's garment trade were willing to join the strike movement.[84] Thus Italian women eventually supported the union movement in the garment industry, but they were slower to do so than their Jewish sisters. Not until the 1920s, when the American-born daughters of Italian parents came of age, did Italian women move into the forefront of the labor struggle.[85]

The sources of Jewish and Italian immigrant women's differing responses to labor organization must be sought in the overlapping contexts of family expectations, political culture, and ethnic community institutions. Cultural, structural, and situational factors shaped the attitudes of both groups.

The image of southern Italian immigrant women as reluctant strikers and unionists grew in large measure from the assumption that Italian family values, especially patterns of patriarchal dominance, precluded female activism.[86] A member of the New York Women's Trade Union League described Italian women as "the oppressed of the race, absolutely under the dominance of men of their family, and heavily shackled by old customs and traditions. They are very much afraid of trade unions."[87] Moreover, the belief that for Italians the family was "sopratutto" (above all else) has contributed to the idea that extrafamilial commitments and involvements such as unionism or radical activism threatened family cohesion and loyalty.[88]

Family values did mediate Italian women's behavior and perceptions. The family orientation among Italian immigrants tended to militate against close contact with outsiders, and women in the group had little freedom to move outside the boundaries of the family unit. In contrast to Jewish females, Italian women were often forbidden to attend meetings at night or had to be chaperoned by fathers and brothers, an obvious constraint on their ability to participate in union activities.[89] Beyond that, an estimated 38–50 percent of Italian females working in the garment trades were married, with domestic obligations that made it as difficult for them to engage actively in the union movement as it was for the tiny proportion of Jewish wives who worked for wages.[90] To complicate matters still further, many Italian wives labored in neighborhood shops on schedules that coincided with their children's schooldays. Tied to a family schedule and limited to neighborhood employment, they could be easily intimidated by bosses who, according to ILGWU business agent Tina Gaeta, "would tell them that if they worked in union shops they would have to pay dues, and travel far [from home]."[91]

The issue of patriarchal authority also circumscribed Italian women's range of choices. ILGWU organizer Grace de Luise-Natarelli, whose father had denounced and disowned her because of her union activities, remembered the bitter clashes between women and their families over the issue of joining a labor organization. At the first organizational meeting of the workers in her Staten Island garment shop, "some of the husbands and some of the parents actually came and dragged out their wives and daughters who were attending . . . because they were against the union."[92]

Even if patriarchal pressures did not always prevent women from joining the union, they could limit the nature and extent of their participation. Grace Grimaldi had worked in a Manhattan blouse factory between 1914 and 1918 under conditions she likened to "slavery." For years she had prayed "for someone to come and help us change the working conditions." But when ILGWU organizers took the factory out on strike, her father prohibited her from walking the picket line because he feared for her safety. So she found other ways to contribute to the struggle. "I used to do behind-the-scenes work in the office." To go out on the picket line, she insisted, "you've got to be a fighter . . . some people are more fighters than others so they take the front."[93]

Family Influences

Nevertheless, family values cut both ways, sometimes constraining and sometimes encouraging labor activism. In her discussion of Italian immigrant women in New York's garment industry, Columba Furio notes that in pro-union households, women were "freed by their men" to join the movement.[94] That seems to have held true among the employees in the New York garment factory where Elizabeth Hasanovitz worked. Describing the dynamics in her workroom, where nearly all the Italians were relatives, she wrote: "Very often you see in a shop a set of finishers who are nearly all Italians . . . if you can persuade one to join the union, you may be sure of getting them all, if you fail with one, you fail with all. It was so in our shop."[95]

A family link to the union movement also characterized Rose and Lena Priola's involvement with the ACW in Chicago, but in their case maternal rather than paternal authority established a legitimating precedent. While working as a finisher in a Chicago factory, their mother had joined the Amalgamated. Rose and Lena followed her footsteps when they helped the union organize fellow workers at Hart, Schaffner & Marx. "She [their mother] used to send us, she used to make us go on the picket line." "I got a kick out of it," Rose remembered, "my sister . . . she's three years older than me . . . my mother used to send me with her so that she wouldn't be alone. I was supposed to be protecting her."[96]

Of course, Italian family authority was not absolute. Columba Furio's study provides numerous examples of Italian women who resisted or defied family authority in order to participate in the union movement. She argues, interestingly enough, that many of those who rebelled in this manner did so in the name of family loyalty, viewing unionism not as "an end itself" but "as a means to protect the family against industrial exploitation." To "preserve the family," she writes, "these women often found it necessary to turn their backs on it."[97]

Jewish families generally imposed fewer restrictions upon their female members than did Italian households. Young Jewish women generally felt freer to maneuver about the city streets and other public settings, enjoyed a greater degree of personal autonomy and independence, and may also have evinced a greater tendency toward social and cultural rebelliousness—including rebellion against patriarchal authority—than their Italian coworkers. Nevertheless, differences in family values among Jewish and Italian immigrants should not be exaggerated. In both groups women usually acted in ways that were consistent with family responsibility. Respect for the wishes of parents and concern for the welfare of the household also shaped the attitudes of Jewish women.

Kin and family sentiments pushed and pulled Jewish women as they did Italian immigrants, sometimes drawing them into the radical and union movements but also tempering their activism. When union organizers began to anticipate the turnout for the 1909 general strike in the New York shirtwaist industry, they worried that despite a nearly unanimous strike vote, some of the young women supporting families would be reluctant to participate.[98] Family responsibilities made women like Jennie Matyas think twice about the consequences of their activism and clearly introduced tensions in other Jewish households where needy parents depended upon their daughters' earnings. Thus when she first joined the strike movement, Matyas hid her involvement from her family. "I didn't dare tell my parents about it because I was sure my mother would be very disturbed and frightened. For one thing, she would be concerned about the possibility of interruption of the pay envelope."[99]

Conversely, parents and relatives who endorsed strikes and unions created a supportive atmosphere within which Jewish daughters might participate in the labor movement, helping to reinforce the messages that young people heard from radical coworkers. Rebecca Holland clearly thought she was affirming family values by joining the movement. "I come from a socialist family. My brother-in-law was a business agent for the Cloakmakers' Union, and all this was part of my blood," she insisted.[100]

One did not have to come from a socialist family to inherit an activist consciousness. Although we cannot determine how many striking daughters came from households where mothers had participated in community-based consumer strikes and boycotts in the years between 1902 and 1908, we may assume that the memory of one's mother or of neighborhood women taking to the streets as strikers on behalf of the household economy must have loomed as an important source of inspiration and affirmation for wage-earning daughters who joined later union campaigns.

Given the economic responsibilities of immigrant daughters to the household, the sympathy and support of parents and close relatives was often crucial to a woman's ability to enter and sustain the struggle for union organization. When Sarah Rozner first went to work for Hart, Schaffner & Marx in 1910, she was "totally ignorant" of the union movement. "When rumors went around about a strike, I knew something was buzzing," she recalled. "When I got home that night, the extra papers were out about a general clothing strike. A group of Jews were gathered in front of our house waiting for the holiday services to begin. I asked my father, what did a strike mean. He knew. He told me that to work when there was a strike was taking the bread out of someone else's mouth, and that was the biggest sin anyone could commit. Weeks went

by and the strike dragged on. I was the main support of the family."
After many weeks out on strike, she recalled, "we couldn't even pay the
eight dollars a month rent, the gas was cut off, and grocery credit
refused." Despite these hardships, her parents' support for the strike
never wavered.

> I told my mother I was going back to work Monday, but first she should go
> with me to a strike meeting. There were speakers of various nationalities
> and religions including one Jewish speaker. I could not imagine going back
> to work after a meeting like this, but still again I told my mother I was
> going back to work. She called me endearing names, and said "Sarah, we'll
> all die before [I'll let] you go back to work."[101]

Thus if Jewish women felt somewhat more independent of family authority than Italians, they still operated within the framework of the
household economy and more often than not heeded the wishes of
parents and relatives. The key difference between these two groups of
women rested largely in the orientation of immigrant families themselves.

Jewish families were far more likely than Italians to sympathize with
the union movement. As a consequence, Jewish daughters moved more
easily into the forefront of labor activism. But family attitudes in both
groups reflected the larger ethnic community culture in which they were
embedded. The differing community orientations of the two groups,
and by extension the differing directions of family sentiment, help
explain why Jewish daughters more readily embraced the union movement.

Ethnic Communities

Italian community support for the movement grew very slowly,
and until the end of World War I many segments of the immigrant
population remained suspicious or hostile to the unions. Those who
favored unionization faced obstacles not encountered by eastern European Jews.

Like their Jewish coworkers, Italian immigrants brought radical traditions with them to the United States. Anarchism, syndicalism, socialism, and what Rudolph Vecoli describes as "a growing class consciousness" had developed among the urban proletariat and peasantry in
northern, central, and southern Italy before the turn of the century. And

like Jewish immigrants, Italian radicals of various political stripes helped build a subculture of radicalism in the New Country.[102] Yet left-wing Italian radicalism was weaker and more seriously divided than the Jewish radical movement, with syndicalists and socialists often competing. Italian socialists worked within the ILGWU, but rebellious Italian anarcho-syndicalists refused to cooperate with AFL affiliates and attempted to build separate and antagonistic garment workers' organizations with the Industrial Workers of the World.[103]

Other institutions and constituencies in the Italian communities undercut the appeal of unions. The "prominenti" (elites) who ran newspapers, employment agencies, and immigrant banks, as well as those who controlled the Italian mutual benefit societies, initially opposed the unions; so did the Catholic clergy. Catholic clergymen took special pains to call attention to the threat that unionism posed to traditional values, stressing that radicals advocated female emancipation and the abolition of the family. Yet what seems to have worried the clergy and the "prominenti" most was the unions' potential to destroy the influence of established community leaders on the immigrant working classes.[104] The increasing support for unions after 1913 had much to do with changes in Italian community organization. Labor contractors no longer controlled the job market; instead Italians went on strike against Jewish and other non-Italian employers, so that the ethnic community was not so divided in its loyalties. And newspaper editors, some of them former labor contractors or friends of contractors, no longer had a reason to oppose the union movement. Eventually, as Edwin Fenton has suggested, Italian-American nationalism supplanted regional loyalties, and many groups including Italian fraternal societies came to regard scabbing as detrimental to the interests of the group.[105]

Beyond the attitudes of the "prominenti" and clergy, part of the issue for Italian garment workers lay in the structure of the garment industry unions themselves. Jews both founded and controlled the ILGWU and, though anxious to organize Italians, jealously guarded the positions of power that would have given Italian workers a sense of security and prestige within the organization. Years of frustrating failure in organizing Italians finally convinced ILGWU leaders that the key to unionizing Italians, or any nationality, was engaging organizers who could speak the same language and who understood the customs and loyalties of the workers.[106] Moreover, it was only after a decade of infighting and repeated demands for Italian "self-government" within the union that separate Italian-language locals were created in the ILGWU. Once Italian members had their own autonomous locals, membership grew steadily. In 1920 the 7,000–member Italian Cloakmakers' Local 48 was the largest in the union. By 1938 Italian Dressmakers' Local 89 was one of the largest union locals in the United States, with more than 40,000 members, most of them women.[107]

The situation in the ACW led to different results. Although eastern European Jews like Sidney Hillman, Joseph Schlossberg, and Dorothy Jacobs dominated the early ACW, almost from the start the Amalgamated emerged as a multi-ethnic institution, with August Bellanca, A. D. Marimpietri, Clara Masilotti, and other Italian radicals playing a central role in the inner circles of power and with Italian-language locals quickly established.[108] Although Italian resentments about "Jewish domination" continued to seethe under the surface, especially among the rank and file, Italian and Jewish "socialist elites" who led the union achieved a remarkable harmony of attitude and purpose and strove to eliminate cultural tensions within the organization.[109] These patterns and policies help explain why Italian women and men responded more readily and enthusiastically to strikes in the men's clothing trades, and why the ACW found it easier to organize Italians than did the ILGWU.

All of this suggests that for Italian women, the critical issues involved in joining the union movement transcended the personal pressures of family roles and patriarchal authority. Both Italian women and Italian men came later to the union movement than Jews did, and the reasons had as much to do with the structures and politics of the immigrant community and the internal organization of the garment unions as with the cultural boundaries of the immigrant family.

If the stereotype of "backward" or "passive" Italian women concealed much about actual behavioral patterns as well as opportunities and influences that conditioned their choices, so too the image of "radical" Jewish women united in militant struggle vastly oversimplifies the responses and outlook of that group. Jews did not stand unanimously behind the radical union movement any more than Italians did. The eastern European Jewish community contained diverse cultural and political constituencies, and its female work force reflected that diversity.

The range of female responses to the union cause was as wide and varied for Jews as it was for Italians. In both cases cultural, structural, and situational factors mediated women's attitudes, shaping a range of responses that varied from dedicated labor militance to outright indifference. On one end of the Jewish spectrum stood the stalwart militants, a small but highly visible minority who closely identified with the cause of socialism and unionism and whose influence far exceeded their numbers. They personified the fighting spirit and idealism associated with the Jewish labor movement, and their involvement was critical to its successes. Even in their own time observers tended to speak of these women in highly romantic terms, citing their heroism, dedication, and willingness to sacrifice for the cause.[110]

At the other end of the spectrum stood Jewish women who resembled those "Americans" whom union leaders viewed as "frivolous." Like the "Alrightniks" derided by *Forward* editor Abraham Cahan for their bourgeois pretensions, some wage-earning daughters with aspirations to upward mobility more or less disassociated themselves from the struggles of the immigrant proletariat. Some, having emigrated from areas of eastern Europe such as Austria-Hungary and Romania where radical movements had made fewer inroads than in Russia and Poland, lacked familiarity with labor organization. If such women did go out on strike, it was sometimes for purely practical, bread-and-butter goals rather than out of a commitment to class struggles or the principles of socialist unionism. Rarely would they take chances. For them, the decision to strike usually came only after a walkout was assured—when peer and community pressure made the consequences of not striking larger than the risks of staying on the job.[111] Between these two poles of indifference and radicalism stood the vast majority of Jewish women, who supported the strike movement but whose political orientation remained more ambiguous. For some, personal goals and aspirations circumscribed a whole-hearted commitment to the union movement. Others were held back by fear and timidity. All of these sentiments mediated Ida Richter's response. Like many others who sympathized with the goals and purposes of the labor movement, she saw unionism as a temporary phase, like wage work itself. "I belonged, after a while to the union," said Richter; "I had marriage in mind so I didn't want to be an ardent member." Initially, she admitted, she had been afraid to go out on strike, afraid of the violence, the clubbings by the police, afraid of being arrested on the picket line. But she had felt "guilty," she said, watching from the window of her shop as her striking coworkers were being "dragged off" in patrol wagons.[112]

For the Ida Richters of the garment industry, as for others, community and family pressures could push and pull them in different directions—either toward or against more active involvement in the union movement. Between guilt and action stood the influence of parents, siblings, landsleit, friends, and neighbors.

The family's cultural orientation played one role in shaping the outlooks and behavior of women, ethnic community attitudes another.

Culturally, socially, and politically the strict Orthodox establishment remained a countervailing force with which socialist unionism had to reckon. Although much reduced in its influence in the New World, especially upon young people, the Orthodox still spoke for a sizable portion of the community. One study published in 1905 estimated that despite a growing drift away from religious practice, at least half of the "maturing" population of East Side immigrants in New York remained within the Orthodox fold, though the following decade doubtless reduced this percentage.[113] The Orthodox press continued to exercise a good deal of influence in the immigrant community. Although the socialist *Jewish Daily Forward* had the largest circulation of all the Yiddish newspapers, boasting a subscription list of 50,000 in 1907, the two dailies representing Orthodox religious interests in New York—the *Yiddishes Tageblatt* and *Morgn Journal*—claimed tens of thousands of subscribers.[114]

The Orthodox outlook on unionism ranged from hostility to qualified support. Some families and individuals viewed the socialist-led garment unions and the radical movement in general with suspicion and fear. Certainly that had been true in Russia, where Fannie Shapiro's Orthodox parents worried that daughters would go off to the big cities, join the radical movement, and "drop religion."[115] Orthodox elders feared that Jewish youth would be corrupted by socialist leaders who, they imagined, were preaching free love and other radical blasphemies sure to undermine the purity of the family and the foundation of the faith.[116]

Such concerns often showed themselves in the anti-unionism of the small landsleit shops where Orthodoxy went hand in hand with employer paternalism. In this environment, where Orthodox bosses and workers belonged to the same landsmanschaftn and synagogue and where religious "services" often punctuated the daily routines of the workshop, labor organization, though not impossible, was sometimes extremely difficult. A letter to the *Forward* by an employee in one such shop complained that all of the workers were Orthodox "fanatics." They had an "organization," with the boss as president and the foreman as treasurer. "Naturally they do not want to hear of a union."[117]

By and large, however, Orthodoxy and unionism were not irreconcilable, and religious beliefs did not in themselves obstruct labor organization. When, for example, 250 Jewish secondhand tailors went out on strike in July 1910, union headquarters closed on Saturdays in honor of the Jewish Sabbath, allowing the strikers to perform their religious duties. The Orthodox among them considered themselves "Jews first of

all," insisting that whether the strike was won or lost, "Jews we remain." But as one observer of their strike noted, the "gigantic labor
movement on the East Side, the tremendous cloak maker walkout, the
powerful campaign carried on by United Hebrew Trades, and the fever
of unionism which has struck New York," swept even tradition-bound
Orthodox tailors into a "general labor uprising."[118] In significant ways
religious and secular notions of social justice complemented each other,
and as several scholars have suggested, this enabled Orthodox workers
to understand labor organization not only as a practical solution to the
material problems of daily existence but as a vehicle for upholding
traditional values.[119]

In America, eastern European Jewish Orthodox leaders and newspapers generally took an ambivalent stance toward the union movement. In the same breath they gave their blessing to striking Jewish
workers and supported the idea of unionization and denounced the
socialist "demagogues" who led the garment unions.[120] Influential Orthodox newspapers such as the *Yiddishes Tageblatt* portrayed the socialist garment union leaders as dangerous missionaries who, like the
Christians, were ready to convert the rank and file to an alien religion.[121]

Yet without question the *Tageblatt* sided with the workers, giving
front-page coverage to the major garment strikes and sympathetically
reporting on the struggles of Jewish women and men to organize.
During the 1913 general strike in New York's white goods industry, for
example, the *Tageblatt* told the strikers' story with elaborate detail,
acknowledging the very low pay of women workers, supporting their
right to fight for a decent standard of living for themselves and the
families they helped sustain, and criticizing the violent behavior of the
local police. Nor, surprisingly, did religious issues interfere with the
paper's support for the strikers. With no hint of disapproval, for example, the paper even reported on union meetings and strike votes taken on
the Sabbath.[122]

Supportive of the strikers in this and other instances, the religious
press and the Orthodox leadership generally tried to play a constructive
and conciliatory role in labor disputes, hoping to mend the conflict
between Jewish workers and Jewish bosses that endangered communal
unity while at the same time arguing that workers deserved better
conditions. Typically, Orthodox spokesmen urged that labor and capital attempt to understand each other. The *Tageblatt* editorialized during
the 1910 New York cloak makers' strike that both sides should "give up
a little" instead of carrying on the fight "to the bitter end." Continued

warfare between workers and bosses, the editor warned, threatened not only the income of thousands of families but the "fate" of "an entire Jewish industry."[123] As a practical matter, however, the goal of community solidarity favored the unions, for as Orthodox leaders frequently acknowledged, Jewish employers often took steps that appeared dangerously divisive.

The fact that most garment industry bosses were Jewish complicated the issue of communal solidarity. Some of the most prosperous manufacturers were assimilated German Jews whose cultural and economic distance from the east Europeans exacerbated worker-employer antagonisms. But growing numbers of employers were Russian Jews. Recently emancipated from the ranks of labor and often veterans of the socialist labor movement, these "Alrightniks" were particularly sensitive to charges of exploiting their former comrades. As co-ethnics, and in the case of the German Jewish employers coreligionists, Jewish bosses found themselves pushed and pulled by the contradictory pressures of religious and ethnic loyalty and economic self-interest. All of this played into the hands of those who supported the union movement. At critical points in the course of a strike, social and moral pressures could be exerted on Jewish employers, as could negative publicity from community leaders.[124] Thus in Chicago the Orthodox Jewish *Daily Courier* refused to carry ads for scab labor, warning Jewish employers against hiring gentile scabs to replace striking Jewish garment workers and accusing manufacturers who did so of behaving like "anti-Semites."[125]

Orthodox leaders accepted the need for unions but attempted to make sure that socialist union leaders did not neglect the religious needs of the rank and file. Orthodox rabbis and other interested parties insisted that, along with other protections offered by the unions, the religious rights of members be guaranteed. In the aftermath of the 1910 New York cloak and suit makers' strike, Orthodox members of the union, with the backing of local rabbis, founded a "Shomer Shabbes" (Sabbath Observers) organization whose purpose was to ensure that members be able to keep the Sabbath and observe all Jewish religious holidays.[126] The secretary of a similar organization wrote to ILGWU president Benjamin Schlesinger in May 1916, urging him to "see to it that the . . . new contracts made with employers when the strike is over, insert a provision that Jewish workingmen desiring to observe the Jewish sabbath and holidays have the full right."[127] The Jewish immigrant community, then, though not united behind the radical union movement, tended to support the right of workers to strike and organize. In contrast to the Catholic church and the Italian "prominenti," who were more likely to oppose the labor movement, even the more culturally conservative elements in the Jewish community appeared ambivalent rather than antagonistic. That support helped ease the way of Jewish daughters into the movement, legitimating their presence on the picket line and creating an environment of community and family sympathy for their activism.

Local Jewish neighborhood community groups and organizations came to the aid of strikers with donations of food, clothing, and other kinds of assistance. Grocers and storekeepers extended credit to striking workers and their families. A shared ethnic-occupational culture helped develop a communal knowledge of exploitative conditions in the garment industry, creating networks of information, a high degree of awareness of and sympathy for the plight of friends, relatives, and neighbors, and a willingness to sacrifice on their behalf.[128] Relatives and landsleit working in similar occupations traded stories about shop conditions, strikes, and union campaigns, all of which helped anchor the labor movement in the context of ethnic community survival. "All the boarders were landsleit," one Jewish immigrant recalled. "The major topics most frequently bantered about concerned the union meetings and sometimes . . . strikes in the needle trades in which everyone worked."[129]

Moreover, with immigrants living and working in close proximity, picketing, parades, and mass meetings melded into neighborhood life, blurring the distinction between participants and nonparticipants. Thousands of striking workers routinely jammed the streets, singing, cheering, and chanting, moving the class struggle outside the confines of shop and factory.[130] A published letter from the father of a striking Jewish shirtwaist worker announcing that his daughter "IS NOT A SCAB!" suggests the interconnections between community solidarity, class identity, and family values in the union movement. Writing to the Socialist *Call* in December 1909, he addressed his comments to the members of the Ladies' Waist Makers' Union in New York:

> Dear Friends—I want to inform you that my daughter Annie is ill and unable to proceed with the work of the struggle that she and you started. I hope she'll be better soon and be able to enter your ranks again. The only thing I want to point out is that SHE IS NOT A SCAB and I hope you will not suspect anything of this kind. In her name I request you to continue the terrible struggle which you have started for decent conditions and humane treatment. Do not lose your spirit of solidarity. . . . Consider yourselves as intelligent self-respecting workers of the organized labor movement![131]

As episodes of working-class communal solidarity, these strikes gathered both wage earners and non—wage earners into the struggle. On the very first day of the 1909 New York waistmakers' uprising, some 15,000 people went out on strike. "The East Side was a seething mass of excited women, girls and men," the *Call* reported. Meeting halls overflowed, with crowds spilling out into the streets. "All over the East Side a sea of excited faces, a mass of gesticulating women and men, blocked the streets."[132] The next day the crowds grew thicker and included both strikers and strike sympathizers. These "vast crowds were as wildly demonstrative as the audience in the [strike] halls. They marched through the streets . . . breaking into storms of applause as the word that another boss had settled with the strikers was passed along," wrote one reporter.[133] Even immigrant mothers and wives, whose busy days revolved around home and neighborhood marketplace, took part in strike activities. "Back at the union halls," an ILGWU official wrote of the 1913 New York white goods strike, "the girls were celebrating. Pianos were thumping. . . . Girls were soon joined by their boyfriends, their mothers and other well wishers and were dancing with whole-hearted abandon."[134]

Wives and mothers took to the streets as well to support the union movement. A giant parade held by striking Cleveland cloakmakers in 1911 included, in addition to thousands of male and female cloakmakers, a large contingent of strikers' wives. "The wives of the strikers marched in a body in the parade with their children," reported Abraham Rosenberg of the ILGWU. "Two wagon loads of children also took part in the parade carrying banners which read, 'Our Fathers and Mothers are Striking to Give Us a Better Education.'"[135]

"Time there was when the East Side woman knew nothing about the union and strikes," announced Pauline Newman during the 1910 cloakmakers' general strike. "But that time is passed. . . . The East Side woman of today is an enthusiastic unionist without belonging to a union and when her husband goes on strike she is with him heart and soul." The tenement stoop, where immigrant wives gathered to exchange news of the strike, had become an important fount of union strength.[136] "The [married] women, even if they did not belong . . . [to] the union, they struggled in [behalf of] the union," Pearl Spenser, veteran of Chicago's garment factories, insisted.[137]

The support of family, neighbors, and friends turned garment strikes into community struggles for working-class dignity and justice, reinforced the efforts of shopfloor organizers, and forged important connections between community political culture and labor organization.

15. Immigrant workers, their families, and friends turn out for a protest parade honoring Charles Lazinskas, who was killed during the 1910 strike of men's clothing workers in Chicago. Chicago Historical Society.

Within this climate of support for working-class rights and social justice, going out on strike amounted to an act of communal solidarity. Even when family economic pressures and more conservative cultural values moderated Jewish women's commitments to labor activism, broad-based community endorsement of strikes and the principles of unionism eased their way into the public political arena of the labor movement.

Garment workers' uprisings transformed the industry. They transformed the immigrant community; and equally important, they transformed the lives of women workers. Jewish daughters who experienced and participated in the tumultuous events of the great uprisings would come to understand not only how their own lives were changing but how they were helping change the lives of others.

6 "As We Are Not Angels"
The New Unionism and the New Womanhood

Standing before a large crowd assembled at New York's Cooper Union in the spring of 1912, a young garment worker named Mollie Schepps delivered an impassioned speech on behalf of working women's right to vote. "Since economic conditions force us to fight our battle side by side with men in the industrial field," working women "cannot play the simple idiot and worship men as heroes." She drove home her point: "As we [women] are not angels, nor are they [men] Gods. We are simply in business together and as such we refuse to play the silent partner any longer."[1]

We know little about Mollie Schepps's life, except that like tens of thousands of Jewish women she worked in New York's shirtwaist trade and was an active member of Local 25 of the International Ladies' Garment Workers' Union, a local with a large female membership and a reputation for labor militance. She also belonged to the organization sponsoring the Cooper Union rally, the Wage Earners' Suffrage League, a group whose membership consisted of women working in shops and factories.[2]

While many favored woman suffrage, most Jewish immigrant daughters of Mollie Schepps's generation did not join pro-suffrage organizations or actively campaign for the vote.[3] And Schepps's speech, with its militant call for equality between the sexes, would have sounded too radical to many of her immigrant sisters. Most of her generation desired a greater voice and expanded rights, including suffrage, without pushing for total equality between the sexes. Nevertheless, the language and central metaphors of the speech grew from understandings shared by most Jewish immigrant daughters. The side-by-side "battle" of women and men for economic survival, the idea that the sexes were "in business" together for that purpose, and the notion that women were no more angelic than men—this was the terminology of a characteristically Jewish construction of gender taking shape among the immigrant generation. Indeed, Mollie Schepps articulated what Jewish women had always known: that the struggle for daily bread took place in partnership with fathers, brothers, and husbands. But she was changing the terms of the discourse, redefining and renegotiating the meaning of that partnership. No longer would young women be content to struggle as the silent half; now they wanted the voice, the recognition, the respect that as working partners they had long been denied. This was a revolution in immigrant women's thinking—one that most of Mollie's Jewish sisters participated in to some degree—a new definition of womanhood being constructed on the foundations of the old.

This reconstruction was part of the emergence of a Jewish immigrant version of "New Womanhood." The concept "New Womanhood" or "New Woman" entered the American vocabulary at the turn of the century. Between the 1890s and the 1920s it was used to portray the continuous, dramatic renegotiation of gender concepts as women experimented with new kinds of public behavior. Used frequently but inconsistently, the concept of the New Woman first described Jane Addams's generation of ambitious, career-oriented, middle-class American women, many of them active in urban reform causes. Later the term was employed to describe an altogether different style of femininity, when the carefree flapper of the 1920s began to challenge old-fashioned notions of female restraint and asexuality with a rebellious style of social and sexual experimentation. Young women also sought to take their place alongside men as companions, pals, and partners, participating socially as well as politically in worlds formerly reserved for men. Observers of social behavior in the 1920s also emphasized the relationship between New Womanhood and the shift toward "companionate marriage"—union based on love, mutual attraction, and consumerism rather than the older standard of matrimony associated with duty, self-sacrifice, and idealized domesticity.[4]

Mollie Schepps and her generation of working-class immigrant daughters developed standards of womanhood that differed from Jane Addams and the flapper. However, it is likely that immigrants and Americans learned something from each other as both cultures reoriented traditional ways to carve out modern sex roles in the first decades of this century.

A Jewish immigrant version of New Womanhood was evident as early as 1902 when journalist Hutchins Hapgood set out to explore "the spirit" of the Lower East Side. The "modern type" of Jewish immigrant woman, Hapgood observed, possessed many "virtues" that might be considered "masculine" in character. By masculine Hapgood meant that these young women were "simple and straightforward," "intensely serious," and "do not 'bank' in any way on the fact they are women." They wanted no special consideration as females and would feel insulted, for example, if their male escorts showed any "politeness growing out of the difference in sex." Some were socialists, others anarchists, many of them sweatshop workers, all passionately interested in radical ideas.[5]

If Hapgood had revisited the topic of immigrant New Womanhood ten years later, he might have noted a less serious side. Well before the appearance of the flapper in the 1920s, immigrant daughters engaged in leisure habits that defied both the norms of the shtetl and the standards of respectable middle-class American morality. Seeking pleasure and male companionship, young female wage earners who went to dancehalls, amusement parks, and theaters, and participated in other forms of mixed-sex leisure, anticipated—even paved the way for—the new feminine styles of the Jazz Age. Like the middle-class bohemian women of Hapgood's world, immigrant daughters were helping to "chart the modern sexual terrain."[6]

Jewish immigrant daughters also helped chart new styles of political behavior for women. For it was garment industry strikers who became role models for American-born middle- and upper-class militant suffragists, activists, and radical feminists of the 1910s. Native-born radical feminists, like Crystal Eastman and Harriet Stanton Blatch, who demanded the right to individual self-fulfillment—economic and political—looked at wage-earning women, with their militant protest styles and their brazen leisure habits, and thought they saw symbols of independent womanhood. Viewed by an earlier generation of female reformers as victims to be pitied, writes Nancy Cott, female wage earners now appeared to modern feminists as "a vanguard to be imitated."[7] Thus as Jewish and other immigrant daughters were reinventing their own ethnic womanhood, they were also inspiring new feminine styles for the American society at large.

Jewish New Womanhood

If Mollie Schepps and her generation of immigrant working women unwittingly influenced changes in the surrounding culture, their kind of New Womanhood was grounded in a framework that had little in common with the world of middle- and upper-class reformers and feminists. It was a framework that was specifically immigrant and Jewish.

A Jewish version of New Womanhood took shape within several overlapping contexts. It was forged out of the changes in social practices encouraged by young working women's involvement in urban mass culture and in the broadened political experience that resulted from their work in the garment industry. The daring of social life and the daring of labor activism each contributed to an easing of the constraints on female behavior. Jewish immigrant youth—male and female—came together as companions in their leisure time and met each other as comrades in the strike movement. The new mood encouraged young women to feel optimistic about making relationships based on a partnership between the sexes, not necessarily an equal partnership but a collaboration that represented a giant step away from the exclusionary patterns of Orthodox Jewish culture. Partnership might be pursued in social life or modern ideas about marriage, and it described the kind of relationship Jewish female activists wanted with men in the civic sphere of the labor movement.

The labor uprisings in the garment industry served as a potent symbol of Jewish women's evolving sense of self. Strikes and union-related activities strengthened and legitimated the female presence in the affairs of the community, creating novel opportunities for the sexes to come together in a mass movement based in class and community interest. Mass strikes had demonstrated to female wage earners the power of collective action. But more important in terms of women's emerging identities, the movement provided young people with an avenue for broadening the scope of feminine roles and responsibilities, one that legitimated a new public visibility and suggested the potential for cooperating with men in the struggle for social change. Long confined to economic and domestic roles, women saw in the labor movement a vehicle for expanding their social and cultural horizons and for joining with men in the civic life of their communities.[8]

Unionism was not the first expression of public political involvement for European-born Jewish women, but it symbolized an important new form of female activism. In the past much of what could be called the public role of Jewish women revolved around their responsibilities as breadwinners, providers, consumers, and dispensers of charity. On various occasions Jewish women acted politically to defend those responsibilities, boycotting high-priced food or protesting high rents and neighborhood evictions.[9] Increasingly these consumer actions meshed with the wider context of radical politics, as immigrant housewives adopted the language and even the tactics of the Jewish labor movement. In 1902, for example, Orthodox Jewish immigrant housewives on New York's Lower East Side staged a consumer boycott to protest the exorbitant price of kosher meat, referring to themselves as "strikers" and to nonparticipants as "scabs."[10] Despite their radical rhetoric and tactics, these protests confirmed traditional gender roles. Though immigrant housewives looted, burned, and rioted against "capitalist" butchers and landlords on behalf of working-class consumers, they did so in the name of customary female responsibilities for maintaining the essentials of daily life—food and shelter—and expressed women's traditional obligations in that realm.[11]

Industrial protest by wage-earning immigrant daughters shared some of the same purposes and had some of the same social dimensions as consumer activism. Both were community projects whose successful outcome depended upon the support of family, kin, and neighbors; both aimed at protecting the public good over the interest of private profiteers. And when young immigrant women went out on strike, they often did so as household providers attempting to improve the family's standard of living. Yet in joining the labor movement, immigrant daughters were doing more than behaving in radical ways to fulfill the "conventional expectations" of women. Unionism symbolized an important further step. It moved the locus and scope of women's activism beyond the household and neighborhood, expanding it in new directions outward into the larger struggle to establish a better social and industrial order. This was a new dimension to Jewish immigrants' political culture. Young women's participation in events that affected communal life involved them in activities that had once been the province of men. The entrance of women into the labor movement thus represented a step toward the integration of the sexes in the mainstream of public life.

Immigrant women's consciousness of their new role and responsibility in public life was an essential element in their activism. Young working daughters recognized that beyond the tangible economic benefits that labor organization would bring to them and their households, the movement also enabled them to act in the service of their class and ethnic group. The language immigrant women used to describe their motivations and goals suggests this transcendent political vision. And it also suggests how women of the immigrant generation integrated politics into the female life cycle, how they combined a commitment to social justice with a sense of their own life course as females.

Acknowledging that they were not permanent wage earners and might not personally benefit from their struggles to build a labor movement, young women often saw themselves as altruistic crusaders for social justice. "It is not for myself, but my heart weeps for the younger girls . . . that they would find life so hard and miserable when they are so young; that they should begin to lose their red cheeks and their hopes from the very moment they land in America," insisted a striking shirtwaist worker as she walked the picket line during the 1909 uprising.[12] "The future generations will bless us for it," Fannia Cohn often heard fellow women unionists say as they spoke of their struggles to build the ILGWU.[13]

Jennie Matyas conceived her role in the labor movement in much the same terms. When she came to America, she knew nothing about socialism or unionism. At first her only ambition was to become a skilled worker. By age fifteen she had succeeded, landing a well-paid position as a sample maker in a dress factory. Although she had few personal complaints about her employer, she grew increasingly disturbed about how other workers were treated, and she wanted to do something about it. In 1913 she attended a pre–general strike meeting of Local 25 in New York, where she listened to ILGWU secretary Abraham Baroff speak about exploitation in the industry. Baroff talked of "changing conditions so that the people who came after us would know a little bit more comfort and ease than we did."

The speech awakened in her a new sense of purpose. "Instantly," she recalled, "I began to see myself as a grown-up who would have to change the world for the children who followed, for the generations that would come after us." At the age of fifteen Jennie Matyas came to believe that "heaven had opened up because I was now really grown up enough to participate in the responsibility of helping to change the world and wipe out misery and poverty."[14]

Union campaigns encouraged such romantic rhetoric. But we cannot dismiss the spirit of self-sacrifice that animated many young female unionists. Most Jewish women would have agreed that joining the union and participating in organizational campaigns would bring them tangible benefits during the four or five years they remained in the work force and would help those workers who came after them. The assumption of this civic responsibility carried with it a new and rewarding sense of female power and importance. More than simply a means of gaining immediate economic and physical protection, activism and unionism became a form of political participation. The flowering of secular radicalism both in eastern Europe and in the immigrant communities of America had convinced many women that helping to change the world was not solely a male prerogative.

On the surface, Jewish women's expressions of altruism and self-sacrifice seem to resemble what historians have labeled the "social housekeeping" role of American middle-class reformers in the Progressive Era. Educated New Women like Jane Addams and Lillian Wald viewed the world less in terms of social class than in categories of gender and built female-centered organizations that would cleanse urban and industrial life of waste, greed, and corruption. They insisted that women of all classes had more in common with one another than with their fathers, brothers, or husbands and believed that as a morally superior "sex group," women were specially suited to be the agents of reform and social change.[15]

Jewish immigrant women were not unfamiliar with this perspective. Certainly it had its analogue among middle-class German Jewish women who were active in early twentieth-century urban reform movements.[16] The contacts that Russian Jewish immigrants had with settlement-house workers and middle-class members of the Women's Trade Union League introduced them to models of American (and Americanized) womanhood that included a commitment to civic "causes," and this familiarity helped counteract traditional Jewish reservations about expanding public roles for women. But as eastern European Jewish immigrant daughters developed a political vision of their own, their understandings and patterns of activism diverged in significant ways from social housekeeping. Jewish immigrant activism sprang from very different roots and carried with it different assumptions about the relationships among gender, community, and politics.

Traditional Orthodox culture had assigned the sexes to masculine and feminine spheres of influence and activity, barring women from the most esteemed pursuits of religious learning and communal authority. In the social spaces occupied by females—the home, the marketplace, the workshops, the women's balcony of the synagogue, the bath-house, and other places where women congregated—a network of female relatives and friends learned to rely on each other for support and assistance and even banded together for political purposes. But this female world lacked the institutional organization typical of western bourgeois women's culture. The political affiliations of working-class Jewish women, as Paula Hyman has pointed out, tended toward informality and spontaneity. Mainly it was more Americanized middle-class German Jewish women who founded their own female institutions.[17] As a group, first-generation Russian Jewish women lacked the sense of moral exceptionalism that undergirded the activism of the social housekeepers and had been central to the development of an independent women's movement in the United States.

Unlike the social housekeepers, eastern European Jewish immigrant women lacked the culturally constructed foundation for the claim that they were acting as morally exalted females on behalf of society. In shtetl tradition it was men, not women, who held the high ground in matters moral, religious, and spiritual. True, striking garment workers had demanded that their employers treat them like "ladies" and insisted upon the same respect and propriety afforded middle-class matrons who did not have to labor in factories. One item on the agenda of their New Womanhood was to get Jewish men to recognize that women as a group deserved a greater regard than misogynist traditions of shtetl culture had bestowed. But for eastern European Jewish women this goal never directly translated into a full-blown political or social movement. Women like Mollie Schepps insisted that females were neither better nor worse than men. As breadwinners, as Jews, as members of a vulnerable class and ethnic community, they stressed the common ground they shared with men. And on that basis they made their claim to civic participation.[18]

Jewish immigrant daughters differed from American reformers in other ways as well. If the prototypical middle-class American reformer before World War I was a single woman who eschewed marriage for a public-spirited career, living and working within a "female" (and often feminist) community, the typical Jewish union member was a teenager with marriage on her mind.[19] In the Old World as in the New, Jewish women's emerging sense of self led neither to commitment to a specific feminist ideology nor to abandonment of fundamental domestic goals. For most Jewish immigrant daughters, neither the inclination toward a total restructuring of male-female relationships nor a commitment to remaining in the work force animated or flowed from their activism. Although the handful of Jewish women who became labor leaders usually chose a union career over married life, Jewish radical tradition certainly offered rank-and-file women other models of female activism. Immigrant daughters familiar with the heroines of the Bund in Russia and Poland knew that many of the most active women in the organization were the wives of male revolutionaries. They had joined the Bund as single women, served as organizers, educators, and propagandists, and then married Jewish comrades and continued their political work in partnership with their husbands, usually deferring to the man's leadership and ideas.[20]

Jewish women garment workers thus encountered two models of female activism—eastern European Jewish socialist and grass-roots American.[21] The German Jewish, female-centered model represented a third, decidedly middle-class model that had much in common with the grass-roots American style. Influenced by middle-class patterns, and sometimes indebted to supporting organizations like the Women's Trade Union League, Russian Jewish immigrant women followed a variety of paths, some closer to the American (i.e., middle-class) model than others. But in the aggregate they forged what can only be considered their own Russian Jewish immigrant version of New Womanhood, based as much on old cultural understandings as on the new lessons of the American experience. Previously excluded from the central discussions of their community, they moved eagerly to take advantage of the opportunities for civic participation that labor activism offered. Whereas American middle-class women had traditionally sought to politicize their role as moral guardians and, at the same time, to differentiate their civic contribution from men's, Jewish daughters aimed to politicize their role as breadwinners, striving to join with men in the common struggles of the working-class immigrant community.

Integration was their goal. But because immigrant women were still evolving in their political identities, their approach to organization remained flexible. Without a long tradition of a "woman" movement to guide them, eastern European Jewish immigrants approached public activism without a well-defined agenda such as the separatist strategies of grass-roots American feminism.[22] With immigrant political culture still in flux, the relationship of Jewish men and women in public life had still to be negotiated. Quite a few Jewish daughters were content to accept a role as junior partners to men. How much authority immigrant women would have and what the limits of their participation might be had not yet been decided.

This negotiation of Jewish women's role in communal life can be seen in the political patterns of the larger immigrant community, on the one hand, and in the union movement, on the other. The attitude of Jews on New York's Lower East Side toward the issue of woman suffrage reveals the degree to which the community recognized the shared responsibilities of men and women in the struggles for family and communal survival. Jewish immigrant women had little doubt about the propriety of votes for their sex. A poll taken on the Lower East Side in 1915 found that 75 percent of Jewish females favored woman suffrage.[23] In two New York State suffrage referenda, in 1915 and 1917, Jewish immigrant election districts (including those on the Lower East Side and Harlem) provided the strongest and most consistent support for suffrage of all Manhattan voters, stronger even than middle- and upper-middle-class native-born Protestant districts—certainly stronger than the Italian vote, which showed pockets of pro-suffrage support but mainly opposed votes for women, and stronger by far than the Irish, who provided the most consistent opposition to the measure. Elinor Lerner, analyzing these voting patterns, has suggested that the distinctive factor in the pro-suffrage vote was the kinds of social contact between males and females in a given ethnic community. Compared with those who opposed suffrage, Jewish men had frequent contact with women in and outside the workplace, especially with female wage earners who worked in the garment trades. Here industrial life and politics tended to be mutually reinforcing.[24]

Yet these understandings reflected more than the shared occupational culture of immigrant men and women. By 1915 the nature of contact between Jewish men and women had evolved so that support for woman suffrage reflected the whole constellation of cultural, social, and political changes inherent in immigrant New Womanhood. By that time women's role in building the garment trades' unions was firmly established. Women had taken the initiative in garment strikes and demonstrated their political usefulness. As a result, both the unions and the wider ethnic community recognized how much they had profited from women's participation in civic life. From a communal standpoint there would be further benefits in women's enfranchisement—most important, a doubling of political strength.[25]

New Womanhood and the New Unionism

It was one thing to support the vote for women, quite another to envision sharing power with them. For the eastern European Jewish immigrant community, votes for women represented not a commitment to full equality but rather the ability of men to accept a limited partnership between the sexes.

The potential for conflict in such an arrangement can be seen best in the labor movement, where the relationship between the garment unions and their young Jewish female constituents illustrates the dilemmas and complexities of Jewish New Womanhood. These unions faced a unique challenge. American unionism had been geared almost exclusively to males. Women, viewed as interlopers in a male world, were often excluded. When accepted, they occupied the margins of union life, typically all but ignored by the male leadership. But this was not possible in the garment industry where women workers were too numerous to ignore and, as we have seen, played a critical role in the mass strike movement that had strengthened union membership and resources.

Thus garment workers' unions were in some respects in a pioneering position. For the first time, two major labor organizations (the ILGWU and the ACW) would have to learn, like it or not, how to accommodate a substantially female membership.[26]

Modeled after fraternal organizations, unions traditionally conducted their business in saloons and other male preserves. The garment unions in the pre–general strike period were no exception. If women were going to play an active part in the labor movement, unions would have to change to meet their particular needs and interests. Moreover, unions would have to face the one issue that had always justified their reluctance to organize women—namely, that most females were temporary workers who did not intend to make a career out of wage work. Labor turnover in this seasonal industry was extremely high for both sexes, but women presented a special problem. Membership in the shirtwaist makers' Local 25 in New York City underwent a complete turnover every three years, a trend that reflected the marriage-mindedness of its largely female Jewish constituents.[27] Getting Jewish women to participate in strikes and to join labor organizations usually presented little problem to organizers, but keeping them active in union affairs was another matter.

Union efforts to meet this challenge yielded mixed results. Male-dominated unions were slow to recognize, and sometimes needed to be pushed to realize, that something had to be done to keep the interest of women members in the business of their organizations. Women unionists continually had to plead to be taken seriously and to insist on programs aimed at strengthening female participation.[28] The unions themselves did little to initiate changes, but they did allow women activists to lay the groundwork for programs that in time helped give the garment unions a look different from other American labor organizations, a look associated with what came to be called the "new unionism."

The new unionism departed from mainstream unionism in several important ways. Anticipating the CIO unions of the 1930s, garment unions organized on an industry-wide basis, breaking the traditional hold of the skilled crafts on the labor movement. Second, unlike mainstream American unionism with its focus on bread-and-butter issues such as wages and hours, the new unionism had a politicized, quasi-socialist goal: to establish a new social order that would empower workers and provide for their welfare on and off the shop floor.[29]

In the garment industry female activists left a deep imprint on the new unionism, both contributing to its development and sometimes running

afoul of its laws. Recognizing that the key to stronger female membership within the garment unions was to infuse their organizations with
the idealism that had characterized the early days of the strike movement, women activists pushed for reforms that would give the union not
only a "body," but a "soul." It was not enough for the union to provide
economic protections; something had to be done to make union membership an intellectually and socially enriching experience.[30]

Fannia Cohn was well aware that overworked and exhausted teenagers might be more enthusiastic about attending union meetings and
other after-work events if they could be promised something beyond the
cut-and-dried business that typified organizational life in mainstream
unions. She had only to listen to the words of Anna Rudnitzky, a
garment worker who complained that "time is passing and everything is
missed. I am not living, I am just working."[31]

This desire on the part of immigrant youth for time for "living" was
an essential preoccupation of their New Womanhood. Single working
girls in search of fun and male companionship sought opportunities to
go dancing after work or to meet with other young people in social
clubs, on the street, and in amusement parks. Others struggled to stay
awake in night schools. The solution to the apathy of young women
dues-payers, some believed, was to find ways of making union life as
enjoyable as the world outside the factory walls. This quest for a
unionism better suited to the needs of its youthful membership ultimately led the ILGWU to develop programs and institutions that
offered members educational and recreational opportunities.

Although early in its history the ILGWU had experimented with
educational programs, not until 1914 were some strides made toward
establishing an on-going commitment to educating workers. Impatient
with the educational work of the International, women activists in the
heavily Jewish shirtwaist workers' Local 25 took matters into their own
hands. Under the direction of Juliet Stuart Poyntz, a Barnard College
history instructor whom they recruited to assist them, members of Local
25 established their own educational department and a program of
classes for New York's shirtwaist and dressworkers which served as a
model for locals in other branches of the women's garment trade.
Following the example of the shirtwaist workers, three New York
ILGWU locals, all of them dominated by men (Local 35, the pressers'
union; Local 9, the finishers' and tailors' union; and Local 1, the cloak
and suit operators' union), organized their own educational programs
between 1915 and 1916.[32] Then in 1918 the ILGWU's Executive Board
established a special educational department for the entire Interna-

tional, with Fannia Cohn serving as secretary. In New York and other cities the department held classes for members, using space provided by the public schools. By 1920, six of New York City's public schools served as "Unity Centers" for the union, offering classes in English, economics, and literature, and also providing space for social and recreational activities.[33] Dances, concerts, outings, and special vacation homes called "Unity Houses" where wage earners and their families could escape the workaday world for a few days of leisure in the mountains of New York or Pennsylvania rounded out the unions' innovative cultural and recreational programs.[34]

The ILGWU pioneered workers' education and recreation, but other garment workers' unions quickly followed its example. In 1917 the United Cloth Hat and Cap Makers' Union developed a comprehensive educational program that also included cultural field trips, concerts, and movies for members and their families. And in the same year the Amalgamated set up similar programs for workers in the men's clothing industry.[35]

These programs were influenced by and appealed to several different constituencies. Clearly they bore the stamp of Progressive reform elements within the labor movement, especially groups like the Women's Trade Union League, which brought a social housekeeping vision to the organizational campaigns. Educational and recreational programs fit within the settlement ideal of uplifting the poor and disadvantaged. Education would create a responsible and intelligent female citizenship in and outside the unions. Unity Houses would encourage female camaraderie and solidarity and would also redirect women's leisure toward what reformers considered respectable and wholesome pastimes. League women believed it was better to see young wage-earning women attend ladies' teas and country weekends in the company of other women than leave them to urban dancehalls and commercial amusement parks.[36]

Conservative union bureaucrats with an eye on the emerging conflict between left-wing and conservative socialism counted other reasons for the special programs of the new unionism. Some ILGWU officials clearly hoped that education would help turn immigrants away from radical "insurgency" and make them orderly and efficient American-style trade unionists, thereby quelling what they perceived as disruptive influences in the ranks.[37]

Ironically, the left wing of the union movement fastened on the radicalizing potential of the Unity Movement. They saw in these new programs a way to bring a humanistic perspective to the labor movement, a means to build class consciousness and solidarity, and the chance to school the rank and file in a radical perspective. This vision of a new unionism was not invented in the United States; it had been tried earlier by Continental socialists, including Jews. As early as the 1870s the German socialist movement established an array of cultural programs—gymnastic competitions, choral and drama societies, schools, and clubs—that comprised what one historian has called an "alternative culture."[38] The underground Jewish labor movement in Russia and Poland never matched these developments, but cultural activities aimed at creating revolutionary consciousness were clearly in evidence. One Jewish immigrant vividly recalled the dramatic club sponsored by the Bundist youth in his shtetl. They performed Jewish folk plays and operettas, using part of the proceeds to help the poor and the sick.[39] And by the time of the mass migration of Jews to the United States, the Bund had already experimented with workers' reading circles.

Immigrant youth brought their own purposes and expectations to the classroom. Though they may have agreed with particular organizers' goals, young people tended to view education programs more as an opportunity for personal and intellectual growth and self-improvement than as a means to develop technical expertise as trade unionists. Attendance records for ILGWU-sponsored schools suggest that most rank-and-file members favored literary and general courses such as English, history, economics, and art appreciation rather than courses in industrial or union-related matters.[40]

What young immigrant women in particular wanted from such programs must be understood within the context of their changing expectations and roles. The quest for education was not limited to Russian Jews, but the cultural orientation of Jewish women figured prominently in the push for expanded union-sponsored courses. It was no accident that the impetus for the educational movement came largely from the young Jewish women in New York Local 25 and reflected in large part experiences and values that immigrants brought with them from Czarist Russia. Always a source of prestige for men in Jewish culture, education had a special meaning for women. A mark of status as well as a potent symbol of freedom and opportunity, it remained for many an unreachable goal. Anti-Semitism in Russia, a strong bias against female education within Old World Orthodox culture, and the hardships of earning a living had conspired against women's dreams of secular education. Education became almost a metaphor for Jewish New Womanhood—a tool in the struggle for integration into civic life, a means to become, in immigrant writer Anzia Yezierska's words, "a person."[41] Education symbolized this broader ambition. "They wanted to get ahead through the union," ILGWU educational director Fannia Cohn explained. "In the U.S. education is not limited to Christians only, as in Czarist Russia. The girls came here with this idea."[42]

Specifically, some women came with the idea that the labor movement stood for workers' education. In the Old World, Bundist educational "circles" led by radical Jewish intelligentsia helped spread literacy and learning to uneducated workers in the Pale of Settlement, providing young seamstresses and factory workers with important opportunities not generally available to laborers or females.[43] Bessie Udin recalled how in 1905 young Bundist organizers "used to come to the towns and open classes for the illiterate."[44] One Jewish woman who led such a study circle described the opening it meant for young women workers, who despite the dangers of being in an illegal movement would gather in the evening to read "forbidden books": "We would sit until one in the morning in a stuffy room . . . and the woman of the house would walk around listening for the police. The girls would listen to the leaders' talk and would ask questions . . . . With what rapt attention they listened to the talks on cultural history, on surplus value . . . wages, life in other lands."[45] Secular education figured so prominently in the organizational tactics of Jewish socialists in eastern Europe that Jewish immigrant girls must have expected the same exciting prospect from the garment unions in America.

By all accounts, the unions succeeded in fulfilling some of these expectations, even though it took years of prodding by women activists such as Fannia Cohn who understood just what was at stake for their immigrant sisters. Union-sponsored forums and classes, Cohn observed, gave Jewish women "a feeling of importance." She was particularly concerned that the ILGWU's educational program be mindful of women workers' need for self-esteem. "There must be no resemblance of patronage or settlement spirit" on the part of the teachers, she wrote to fellow Jewish unionist Rebecca Holland in 1924.[46] Determined to make education a reality for the immigrant women in her union, Cohn went about her duties with what ILGWU official Gus Tyler called "a quiet, matronly air of *chutzpah*." She would approach the head of Columbia University's history department and say: "My name is Fannia Cohn. I come from the garment workers, the girls. They want to know about history. I want you should come and give me a lecture."[47]

These efforts helped create a sense among the membership that union organizations were committed not only to bread-and-butter issues but to the personal growth of the members. Mollie Friedman, a member of shirtwaist workers' Local 25, put it this way in a speech she made at the AFL convention in 1918: "Working at the machine or sticking pins in dresses does not do much for the education of the [union] members. . . . Our international found out that teaching girls how to picket a shop was not sufficient, and they taught us how to read books." Having the opportunity to attend union-sponsored classes profoundly affected her outlook. "When I was asked to join the union, I felt I had to join it, but now I feel I would give my life for an organization that will educate its members."[48]

As immigrant women struggled to negotiate their role in civic life, they could count such developments as significant milestones. The educational and recreational activities of the new unionism represented, in part, an accommodation to young people's needs and suggested how the numerical strength of female membership and the persistence of women activists could generate important changes in the union movement. But there were limits to how far unions were willing to go. Other venues of union life presented a more complex and contradictory picture. Both major garment unions were only marginally receptive to female leadership, and women made little headway breaking into the top echelons of organizational power. Yet the picture of women's union experience is distorted if we begin by examining these exclusionary patterns at the highest level of union bureaucracy. To do this is to ignore what many rank-and-file women saw as an important source of their own influence.

Female Unionism at the Point of Production

It is lower down the ladder, at the shopfloor level—at the point of production—where we can look to find another, equally revealing portrait of female unionism. In the daily affairs of the shop women union members seized a significant degree of responsibility and authority. It was on the job that the voice of New Womanhood was strongest. On the shop floor union membership represented a kind of citizenship for women, a citizenship that gave some women the chance to assume positions of authority that enhanced their sense of self-importance and esteem. During strikes women had served as picket captains and had taken charge at strike headquarters and union halls. In the poststrike period women held offices in their local unions and were often elected to serve on price committees in their factories, where they attempted to negotiate equitable piecerates for each new garment to be produced. As one Jewish immigrant woman put it, "I didn't take too much part in [union] organizing, but I did help maintain the shop in union conditions while I worked. I was [on] a price committee, and the boss was very annoyed with me because I was fighting for a [better] price."[49]

The rank-and-file women with the greatest influence at the shop level of union organization were the Chairladies. Elected by the workers in the shop, the Chairlady served as the voice of the union on the shop floor. It was her responsibility to make sure that fellow workers understood the rules and regulations of a union shop and to see that both workers and employers abided by contract obligations. Thus the Chairlady, though not paid for her duties, carried a great deal of authority in labor-related matters on the shop floor and consequently held a good deal of prestige among her coworkers. Fannie Shapiro recalled the tremendous sense of responsibility and self-importance that she and other Chairladies felt: "When you're shop chairlady, you belong to the union. Sometimes a strike came up. You have to go on the stage and take the floor and explain what's happening."[50] A Chairlady, claimed another, had "so many things to think about. . . . You feel the responsibility for each worker and above all responsibility for the life of the union."[51]

The Chairladies were not alone in taking authority over the conditions of work in union shops. In the aftermath of the great organizing strikes the rank and file, both women and men, struggled to exercise influence over the shop environment. Historians have noted the tendency of male workers to seize authority in poststrike situations, which are often characterized by protracted militance. In the garment industry women also played this role. The same exhilarating sense of power and possibility came to women, who returned to the workroom with a new self-confidence and a growing combativeness. Just as Jewish daughters felt entitled to walk the picket line, so too they considered it as much their right as their male coworkers' and union officers' to define the nature of a union shop. Daily, on the shop floor, they found ways to assert their citizenship within the unions.

Union contracts provided the context for this exercise of power. Such contracts included the ill-fated "Protocols of Peace" in the women's garment industry and similar agreements in the men's clothing industry. These agreements spelled out the responsibilities of employers and the rights of workers regarding sanitation, hours, pay scales, and "treatment." On the lookout for employer violations of union contracts or, in some cases, ignoring the rule of law by asserting other forms of justice, women collectively challenged practices that as unorganized individuals they had been helpless to change. In the process they translated the idealism that had animated their picket lines into a heightened spirit of defiance on the shop floor.

Women's work groups, always a potential source of rebellion, became hives of resistance to the arbitrary power of supervisors and employers and also to what some considered cumbersome union procedures. Anxious to assert a degree of control at work, young rank-and-file women set out to test the limits of the new unionism. Their combative spirit apparently knew few bounds, threatening at times to destabilize the unions themselves. Many union agreements outlawed strikes and work stoppages. Both garment workers' unions had pledged along with employers to replace industrial chaos and conflict with "law and order" by mutual cooperation and decision making. In the "Protocols of Peace" reached with New York women's clothing manufacturers between 1910 and 1916, and in similar agreements negotiated by the unions in the men's clothing industry after the great Chicago strikes of 1910 and 1915, employers and unions jointly would govern the shop floor under the principle of "industrial democracy." A system of "impartial" Grievance and Arbitration Boards (Trade Boards in the Men's Clothing Industry) investigated shopfloor disputes and contract violations, attempting to reach a settlement that would forestall further conflict. Price Committees, consisting of union and employer representatives, set piecerates, and in the women's garment industry Joint Boards of Sanitary Control oversaw the maintenance of shop safety and sanitation. Rather than establish closed, "union" shops, these Protocols provided for "preferential union shops." In exchange for disciplining the rank and file, unions were assured their members would receive preference in hiring.[52]

The new protections, while not ideal, were major gains to workers accustomed to the arbitrary power of employers. One Jewish immigrant said that now the bosses "couldn't tell you to go if they didn't want you, they had to have a very good reason."[53] Before unionization, another Jewish woman insisted, "if the bosses didn't like a girl they sent her down [fired her]. They couldn't do it after [the union came in]. They can't send down anybody they want. If a boss had a little thing, he don't like a girl, she don't make good work. . . . But you know they couldn't do it now."[54] Describing women's expanded sense of rights and responsibilities on the job, one woman recalled that in the days before the union, the employers "could do anything they wanted." But after the union came in, the women could "do something" to control their working conditions.[55] When a boss acted in ways that did not meet with workers' approval, she boasted, "we made a stoppage, the whole shop stopped. . . . That was a good union shop. I loved it—a stoppage for nothing. If he didn't do the right thing—a stoppage!"[56]

As this last statement suggests, however, women frequently side-stepped prescribed grievance procedures—a stoppage, though illegal under the new contract rules, was quicker and often more effective. A shop Chairlady for the Amalgamated Clothing Workers at Hart, Schaffner & Marx, Sarah Rozner often disobeyed·procedural rules. "We had specifically written in the agreement, no stoppages. So when I see that the examiner is abusing the workers, *although I wasn't an officer*, if I saw that something is wrong, I would instigate a work stoppage. I would find one confidential person, maybe two, and nobody would ever find out who it was who was making stoppages. To improve conditions, whatever it was, concerning prices or conditions. I used to do that . . . I knew it was wrong, [but] the worker was abused. It was against the union rule. I made my own rules."[57] In some workrooms violation of union rules and defiance against employers in the form of illegal work stoppages—described by one observer as "shop mutinies"—became almost a way of life in the years after the big organizational drives.[58]

Such turbulence cannot be attributed to one particular segment of the work force or to one set of concerns. Certainly, as Steve Fraser's study of the Amalgamated has shown, it was characteristic of older skilled male immigrants who attempted to defend artisanal privileges and customs threatened by new, union-negotiated work rules.[59] But women workers, many of them lacking artisanal traditions, also defied no-strike contracts and violated union rules to defend established work cultures and to assert union power in their own way. For example, Mollie Steinholtz, who became Chairlady for the armhole-basting shop at Hart, Schaffner & Marx in 1915, admitted that the women in her shop frequently violated union rules by working during the lunch hour, some of them eating at their machines—a traditional practice for piece-workers—in order to boost their earnings.[60]

The practices of pieceworkers were also at stake when Chairlady Celia Foreman led a shop protest against the lunchtime rule the ILGWU had negotiated to standardize the working day at the Aero Shirtwaist factory in 1914. She had complained that the rule was arbitrary, insisting that neither she nor the other "girls" would give it serious consideration. Refusing to obey, she remained at her sewing machine during the lunch break and as a result was ordered to leave the shop. When the employer came in on Monday morning after the incident, he noticed "a commotion in the factory." The women refused to work unless the Chairlady was reinstated. "They sat around for about ten or fifteen minutes and didn't budge." Consequently they were all fired but were allowed to return to the factory later that afternoon. Several days later another women defied the rule, and the workers staged a stoppage in her defense.[61]

Explaining the shopfloor militance of union women, Belle Israels, grievance clerk in the dress and shirtwaist industry under the Protocol, observed that "any change in the factory brings about a certain attitude of defiance. . . . Rules are sometimes made where a firm decides that each operation as it passes through each group of people in the factory shall be checked in some way. A girl is required to sign tickets she never signed before. Frequently there is a protest."[62]

Another explanation for rank-and-file insurgency—one favored by union leaders who struggled continually to get workers to honor the contract—was that the militance stemmed from the revolutionary agitation of left-wing socialists. The radicals argued that any contract that signed away the right to strike amounted to class collaboration. In a speech to the 1910 convention ILGWU general secretary John Dyche warned that "our *kampflustig* [hot-headed] members" refuse to accept the "limitations" of unionism and "have their heads full of revolutionary stuff which they read in the Jewish radical press."[63]

To some degree he was right. Left-wing radicalism undoubtedly played a part in the climate of conflict. But workers did not need a well-developed ideological posture to engage in insurgent behavior. Often it came down to the desire of newly unionized immigrants to assert their collective will. As a method of doing so, the strike was so firmly rooted in east European Jewish working-class and artisanal traditions, and now, in the garment industry's work culture, that no other tactic had as much appeal. That was true for the women working at the Bijou Waist Company—the scene of many bitter confrontations during the 1909 shirtwaist strike and the site of more arrests and clubbings than any other New York waist factory. There the discharge of one "girl," whatever the cause, would create a backlash among the other workers who came in the morning, "sat down to the machines . . . but wouldn't start to work." Most of the trouble, the owner of the firm maintained, was the fault of the Chairlady who represented the union in the shop.[64]

Women participated in work stoppages for the reasons men did—to defend old practices and to extend benefits and protect wages.[65] Overall, women's insurgency can be read as a statement that they intended to have a direct, decision-making role in the affairs of union shops. Like their male counterparts, rank-and-file women felt entitled to recognition and involvement and to a voice in those issues which directly concerned their work lives. If women's protests violated union rules, they were also meant to assert something more positive. Through these protests newly unionized women conveyed to employers and to union bureaucrats alike the potent new confidence that labor organization bestowed on the most vulnerable sector of the working class.

Experimenting with Separatism

The power that unionized women often exercised at the level of the shop floor did not, however, readily translate up the ladder of union bureaucracy. The nagging fact remained that women had little say in the making of national union policy or the structuring of union life, and they generally fared less well than men in the bread-and-butter gains that contracts provided. Neither the ILGWU nor the Amalgamated stood fully behind the principle of equal pay for equal work. Some contracts actually reinforced entrenched patterns of gender discrimination, stipulating lower minimums for women who performed the same work as men.[66] Lottie Spitzer recalled how officials at the Amalgamated's Chicago office condoned the discriminatory practices of employers. When she complained to the union that she was being paid less than a male coworker for the same task, the union refused to defend her. "The Union told me, 'Well, he is a man, and this is a woman's pay.' There were a lotta women like I. They did men's work and they got girl's pay. I don't know whether the union wasn't strong enough to fight for it. Or they wanted to get along with the companies."[67]

Despite their majority in the garment unions, only a handful of women rose to positions of national union power where they might have rectified such inequities. Women may have pioneered and staffed educational programs, but the union executive boards—their controlling bodies—were largely run by men. Between 1916 and 1924 Fannia Cohn served as the lone female voice on the ILGWU's General Executive Board (GEB), even though the union's membership was two-thirds female. The ACW, the younger and in some respects more progressive union, still had only a small corps of women in the leadership. Bessie Abramovitz sat on the arbitration board that handled workers' grievances with Hart, Schaffner & Marx in Chicago and also served as secretary-treasurer of ACW District Council No. 6 in that city. Eventually she secured a seat on the union's powerful General Executive Board. Twenty-two-year-old Latvian-born Dorothy Jacobs, another charter member of the ACW and organizer of the buttonhole makers' local in Baltimore, served on the ACW Joint Board in that city and in 1916 was elected to the Amalgamated's General Executive Board, succeeding Abramovitz who had withdrawn from the board when she married union president Sidney Hillman that year. When Jacobs married August Bellanca in 1918, she gave up her seat on the GEB. "Health reasons" provided the official explanation for her resignation. But perhaps, as for Bessie Abramovitz, her departure from the center of union power symbolized a concession to what might have been perceived as conflict of interest in a husband-wife leadership team. Mamie Santora, like Jacobs an enthusiastic advocate of women's rights, succeeded her on the GEB.[68]

Here and there a woman occupied a position of power and authority above the level of the shop floor, but she was the exception, not the rule. A handful of women in both unions served as full-time, salaried organizers. But even in locals where women outnumbered men, such as white goods Local 62 and shirtwaist Local 25, some of the officers were female but the president was always a male.[69] Even as members of the garment unions addressed one another with the socialist terms "brother" and "sister," clearly these were still big brothers and little sisters. Overall, the small number of women in the inner circles of the Amalgamated and the ILGWU stood in dramatic contrast to the subordinate role played by the masses of female dues-payers who had pioneered the union movement during the general strikes.

Immigrant women responded to the issue of subordination within the unions in a variety of ways, ranging from passive acceptance to militant rebellion. In attempting to reconcile their idealistic vision of helping to change the world with the real limits that union officials placed on the female voice within the movement, the more radical and active women steered an uneasy course between their commitment to class solidarity and the promises of feminist reform.

From about 1913 on, as the woman question began to rock the boat of union politics, a small but vocal cadre of Jewish feminists pressed for a greater measure of equality within the ILGWU and later in the Amalgamated. Like immigrant women in the Socialist party, Jewish feminists in the garment workers' unions saw themselves first and foremost as workers dedicated to class issues. Thus they faced a dilemma: how to advance the status of women within a workers' organization without undermining what they considered their highest priority, class solidarity.[70]

Immigrant activists divided on the question of what kind of strategy would best advance women's position in the unions. The one path that had proved so useful to earlier generations of female (and feminist) reformers in the United States, and which some Jewish women de-

16. Executive Board, Local 25 of the ILGWU, 1912. Clara Lemlich, a leader of the 1909 shirtwaist workers' uprising, is standing in the back row, third from left. International Ladies' Garment Workers' Union, Labor-Management Documentation Center, Cornell University.

fended—separate female institutions—fit uncomfortably in the class and ethnic frameworks of immigrant unionism.

The question of whether to try to integrate women into male-dominated organizations or to form semi-autonomous women's institutions plagued both the union and the socialist movements in this period. In the Socialist party a vocal faction of American-born women advocated the path followed by the social housekeepers—separate female organizations that would advance women's equality in the party, assure female autonomy, and celebrate what they considered women's special virtues.[71] In the union movement such views were shared by many middle-class members of the Women's Trade Union League as well as by some

Jewish working women active in the League, among them Pauline Newman.[72]

Middle-class allies in the WTUL tried to impress upon young female garment workers that they might gain more from union membership if they abandoned their dependence on what New York League secretary Helen Marot called the "incompetent" Russian Jewish men who led the garment unions. Instead, she argued, they ought to rely on their own feminine resources.[73] The League, however, was in a delicate position. Afraid of alienating the American Federation of Labor with tactics that smacked of "dual unionism," the League never openly advocated separatist schemes, even if they were privately discussed. Within League circles it was widely believed that women's power and agency in the labor movement could be enhanced though separate female institutions.[74] WTUL activist Alice Henry let her separatist preferences show when she insisted in her 1915 analysis, *The Trade Union Woman*, that girls would be "happier" in their own "women's local." There they could run their own meetings and hold them when and wherever they chose. And following the woman-as-moral-superior logic of the social housekeepers, Henry suggested that women's special qualities made them best suited to be the "main leaders" and "teachers" of other union women. "Women have always been the teachers of the race," she insisted. "Whenever woman has been left to self-development on her own lines her achievements have always been in the constructive direction." Woman as "wise and patient" teacher was "urgently needed" in the labor movement.[75] The "very fact that they are women" with distinctly "feminine, and especially maternal qualities," Henry believed, made them uniquely suited to domesticate the labor unions. Someday men would come to appreciate how the union could become "the larger home."[76]

Henry and most middle-class allies in the League would have agreed with an editorial in the *Ladies' Garment Worker* in August 1914 that argued it was not "normal" for "tens of thousands of girls, many of them possessing active minds and intelligence," to be "thrown upon the leadership of a comparatively small number of men in the trade." The writer, Constance Denmark, proposed that foreign-language locals in the New York dress and shirtwaist unions should be abolished in favor of mixed-nationality women's branches. Once organized into a solidly female branch, she said, "the women . . . would have a better chance to assert themselves, learn their own strength, and the ways and means to govern themselves."[77]

For evidence, one had only to turn to the so-called American unions, a

term used in a 1911 government study to describe trade unions dominated by native-born (hence "American") women. In such organizations, the study concluded, women were most likely to be found "organizing their own affairs." By contrast, in most unions with large
immigrant populations, even where women were the majority of members, men provided leadership and held the reigns of power.[78]

As idealistic immigrant women faced a male leadership that paid only
lip-service to the notion of male-female comradeship and continued to
discriminate against women, some began to follow the path of American and Americanized feminists. They advocated that the garment
unions experiment with separate women's organizations. Union militants with feminist leanings, like Pauline Newman, as well as others
who had worked closely with the Women's Trade Union League felt that
ILGWU women might benefit if the locals established separate men's
and women's branches. They argued, tellingly, that the mixed-sex locals
were losing the participation of female members who felt shut out or
intimidated. Too often, they pointed out, women either neglected to
attend local meetings or, if they did attend, felt too shy to speak because
of the dominating presence of males. "We all know that girls feel more
at home among themselves than among men. . . . When they meet
together with men, they hardly get a chance to express their opinion on
questions which concern them," ILGWU activist and WTUL member
Newman explained.[79] The problem, as she saw it, was that women
unionists felt "swallowed up in a sea of masculinity."[80]

Newman was hardly typical. Most Jewish immigrant women,
whether activists or rank-and-file dues-payers, lacked experience in the
organized female political networks that would have taught them the
value of autonomous women's institutions.[81] And the minority who
came to advocate separatism tended to see it not as an institutional
expression of female difference, or what some historians have called
"women's culture," but as a "tactical expedient" toward integration
into the organizational mainstream. As it was for immigrant women in
the Socialist party, separatism in the garment unions was pragmatic
rather than ideological.[82] Those immigrants who spoke about the necessity of women's organizations in the labor movement were quite
clear about their rationale. They spoke as had Mollie Schepps, not in
terms of their gender differences with men but of their common experiences and struggles as wage earners and providers. They wanted to enter
the labor movement on the same terms as men, but they recognized the
need to narrow the gap between ideals and realities.

Separation seemed to belie the commonality that Jewish women and men shared as wage earners and as members of a class-based ethnic community. Nevertheless some feminists in the union conceived of this strategy as a practical intermediate step toward the political partnership they were seeking. Explaining to ACW General Secretary Joseph Schlossberg why a "woman's local" seemed abnormal but necessary in Chicago, Raissa Lomonossoff, the Russian-born educational director of the union in that city, blamed the cultural climate in the United States. "Last Fall," she said, "when Mr. Hillman . . . asked whether I could take part in organizing a woman's local . . . I could not give any answer at that time, as in my mind I could not find any reason for having separate locals for men and women. Being a Russian, I was inclined to believe that if men and women work together, they can meet together also, and respect each other's opinions." In Chicago, she insisted, the situation was very different. "The men are very 'nice' to women, but when it comes to business matters the women are being pushed aside." Such conditions were not "normal," she said, especially in labor organizations "on which we all build our hopes for a better world to live in."[83]

Sarah Rozner agreed. Writing to Sam Levin, the manager of the Chicago Joint Board of the ACW, whom she blamed for much of the discrimination in the union, Rozner insisted that women wanted only "whatever is duly coming to us!" By this she meant that women unionists had "to be brought into the fold." She assured him that women who advocated separate locals "are not interested in creating a sex issue in our organization. If anything, we want to do away with it as much as possible. . . . We care not for special privileges. We want to be looked upon as part and parcel of our organization."[84]

Although some male leaders in the Amalgamated saw separate women's locals as subversive or divisive to the union, women themselves viewed them not as antagonistic but as alternative modes of organization. Rose Priola Falk, an Italian garment worker who joined the ACW women's local in Chicago, recalled that women's first loyalty had been to the union itself, and despite men's criticisms to the contrary the local stood behind the Amalgamated "a hundred percent." Elaborating, she maintained that "the men were the ones that led the parade, but when it came to actually doing the work, it was the women that put in all the hours and all the hard work." But, she added, women gladly sacrificed for their organization, even when they got second billing. "We weren't doin' it for our personal [gain] . . . we believed in what the union was doing."[85]

It took considerable agitation on the part of feminists to convince union leaders of the merits of separate organizations. In the ILGWU the

huge New York shirtwaist workers' Local 25, which previously had
been subdivided into three separate language branches (Yiddish, Italian,
and English) tried to accommodate women's concerns by organizing
separate female branches instead.[86] To answer the cry for reform in the
organization of New York cloakmakers, the ILGWU reorganized Local
9 in 1913, reassigning 4,000 female cloak finishers to their own Ladies
Branch of that Local. When Rose Kaplan joined Local 9, she was told
that the women met separately "because the men didn't behave nicely"
and talked in ways that were insulting to women.[87]

The Amalgamated was more reluctant to pursue this tack and waited
until 1917 before trying anything similar. Baltimore organizer Dorothy
Jacobs Bellanca, ever sensitive to the need to address gender tensions
within a union dedicated to class solidarity, advocated the division of
existing mixed-sex locals into men's and women's branches (as the
ILGWU had done). She believed the separate branches would enable
women to strengthen their ranks without threatening the established
locals.[88] But instead, feminist activists in the ACW eventually bolted the
parent locals and founded separate women's locals that cut across
occupational and ethnic lines and brought together all female workers
in the men's clothing industry within a particular city.

The first of these women's locals was founded in Rochester, New
York, in 1917 and was followed shortly by another in New York City.[89]
In Chicago, the center of the Amalgamated's strength, the women's local
did not emerge until 1920, though some groundwork had been laid a
few years earlier. In 1917 Chicago feminists close to the labor movement launched the Girls' Civic and Educational Club, which reformer
Grace Abbott hailed as "a new radical organization free from those
prejudices and traditions which hamper some of the older organizations." The intent of the club was to train female unionists in parliamen-
tary law "so that ignorance of mere procedure would never keep them
from taking part in discussions that may come up in meetings which
they attend."[90] But the new club could not overcome the more serious
obstacles to women's equality within the union movement. The limits of
its effectiveness became clear at the Amalgamated's 1920 national convention in Boston. Several women from different Chicago locals ran as
delegates to the convention, but all were defeated. [91]

For Sarah Rozner, who lost in the election, it was a disillusioning
moment. "It began to dawn on me what it was all about as far as the
women were concerned," Rozner recalled. "Up to that time I was
mainly class conscious, but when I saw that they [the men] were so
ruthless, so indifferent to . . . the women, I thought how can we stand by

and ignore it?"[92] In response Rozner, Nettie Richardson, and other disgruntled members founded ACW women's Local 275, an organization open to women clothing workers from all occupational and ethnic groups in Chicago but primarily drawing its members from coatmakers' Local 39.[93]

At the outset a main concern among ACW feminists in Chicago was to find a way to increase female representation in the decision-making process. As Sarah Rozner explained it, "every local has the prerogative of having their own convention delegates and of nomina[ting] a business agent, so if there was a woman's local, then there would *have* to be women delegates, there would *have* to be a woman business agent."[94]

The women's locals and branches yielded mixed results. Never as popular with the rank and file as their organizers had hoped, the separate organizational units did accomplish some of their central purposes and put pressure on the male-dominated hierarchy to recognize the needs and ambitions of women. The ILGWU "ladies'" branches faced the problem of official hostility from parent locals (some of them foreign-language locals with strong ethnic loyalties) and from the General Executive Board, finally getting caught up in a tug of war between left- and right-wing factions within the union.

Part of the problem was structural. Though beneficial from the standpoint of involving more women in union activities, the ladies' branches of the ILGWU conferred little additional power on female members. Although they sent representatives to the Executive Board of their local, the ladies' branches did not have their own officers and thus remained separate but unequal organizations.

When Rose Kaplan and other left-wing women in the ILGWU recognized that separatism could lead to further exclusion of women and of the left from the mainstream of union life, they advocated reintegration. Indeed, by 1920 Kaplan and other radicals in the ladies' branch of New York's Local 9 were moving to abolish sex divisions, arguing that separate organizations discriminated against women. "Our interests are not different from the men. And they [the women] want to be [together with them] so that they could discuss matters in the shop, the prices and all like that," she explained.[95]

But discrimination was not the only concern. By the early 1920s larger political undercurrents coincided with women's cynicism. The defensive position of left-wing unionism in an increasingly conservative political environment, and the internal struggles between socialists and communists within the union, threatened to tear the ILGWU apart and created contrary pressure for internal cohesion and unity. Separatism of

17. The past and present of the Amalgamated Clothing Workers are captured in this photograph of union pioneer Sarah Rozner with Adelia Bailey. In 1961 Bailey won a scholarship to a training program that Rozner had founded to promote female leadership in the union. *The Advance*, July 1, 1961. Amalgamated Clothing Workers of America Records, Labor-Management Documentation Center, Cornell University.

any kind threatened the very survival of the organization. With political pressures escalating and separatist experiments only marginally successful, even such life-long activists and advocates of women's rights as Fannia Cohn were insisting that the sexes had "much in common" and ought not to be separated into male and female organizations.[96]

The Amalgamated gave its female locals more of a chance, and because they established separate gender locals with their own officers, they were a more potent force for change than the women's branches in the ILGWU. The impact of the Chicago women's local, even with a very small membership, could hardly be denied. "Already the men are being stirred up," Raissa Lomonossoff insisted in the spring of 1920, just weeks after women's Local 275 was founded. "Local 39 is sending two alternative women delegates, and Local 152 is sending one to the Boston Convention. The Women's Local is sending three . . . and so instead of having only one woman delegate from Local 144, we are going to have seven," she proudly announced.[97] Some who joined the women's local in Chicago also recalled the expanded social and cultural benefits that accrued from membership. "We had a dramatic club, we had a choir . . . we taught ballet," said Rose Priola Falk, adding that the only cultural activities the male-dominated locals supported were concerts and dances.[98]

Nevertheless, successes, especially in attracting members, were still very limited. At its founding in 1920, Local 275 had about four hundred members, a small but visible cadre who claimed to speak on behalf of some twenty thousand women, mostly immigrants, who paid dues to other ACW locals in Chicago. Although we do not know the ethnic makeup of the original membership in Local 275, if Jewish daughters other than Sarah Rozner did join, they apparently preferred to keep a low profile. Nettie Richardson, a Chicago-based organizer and founding member, reported not long after the women's local was organized that of the "dozen very active girls" who were "working their heads off to make the local a success, . . . none [were] Jewish."[99] Joining a women's local meant deserting one's parent union, an act that made many women uneasy and fearful of being penalized or ostracized.[100] Agnes Budilovsky, a Polish immigrant woman active in Chicago pants makers' Local 144 at Hart, Schaffner & Marx, said that women like herself remained in their parent locals because they did not want to jeopardize the strength and integrity of long-established organizations. As a compromise she regularly attended the social and cultural activities sponsored by women's Local 275.[101]

Ethnic values and allegiances served to anchor female membership in parent locals. The situation in Rochester provides a good example. In 1924 women, who comprised 60 percent of the ACW's dues-payers in Rochester, responded quite enthusiastically to women's Local 244, swelling its membership to 1,300. Nevertheless, almost twice as many female members of the ACW in that city belonged to mixed-sex locals, including Polish and Italian locals, with the bulk of female members (about 1,500) concentrated in Italian Local 202.[102] At a time when ethnic rivalries continued to plague the garment unions, group loyalty remained a more compelling principle to most immigrant women than cross-ethnic gender solidarity.

With regard to Jewish immigrants, separatist experiments suffered from a deeper, more revealing problem. The exceptional strength of female activism in the Jewish immigrant community makes it difficult to understand why so many would be content to follow men's leadership in the unions rather than insist upon female organizations freer from male control. Ultimately, the overlapping values of eastern European Jewish working-class culture and immigrant New Womanhood undermined the appeal and the effectiveness of separatism. The conditional endorsement of Jewish activists like Dorothy Jacobs Bellanca and Fannia Cohn, who viewed this mode of organization as a temporary expedient on the road to full integration of women, found little resonance among the rank and file. This was because rank-and-file women were often less willing than female leaders to jeopardize common goals of ethnic and class unity for gender equity. Equally important, rank-and-file immigrant daughters were often willing to settle for the limited nature of citizenship that union membership provided.

Jewish women's activism grew out of the genuine excitement of joining an enterprise that included both sexes. For most Jewish daughters, "junior" partner status in the labor movement was preferable to a return to the gender separation that had limited their access to public life and underscored their cultural inferiority in the shtetl. Their kind of New Womanhood had brought them into the gender-integrated world of dating and commercial leisure. It had enabled them to walk the picket line and fight for their rights as workers in the same manner as their male coworkers in the shops. To return to a world that isolated the sexes would have been to take a step backward to the world of their mothers and grandmothers, a world defined by the exclusionary, misogynist traditions of Old World culture. As Jewish New Women they looked forward to a world of mutuality and sharing, willing in the short term to accept the imperfections of a junior partnership with men.

Mollie Wexler, who had first joined the radical movement as a teenager in Poland and who became a full-time organizer for the ILGWU in 1917, recalled that neither she nor most other immigrant women worried much about the dominant role of men in the union. "We weren't discussing it," she said of the problem of male leadership. Interviewed in 1972, she knew too well the distance between her own youthful political vision and the much more radical agenda of the new feminist revolution of the 1960s and 1970s. Looking back at her own experience in the union movement, she stressed how her generation had more limited expectations. At that time, she insisted, "we took it for granted that the men had the stronger personalities and through them we'll get somewhere.... We admired [them], we appreciated it, praising the men that do so much for us, being lucky that they take our interest in their mind."[103]

Yet Mollie Wexler had once stood at the vanguard of her own immigrant generation. She was a living example of Jewish New Womanhood. A full-time union organizer and a woman with a voice in her community's civic life, she was far more modern and liberated from patriarchal tradition than the mother she left behind in Poland when she came to the United States as a teenager. And yet she still deferred to the leadership of the men, willing to serve as a junior partner, less than equal but still not silent.

An Unsettled Generation

The evolving nature of Jewish New Womanhood seems paradoxical. Teenage girls came to this country, worked in the garment industry, went out on strike, briefly became involved in union activities, married, and settled into domestic life. Such a trajectory was typical, containing all of the compelling experiences of immigrant women's lives—work, the labor movement, marriage, motherhood. This life course pulled Jewish daughters in seemingly contradictory directions. On the one hand, the labor movement expanded the female sphere, giving women a greater (one might say an official) role in the civic life of the Jewish community. And work, traditionally a source of social identity for eastern European Jewish women, conferred upon immigrant daughters a sense of competence and, for some, a feeling of self-worth that came from knowing they could earn a living if they had to. At the same time, however, young women aspired to a romantic version of marriage.

Each aspect of the life course represented a source of female esteem but for different reasons. One image emphasized women's ability to fight side by side with men to help earn a living and to struggle for workers' rights. The other stressed the respectability and romantic promise that women sought in the role of modern wife-companion. Radical politics and labor activism provided a novel source of recognition for women's abilities and expanded their presence in civic life. It countered the notion of female inferiority, provided a greater sense of gender equality, and stressed that women were capable of improving the social order. The ideal of romantic marriage held out a desirable alternative to traditional Jewish marriage arrangements, because it substituted love and attraction for "yichus" (prestige), and it translated the notion of comradeship and partnership into the domestic setting.

As sources of female identity, these models of womanhood complemented each other. But they also stood in tension. And it is that tension, and the ways in which daughters of the shtetl struggled with it, which makes their generation so significant for understanding the relationship between immigrant experience and women's history. Jewish immigrant daughters were unsettled in their relationship to this country and unsettled about which vision of New Womanhood they would claim. Pulled between the desire to participate in the world outside the home and the equally compelling world of domestic respectability, the life course of this generation moved not in a straight line toward one identifiable model but back and forth like a pendulum.

The question of married women's work was never definitively resolved for this generation. Jewish wives who had been working daughters continued to grapple with social and economic questions related to this issue. Most quit their jobs when they married, but it is difficult to determine how they made their choices about leaving work. Some women insisted that they resented leaving their jobs and agreed to do so only because of pressure from their husbands and relatives.[104] In general, Jewish immigrants aspired to "middle-class" notions of respectability which stressed that married women remain at home. However, there is evidence that in some households of newlyweds in the early 1920s, the pressure to conform came from husbands rather than wives. Their mothers in the Old Country may have served as breadwinners, but many of these new-style husbands were adamant that their wives should not. As one Russian Jewish garment worker who married at about the time of World War I put it: "I stopped [working] . . . because my husband objected . . . the prestige of the man demanded that I stay home."[105] Dora Bayrack remembers the tension created by her conflicting views. Preferring to go back to work, she suggested to her husband that they hire someone to take care of their baby. "He thought I was crazy. He made a living, he had enough, so it was an offense to him."[106] Another immigrant woman, who quit her job but helped her husband in his business, regretted she had not remained in the garment industry because she expected that one day she would have become a designer. "That's what I was hoping for," she recalled.[107]

Unresolved feelings combined with economic necessity to lead Jewish wives in and out of the work force as circumstances dictated. Many, like Lottie Spitzer, a veteran of the campaigns to organize Chicago clothing workers, helped their husbands in business and tried to return to outside wage work during the Great Depression, when her children were older and when conditions created greater economic need in the household. Recalling her days as a newlywed she said, "I missed [outside] work an

awful lot." But her husband had insisted she remain at home. "When my
girl was eleven . . . it was seventeen years I was away from work . . . I said
I'm not stayin' home anymore. First of all, I had in my mind to give the
children a good education . . . my husband didn't make much. So I
wanted to help out."[108]

But it was not only Depression-era financial burdens that pulled
young married women toward the breadwinning role. Old patterns died
hard for both men and women in this generation. Husbands and wives
struggled to mesh modern concepts of respectability with the requirements of daily existence and the pressures for upward mobility. Even as
they claimed to accept the standards of respectability that required
wives to abandon wage work, some married women—particularly
those whose husbands were moving out of the wage-earning class into
the world of small business entrepreneurship—adopted a modified version of domesticity that kept the old breadwinning partnership alive.

That was true for Mollie Linker, a young women who had come to
this country at the age of thirteen and led several hundred garment
workers out on strike before she married at the age of eighteen. Her
marriage was not to mimic the standard American middle-class model
of domestic life. From the start of her marriage she went to work in her
husband's candy store, standing "side by side" in the store with him for
the next fifty-five years.[109] Like their mothers and grandmothers before
them, Jewish daughters who married around the time of World War I
differentiated between laboring in a family business and going out to
perform wage work. The first was a long-standing tradition among
married women, the second had to be justified according to circumstance.

Jewish daughters moved in and out of political life as easily as they
dropped in and out of breadwinning. In that sense, too, their marriages
differed from our images of middle-class companionate marriage in the
1920s. The classic portrait of this new marital style in the post–World
War I period has couples sharing recreational and social interests, but
women spending their energies in consumerism to the exclusion of civic
and political commitments. Recent work in women's history suggests,
however, that female activism—socialist, feminist, and reformist—
remained alive and well in the interwar period.[110] Former garment
workers may have become less active, but they certainly did not trade
married life for political passivity. When Jewish immigrant daughters
married, as most did, they did not cease to believe in the "movement,"
nor did they leave their politics behind in the garment factories. Home
and family responsibilities pushed activism to the background, yet

larger political commitments and visions still informed their lives. When he visited the Jewish quarter on the Lower East Side early in the century, journalist Hutchins Hapgood observed that "many of these women, so long as they are unmarried, lead lives thoroughly devoted to 'the cause,' and afterwards become good wives and fruitful mothers, and urge on their husbands and sons to active work in the movement."[111]

For some women, marriage actually heightened political awareness and engagement, particularly when husbands were active in the labor and radical movements. One Jewish immigrant who had joined the shirtwaist makers' union when she was single admitted that it was only after she married her "politically conscious" husband that she began to "develop politically."[112] Moreover, once the children had grown enough to allow a flexible domestic schedule, women who remained involved sometimes found they had more time for political activities than their husbands did. The men had to labor twelve or fourteen hours a day, said one former garment union activist, "whereas we housewives, as much as we were occupied, we could steal some of our time and devote it to" political work.[113]

Both the Socialists and the Communists supported married women's involvement in political struggle. In the late teens and the 1920s the socialist *Jewish Daily Forward* featured articles that condemned kitchen "slavery" and urged housewives not to let the drudgery of housework sap vital energy that might be directed to helping the working-class movement.[114] Some Jewish wives heeded this call, retaining their union membership and participating in various activities. A few even continued to work as union organizers after they married. Issues of importance to the family and community periodically brought married women back into the political fray as fundraisers, campaigners, and sometimes as agitators. More often than not married life shifted the arena of politics away from the union itself toward a more general involvement in socialist and Jewish "causes" and crises. That was especially true during the 1930s, when Depression-era conditions rekindled the political hopes of the left, and some Jewish women found themselves on the barricades once again. During the Depression widespread suffering in working-class neighborhoods sent many former garment workers back to the streets to fight evictions and struggle for the rights of the unemployed.[115]

Yet even the idealistic socialists at the *Forward* recognized that most working class wives remained, as one writer put it, "tied down to the house and kitchen."[116] Whatever their inclinations, more often than not married women stood on the political sidelines, rarely engaging as directly in the struggle as they had when they were single wage earners. As wives and mothers, they were absorbed by new pressures and preoccupations; new concerns about households, husbands, and children pushed politics into the background, though never completely out of sight.

The experiences and values of this generation of Jewish immigrant women suggest that work, activism, and domesticity were never clearly demarcated stages in the life cycle. Immigrant women moved in and out of work and politics. Their female identities were complex and fluid. It would be their daughters, the next generation, those born in the United States during the 1920s and 1930s, who would begin to feel more at home with the cult of domesticity—what Betty Friedan calls the "happy housewife heroine" role. This gap between immigrant mothers and Betty Friedan's generation of American-Jewish daughters was best expressed by a former garment worker born in Poland who said: "My husband considered me aggressive and so does my daughter." Nevertheless, like others of her background she had always taken pride in this trait. And in her old age she insisted, "Only through my aggressiveness am I protected."[117]

A transitional sense of cultural identity located this generation of immigrant women partly on the terrain of what historians of the 1920s call the New Womanhood, partly in a framework wholly their own. Daughters of the Old World, they were still in the process of inventing the New.

Notes

Introduction

1. Interview with Mollie Linker in Sydelle Kramer and Jenny Masur, eds., *Jewish Grandmothers* (Boston, 1976), pp. 93, 96–97, 102.

2. Joseph Schlossberg, *The Rise of the Clothing Workers*, Amalgamated Educational Pamphlets 1 (New York, 1924), p. 5 (italics mine).

3. Quoted in Hilda W. Smith, ed., *The Workers Look at the Stars* (New York: Vineyard Shore Workers' School, 1927), preface.

4. The most significant studies of immigrant women include Charlotte Baum, Paula Hyman, and Sonya Michel, *The Jewish Woman in America* (New York, 1975); Elizabeth Ewen, *Immigrant Women in the Land of Dollars: Life and Culture on the Lower East Side, 1890–1925* (New York, 1985); Judith E. Smith, *Family Connections: A History of Italian and Jewish Immigrant Lives in Providence, Rhode Island, 1900–1940* (Albany, N.Y., 1985); Virginia Yans-McLaughlin, *Family and Community: Italian Immigrants in Buffalo, 1880–1930* (Ithaca, N.Y., 1977); and Hasia Diner, *Erin's Daughters in America: Irish Immigrant Women in the Nineteenth Century* (Baltimore, Md., 1983).

5. Some of the best recent studies of working-class women's culture—Kathy Peiss, *Cheap Amusements: Working Women and Leisure in Turn-of-the-Century New York* (Philadelphia, 1986); Joanne J. Meyerowitz, *Women Adrift: Independent Wage Earners in Chicago, 1880–1930* (Chicago, 1988); Leslie Woodcock Tentler, *Wage-Earning Women: Industrial Wage Work and Family Life in the United States, 1900–1930* (New York, 1979)—devote little attention to the ways in which particular ethnic group values shaped a variety of working-class experiences for women. One very important exception is the pioneering work of Alice Kessler-Harris, "Organizing the Unorganizable: Three Jewish Women and Their Union," *Labor History* 17 (Winter 1976); another is Tamara K. Hareven, *Family Time and Industrial Time* (Cambridge, 1982).

6. Oscar Handlin, *The Uprooted: An Epic Story of the Great Migrations That*

Made the American People (Boston, 1951), and Moses Rischin, *The Promised City: New York's Jews, 1870–1914* (Cambridge, Mass., 1962), both present an image of immigrants as culturally dislocated. Historians who have stressed the ability and desire of newcomers to cleave to the old ways include Yans-McLaughlin, *Family and Community*, and Rudolph Vecoli, "The Contadini in Chicago: A Critique of *The Uprooted,*" *Journal of American History* 51 (1964): 404–17. This framework has also been influential in labor history and was central to the work of Herbert Gutman. See "Work, Culture, and Society in Industrializing America, 1815–1919," in Gutman, *Work, Culture, and Society* (New York, 1977), pp. 3–78. More recently historians have taken a middle ground, acknowledging not only the alienation and loss felt by immigrants but also the significant continuities between Old and New World experiences. See, for example, Dino Cinel, *From Italy to San Francisco: The Immigrant Experience* (Stanford, Calif., 1982); John Bodnar, *The Transplanted: A History of Immigrants in Urban America* (Bloomington, Ind., 1985); and Donna R. Gabaccia, *From Sicily to Elizabeth Street: Housing and Social Change among Italian Immigrants, 1880–1930* (Albany, N.Y., 1984).

7. For a critique of the concepts of tradition and modernity in labor history, see Daniel Rodgers, "Tradition, Modernity, and the American Industrial Worker: Reflections and Critique," *Journal of Interdisciplinary History* 7 (Spring 1977): 655–81. As I hope to make clear, I am not using the standard measures of "modernity" (faith in science, progress, rationality, etc.) to describe the Jewish orientation. Rather, I am trying to suggest other possible ways in which this group looked forward rather than backward. For an important theoretical treatment of the meanings of modernity for Jews see Steven Cohen, *American Modernity and Jewish Identity* (New York, 1983), pp. 7–23. Also helpful is Steve J. Zipperstein, *The Jews of Odessa: A Cultural History, 1794–1881* (Stanford, Calif., 1985).

8. Sydney Stahl Weinberg argues that immigrant women "defined themselves within the domestic sphere regardless of whether or not they worked for wages." She insists that Jewish women's interests revolved almost exclusively around the home and interpersonal relationships rather than "external accomplishments": *World of Our Mothers* (Chapel Hill, N.C., 1988), p. xx. Even Elizabeth Ewen's superb history of Italian and Jewish working-class women, which acknowledges the relationship between domestic and nondomestic experience, devotes only a scant last chapter to the world of industrial wage work. My own views support those of Sarah Eisenstein, whose essays in *Give Us Bread, but Give Us Roses: Working Women's Consciousness in the United States, 1890 to the First World War* (London and Boston, 1983) stress the formative impact of wage work outside the home on female consciousness and identity.

9. To date there is still no full-scale treatment of Jewish immigrant women in the garment industry or as industrial wage workers. But some significant studies treat various aspects of this experience: Kessler-Harris, "Organizing the Unorganizable"; Nancy Schrom Dye, *As Equals and as Sisters: Feminism, Unionism, and the Women's Trade Union League in New York* (Columbia, Mo., 1980); and several of the essays in Joan M. Jensen and Sue Davidson, eds., *A Needle, a Bobbin, a Strike: Women Needleworkers in America* (Philadelphia, 1984).

10. See, for example, Tentler, *Wage-Earning Women*, and Patricia A. Cooper, *Once a Cigar Maker: Men, Women, and Work Culture in American Cigar Factories,*

1900–1919 (Urbana, Ill., 1988). Studies that reveal the overlapping cultures of male and female wage work include Mary H. Blewett, *Men, Women, and Work: Class, Gender, and Protest in the New England Shoe Industry, 1780–1910* (Urbana, Ill., 1988), and Nancy A. Hewitt, "'The Voice of Virile Labor': Labor Militancy, Community Solidarity, and Gender Identity among Tampa's Latin Workers," in Ava Baron, ed., *Work Engendered: Toward a New Understanding of Men, Women, and Work* (Ithaca, N.Y., forthcoming).

11. The view of women workers as indifferent and unambitious has been most forcefully articulated in Tentler's *Wage-Earning Women*. In contrast, Sarah Eisenstein suggested that young working women were probably more job-conscious than was previously recognized. Though her study is more theoretical than empirical, her insights bear further exploration. See *Give Us Bread, but Give Us Roses*. Important insights into the work identities and job consciousness of women in various occupations are found in Susan Porter Benson, "'The Customers Ain't God': The Work Culture of Department-Store Saleswomen, 1890–1940," in Michael H. Frisch and Daniel J. Walkowitz, eds., *Working-Class America* (Urbana, Ill., 1983); Tamara K. Hareven and Randolph Langenbach, *Amoskeag: Life and Work in an American Factory-City* (New York, 1978); Cooper, *Once a Cigar Maker*; and Blewett, *Men, Women, and Work*.

12. Older accounts include Melvyn Dubofsky, *When Workers Organize: New York City in the Progressive Era* (Amherst, Mass., 1968), and Louis Levine, *The Women's Garment Workers* (New York, 1924).

Chapter 1. *"A Girl Wasn't Much"*

1. For an overview of the traditional role of the Jewish wife in the shtetl see May Edel, "Marriage and the Family," unpub. doc. J-77, vol. 7, n.d. (c. 1949), Columbia University Research in Contemporary Cultures Collection, Institute for Intercultural Studies, Manuscripts Division, Library of Congress (hereafter cited as RCC). See also Mark Zborowski and Elizabeth Herzog, *Life Is with People: The Jewish Little Town of Eastern Europe* (New York, 1952); Charlotte Baum, Paula Hyman, Sonia Michel, *The Jewish Woman in America* (New York, 1976), especially p. 76; and Charlotte Baum, "What Made Yetta Work? The Economic Role of Eastern European Jewish Women in the Family," *Response* 18 (1973): 33–34.

2. For a general yet overly romanticized description of shtetl life see Zborowski and Herzog, *Life Is with People*. See also Elias Tcherikower, ed., *The Early Jewish Labor Movement*, trans. and rev. Aaron Antonovsky (New York, 1961), pp. 3–12; Abraham Ain, "Swislocz: Portrait of a Shtetl," *YIVO Annual of Jewish Social Science* 4 (1949); and Yitzack Yankev Doroshkin, "From Zhitkovitch—through the World: Episodes from My Life," unpub. autobiography, Archives of the YIVO Institute for Jewish Research, New York.

3. Zborowski and Herzog, *Life Is with People*, pp. 86–87.

4. Interview with Dora Bayrack by the author, June 8, 1981, Santa Monica, Calif. For further discussion of this issue see Celia S. Heller, *On the Edge of Destruction: Jews of Poland between the Two World Wars* (New York, 1980), p. 154.

5. The custom of eating days for Yeshiva students is discussed in Zborowski

and Herzog, *Life Is with People*, p. 100, and Abraham Cahan, *The Education of Abraham Cahan*, trans. Leon Stein, Abraham P. Conan, and Lynn Davison from the Yiddish autobiography (Philadelphia, 1969), pp. 68–70.

6. Yiddish writer I. L. Peretz sarcastically criticized this way of thinking in his story "Domestic Happiness," which is excerpted in Ronald Sanders, *The Downtown Jews* (New York, 1969), p. 350.

7. Interview with Ida Richter in Sydelle Kramer and Jenny Masur, eds., *Jewish Grandmothers* (Boston, 1976), p. 125.

8. On the folk culture of the shtetl and the rewards of female labor see Ruth Rubin, ed., *A Treasury of Jewish Folk Song* (New York, 1950), pp. 15, 33; also Mirian Shomer Zunser, *Yesterday: A Story of Three Generations of Jewish Life* (New York, 1939), p. 7; Zborowski and Herzog, *Life Is with People*, pp. 83, 131; and Baum, Hyman, and Michel, *The Jewish Woman in America*, pp. 67–68.

9. Fannie Edelman, *The Mirror of Life: The Old Country and the New*, trans. Samuel Pasner (New York, 1961), pp. 18–19.

10. Unpub. doc. J-P 343, vol. 10, July 1949, p. 10, RCC. See also Samuel H. Cohen, *Transplanted* (New York, 1937), pp. 18–19. Celia Heller's research indicates that this pattern persisted into the interwar period of the 1920s and 1930s. See *On the Edge of Destruction*, p. 154.

11. Eva Broido, *Memoirs of a Revolutionary*, trans. and ed. Vera Broido (New York, 1967), p. 2. See also Leonard S. Kahn, "The Role of the Family in the Adjustment of the Jewish Immigrant in the United States," M.A. thesis, Columbia University (Sociology), 1952, p. 2; Cohen, *Transplanted*, p. 10; and Rubin, *Treasury of Jewish Folk Song*, pp. 15, 33.

12. Zunser, *Yesterday*, pp. 153–54.

13. For a precise breakdown of Jewish occupations as enumerated in the Russian census of 1897 see U.S. Congress, Senate, *Reports of the Immigration Commission*, vol. 12, "Emigration Conditions in Europe," 61st Cong., 3d sess., Senate Doc. 748 (Washington, D.C., 1911), pp. 290–91, and I. M. Rubinow, "Economic Conditions of the Jews in Russia," *Bulletin of the Bureau of Labor* 72 (1907). See also Ain, "Swislocz," pp. 101–6; unpub. doc. J-R 61, vol. 5, Aug. 20 and 24, 1947, pp. 1–8, RCC.

14. See Tcherikower, *Early Jewish Labor Movement*, pp. 12–26; Salo W. Baron, *The Russian Jew under the Tsars and Soviets*, 2d ed. (New York, 1976), pp. 80–81; Hirsh Abramovitch, "Rural Jewish Occupations in Lithuania," *Yivo Annual of Jewish Social Science* 2–3 (1947–48): 205–20; E. Eisenberg, ed., *Plotsk: A History of an Ancient Jewish Community in Poland* (Tel Aviv, 1967), p. 23; Tooretz-Yeremitz Societies, *Book of Remembrance, Tooretz-Yeremitz* (Tel Aviv, 1977), p. 75; and Ezra Mendelsohn, *Class Struggle in the Pale: The Formative Years of the Jewish Workers' Movement in Tzarist Russia* (Cambridge, 1970), chap. 1. On the situation in Galicia see Samuel Joseph, *Jewish Immigration to the United States from 1881 to 1910*, Studies in History, Economics and Public Law 145, Columbia University (New York, 1914), p. 51.

15. For a good overview of residence restrictions see Joseph, *Jewish Immigration to the United States*, pp. 57–58. The Pale of Settlement included the following areas: in Lithuania the provinces (*gubernias*) of Vilna, Grodno, and Kovno; in White Russia the provinces of Minsk, Vitebsk, and Mogilev; in southwestern Russia

the provinces of Volhynia, Podolia, Kiev (except the city of Kiev), Chernigov, and Poltava; in southern Russia the provinces of Bessarabia, Kherson, Ekaterinoslav, and Taurida (except the city of Yalta); in Poland the provinces of Warsaw, Kalisz, Kielce, Lomza, Lublin, Petrikau, Plock (Polotzk), Radom, Suwalki, and Siedlec.

16. Arcadius Kahan, "The Impact of Industrialization in Tsarist Russia on the Socioeconomic Conditions of the Jewish Population," in Kahan, *Essays in Jewish Social and Economic History*, ed. Roger Weiss (Chicago, 1986), pp. 6, 49–51, 64 n.10. Kahan's figures may also fall short since it is not clear whether he included women who assisted their husbands in small businesses or craft enterprises on a part-time basis.

17. Kahan, "Impact of Industrialization in Tsarist Russia," pp. 64–65 n.10.

18. For further discussion of the flexibility of gender roles in the Jewish family in eastern Europe, see Ruth Landes and Mark Zborowski, "Hypothesis concerning the Eastern European Jewish Family," *Psychiatry* 13 (1950): 447–64.

19. Joan W. Scott and Louise A. Tilly, *Women, Work, and the Family* (New York, 1978), pp. 44–47, discuss the situation in western European families.

20. The song appears in Ruth Rubin, *Voices of a People*, 2d ed. (New York, 1973), pp. 112–13.

21. The memoirs and oral histories of Jewish immigrants are replete with descriptions of women's commercial activities in eastern Europe. See for example Pearl Halpern interview, Irving Howe Collection, YIVO Archives; unpub. autobiographies of Sara Abrams and Rebecca August, YIVO Archives; Cohen, *Transplanted*, p. 18; and Lucy Robins Lang, *Tomorrow Is Beautiful* (New York, 1948), p. 11.

22. Cahan, *Education of Abraham Cahan*, p. 18; see also Mary Antin, *The Promised Land* (Boston, 1912), pp. 65–66.

23. Interview 1 with Lottie Spitzer by Kristine Feichtinger, p. 16, July 18, 1974, and 5, p. 1, Sept. 13, 1974; Interview with Rebecca Holland (Goldberg) by Patti Pricket, Nov. 12, 1974, tape 1, side A, Feminist History Research Project Collection, "Women in the Labor Movement," Topanga, Calif., Sherna Gluck, Director. Hereafter cited as FHRP.

24. Edelman, *The Mirror of Life*, pp. 21–22. On the general phenomenon of "absentee husbands" see May Edel, "Marriage and the Family," unpub. doc. J-77, vol. 7, p. 16, RCC; unpub. doc. J-R 32, vol. 2, Aug. 7, 1947, p. 4, RCC; Abramovitch, "Rural Jewish Occupations in Lithuania," pp. 206, 209; Kahn, "Role of the Family," p. 18; and Rebecca August, unpub. autobiography, YIVO Archives.

25. Isaac Meier Dick, *Feigele der Maggid* (Vilna, 1860), as quoted in Baron, *The Russian Jew*, p. 88.

26. Lottie Spitzer interviews 1 and 5, FHRP; interview with Pearl Halpern, p. 16, Irving Howe Collection, YIVO Archives.

27. Rose Pesotta, *Days of Our Lives* (Boston, 1958), p. 76.

28. See Zborowski and Herzog, *Life Is with People*, p. 247.

29. Unpub. doc. J-R 32, vol. 2, April 1949, p. 1, RCC.

30. As quoted in Zborowski and Herzog, *Life Is with People*, p. 251. Abramovitch, "Rural Jewish Occupations in Lithuania," p. 217, insists that only the "poorest" girls became domestic servants. It is likely that the disdain for domestic service was strong among the *balebatim*, or middle-class Jews, who valued indepen-

dence. The great number of female domestics in the Pale suggests that the stigma did not outweigh the need to work. On attitudes toward domestic service in western Europe see Theresa McBride, "The Long Road Home: Women's Work and Industrialization," in Renate Bridenthal and Claudia Koonz, eds., *Becoming Visible: Women in European History* (Boston, 1977), esp. p. 289.

31. The pattern of going to another city to work as a domestic is mentioned in Spitzer interview 5, p. 4, FHRP. The Russian census of 1897 counted 113,740 Jewish female domestic servants. It did not list ages or marital status. See *Reports of the Immigration Commission* 12: 290–91. On marriage patterns of domestics see Abramovitch, "Rural Jewish Occupations in Lithuania," p. 217.

32. Kahan, "Impact of Industrialization in Tsarist Russia," p. 65, n. 14.

33. Unpub. doc., J-P 326, Interview 3, p. 19, May 1949, RCC.

34. Unpub. doc. J-R 344, Interview 2, p. 6, vol. 7, July 1949, RCC.

35. Interview with Dora Bayrack by the author; Weber and Kempster, "Letter from the Secretary of the Treasury Transmitting a Report of the Commissioners of Immigration upon the Causes Which Incite Immigration to the United States," Exec. Doc. 235, part I, vol. I, House of Representatives, 52d Cong., 1st sess. (Washington, D.C., 1892), p. 42. Hereafter cited as "Weber-Kempster Report." The yellow ticket allowed a prostitute to live anywhere in the Russian Empire.

36. Jewish Colonization Association, *Recueil de matériaux sur la situation économique des Israelites de Russie*, 2 vols. (Paris, 1906–8), 1: 254, 258, 285, 369–70, describes other trades for women. Hereafter cited as *Recueil de matériaux*. See also "Weber-Kempster Report," pp. 85, 87; Mendelsohn, *Class Struggle in the Pale*, pp. 23–25, 93; Rubinow, "Economic Condition," pp. 541, 546; Max Sandin, unpub. autobiography, p. 3, YIVO Archives; Gutrajman, "A Woman's Story," unpub. autobiography, pp. 96–97, YIVO Archives; and Records of the Women's Bureau, Schedule #7-2-85 (Dora Garber), unpub. materials for Bulletin 74, Record Group 86, National Archives.

37. J.C.A., *Recueil de matériaux*, 2: 204.

38. Shmarya Levin, *The Arena*, trans. Maurice Samuel (New York, 1932), p. 53; "Weber-Kempster Report," pp. 73, 75. Ezra Mendelsohn called the female tobacco workers the first real Jewish "proletariat" in Russia: *Class Struggle in the Pale*, pp. 25–26.

39. Rubinow, "Economic Condition," p. 546. On Dvinsk see Max Sandin, unpub. autobiography, YIVO Archives.

40. Rubinow, "Economic Condition," p. 526; Mendelsohn, *Class Struggle in the Pale*, p. 23. The Jewish Colonization Association estimated that in 1898 about 13,000 women and girls worked for industrial manufacturers either in factories or at home.

41. Jacob Lestshinsky, "Industrial and Social Structure of the Jewish Population of Interbellum Poland," YIVO *Annual of Jewish Social Science* 11 (1956–57): 249.

42. For a thorough discussion of Jewish female artisans in the Pale, see J.C.A., *Recueil de matériaux* 1: 251, 255, 285 and passim; 2: table 53. In 1898 the total number of female artisans counted was 76,548. The total number of women in the clothing trades was 53,964. The JCA did not provide data for age or marital status of these women, but it is likely that apprentices and assistants tended to be young unmarried women and girls. The total number of apprentices (16,792) and the total

number of assistants (19,123) were 67 percent of women in these trades. On the problem of underreporting and undercounting of employment see Kahan, "Impact of Industrialization in Tsarist Russia," pp. 6–9.

43. See Mark Wischnitzer, *A History of Jewish Crafts and Guilds* (New York, 1965), p. 244.

44. Ibid., p. 255; Baron, *The Russian Jew*, p. 113.

45. Unpub. doc. J-R 61, vol. 5, Aug. 1947, p. 2, RCC.

46. J.C.A., *Recueil de matériaux*, 1: 242; *Reports of the Immigration Commission*, 12: 290–91.

47. See Ain, "Swislocz," p. 107; Raphael Mahler, "The Economic Background of Jewish Migration to the United States," *YIVO Annual of Jewish Social Science* 7 (1952): 263; J.C.A., *Recueil de matériaux*, 1: 334–35.

48. See *Reports of the Immigration Commission*, 12: 306; Mendelsohn, *Class Struggle in the Pale*, pp. 10–11; and Gutrajman, "A Woman's Story," unpub. autobiography, p. 98, YIVO Archives.

49. On the size of shops in the clothing trades in Russia and Poland see J.C.A., *Recueil de matériaux*, 1: 252–53, 295. The largest artisan workshops were in Poland (3.2 workers on the average) and the smallest in Lithuania (2.1 workers). See also Mendelsohn, *Class Struggle in the Pale*, pp. 9–10; Rubinow, "Economic Condition of the Jews in Russia," p. 523; Doroshkin, "From Zhitkovitch," unpub. autobiography, p. 15, YIVO Archives; Brucha Gutrajman, "A Woman's Story," unpub. autobiography, pp. 94–95, YIVO Archives; W. E. Rabinowitch, ed., *Pinsk Historical Volume: History of the Jews of Pinsk* (Tel Aviv, 1973), p. 52; *Reports of the Immigration Commission*, 12: 306–7; Jacob Bross, "The Jewish Labor Movement in Galicia," *YIVO Annual of Jewish Social Science* 5 (1950): 58; and Beatrice Baskerville, *The Polish Jew* (New York, 1906), p. 43.

50. Cahan, *Education of Abraham Cahan*, p. 60.

51. Brucha Gutrajman, "A Woman's Story," unpub. autobiography, p. 88, YIVO Archives.

52. "Songs of the Needle-Trade Workers," collected and trans. Sam Schwartz, unpub. typescript, W.P.A. Federal Writers' Project, New York City Folklore, Archive of Folksong, drawer 38–2, Library of Congress.

53. Sholom Asch, *The Mother*, trans. Nathan Asubel (New York, 1930), p. 63. The novel was originally published in Yiddish in 1925. See also Sarah Reznikoff, "Early History of a Seamstress," in Charles Reznikoff, *Family Chronicle* (New York, 1963), pp. 43–44.

54. Fannie Shapiro interview, Jenny Masur Papers, YIVO Archives. A somewhat edited version appears in Kramer and Masur, eds., *Jewish Grandmothers*.

55. Abraham Bisno, *Union Pioneer* (Madison, Wisc., 1967), p. 6. According to Sara Abrams, with compulsory military service required of Jews in eastern Europe, and with many young people marrying at the time of a young man's call to service, "it was not uncommon for women to be taught trades with an eye to self-reliance." Unpub. autobiography, p. 1, YIVO Archives.

56. On the importance of the dowry see Edel, "Marriage and the Family," unpub. doc. J-77, vol. 7, pp. 1–2, RCC; Zborowski and Herzog, *Life Is with People*, p. 273. On charitable provisions for the dowries of poor girls see Tcherikower, *Early Jewish Labor Movement*, p. 7.

57. Many of these seamstresses' songs traveled from Russia to New York City, where they were sung by immigrant garment workers. See Schwartz, "Songs of the Needle-Trade Workers," W.P.A. Archive of Folksong, Library of Congress. A somewhat different version of the song appears in Rubin, *Voices of a People*, p. 344.

58. Rose Cohen, *Out of the Shadow* (New York, 1918), p. 29.

59. Reznikoff, "Early History of a Seamstress," pp. 30, 45. Zborowski and Herzog observed that women of any social class had much in common with the *proste*. Neither were known for their education, and both were viewed as excitable and unrestrained in their behavior when compared to the dignity of the scholar. *Life Is with People*, p. 151.

60. Elizabeth Hasanovitz, *One of Them: Chapters from a Passionate Autobiography* (New York, 1918), p. 10. See also interview with Jennie Matyas, "Jennie Matyas and the I.L.G.W.U.," by Corinne Gilb, 1955, p. 8, Institute of Industrial Relations, University of California, Berkeley. Hereafter cited as Jennie Matyas interview. Jacob Lestchinsky insists that factory work for women was seen as objectionable but that industrial homework had more respectability for Orthodox Jews. "The Industrial and Social Structure of the Jewish Population of Interbellum Poland," p. 249.

61. Leon Kobrin, *A Lithuanian Village* (1920), trans. Isaac Goldberg (New York, 1927), p. 3.

62. Unpub. doc. J-R 309, vol. 11, April 1949, p. 1, RCC. On the association between loss of family dignity and children learning a trade or becoming workers, see Ephraim E. Lisitzky, *In the Grip of Crosscurrents* (New York, 1959), p. 104; Joseph Bennett, *The Life of an Immigrant* (Atlantic City, N.J., 1937), p. 37; Isaac S. Pomerance, "Autobiographical Notes," unpub. autobiography, p. 20, YIVO Archives; and Michael Charnofsky, *Jewish Life in the Ukraine: A Family Saga* (New York, 1965), p. 79.

63. J.C.A., *Recueil de matériaux*, 1: 251, 255.

64. The case history is discussed in Edel, "Marriage and the Family," unpub. doc. J-77, p. 4, RCC.

65. Sherna Gluck, ed., "What Is It We Want Brother Levin?: Reminiscences of a Non-Conforming Shop Girl, 1872–1976," unpub. ms. in author's possession, pp. 1, 4. Gluck's paper is based on summaries of her interviews with Rozner and Rozner's own diaries.

66. Ain, "Swislocz," p. 200.

67. Interview with Mollie Wexler by Sherna Gluck, tape 1, side A, November 22, 1972, FHRP.

68. Interview with Rose Kaplan (Himmelfarb) by Sherna Gluck, tape 1, side A, March 13, 1975, FHRP. See also Reznikoff, "Early History of a Seamstress," p. 30.

69. Quoted in Kahn, "Role of the Family," p. 17. See also S. L. Hoffman, *Autobiography of S. L. Hoffman* (New York, 1967), pp. 36–37; Alexander S. Miller, "And Poverty Was Their Lot," in *Memorial Book, Dobromil*, Dobromiler Society in New York (Tel Aviv, 1963), pp. 38–40; and Records of the Women's Bureau, Schedule #7-2-128 (Esther Costin), unpub. materials for Bulletin 74, Record Group 86, National Archives.

70. See for example, Antin, *The Promised Land*, p. 149; Doroshkin, "From Zhitkovitch," unpub. autobiography, pp. 15, 33, YIVO Archives.

71. Gutrajman, "A Woman's Story," unpub. autobiography, pp. 88–89, YIVO Archives.

72. Ibid., p. 89.

73. Ibid., pp. 97–98. On violence in the workshops see Max Sandin, unpub. autobiography, pp. 5–6, YIVO Archives; Mendelsohn, *Class Struggle in the Pale*, p. 8. The example of a tailor beating a young female apprentice is quoted in Kahn, "Role of the Family," p. 17.

74. Interview with Mollie Wexler by Sherna Gluck, tape 1, side 1, FHRP. On working hours in general see Mendelsohn, *Class Struggle in the Pale*, pp. 11–12; *Reports of the Immigration Commission*, 12: 306–7.

75. Unpub. doc. J-R 38, vol. 2, p. 2, Aug. 18, 1947, RCC.

76. Mendelsohn, *Class Struggle in the Pale*, p. 87. See also J.C.A., *Recueil de matériaux*, 1: 395; Ain, "Swisloez," p. 114; and Baskerville, *The Polish Jew*, p. 43.

77. Unpub. doc. J-R-38, vol. 2, Aug. 18, 1947, p. 3, RCC.

78. Both songs are in Rubin, ed., *A Treasury of Jewish Folksong*, p. 97.

79. I. L. Peretz, "The Three Seamstresses," in Joseph Leftwich, ed., *The Golden Peacock: A World Wide Treasury of Yiddish Poetry* (New York, 1961), p. 77.

80. Mollie Wexler interview, tape 1, side A, FHRP.

81. Ibid.

82. Ibid.; Doroshkin, "From Zhitkovitch," p. 33, YIVO Archives, suggests that boys also first learned hand sewing and later how to use a machine.

83. Rozner is quoted in Gluck, ed., "What Is It We Want Brother Levin?" pp. 4–5.

84. "Weber-Kempster Report," p. 73.

85. Mollie Wexler interview, tape 1, side 1, FHRP.

86. See Tcherikower, *Early Jewish Labor Movement*, pp. 23–24; Mendelsohn, *Class Struggle in the Pale*, p. 3; and Joseph, *Jewish Immigration to the United States*, pp. 60–61.

87. See Tcherikower, *Early Jewish Labor Movement*, pp. 23–24; *Reports of the Immigration Commission*, 12: 275.

88. See "Weber-Kempster Report," pp. 39, 53–57, 66; *Reports of the Immigration Commission*, 12: 276, 318.

89. "Weber-Kempster Report," p. 66; Tcherikower, *Early Jewish Labor Movement*, pp. 12–13; Baron, *The Russian Jew*, p. 86. See also Ain, "Swisloez," p. 220; Henry J. Tobias, *The Jewish Bund in Russia from Its Origins to 1905* (Stanford, Calif., 1972), p. 7; and Jacob Bross, "The Jewish Labor Movement in Galicia," *YIVO Annual of Jewish Social Science* 5 (1950): 58. Raphael Mahler, "The Economic Background of the Jewish Migration from Galicia to the United States," *YIVO Annual of Jewish Social Science* 7 (1952): 259, discusses the impact of commercial and industrial development outside the Pale, where Jewish artisans and traders faced similar problems of economic displacement.

90. Mendelsohn, *Class Struggle in the Pale*, pp. 15–16; Baron, *The Russian Jew*, p. 96; Mahler, "Economic Background," p. 259; and Societies of Former Residents of Kalish, *The Kalish Book* (Tel Aviv, 1968), pp. 73–75, 78. Kalish (Kalisz), a town in Poland, saw its lace industry mechanized and taken over by large industrialists.

91. See Mendelsohn, *Class Struggle in the Pale*, p. 11 and passim. See also Rubinow, "Economic Condition of the Jews in Russia," pp. 519–20.

92. Levin, *The Arena*, pp. 238–39; Mendelsohn, *Class Struggle in the Pale*, pp. 18–23; Baskerville, *Polish Jew*, p. 50; Tobias, *The Jewish Bund in Russia*, p. 9; and "Weber-Kempster Report," p. 66.

93. Baskerville, *Polish Jew*, pp. 44–46, 50. See also J.C.A., *Recueil de matériaux*, 2: 210; Mendelsohn, *Class Struggle in the Pale*, pp. 21–23.

94. Mendelsohn, *Class Struggle in the Pale*, pp. 114–15; Ain, "Swislocz," pp. 225–26. Even in the interwar period in Poland, shops employing Jews tended to be relatively small and unmechanized. See *Zydowskie Przedsiebiorstwa Przemyslowe w Polsce, Wdlug ankietyz 1921 Roku* (Jewish industrial establishments in Poland, surveyed in 1921), 9 vols., compiled under the supervision of Eliezer Heller (Warsaw, 1922); printed in Polish, Yiddish and English. Of particular interest are the tables for the Bialystok region, vol. 3, Tables IV, V, VI, which show that only in the textile industry did Jews use motor-driven machinery to any great extent and that Jews generally worked in very small shops. On the relative security of small-town versus big-city artisans see Kahan, "Impact of Industrialization in Tsarist Russia," pp. 25–26.

95. See Mahler, "Economic Background of the Jewish Migration from Galicia," pp. 261–63, and Joseph, *Jewish Immigration to the United States*, p. 68.

96. "Weber-Kempster Report," pp. 66, 67, 84.

97. Ibid., p. 84.

98. On the impact of the Kishinev pogrom see Tobias, *The Jewish Bund in Russia*, pp. 222–23.

99. My understanding of the Haskalah owes much to Steven J. Zipperstein's *The Jews of Odessa: A Cultural History, 1794–1881* (Stanford, Calif., 1985), esp. chap. 1. See also Jacob F. Raisin, *The Haskalah Movement in Russia* (Philadelphia, 1913), and Howard Morely Sachar, *The Course of Modern Jewish History* (New York, 1958), pp. 199–219.

100. On the Haskalah critique of unproductive men see Ruth Adler, *Women of the Shtetl through the Eyes of Y. L. Peretz* (Rutherford, N.J., 1980), pp. 34–71 and passim. See also Sachar, *Course of Modern Jewish History*, p. 201.

101. Zipperstein, *The Jews of Odessa*, pp. 11–13; Heller, *On the Edge of Destruction*, p. 31; and Baum, Hyman, and Michel, *The Jewish Woman in America*, p. 72.

102. Zunser, *Yesterday*, p. 66. See also Reznikoff, "Early History of a Seamstress," pp. 23–24; Baum et al., *The Jewish Woman*, pp. 60–61; Levin, *The Arena*, pp. 218–20; Rachel Greb, "Difficulties in Entering School," *Spring Magazine*, Affiliated Summer School for Women Workers in Industry (April 1929), p. 15, in Hilda Smith Papers, Box 24, Schlesinger Library, Radcliffe; and Harry Mann, "A Landsman from Skvira," unpub. autobiography, p. 1, YIVO Archives.

103. Baum, Hyman, and Michel, *The Jewish Woman in America*, pp. 71–73.

104. For a detailed discussion of this theme see Adler, *Women of the Shtetl through the Eyes of Y. L. Peretz*, pp. 22–25, 26–71. See also David G. Roskies, "Yiddish Popular Literature and the Female Reader," *Journal of Popular Culture* 10 (Spring 1977): 852–58.

105. Adler, *Women of the Shtetl*, pp. 23, 59–60. See also David Biale, "Childhood, Marriage, and the Family in Eastern Europe," in Steven M. Cohen and Paula E. Hyman, eds., *The Jewish Family: Myths and Realities* (New York, 1986). Domes-

ticity was the model of femininity in middle-class German Jewish families. On this theme see Marion Kaplan, "Priestess and Hausfrau: Women and Tradition in the German-Jewish Family," also in Cohen and Hyman.

106. On the relationship between Haskalah, Zionism, and socialism see Jonathan Frankel, *Prophecy and Politics: Socialism, Nationalism, and the Russian Jews, 1862–1917* (Cambridge, 1981), pp. 29–31, 33–43, and passim; Sachar, *Course of Modern Jewish History*, pp. 287–88; and Tobias, *The Jewish Bund in Russia*, pp. 9, 11.

107. The two most important studies of the Bund are Mendelsohn, *Class Struggle in the Pale*, and Tobias, *The Jewish Bund in Russia from Its Origins to 1905*.

108. Gerald Sorin, *The Prophetic Minority: American Jewish Immigrant Radicals, 1880–1920* (Bloomington, Ind., 1985), p. 18. See also Heller, *On the Edge of Destruction*, pp. 41–42.

109. The major work on Zionism and Socialism is Frankel, *Prophecy and Politics*. A summary of the Zionist-Socialist tensions can be found in Sachar, *Course of Modern Jewish History*, pp. 293–94.

110. Tobias, *The Jewish Bund in Russia*, traces these developments in great detail. See especially chapters 14–16.

111. Interview with Bessie Udin by Sherna Gluck, tape 1, side 1, FHRP.

112. Tobias, *The Jewish Bund in Russia*, p. 7; Mendelsohn, *Class Struggle in the Pale*, p. ix.

113. In their discussion of *sheyne* and *proste* status among eastern European Jews, Zborowski and Herzog distinguish between the "people of the week," those who made a living with their hands, and "people of the Sabbath," those who were primarily engaged in study and prayer. The *balebatim* (bosses) and middle-class merchants fell somewhere between the two but were generally believed to be closer to the sheyne (beautiful Jews). *Life Is with People*, pp. 142–43. See also unpub. doc. J-P 326, vol. 10, May 1949, pp. 16–18; J-R 345, vol. 7, July 1949, p. 5; J-R 309, vol. 11, April 1949, pp. 1–2; and J-R 312, vol. 11, p. 1, RCC.

114. Unpub. doc. J-R 82, vol. 10, Oct. 9 and 13, 1947, p. 10, RCC. See also Kahn, "Role of the Jewish Family," pp. 21–22.

115. Interview with May Horowitz by the author, June 7, 1981, Los Angeles.

116. Interview 5 with Lottie Spitzer by Kristine Feichtinger, Sept. 13, 1974, p. 4, FHRP.

117. Zunser, *Yesterday*, p. 49.

118. Unpub. doc. J-R 149, vol. 7, Feb. 12 and 13, 1948, p. 7, RCC. See also Zunser, *Yesterday*, p. 58.

119. See Mendelsohn, *Class Struggle in the Pale;* Tobias, *Jewish Bund in Russia.*

120. See Tobias, *Jewish Bund in Russia*, p. 44; Baum, Hyman, and Michel, *The Jewish Woman in America*, pp. 77–78, 87; J. S. Hertz, comp., *Der Bund in Bilder* (New York, 1958), pp. 17, 41, 50, 60; Norma Fain Pratt, "Culture and Radical Politics: Yiddish Women Writers, 1890–1940"; and Harriet Davis-Kram, "The Story of the Sisters of the Bund," *Contemporary Jewry* 5 (Fall/Winter 1980): 27–43.

121. Davis-Kram, "The Story of the Sisters of the Bund"; Tobias, *Jewish Bund in Russia*, pp. 41–44; and Baum et al., *The Jewish Woman in America*, p. 77.

122. The song appears in Rubin, *Voices of a People: The Story of Yiddish Folksong*, p. 296. Rubin translates "ale" as "all men," but the term commonly refers to "all people" and is a genderless concept.

123. Tobias, preface to *Jewish Bund in Russia*, has a rendition of the "Oath," as does Pratt, "Culture and Radical Politics," p. 74.

124. Interview with Mollie Wexler by Sherna Gluck, tape 1, side A, FHRP.

125. Mendelsohn, *Class Struggle in the Pale*, pp. 153–54. See also Samuel A. Portnoy, *Vladimir Medem: The Life and Soul of a Legendary Jewish Socialist* (New York, 1979), pp. 235–36, a translation of Medem's autobiography, *Fun Mayn Lebn*.

126. Gutrajman, "A Woman's Story," unpub. autobiography, YIVO Archives. On the Bund as a generational rebellion see Tobias, *The Jewish Bund in Russia*, pp. 44–45, 236–37.

127. Michael Charnofsky, *Jewish Life in the Ukraine: A Family Saga* (New York, 1965), p. 104.

128. Unpub. doc. J-R-31, vol. 2, Aug. 3, 1947, p. 11, RCC.

129. Pesotta, *Days of Our Lives*, p. 169.

130. Eva Broido, *Memoirs of a Revolutionary* (New York, 1967), pp. 5–6. For an important discussion of Bundist women see Harriet Davis-Kram, "Jewish Women in Russian Revolutionary Movements," M.A. thesis, Hunter College, 1970, and her summary article "The Story of the Sisters of the Bund."

131. Fannie Shapiro recalled the tensions in her family when she threatened to go off to a neighboring city to become a worker. "My people wouldn't let me go because at that time . . . socialism and many other progressive things were coming to life." Her mother feared that she would "become a socialist and drop religion." Interview in Kramer and Masur, eds., *Jewish Grandmothers*, p. 7.

132. Quoted in Kahn, "The Role of the Family in the Adjustment of the Jewish Immigrant," pp. 18–19.

133. As quoted in Nora Levin, *While Messiah Tarried: Jewish Socialist Movements, 1871–1917* (New York, 1977), p. 248.

134. Unpub. doc. J-R 31, p. 10, Aug. 3, 1947, RCC.

135. Tobias, *Jewish Bund in Russia*, pp. 295–311.

136. Ibid., pp. 140, 239–40, 246, 312–13, 339; Levin, *While Messiah Tarried*, pp. 348–59.

137. Interview with Dora Bayrack by the author.

138. Simon Kuznetz, "Immigration of Russian Jews to the United States: Background and Structure," in *Perspectives in American History* 9 (1975): 36, 93–94, 96, 98, 104–5, 116–17; Joseph, *Jewish Immigration to the United States*, pp. 66, 95, 189; Rubinow, "Economic Condition of the Jews in Russia," pp. 492, 495, 504–5, 520; and *Reports of the Immigration Commission*, 12: 326. For somewhat different views see Tcherikower, *Early Jewish Labor Movement*, pp. 71–72; Irving Howe, *World of Our Fathers* (New York, 1976), pp. 58–59.

139. Mollie Linker interview in Kramer and Masur, eds., *Jewish Grandmothers*, p. 92; see also Isaac S. Pomerance, "Autobiographical Notes," unpub. autobiography, p. 22, YIVO Archives.

140. "Weber-Kempster Report," p. 69. See also Tobias, *The Jewish Bund in Russia*, p. 10; Rubinow, "Economic Condition of the Jews in Russia," p. 677.

141. "Weber-Kempster Report," p. 56.

142. Ibid., p. 83.

143. Antin, *The Promised Land*, p. 22.

144. Interview with Celia R., in Elizabeth Howe Bliss, "Intimate Studies in the Lives of Fifty Working Girls," M.A. thesis, Columbia University, 1915, p. 85. See also Cahan, *Education of Abraham Cahan*, p. 216; Joseph Bennett, *The Life of an Immigrant* (Atlantic City, N.J., 1937), p. 31.

145. Rubin, *Treasury of Jewish Folk Song*, p. 24.

146. Doroshkin, "From Zhitkovitch," p. 60, YIVO Archives. See also Bennett, *The Life of an Immigrant*, p. 31.

147. "Weber-Kempster Report," p. 73. *Reports of the Immigration Commission*, 12: 309, compares the cost of living in Russia and the United States.

148. See for example Ella Wolff and Abraham Mendelowitz interviews, Amerikaner Yiddishe Geshikhte Bel-Pe; Isaac S. Pomerance, "Autobiographical Notes," unpub. autobiography, p. 22; Morris Gordasky questionnaire, "Questionnaires for Union Members" (unpub.) 1955, Aaron Antonovsky Papers; all in YIVO Archives.

149. Joseph Morgenstern, *I Have Considered My Days* (New York, 1964), p. 94; Isaac Pomerance, "Autobiographical Notes," p. 22, YIVO Archives.

150. Rose Pesotta, *Bread upon the Waters* (New York, 1944), p. 4.

151. Quoted in Nancy L. Green, *The Pletzl of Paris: Jewish Immigrant Workers in the Belle Epoque* (New York, 1986), p. 24.

152. Edelman, *The Mirror of Life*, p. 22. See also Charnofsky, *Jewish Life in the Ukraine*, p. 104. For a moving reflection on the psychological boundaries of Jewish family life and the longing for freedom see Broido, *Memoirs of a Revolutionary*, pp. 5–6.

153. Antin, *The Promised Land*, pp. 150–51.

154. Interview with Sophie S., in Elizabeth Howe Bliss, "Intimate Studies in the Lives of Fifty Working Girls," p. 91.

155. Letter to the *Jewish Daily Forward* (1909), quoted in Isaac Metzger, ed., *A Bintl Brief* (New York, 1971), p. 99.

156. Interview with Mollie Wexler by Sherna Gluck, tape 1, side A, FHRP.

157. Interview with Dora Bayrack by the author.

158. Fannie Shapiro interview in Kramer and Masur, eds., *Jewish Grandmothers*, p. 10.

159. On inter and intraregional migration compared to overseas migration see Kahan, "The Impact of Industrialization in Tsarist Russia," pp. 31–33. On the number of women in the Jewish migration to the United States see Joseph, *Jewish Immigration to the United States*, p. 43. For comparative statistics on women emigrating to the United States see Hasia Diner, *Erin's Daughters in America: Irish Immigrant Women in the Nineteenth Century* (Baltimore, 1983), p. 31. On the return rate of various immigrant groups see John Bodnar, *The Transplanted: A History of Immigrants in Urban America* (Bloomington, Ind., 1985), p. 53, and Joseph, *Jewish Immigration*, p. 134, for Jewish return rates. Joseph's figures are for the years 1907–8.

160. Letter to the *Jewish Daily Forward*, July 9, 1917, quoted in Robert E. Park and Herbert A. Miller, *Old World Traits Transplanted* (New York, 1921), p. 62.

161. The family history is described in Leon Stein, *The Triangle Fire* (Philadelphia, 1962), p. 132.

162. Diner, *Erin's Daughters in America*, chap. 2.

163. Council of Jewish Women, New York Section, Report of Agent, Immigra-

tion Station, April 1909–March 1910, in Baron de Hirsch Fund Papers, Record Group I-80, Box 55, American Jewish Historical Society, Brandeis University, Waltham, Mass. During these years an agent from the Council of Jewish Women kept track of incoming Jewish female immigrants at Ellis Island and attempted to assist them with deportation problems, housing, and transportation. For a description of the port work undertaken by the New York Section of the Council of Jewish Women, see Henry L. Sabsovich to Eugene S. Benjamin, July 24, 1911, in Baron de Hirsch Fund Papers, R.G. I-80, Box 37, American Jewish Historical Society. On Jewish immigrant women interviewed in Chicago see Viola Paradise, "The Jewish Immigrant Girl in Chicago," *The Survey* 30 (Sept. 6, 1913): 699–700; *Annual Report of the Commissioner General of Immigration* (Washington, 1910), pp. 24–25.

164. Hasanovitz, *One of Them*, p. 214.

Chapter 2. Mothers and Daughters

1. Elizabeth Hasanovitz, *One of Them: Chapters from a Passionate Autobiography* (New York, 1918), pp. 41–42.

2. Interview with Mollie Wexler by Sherna Gluck, tape 1, side A, Nov. 22, 1972, Feminist History Research Project Collection, "Women in the Labor Movement," Topanga, Calif. Hereafter cited as FHRP.

3. Interview with Rose Kaplan (Himmelfarb) by Sherna Gluck, tape 1, side A, March 13, 1975, FHRP.

4. Emma Goldman, *Living My Life*, ed. Richard and Anna Maria Drinnon (New York, 1977), p. 11.

5. See Elias Tcherikower, ed., *The Early Jewish Labor Movement in the United States*, trans. and rev. Aaron Antonovsky (New York, 1961), p. 115.

6. Mary Grace Worthington, *Fifty Benevolent Social Institutions in or near New York: A Brief Guide for Visitors* (New York, 1915), pp. 46–47, has a good description of the way immigrants were processed at Ellis Island. See also Philip Taylor, *The Distant Magnet: European Emigration to the U.S.A.* (New York, 1971), chap. 7, which describes the procedures for quarantine of immigrants. On Jewish detainees see Henry L. Sabsovich (Hebrew Sheltering and Immigrant Aid Society) to Eugene S. Benjamin, July 24, 1911, in Baron de Hirsch Fund Papers, Box 37, Record Group I-80, American Jewish Historical Society, Brandeis University, Waltham, Mass. Hereafter cited as AJHS.

7. Unpub. autobiography of Sara J. Abrams, p. 3, YIVO Archives, New York.

8. The absence of formal record keeping meant that there were no birth certificates for most women born in eastern Europe. Some women had their fathers write letters to port authorities claiming they were sixteen years old. There was no way to prove a woman's age, however.

9. See Council of Jewish Women, "From the Report of the Executive Secretary," *Proceedings*, Fifth Triennial Convention (Cincinnati, 1908), p. 152; Grace Abbott, *The Immigrant and the Community* (New York, 1917), pp. 55–56, 67; and Viola Paradise, "The Jewish Immigrant Girl in Chicago," *The Survey* 30 (Sept. 6, 1913): 699–704.

10. Sydney Stahl Weinberg, *World of Our Mothers* (Chapel Hill, N.C., 1988), p. 78.

11. Interview with Lottie Spitzer by Kristine Feichtinger, Interview 5, p. 10, Sept. 13, 1974, FHRP.

12. Fannie Shapiro interview, in Sydelle Kramer and Jenny Masur, eds., *Jewish Grandmothers* (Boston, 1976), p. 9. See also the original interview in Jenny Masur Papers, YIVO Archives.

13. See Young Women's Christian Association, Department of Immigration and Foreign Born Women, *Reports*, Dec. 10, 1911, YWCA Archives, New York. See also Rose Sommerfeld (National Council of Jewish Women) to Mr. Gold, Dec. 3, 1905, Baron de Hirsch Fund Papers, Box 56, AJHS, Brandeis University.

14. Sylvia Bernstein interview, in Joan Morrison and Charlotte Fox Zabusky, *American Mosaic: The Immigrant Experience in the Words of Those Who Lived It* (New York, 1980), pp. 85–86.

15. Interview 1 with Mollie Wexler, side 1, FHRP.

16. Samuel Joseph, *Jewish Immigration to the United States from 1881 to 1910* (New York, 1914), p. 149; Charles Bernheimer, ed., *The Russian Jew in the United States* (New York, 1905), pp. 43–59.

17. Abraham Cahan, *The Education of Abraham Cahan*, trans. Leon Stein et al. (Philadelphia, 1969), pp. 215–16, 220.

18. See Allon Schoener, ed., *Portal to America: The Lower East Side, 1870–1925* (New York, 1967), pp. 210–11; and Edward E. Pratt, *Industrial Causes of Congestion of Population in New York City*, Studies in History, Economics and Public Law 43, Columbia University (New York, 1911), pp. 30–34.

19. Isidore Wisotsky, "Such a Life," unpub. autobiography, p. 1, YIVO Archives.

20. Julius S. Baker, "The Life Story of Yudel Shmerl, from Birsze, Lithuania to Baltimore, Maryland, U.S.A.," unpub. autobiography, pp. 62–63, YIVO Archives.

21. Interview with Pauline Newman, Amerikaner Yiddishe Geshikhte Bel-Pe, Jan. 19, 1965, p. 2, YIVO Archives.

22. Rose Cohen, *Out of the Shadow* (New York, 1918), p. 71.

23. "Jennie Matyas and the I.L.G.W.U.," interview with Jennie Matyas by Corinne Gilb, p. 12, Industrial Relations Library, University of California, Berkeley (hereafter cited as Jennie Matyas interview).

24. Good descriptions of Jewish immigrant ghettos can be found in Moses Rischin, *The Promised City: New York's Jews, 1870–1914* (Cambridge, Mass., 1962); Louis Wirth, *The Ghetto* (Chicago, 1928, repr. 1956); Charles Bernheimer, ed., *The Russian Jew in the United States* (Philadelphia, 1905); and in the autobiographies and reminiscences of immigrants.

25. Boris Bogin, *Born a Jew* (New York, 1930), in Harold U. Ribalow, ed., *Autobiographies of American Jews* (Philadelphia, 1973), p. 380.

26. *Hull House Maps and Papers by the Residents of Hull House Social Settlement* (Chicago, 1905), pp. 17–19. See also Tomas Jesse Jones, *The Sociology of a New York City Block*, Columbia University Studies in History, Economics and Public Law (New York, 1904); Wirth, *The Ghetto*, pp. 229–30.

27. Abraham Cahan, "Yekl, a Tale of the New York Ghetto" (1896), reprinted in Abraham Cahan, *Yekl and the Imported Bridegroom and Other Stories of Yiddish New York* (New York, 1970), pp. 13–14. See also Rischin, *Promised City*, pp. 77–78; U.S. Congress, Senate, *Reports of the Immigration Commission*, vol. 1,

"Immigrants in Cities," 61st Congress, 2d sess. (Washington, D.C., 1911), p. 166; Wirth, *The Ghetto*, pp. 226–27.

28. See Rischin, *Promised City*, pp. 104–5; Irving Howe, *World of Our Fathers* (New York, 1976), pp. 183–90; *The Jewish Communal Register* (Kehilla) (New York, 1918), p. 733; and Arthur A. Goren, *New York Jews and the Quest for Community: The Kehilla Experiment, 1908–1922* (New York, 1970), pp. 20–22.

29. On the relations between German and Russian Jews in New York see Rischin, *Promised City*, chap. 6; Abraham Cahan, *Education*, p. 223.

30. Cahan, *Education*, pp. 218–19, 400.

31. See Pratt, *Industrial Causes of Congestion of Population*, pp. 30–34; Robert Coit Chapin, *The Standard of Living among Workingmen's Families in New York City* (New York, 1909), p. 789. See also Bernheimer, ed., *The Russian Jew in the United States*, p. 286. For details on the actual cost of housing in various cities where immigrants settled see *Reports of the Immigration Commission*, "Immigrants in Cities," 1: 112.

32. *Reports of the Immigration Commission*, "Immigrants in Cities," 1: 160–61, describes typical New York tenement houses. By 1901 the New York City Tenement Laws required that new buildings have indoor plumbing and adequate light and ventilation. In other cities conditions varied. In Chicago immigrants often lived either in tenement houses or in low frame "shanties"; see 1: 249–50. In Philadelphia, conditions were sometimes better. Instead of tenements, immigrants in the southeastern section of the city rented private houses, although sometimes more than one family shared a house. See Bernheimer, ed., *The Russian Jew in the United States*, pp. 304–5.

33. Jennie Matyas interview, pp. 17–18.

34. The incident is discussed in Abbott, *The Immigrant and the Community*, p. 63.

35. Marie Ganz with Nat Ferber, *Rebels into Anarchy, and Out Again* (New York, 1920), pp. 3–4.

36. Rose Schneiderman with Lucy Goldthwaite, *All for One* (New York, 1967), pp. 23–24.

37. See Isidore Wisotsky, unpub. autobiography, p. 4, YIVO Archives; Max Sandin, unpub. autobiography, pp. 5–6, YIVO Archives; and Naomi Chaitman, "The House," Oct. 20, 1948, unpub. doc. J-296, vol. 15, Columbia University Research on Contemporary Cultures, Institute for Intercultural Studies, Manuscripts Division, Library of Congress. Hereafter cited as RCC.

38. Quoted in Ezra Mendelsohn, *Class Struggle in the Pale: The Formative Years of the Jewish Workers' Movement in Tsarist Russia* (Cambridge, 1970), p. 113.

39. On Vilna apartment houses see Cahan, *Education*, p. 12.

40. Interview with Zena Druckman by Sally Hanelin, Feb. 4, 1977, Judah Magnes Museum, Western Jewish History Collection, Berkeley, Calif.

41. Mary Antin, *The Promised Land* (Boston, 1911), p. 184, italics added.

42. Interview with Ella Wolff, Amerikaner Yiddishe Geshikhte Bel-Pe, Dec. 27, 1963, p. 1, YIVO Archives. For similar concerns about "freedom" see the unpublished autobiographies of Philip Armon, p. 11, and Isaac Pomerance, p. 23, YIVO Archives.

43. Quoted in Elizabeth Howe Bliss, "Intimate Studies in the Lives of Fifty Working Girls" (M.A. thesis, Columbia University, 1915), p. 91.

44. The accommodations for boarders are colorfully described by Charles Zimmerman, interview, Amerikaner Yiddishe Geshichte Bel-Pe, Nov. 13, 1964, p. 3, YIVO Archives.

45. Headworker, College Settlement, et al. to Eugene S. Benjamin, Feb. 13, 1913, in Baron de Hirsch Fund Papers, Box 58, AJHS. For insights into the concerns of middle-class reformers about the moral condition of female boarders see Mary Antin to Eugene F. Benjamin, n.d. (c. 1911), Baron de Hirsch Fund Papers, Box 58. Antin worried that young women were being subjected to overcrowding, vulgar language, and lewd behavior in the homes of strangers.

46. Bliss, "Intimate Studies in the Lives of Fifty Working Girls," p. 86.

47. Interview 6 with Lottie Spitzer by Kristine L. Feichtinger, Nov. 11, 1974, pp. 4–5, FHRP.

48. Interview with Fannie Shapiro, in Kramer and Masur, eds., *Jewish Grandmothers*, p. 11; see also interview 6 with Lottie Spitzer by Feichtinger, pp. 4–5, FHRP; Leslie Woodcock Tentler, *Wage-Earning Women: Industrial Work and Family Life in the United States, 1900–1930* (New York, 1979), pp. 117–19.

49. Sarah Reznikoff, "Early History of a Seamstress," in Charles Reznikoff, *Family Chronicle* (New York, 1963), p. 79.

50. Marie S. Orenstein, "How the Working Girl of New York Lives," New York (State) Factory Investigating Commission, *Fourth Report* (Albany, 1915), p. 1700. See also Elizabeth Beardsley Butler, *Women and Trades: Pittsburgh, 1907–1908* (New York, 1909), p. 125; Joanne J. Meyerowitz, *Women Adrift: Independent Wage-Earners in Chicago, 1880–1930* (Chicago, 1988), p. 72.

51. See Bliss, "Intimate Studies in the Lives of Fifty Working Girls," pp. 90–91; Meyerowitz, *Women Adrift*, pp. 71–72.

52. Bliss, "Intimate Studies," p. 90; Tentler, *Wage-Earning Women*, pp. 117–19.

53. Council of Jewish Women, *Proceedings*, Fifth Triennial Convention, p. 171; Rudolph Glanz, *The Jewish Woman in America*, vol. 2: *The Eastern European Jewish Woman* (New York, 1976), pp. 35, 161; and Meyerowitz, *Women Adrift*, pp. 47, 79. Compare the descriptions of public lodging houses in Dorothy Richardson, *The Long Day* (1905), reprinted in William O'Neill, ed., *Women at Work* (New York, 1970).

54. On destabilization the classic work is Oscar Handlin, *The Uprooted* (Boston, 1951). Historians who have stressed the uses of tradition in adapting to change include Virginia Yans-McLaughlin, *Family and Community: Italian Immigrants in Buffalo, 1880–1920* (Ithaca, N.Y., 1977); Judith E. Smith, *Family Connections: A History of Italian and Jewish Immigrant Lives in Providence, Rhode Island, 1900–1940* (Albany, N.Y., 1985); Dino Cinel, *From Italy to San Francisco: The Immigrant Experience* (Stanford, Calif., 1982); John Bodnar, "Immigration, Kinship, and the Rise of Working-Class Realism," *Journal of Social History* 14 (Fall 1980): 46–65; Tamara K. Hareven, *Family Time and Industrial Time* (Cambridge, 1982); and Corinne Azen Krause, "Urbanization without Breakdown: Italian, Jewish, and Slavic Immigrant Women in Pittsburgh, 1900–1945," *Journal of Urban History* 4 (May 1978): 291–305.

55. Yans-McLaughlin, *Family and Community*, p. 20; Cinel, *From Italy to San Francisco*, p. 259.

56. Smith, *Family Connections*, pp. 23–24.

57. Chapin, *Standard of Living*, p. 245. Chapin's estimates are for 1907.

58. *Reports of the Immigration Commission*, "Immigrants in Cities," 2: 546.

59. "Synopsis of the Census of Jews in the 7th–10th & 13th Wards in the City of New York Taken in August, 1890," Baron de Hirsch Fund Papers, Box 16, AJHS. See also Isaac M. Rubinow's figures for Jewish occupations in New York, in Bernheimer, *Russian Jew in the United States*, p. 112. He estimated that 53 percent of Russian Jewish men were garment workers as were 77 percent of the working women. Thomas Kessner, *The Golden Door: Italian and Jewish Immigrant Mobility in New York City, 1880–1915* (New York, 1977), pp. 59–61, found that in 1880 more than 4 percent of Jews had low white-collar jobs including positions in petty commerce and small business, whereas 56 percent did manual labor.

60. In Chicago 45 percent of Russian Jewish male heads of household were in business for profits; in Philadelphia, 48 percent; and in New York, 26 percent. *Reports of the Immigration Commission*, "Immigrants in Cities," vol. 1: Table 62, p. 309, Table 56, p. 217, Table 53, p. 397.

61. See Kessner, *Golden Door*, pp. 60–65; Howe, *World of Our Fathers*, pp. 164–65; Herbert Gutman, *The Black Family in Slavery and Freedom* (New York, 1977), Appendix G, p. 527. Gutman found that out of a sample of 5,590 household heads from the New York State census of 1905, 12 percent of Jews were in some kind of business. Using the same census, Kessner's sample of 936 Jewish household heads revealed that 30.8 percent reported their occupation as commerce. The Immigration Commission's 1911 study "Immigrants in Cities," vol. 1, found that 7 percent of Jewish male household heads were "peddlers and proprietors." See pp. 216–17. Although the statistics vary on the number of people in commercial occupations, it is still clear that the vast majority of Jewish household heads did manual labor in the early twentieth century.

62. This was true for most working-class families regardless of nationality. See Chapin, *Standard of Living*; and Tentler, *Wage-Earning Women*, pp. 218–19.

63. *Reports of the Immigration Commission*, "Immigrants in Cities," vol. 1: Table 70, p. 231, Table 71, p. 232.

64. Charles Bernheimer, "Lower East Side Dwellers," in *University Settlement Studies, Twenty-First Annual Report of the University Settlement Society, New York, 1907* (New York, 1908), p. 32.

65. The census sample is from Thomas Kessner and Betty Boyd Caroli, "New Immigrant Women at Work," *Journal of Ethnic Studies* 5 (Winter 1978): 24–26. Kessner and Caroli found that in both the 1880 and the 1905 samples for New York, 6 percent of Italian wives were working.

66. The Commission data were actually gathered in 1907–8. "Immigrants in Cities," vol. 2, Table 401, pp. 546–47. See also U.S. Congress, Senate, *Report on Condition of Woman and Child Wage-Earners in the United States*, vol. 2, Senate Doc. 645, 61st Cong., 2d sess. (Washington, D.C., 1911), Tables XII, XXVIII, pp. 66–67, 221, 364–65, 836–37; Caroline Manning, *The Immigrant Woman and Her Job*, U.S. Department of Labor, Women's Bureau, Bulletin 74 (Washington, D.C.,

1930). Manning's survey of immigrant women at work in Philadelphia between 1923 and 1925 shows that Jewish and Italian wives were the least likely of all immigrants to be working for wages. For a good discussion of the relationship between husband's income and the tendency of married women to work, see Elizabeth H. Pleck, "A Mother's Wages: Income Earning among Married Italian and Black Women, 1896–1911," in Elizabeth H. Pleck and Nancy F. Cott, eds., *A Heritage of Her Own: Towards a New Social History of American Women* (New York, 1979), pp. 367–92.

67. The Immigration Commission does not provide data on desertion rates, but the *Report on Condition of Woman and Child Wage-Earners in the United States*, 2: 635, suggests that Jewish households had a much higher rate of deserted or widowed wives (24 percent) than Italians (12 percent). Reena Sigman Friedman, who has studied the question of Jewish immigrant desertion, attributes the high rate of male deserters to the long separation endured by families when men emigrated to America before their wives and to the consequent impatience of more Americanized husbands with the slower assimilation of wives. The desertion problem reached alarming dimensions in the period between 1900 and 1911, when about 15 percent of the annual budgets of Jewish charities was devoted to desertion cases. In 1911 a National Desertion Bureau was established to coordinate efforts to cope with the problem. See Friedman, " 'Send Me My Husband Who Is in New York City': Husband Desertion in the American Jewish Immigrant Community, 1900–1926," *Jewish Social Studies* 44 (Winter 1982): 1–18.

68. *Reports of the Immigration Commission*, "Immigrants in Cities," vol. 1: Table 401, pp. 546–47, Table 79, p. 139, Table 46, p. 87. Cities surveyed were New York, Philadelphia, Boston, Chicago, Buffalo, Cleveland, and Milwaukee. Judith Smith also found a different pattern for Providence. There Italians were more likely to keep boarders than Jews, but both groups preferred to give the wage-earning role to daughters rather than mothers. *Family Connections*, pp. 62–77. See also Miriam Cohen, "Italian-American Women in New York City: From Workshop to Office," in Milton Cantor and Bruce Laurie, eds., *Class, Sex, and the Woman Worker* (Westport, Conn., 1977).

69. U.S. Congress (Senate), *Report on Condition of Woman and Child Wage-Earners in the United States*, vol. 2 (Men's Ready Made Clothing Industry) (Washington, D.C., 1911), p. 540, Table 3. See also pp. 635, 653, Table 28. Cities include New York, Chicago, Baltimore, and Rochester. For another set of data covering Jewish and Italian families over a much longer time (1915–40), see Smith, *Family Connections*, pp. 76–77.

70. Virginia Yans-McLaughlin notes in the case of Buffalo Italians that even though many wives were engaged in part-time work in canneries, this wage-earning activity was not often reported to census takers. *Family and Community*, p. 202.

71. For similar behavior among southern Italians, see Virginia Yans-McLaughlin, "Italian Women and Work: Experience and Perception," in Cantor and Laurie, eds., *Class, Sex, and the Woman Worker*.

72. Interview with Florence Beer by the author, Los Angeles, Calif., June 8, 1981. On the need for a wife to protect her modesty in the presence of other men, and the probability that this was a restraint on a wife's ability to work in a factory, see Kessner and Caroli, "The New Immigrant Woman at Work," p. 25.

73. Yans-McLaughlin, *Family and Community*, pp. 180–83; and "Italian Women and Work: Experience and Perception."

74. Rose Pesotta, *Days of Our Lives* (Boston, 1958), p. 172.

75. See A. H. Fromenson, "Some Real Needs of the East Side," *Jewish Charity* 3 (Feb. 1904): 105–8; Abraham Osuroff, "Jewish Day Nurseries," in *Jewish Communal Register* (Kehilla), p. 1027. For a good discussion of the lack of adequate childcare arrangements for urban working women in general, see Tentler, *Wage-Earning Women*, pp. 161–65.

76. Mary Kingsbury Simkhovitch, *The City Worker's World in America* (New York, 1917), p. 105.

77. Anzia Yezierska, *Bread Givers* (1925; repr. New York, 1975), p. 8.

78. Elizabeth Ewen, *Immigrant Women in the Land of Dollars: Life and Culture on the Lower East Side, 1890–1925* (New York, 1985), pp. 149–55.

79. Jennie Matyas interview, p. 18.

80. For a comparison of the earnings of homeworkers and factory workers in the men's clothing industry, see *Report on Condition of Woman and Child Wage-Earners*, 2: 220.

81. Ephraim Wagner, "The Village Boy," unpub. autobiography, p. 156, YIVO Archives. See also Kessner, *The Golden Door*, p. 76.

82. Elizabeth Stern, *My Mother and I* (New York, 1917), p. 21.

83. Cohen, *Out of the Shadow*, p. 73.

84. See *Reports of the Immigration Commission*, "Immigrants in Cities," vol. 1: Summaries of Seven Cities, Table 50, pp. 94–95. See also *Report on Condition of Woman and Child Wage-Earners*, 2: 221, 374; United States Commission on Industrial Relations, *Reports*, vol. 2: "Men's Garment Trades in New York City," Senate Doc. 415, 64th Cong., 1st sess. (Washington, 1916), pp. 2004, 2018, 1794, 2013. On family shops see Abraham Bisno, *Union Pioneer* (Madison, Wisc., 1967), p. 48.

85. *Report on Condition of Woman and Child Wage-Earners*, 2: 221. See also Mary Van Kleeck, "Child Labor in Home Industries," in National Child Labor Committee, *Child Employing Industries*, Proceedings of the Sixth Annual Conference, Boston, January 1910 (New York, 1910), p. 148. Van Kleeck notes that most homeworkers in New York were Italians, as does Kessner, *The Golden Door*, pp. 73–74.

86. Elizabeth C. Watson, "Homework in the Tenements," *The Survey*, Feb. 4, 1911, p. 774. See also *Reports of the Immigration Commission*, "Immigrants in Cities," vol. 1, Table 52, p. 96.

87. See Willett, *Employment of Women in the Clothing Trade*, p. 253; Kessner, *The Golden Door*, p. 76. Barbara Klazynska discusses the importance of Italian *padrones* in distributing homework to Italian women in their apartments. Usually the women were family or friends of the padrone or lived in the same building with him. She notes that the same padrone who found homework for women in Philadelphia found jobs for men on the railroads. See "Why Women Work: A Comparison of Various Groups—Philadelphia, 1910–1930," *Labor History* 17 (Winter 1976): 76–78.

88. *Reports of the Immigration Commission*, "Immigrants in Cities," vol. 2, Table 401, p. 546.

89. See unpub. doc. J-R 301, vol. 11, April 1, 1949, p. 1, RCC; and Bisno, *Union Pioneer*, p. 16, on the practice of taking in boarders in eastern Europe.

90. Unpub. doc. J-R 344, vol. 7, July 1949, pp. 1–2, RCC.

91. Tape I-117, New York City Immigrant Labor History Project of the City University Oral History Research Project, Robert F. Wagner Labor Archives, Bobst Library, New York University. Hereafter cited as NYCILHP.

92. For an elaboration of the work/business distinction among Jewish immigrants, see my Ph.D. diss., "The Working Life of Immigrants: Women in the American Garment Industry, 1880–1920" (University of California, Berkeley, 1983). Sydney Weinberg has subsequently discussed this theme in *World of Our Mothers* (Chapel Hill, N.C., 1988), pp. 238–39.

93. Interview with Pearl Kramer (pseud.) by the author, Los Angeles, Calif., June 8, 1981.

94. Interview with Mollie Millman (pseud.) by the author, Oakland, Calif., Nov. 4, 1980.

95. Interview with Mollie Linker, in Kramer and Masur, eds., *Jewish Grandmothers*, p. 100.

96. Interview with May Horowitz by the author, Los Angeles, June 7, 1981. See also Sara Abrams, unpub. autobiography, p. 3, YIVO Archives, and Baum et al., *The Jewish Woman in America*, p. 98.

97. Charlotte Baum, "What Made Yetta Work? The Economic Role of Eastern European Jewish Women in the Family," *Response* no. 18 (Summer 1973): 36. Judith Smith's sample of the occupations of 72 Jewish wives in Providence covers 1915–40 and shows that 11 percent listed their occupation as "storekeeper." *Family Connections*, p. 77.

98. Percentages are as follows: Chicago 45 percent (vol. 1, Table 62, p. 309), New York 26 percent (vol. 1, Table 56, p. 217), Philadelphia 48 percent (vol. 1, Table 53, p. 397), *Reports of the Immigration Commission*, "Immigrants in Cities."

99. *Jewish Daily Courier*, July 8, 1912, trans. in Works Progress Administration, Foreign Language Press Survey, Box 24, Regenstein Library, University of Chicago.

100. Wirth, *The Ghetto*, p. 236; Baum et al., *The Jewish Woman in America*, p. 100, describes the scene on New York's East Side.

101. Yans-McLaughlin, *Family and Community*, pp. 214–15.

102. *Sholom Aleykhem tsu Immigranten*, Educational Alliance (New York, 1903), pp. 36–37.

103. Abraham Cahan, *The Rise of David Levinsky* (1917; repr. New York, 1960), pp. 96–97.

104. Yezierska, *Bread Givers*, p. 48. For insights into the position of the Torah scholar and the rabbi in America see Hutchins Hapgood, *The Spirit of the Ghetto* (1902; repr. Cambridge, Mass., 1967), pp. 44–70.

105. Interview with May Horowitz by the author.

106. On the image of the "lady" in Jewish immigrant fiction, see Baum et al., *The Jewish Woman in America*, pp. 193–204.

107. Figures for seven cities total 101 percent due to rounding. The Boston figures, calculated from several related tables, show 359 women age 16 or older, of whom 113 or 31.5 percent worked. See vol. 2, Table 397, p. 505, "Immigrants in

Cities." Of the same 359 women, 81 were single and 278 were married or widowed (vol. 2, Table 8, p. 29). The commission reported that 14.6 percent of Jewish wives in Boston worked (vol. 1, Table 60). This means that there were 41 working wives and 72 unmarried working women in the sample. These 72 unmarried working women equal 89 percent of all single women in the sample. Although exact statistics on the percentage of unmarried daughters in the other six cities are not available, the overall rate of female employment in each city is comparable to Boston. Yet outside of Boston, the rate of married women's employment is often lower. This suggests that unless the ratio of married to unmarried women in Boston was unique, the proportion of unmarried working daughters in these cities should have been just as high.

108. The remaining 53 percent of girls aged 14–15 were in school. See "Immigrants in Cities," vol. 2, Table 398, p. 521. Thirty-three percent of Jewish boys in the same age group were at work (Table 398, p. 513).

109. The census material appears in Howe, *World of Our Fathers*, p. 142.

110. Mark Zborowski and Elizabeth Herzog, *Life Is with People: The Jewish Little Town of Eastern Europe* (New York, 1952), p. 347.

111. On the place of women in the synagogue see May Edel, "Marriage and the Family," unpub. doc. J-77, vol. 7, n.d., p. 18, RCC.

112. Zborowski and Herzog, *Life Is with People*, pp. 348–49, 278–79, 285.

113. Ibid., pp. 278–79.

114. In eastern Europe the forces of modernization led some women to abandon Orthodox customs. Even so, there was still a strong community sentiment favoring traditional ways. Women in Europe who did not go to the *Mikveh* or who wore their own hair were clearly in conflict with the force of tradition. See Lucy Robins Lang, *Tomorrow Is Beautiful* (New York, 1948), p. 9. Among immigrant wives in America, the first step toward assimilation was usually abandoning Old World styles of dress, including the wig. This did not mean, however, that the fundamental notion of a married woman's need for modesty and piety was abandoned as well. On the dress and customs of Orthodox women in America see Hapgood, *Spirit of the Ghetto*, pp. 73–76.

115. May Edel, "Marriage and the Family," unpub. doc. J-R 32, p. 8, RCC. See also Pesotta, *Days of Our Lives*, pp. 169, 172.

116. The cases handled by the Joint Relief Committee and a summary of their conclusions about the economic role of Jewish and Italian immigrant daughters are found in "Report of the Joint Relief Committee, Ladies Waist and Dressmakers' Union, Local 25, on the Triangle Fire Disaster" (New York, Jan. 15, 1913). A copy of the report is in the Archives of the International Ladies' Garment Workers' Union, Catherwood Library, Cornell University. See also Elizabeth Dutcher, "Budgets of the Triangle Fire Victims," *Life and Labor* 2 (Sept. 1912), and "Visitors' Reports on Triangle Fire Victims and Their Families," in Leonora O'Reilly Papers (Reel 13), Schlesinger Library, Radcliffe College.

117. Dutcher, "Budgets of the Triangle Fire Victims," pp. 265–66. See also "Report of the Joint Relief Committee," p. 8; Leon Stein, *The Triangle Fire* (Philadelphia, 1962), pp. 124–25.

118. "Report of the Joint Relief Committee," p. 12.

119. Ibid., p. 24.

120. Dutcher, "Budgets of the Triangle Fire Victims," p. 267.

121. *Report on Condition of Woman and Child Wage-Earners*, vol. 1, "Men's Ready Made Clothing Industry," Table 27, pp. 782–819; figures were taken from tables on New York and Philadelphia. In all cities surveyed by the Labor Bureau, 70 percent of Jewish fathers were employed, and 97 percent of Jewish women over age 16 were employed. The majority of Jewish families included in this study had one or more working daughters (see pp. 634–37). The data were collected in 1908. See also *Reports of the Immigration Commission*, vol. 1, "Immigrants in Cities," pp. 232–33. The Immigration Commission data on New York City show that among Jewish immigrants only 20 percent of the 296 Russian Jewish fathers surveyed could support their families without the help of working children. The study also found that more than any other group, Jews depended on the wages of their children. For a summary of contemporary studies on the family contributions of young working women, see Tentler, *Wage-Earning Women*, pp. 87–93, 218–19. Tentler does not break down her analysis by ethnic groups, however.

122. *Report on Condition of Woman and Child Wage-Earners*, vol. 2, Table 13, pp. 652–53. Jewish daughters gave an average of 89 percent of their earnings to the family fund, sons only 70 percent.

123. Records of the U.S. Department of Labor, Woman's Bureau, unpub. material for Bulletin 74, Schedule 7-1-7, Record Group 86, National Archives.

124. Interview with Mollie Millman by the author.

125. Interview with Nettie Licht by the author, Redondo Beach, Calif., Nov. 25, 1978.

126. "Arbitration Proceedings between the Ladies' Dress and Waist Manufacturers Association and the International Ladies' Garment Workers' Union," Feb. 5 and 7, 1916, New York. Unpub. transcript, International Ladies' Garment Workers' Union, Research Dept., New York. The union surveyed the living conditions and expenses of 700 single women in the New York shirtwaist factories. The majority were Jewish.

127. Interviews with Nettie Licht and Mollie Millman by the author.

128. *Report on Condition of Woman and Child Wage-Earners*, "Men's Ready Made Clothing Industry", vol. 2, Table 13, pp. 652–53.

129. "The 1909 Strike" (anon.), in Andria Taylor Hourwich and Gladys L. Palmer, eds., *I Am a Woman Worker: A Scrapbook of Autobiographies* (mimeographed), Affiliated Schools for Workers, Inc. (New York, 1936), p. 111.

130. Interview with Dora Bayrack by the author.

131. Cohen, *Out of the Shadow*, pp. 69–70.

132. Unpub. doc. J-198, vol. 12, 1949, pp. 3, 5, RCC.

133. Interview with Fannie Shapiro, in Kramer and Masur, eds., *Jewish Grandmothers*, p. 10.

134. U.S. Department of Labor, Woman's Bureau, unpub. material for Bulletin 74, Schedule 7-2-214, Record Group 86, National Archives.

135. See Forest Chester Ensign, *Compulsory School Attendance and Child Labor* (Iowa City, 1921), p. 134; Selma Berrol, "Education and Economic Mobility: The Jewish Experience in New York City, 1880–1920," *American Jewish Historical Society Quarterly* 65 (March 1976): 259; Jeremy P. Felt, *Hostages of Fortune: Child Labor Reform in New York* (Syracuse, N.Y., 1965), chap. 5; and Miriam

Cohen, "Changing Educational Strategies among Migrant Generations: New York Italians in Comparative Perspective," p. 13, paper delivered at the annual meeting of the American Historical Association, San Francisco, Dec. 1978.

136. Ella Wolff interview, p. 1, Amerikaner Yiddishe Geshikhte Bel-Pe, YIVO Archives. See also Rebecca August, unpub. autobiography, p. 1, YIVO Archives.

137. Among daughters born in Europe (first generation), 53 percent of the 14- and 15-year-olds were at school, and 39 percent worked. Among native-born daughters of immigrant parents (second generation), 62 percent in the same age group were in school and only 26 percent worked. A small number of girls in both generations were reported "at home." See *Reports of the Immigration Commission*, "Immigrants in Cities," vol. 2, Table 398, and vol. 1, Table 75, p. 134. Settlement house worker Lillian Wald noted in 1893 that there were many Jewish families on New York's Lower East Side who completely neglected their children's schooling. There were "entire families," she found, where not one child had even stepped into a schoolroom. Lillian Wald to Jacob Schiff, Oct. 2, 1893, Case Reports, Box 2, Lillian Wald Papers, New York Public Library. According to Selma Berrol, "Education and Economic Mobility," the number of Jewish immigrant children in school varied with the time of immigrant arrival and the force of the law. See also Tentler, *Wage-Earning Women*, pp. 93–96.

138. Antin, *Promised Land*, pp. 200–201.

139. Interview with Mollie Linker, in Kramer and Masur, eds., *Jewish Grandmothers*, p. 94.

140. Jennie Matyas interview, pp. 20, 58.

141. Sara Abrams, unpub. autobiography, p. 12, YIVO Archives. For fictional treatments of this theme see Arthur Bullard [Albert Edwards], *Comrade Yetta* (New York, 1913); Bertha Levy, "Regina's Disappointment," *The Ladies' Garment Worker* 4 (Sept. 1913).

142. Letter to the *Jewish Daily Forward*, quoted in Metzker, *A Bintl Brief*, pp. 65–66.

143. Records of the Department of Labor, Woman's Bureau, unpub. material for Bulletin 74, Schedules 7-6-447; 7-2-241 (Tannenbaum), Record Group 86, National Archives. See also Bliss, "Intimate Studies in the Lives of Fifty Working Girls," p. 101.

144. "How and Why I Chose My First Job," *The Bryn Mawr Daisy* 2 (June 8, 1922): 5. Bryn Mawr School for Women Workers, Hilda Smith Papers, Schlesinger Library, Radcliffe College.

Chapter 3. Unwritten Laws

1. Sam Liptzin, *Tales of a Tailor: Humor and Tragedy in the Struggles of the Early Immigrants against the Sweatshop*, trans. Max Rosenfeld (New York, 1965), pp. 71–72.

2. See *Reports of the Immigration Commission*, vol. 11, "Immigrants in Industry" (Clothing Manufacture), 61st Cong. (Senate), 2d sess. (Washington, D.C., 1911), pp. 259, 266–69; Irving Howe, *World of Our Fathers* (New York, 1976), p. 154; and Niles Carpenter, *Immigrants and Their Children*, Census Monographs 7 (Washington, D.C., 1927), p. 287. A good overview of the growth of the

garment industry work force is *Census Reports* 11, Twelfth Census of the United States (1900), Manufactures, part III, Special Reports on Selected Industries (Clothing) (Washington, D.C., 1902).

3. For a contrasting view emphasizing a distinct, sex-segregated labor market for young working women see Leslie Woodcock Tentler, *Wage-Earning Women: Industrial Work and Family Life in the United States, 1900–1930* (New York, 1979), p. 14. Tentler's study was not industry-specific but looked at women wage earners in the aggregate. Certainly there are examples of occupations and industries employing both sexes which did have distinct boundaries between men's and women's work. For example, Patricia Cooper found that in this period, most women in the cigar industry occupied a separate labor market, working on cheap cigars in sex-segregated factories. *Once a Cigar Maker: Men, Women, and Work Culture in American Cigar Factories, 1900–1919* (Urbana, Ill., 1987), pp. 161–62.

4. On the emergence and development of the American garment industry see Egal Feldman, *Fit for Men: A Study of New York's Clothing Trade* (Washington, D.C., 1960), esp. pp. 1–10, 90–111; Louis Levine, *The Women's Garment Workers* (New York, 1924), pp. 1–17; Joel Seidman, *The Needle Trades* (New York, 1942), pp. 3–30; *Census Reports* 9, Twelfth Census (1900), Manufactures, part III, Special Reports on Selected Industries (Clothing); Jesse E. Pope, *The Clothing Industry in New York* (Columbia, Mo., 1905), chap. 1; and Steve Fraser, "Combined and Uneven Development in the Men's Clothing Industry," *Business History Review* 57 (Winter 1983): 522–47.

5. See *Census Reports* 9, Twelfth Census (1900), Manufactures, part III, Special Reports on Selected Industries (Clothing), p. 299; U.S. Bureau of Labor, *Regulation and Restriction of Output*, Eleventh Special Report of the Commissioner of Labor (Washington, D.C., 1904), pp. 537–39, 551. For a good overview of the impact of technology on the evolution of the clothing industry see Rosara Lucy Passero, "Ethnicity in the Men's Ready-Made Clothing Industry, 1880–1940: The Italian Experience in Philadelphia" (Ph.D. diss., University of Pennsylvania, 1978), pp. 26–30.

6. Seidman, *The Needle Trades*, Appendix, Table 1, p. 335, Table 6, p. 340; Feldman, *Fit for Men*, pp. 93, 100, 110; Pope, *The Clothing Industry in New York*, pp. 3, 23–24; and Twelfth Census, vol. 9 (1900), Special Reports (Clothing).

7. See *Reports of the Immigration Commission*, "Immigrants in Industry," p. 271, Table 13, p. 282; U.S. Congress, Senate, *Report on Condition of Woman and Child Wage-Earners in the United States*, vol. 2, 61st Cong., 2d sess. (Washington, D.C., 1911), pp. 46–47, 57; U.S. Commission on Industrial Relations, *Reports*, vol. 2, "Men's Garment Trades in New York City," 64th Cong., 1st sess. (Washington, D.C., 1916), pp. 2016, 2032; Mary Van Kleeck, "Women and Children Who Make Men's Clothing," *The Survey* 26 (April 1, 1911): 68; *Special Report on Sanitary Conditions in Shops of the Dress and Waist Industry*, May 1913, A Preliminary Report of the Joint Board of Sanitary Control in the Dress and Waist Industry (New York, 1913), p. 7; and George M. Price, "A General Survey of the Sanitary Conditions in the Cloak Industry," *First Annual Report of the Joint Board of Sanitary Control in the Cloak, Suit, and Skirt Industry of Greater New York* (New York, 1911), p. 39.

8. Arcadius Kahan, "Economic Opportunities and Some Pilgrims' Progress:

268 Notes to Chapter 3

Jewish Immigrants from Eastern Europe in the U.S., 1890–1914," Journal of Economic History 38 (March 1978): 235–51; Elias Tcherikower, ed., The Early Jewish Labor Movement in the United States, trans. and rev. Aaron Antonovsky (New York, 1971), pp. 163, 174; Pope, The Clothing Industry in New York, pp. 27, 52–53, 63; Levine, The Women's Garment Workers, p. 17; Wilfred Carsel, A History of the Chicago Ladies' Garment Workers Union (Chicago, 1940), pp. 4–7; and Passero, "Ethnicity in the Men's Clothing Industry," pp. 36–37.

9. Schlesinger is quoted in "Manufacturers, Contractors, and Sub-Manufacturers in the Cloak Trade," trans. of article from the *Jewish Daily Forward,* June 10, 1913. Copy in Paul Abelson's papers, Box 9, Labor Management Documentation Center (LMDC), Catherwood Library, Cornell University.

10. Data from the 1914 Federal Census of Manufactures are discussed in detail in J. M. Budish and George Soule, *The New Unionism in the Clothing Industry* (1920; repr. New York, 1968), pp. 33–34. Figures on the size of firms at the turn of the century can be found in *Census Reports,* Twelfth Census (1900), Special Report on Selected Industries, Tables 4 and 17. See also B. M. Selekman et al., *Regional Plan, the Clothing and Textile Industries in New York and Its Environs* (New York, 1925), pp. 21–22, 34, 54–55, 60; Seidman, *Needle Trades,* p. 120; and New York (State) Factory Investigation Commission, *Preliminary Report* 2 (Albany, 1916), p. 581. A good source for comparing the small size of garment factories to the scale of operations in other American industries is Daniel Nelson, *Managers and Workers: Origins of the New Factory System in the United States* (Madison, Wisc., 1975), pp. 3–5.

11. Steve Fraser provides an important analysis of the decentralized development of the industry and the implications for the kinds of immigrant business cultures that evolved. See "Combined and Uneven Development in the Men's Clothing Industry."

12. On the business practices that fostered decentralization see Levine, *The Women's Garment Workers,* pp. 383–89; Seidman, *The Needle Trades,* pp. 4–5, 9–10; Selekman et al., *Regional Plan of New York and Its Environs,* pp. 21–22, 34, 54–55, and passim; Fraser, "Combined and Uneven Development."

13. Abraham Bisno, *Union Pioneer* (Madison, Wisc., 1967), p. 48.

14. New York Women's Trade Union League, "Unpublished Investigation," n.d. [c. 1914], p. 9, copy in Mary Dreier Papers, Box 9, Schlesinger Library, Radcliffe College.

15. See Levine, *Women's Garment Workers,* p. 170; Melech Epstein, *Jewish Labor in the U.S.A.: An Industrial, Political and Cultural History of the Jewish Labor Movement, 1882–1914* (2 vols. in 1) (New York, 1969), p. 395.

16. Abraham Cahan, *The Rise of David Levinsky* (1917; repr. New York, 1960), p. 373.

17. Jacob Riis, *How the Other Half Lives: Studies among the Tenements of New York* (1890; repr. New York, 1971), p. 97.

18. Goldie Share, "My First Job," *Bryn Mawr Daisy* 2 (June 8, 1922), Hilda Smith Papers, Schlesinger Library, Radcliffe College.

19. Questionnaires for Union Members, Aaron Antonovsky Papers, YIVO Archives, New York City.

20. Interview with Mollie Steinholtz by Taffie Viner, tape 1, side A, March

1974, Feminist History Research Project, Topanga, Calif. Hereafter cited as FHRP.

21. Records of the U.S. Department of Labor, Woman's Bureau, unpub. material for Bulletin 74, Schedules 7-2-137 and 7-2-135, Record Group 86, National Archives.

22. Ibid., Schedule 7-2-127.

23. Interview 1 with Lottie Spitzer by Kristine Feichtinger, side A, July 18, 1974. FHRP.

24. Riis, *How the Other Half Lives*, pp. 91–92; William Leiserson, "History of the Jewish Labor Movement in New York" (M.A. thesis, Columbia University, 1908). A copy is in the YIVO Archives. An excerpt is printed in Leon Stein, *Out of the Sweatshop: The Struggle for Industrial Democracy* (New York, 1977), pp. 41–42; See also Epstein, *Jewish Labor in the U.S.A.*, pp. 100–101; Cahan, *The Education of Abraham Cahan*, p. 220. Sam Liptzin, in his reminiscences about New York's tailoring trade, claims that the Hester Park pig market got its name because everything, including "scab" labor, could be purchased there. See *Tales of a Tailor*, p. 22.

25. Joseph Breslau, "A Presser's Past," in *Garment Workers Speak*, I.L.G.W.U. Education Department, n.d. [c. 1938], in Fannia Cohn Papers, Box 12, New York Public Library; Ephraim Wagner, "The Village Boy," unpub. autobiography, p. 165, YIVO Archives; Selig Perlman, "Unorganized Labor Exchanges in New York," unpub. testimony, U.S. Commission on Industrial Relations, *Reports*, 1912–15, microfilm reel 5, LMDC, Catherwood Library, Cornell University. On the *birze* see Henry J. Tobias, *The Jewish Bund from Its Origins to 1905* (Stanford, Calif., 1972), p. 101.

26. Rose Schneiderman with Lucy Goldthwaite, *All for One* (New York, 1967), pp. 35, 43; Sara Abrams, unpub. autobiography, p. 13, YIVO Archives; Wilfred Carsel, *A History of the Chicago Ladies' Garment Workers Union*, p. 7; and Tcherikower, ed., *Early Jewish Labor Movement*, p. 143. The job placement activities of Jewish charities are chronicled in *The Jewish Communal Register* (Kehilla) (New York, 1918).

27. Advertisements for jobs in garment shops and factories appeared regularly in the classified ads of the *Jewish Daily Forward*. The examples used here appear in the classified ad page for Feb. 1, 1909. The gap between the promise and reality of job advertisements is discussed in the unpublished autobiography of Isidore Wisotsky, "Such a Life," p. 88, YIVO Archives; see also Louise Odencrantz, *Italian Women in Industry: A Study of Conditions in New York City* (New York, 1919), pp. 43–44.

28. U.S. Department of Labor, Woman's Bureau, unpub. material for Bulletin 74, Schedule 7-2-165, Record Group 86, National Archives. Another description of the search for work in neighborhood shops can be found in Bessie Kriegberg, unpub. autobiography, p. 286, YIVO Archives.

29. Philip Armon, unpub. autobiography, p. 4, YIVO Archives.

30. U.S. Department of Labor, unpub. material for Bulletin 74, Schedule 7-2-173, Record Group 86, National Archives.

31. Although there has been much debate among feminist scholars about the origins of sex-typing in industry, only a few studies look at the problem from a historical, industry-specific perspective. These include Ruth Milkman, *Gender at Work* (Urbana, Ill., 1987); Ava Baron, "Women and the Making of the American

Working Class: A Study of the Proletarianization of Printers," *Review of Radical Political Economies* 14 (Fall 1982): 23–42; Patricia Cooper, *Once a Cigar Maker: Men, Women, and Work Culture in American Cigar Factories, 1900–1919* (Urbana, Ill., 1987); and Mary Blewett, *Men, Women, and Work: Class, Gender, and Protest in the New England Shoe Industry, 1780–1910* (Urbana, Ill., 1988).

32. On developments in the United States see Helen Sumner, *History of Women in Industry*, in *Report on the Condition of Woman and Child Wage-Earners*, 11 (Washington, D.C., 1910), p. 144; Feldman, *Fit for Men*, pp. 93–111; Robert James Myers, "The Economic Aspects of the Production of Men's Clothing (with Particular Reference to the Industry in Chicago)" (Ph.D. diss., University of Chicago, 1937), pp. 67–84.

33. U.S. Bureau of Labor Statistics, *Bulletin* 143, p. 159. One immigrant woman claimed that most workers in the children's dress industry had sewn the entire garment. Tape I-108, New York City Immigrant Labor History Project (NYCILHP), Wagner Archives, Bobst Library, New York University.

34. See Hirsch Abramovitch, "Rural Jewish Occupations in Lithuania," *YIVO Annual of Jewish Social Science* 2–3 (1947–48), esp. p. 206; Jewish Colonization Association, *Recueil de matériaux sur la situation économique des Israelites de Russie* (Paris, 1906–8), 2 vols., 1: 246. Even in the city of Moscow (off-limits to most Jewish workers), the largest ready-made clothing manufacturers refrained from introducing an extensive subdivision of labor and used hand workers more often than machine operators. See E. A. Oliunina, "The Tailoring Trade in Moscow and the Villages of Moscow and Riazan Provinces: Material on the History of Domestic Industry in Russia" (Moscow, 1914), trans. and ed. Victoria E. Bonnell in *The Russian Worker: Life and Labor under the Tsarist Regime* (Berkeley, Calif., 1983), pp. 154–83.

35. Tentler, *Wage-Earning Women*, p. 31.

36. Bisno, *Union Pioneer*, p. 237.

37. Ibid. See also U.S. Bureau of Labor, Eleventh Special Report, *Regulation and Restriction of Output*, p. 548; *Report on Condition of Woman and Child Wage-Earners*, 2, "Men's Ready-Made Clothing," p. 424 and passim; *Report of the Industrial Relations Commission on the Relations and Conditions of Capital and Labor*, 7, Clothing Manufacture (Sweatshops), 56th Cong. (House), 2d sess. (Washington, D.C., 1901), p. 187; and Edna Bryner, *The Garment Trades* (Cleveland, 1916), p. 13.

38. Bisno, *Union Pioneer*, p. 237.

39. U.S. Bureau of Labor, Eleventh Special Report, *Regulation and Restriction of Output*, p. 548. See also Ernest Poole, "Task Work Bowing to Factory System," *The Outlook* (Nov. 21, 1903), repr. in Allon Schoener, ed., *Portal to America: The Lower East Side, 1870–1925* (New York, 1967), pp. 169–70.

40. Section work was common in workrooms turning out cheap or standardized garments. It was especially important in the making of men's clothing, undergarments, and certain types of shirtwaists. But the actual organization of work varied dramatically from one shop to the next. See the descriptions in Pearl Goodman and Elsa Ueland, "The Shirtwaist Trade," *Journal of Political Economy* (Dec. 1910): 818–19; *Report on Condition of Woman and Child Wage-Earners*, 2: 447, 462; and Pope, *The Clothing Industry in New York*, pp. 70–71.

41. Cleo Murtland, "A Study of the Dress and Waist Industry for the Purpose of

Industrial Education" (Appendix I), U.S. Bureau of Labor Statistics, *Bulletin* 145 (Washington, D.C., 1914), pp. 157–59; Katherine Tyng, "The Processes and Organization of Work in Dress and Waist Manufacture," *Special Report on Sanitary Conditions in the Dress and Waist Industry,* May 1913, A Preliminary Report of the Joint Board of Sanitary Control in the Dress and Waist Industry (New York, 1913); and New York (State) Factory Investigating Commission, *Preliminary Report,* 3 (Albany, 1912), p. 1784.

42. Marie Ganz with Nat Ferber, *Rebels into Anarchy and Out Again* (New York, 1920), pp. 93–94.

43. As reported by Mary Van Kleeck, *A Seasonal Industry: A Study of the Millinery Trade in New York* (New York, 1917), pp. 148–49.

44. *Proceedings of the Council of Jewish Women,* Fifth Triennial Convention, 1908, Cincinnati, Ohio, p. 155. See also Odencrantz, *Italian Women in Industry,* for similar problems experienced by Italians in adjusting older work patterns to new industrial routines.

45. Viola Paradise, "The Jewish Immigrant Girl in Chicago," *The Survey* 30 (Sept. 6, 1913): 701.

46. On women needleworkers and female craft traditions in southern Italy see Columba Marie Furio, "Immigrant Women and Industry: A Case Study. Italian Immigrant Women in the Garment Industry, 1890–1950" (Ph.D. diss., New York University, 1979), p. 58, and Elizabeth Ewen, *Immigrant Women in the Land of Dollars: Life and Culture on the Lower East Side, 1890–1925* (New York, 1985), pp. 244–45.

47. Interview with Mollie Wexler by Sherna Gluck, tape 1, side B, Nov. 22, 1972, FHRP.

48. Ibid.; see also "The Wrapper Industry," *The Ladies' Garment Worker* 1 (Oct. 1910): 2.

49. Interview with Lottie Spitzer by Kristine Feichtinger, Interview 1, p. 1, FHRP.

50. F. E. Sheldon, *A Souvenir Journal of the Strike of the Ladies Waistmakers' Union* (New York, 1910), pp. 2–3; Elizabeth Hasanovitz, *One of Them: Chapters from a Passionate Autobiography* (Boston, 1918), p. 55.

51. See the statement by a former employee of the Triangle Shirtwaist Co. in Leon Stein, *The Triangle Fire* (Philadelphia, 1962), p. 161. See also Hasanovitz, *One of Them,* p. 120.

52. U.S. Commission on Industrial Relations, *Reports,* 2: 2011.

53. U.S. Bureau of Labor Statistics, *Bulletin* 146, "Wages and Regularity of Employment and Standardization of Piece Rates in the Dress and Waist Industry: New York City" (Washington, D.C., 1914), pp. 145–48; U.S. Commission on Industrial Relations, *Reports,* 4 (The Women's Garment Industry in Philadelphia), Becky Stein Testimony, p. 3156.

54. "Jennie Matyas and the I.L.G.W.U.," interview with Jennie Matyas by Corinne Gilb, p. 31, Industrial Relations Library, University of California, Berkeley. (Hereafter cited as Jennie Matyas interview.)

55. Hasanovitz, *One of Them,* p. 120.

56. On the cigar industry see Cooper, *Once a Cigar Maker,* esp. chap. 6. On printers see Baron, "Women and the Making of the American Working Class."

57. On this point see Mary Christine Stansell, "Women of the Laboring Poor in

New York City, 1820–1860" (Ph.D. diss., Yale University, 1979), pp. 62–63, 111–12; Feldman, *Fit for Men,* pp. 95, 98; Bruce Laurie, *The Working People of Philadelphia, 1800–1850* (Philadelphia, 1980), p. 86; and Pope, *The Clothing Industry in New York,* pp. 13, 21.

58. I am grateful to costume historian Pat Trautman at the University of Connecticut for this information.

59. Stansell, "Women of the Laboring Poor," pp. 62–63.

60. Sumner, *History of Women in Industry,* p. 144.

61. This transition appears to have begun during the Civil War, when machine production of women's clothing brought unskilled men into traditional women's trades such as dressmaking. See Alice Kessler-Harris, *Out to Work: A History of Wage-Earning Women in the United States* (New York, 1982), p. 78.

62. Nancy Green found a similar pattern in the development of the ready-made women's clothing industry in turn-of-the-century Paris, where east European Jewish immigrant tailors came to dominate a trade that had been the traditional province of French women. Green notes that in Paris, women's-wear tailors mainly came from eastern and central Europe, where men had always sewn women's clothes. Nancy L. Green, *The Pletzl of Paris: Jewish Immigrant Workers in the Belle Epoque* (New York, 1986), pp. 39–41. A fascinating firsthand account of a Jewish tailor making custom-produced clothing for men and women in a small Jewish shtetl can be found in Tape I-134, NYCILHP, Wagner Archives, New York University. On the movement of immigrant men into the women's ready-made clothing industry in the United States see Levine, *Women's Garment Workers,* pp. 13, 171; U.S. Commission on Industrial Relations, *Reports,* 4: 3158–62; and *Census Reports* 9, Twelfth Census (1900), Manufactures, part III, pp. 283, 300.

63. According to the manager of the New York Joint Board of the Cloak Makers' Union, immigrant men who had completed their tailoring apprenticeships in the Old Country were the main source of new recruits in the shops. Geo. Wishnak to H. L. Sabsovich, Sept. 15, 1914, Baron de Hirsch Fund Papers, Box 56, American Jewish Historical Society, Brandeis University. Costume historians Claudia B. Kidwell and Margaret C. Christman argue that because making women's suits involved the same "tailoring techniques" used in sewing men's suits, these garments "had to be made by a male tailor" rather than a female dressmaker. *Suiting Everyone: The Democratization of Clothing in America* (Washington, D.C., 1974), p. 143. A similar process of native-born women's displacement by skilled male needle workers from eastern and southern Europe occurred in the shoemaking industry in New England. See Mary Blewett, *Men, Women, and Work: Class, Gender, and Protest in the New England Shoe Industry, 1780–1910* (Urbana, Ill., 1988), pp. 317–18.

64. See George M. Price, "A General Survey of the Sanitary Conditions of the Cloak Industry," *First Annual Report of the Joint Board of Sanitary Control* (New York, 1911), p. 39; Levine, *Women's Garment Workers,* p. 11; "Proceedings of Arbitration Board on Working Conditions to Be Established in the Cloak, Suit and Skirt Industry of Chicago," Sept. 14, 1915, p. 26, transcript in Paul Abelson Papers, Labor-Management Documentation Center (LMDC), Catherwood Library, Cornell University; and U.S. Department of Labor, Bureau of Labor Statistics, *Bulletin* 183, "Regularity of Employment in the Women's Ready-to-Wear Garment Industries" (Washington, D.C., 1916), p. 17.

65. Interview with Rose Kaplan (Himmelfarb) by Sherna Gluck, Interview 1, side A, March 13, 1975, FHRP.

66. *Report on Condition of Woman and Child Wage-Earners*, 2: 38.

67. Liptzin, *Tales of a Tailor*, p. 71. See also Mabel Hurd Willett, *Women in the Clothing Trade* (New York, 1902), p. 68.

68. *Report on Condition of Woman and Child Wage-Earners*, 2: 444, 464, 471; Willett, *Women in the Clothing Trade*, pp. 54, 68–71. A similar pattern of ethnic variation in the handling of machine work occurred in Philadelphia. See Passero, "Ethnicity in the Men's Ready-Made Clothing Industry," pp. 224–26.

69. *Report on Condition of Woman and Child Wage-Earners*, 2: 431–33.

70. Van Kleeck, "Women and Children Who Make Men's Clothes," p. 67.

71. *Report on Condition of Woman and Child Wage-Earners*, 2: 445–51.

72. Interview with Lottie Spitzer by Kristine Feichtinger, Interview 1, p. 4, and Interview 7, p. 13, FHRP.

73. *Report on Condition of Woman and Child Wage-Earners*, 2: 478–80.

74. Interview with Agnes Budilovsky and Rose Falk by Kristine Feichtinger, Sept. 5, 1974, Interview 1, p. 2, FHRP. See also *Report on Condition of Woman and Child Wage-Earners*, 2: 463–64, 471–75.

75. Historians have overemphasized the dead-end nature of women's factory work. See, for example, Tentler, *Wage-Earning Women*, chap. 1. David Montgomery's recent study of skilled and unskilled factory workers restates the dead-end argument by noting that "the factory offered no prospects of a better job to the [female] pieceworker aside from a handful of positions as forewoman or trouble shooter . . ." (Montgomery, *Fall of the House of Labor* [Cambridge, 1987], p. 135).

76. See George M. Price, "Ten Years of Sanitary Self Control," *Tenth Annual Report of the Joint Board of Sanitary Control in the Cloak, Suit and Skirt, and the Dress and Waist Industries* (New York, 1921), p. 29; Levine, *Women's Garment Workers*, pp. 219–20.

77. Cleo Murtland, "A Study of the Dress and Waist Industry for the Purpose of Industrial Education," p. 159 and passim.

78. Minutes of the Joint Board of Grievances in the Dress and Waist Industry, Chief Clerk's Investigation, March 19, 1914, pp. 315–17 (transcript), ILGWU Research Dept., New York City.

79. Ibid., pp. 155–68. Immigrant women sometimes spoke of their ambitions to become designers. For example, tape 2, I-2, NYCILHP, Wagner Archives, Bobst Library, New York University.

80. Progressive-Era investigations provide a great deal of aggregate data, but I have been unable to locate records of individual manufacturers except the scattered data that appear in union conciliation and arbitration records from the Protocol period. Even corporate giants like Hart, Schaffner & Marx have not retained payroll and other employee data from before the 1930s.

81. For an overview of this literature see Sarah Eisenstein, *Give Us Bread, but Give Us Roses: Working Women's Consciousness in the United States, 1890 to the First World War* (London, 1983), chap. 4.

82. For an analysis of very similar patterns and ideologies of gender stereotyping in another industry see Ruth Milkman, "Redefining 'Women's Work': The Sexual Division of Labor in the Auto Industry during World War II," *Feminist*

Studies 8 (Summer 1982): 337–72, and *Gender at Work*. Milkman also explores the need of employers and observers to construct gender stereotypes for jobs that could be performed easily by both sexes.

83. Milkman, *Gender at Work*.

84. J. W. Schereschewsky, "The Health of Garment Workers," *Studies in Vocational Diseases,* Public Health Bulletin 71, U.S. Public Health Service (Washington, D.C., 1915), p. 39; and *Report on Condition of Woman and Child Wage-Earners,* 2: 443.

85. *Report on Condition of Woman and Child Wage-Earners,* 2: 456–57.

86. Ibid., pp. 463–64, 471–72, 508.

87. Schereschewsky, "The Health of Garment Workers," pp. 39–40.

88. Ibid., p. 40.

89. Ibid., pp. 39–40; U.S. Department of Labor, Bureau of Labor Statistics, *Bulletin* 146, "Wages and Regularity of Employment and Standardization of Piece Rates in the Dress and Waist Industry: New York City" (Washington, D.C., 1914), p. 30.

90. Bureau of Labor Statistics, *Bulletin* 146, p. 30.

91. Ibid.

92. U.S. Department of Labor, Bureau of Labor Statistics, *Bulletin* 147, "Wages and Regularity of Employment in the Cloak, Suit, and Skirt Industry" (Washington, D.C., 1915), p. 123.

93. Ibid., pp. 107, 123, 127.

94. Liptzin, *Tales of a Tailor,* p. 245.

95. In an important theoretical discussion of the division of labor by sex, Heidi Hartmann has suggested that male workers (and not just capitalist employers) have played a critical role in erecting and maintaining a division of labor that subordinates women and bolsters patriarchy. "Capitalism, Patriarchy, and Job Segregation by Sex," *Signs* 1 (Summer 1976): 137–69. Alice Kessler-Harris also provides an important discussion of this issue, noting too that women themselves had their own criteria about suitable feminine occupations. See *Out to Work,* pp. 136–41.

96. Established craft unions protected "male" skills by passing them on to young men rather than women, and they supported protective legislation as a way of limiting women's presence in various trades. Hartmann, "Capitalism, Patriarchy, and Job Segregation by Sex"; Alice Kessler-Harris, "Where Are the Organized Women Workers?" in Nancy F. Cott and Elizabeth H. Pleck, eds., *A Heritage of Her Own* (New York, 1979), pp. 347–48, 357, 359.

97. U.S. Department of Commerce, Bureau of the Census, *Earnings of Factory Workers 1899 to 1927: An Analysis of Payroll Statistics,* Census Monographs 10 (Washington, D.C., 1929), p. 110.

98. *Report on Condition of Woman and Child Wage-Earners,* vol. 2, p. 130–31.

99. Ibid., p. 155.

100. Ibid., p. 184; see also Bureau of Labor Statistics, *Bulletin* 146, Table 15, p. 45, Table 17, p. 47, and passim.

101. Morris Hillquit, council for the ILGWU, voiced a common assumption that men had greater speed than women sewing-machine operators. "Arbitration to Settle and Adjust the Disagreements Now Existing between the Manufacturers and Employees in the Waist, Dress and Children's Dressmaking Industries in the City of

Philadelphia," Jan. 17, 1916, transcript in ILGWU Archives, LMDC, Catherwood Library, Cornell University. See also Bureau of Labor Statistics, *Bulletin* 146, pp. 34–35.

102. Statements of Striking Garment Workers, Chicago, Men's Garment Strike, 1910, unpub. typescript, National Women's Trade Union League Papers, Reel 4, Schlesinger Library, Radcliffe College.

103. Interview with Rose Soskin in Kramer and Masur, eds., *Jewish Grand-mothers*, p. 41.

104. Van Kleeck, "Women and Children Who Make Men's Clothes," p. 66.

105. "Statement on the Strike of the 35,000 Unorganized Garment Workers of Chicago," n.d. [1910], Women's Trade Union League of Chicago, National Women's Trade Union League Papers, Reel 4, Schlesinger Library, Radcliffe College.

106. *Report on Condition of Woman and Child Wage-Earners*, 2: 194.

107. U.S. Commission on Industrial Relations, *Reports*, 4, "The Women's Garment Industry in Philadelphia," p. 3118. See also Tentler, *Wage-Earning Women*, p. 21.

108. Hasanovitz, *One of Them*, p. 116.

109. Jennie Matyas interview.

110. See for example Bureau of Labor Statistics, *Bulletin* 147, pp. 106–7; *Bulletin* 175, p. 23.

111. Tentler, *Wage-Earning Women*, pp. 32–33, 80, and passim. My own findings support the conclusions of Sarah Eisenstein, who argued that wage-earning women had a strong work-centered identity and were quick to defend their right to employment and to decent wages. *Give Us Bread, but Give Us Roses*, pp. 22–25.

112. On Italian dressmakers and seamstresses see Columba Marie Furio, "Immigrant Women and Industry: A Case Study. Italian Immigrant Women and the Garment Industry, 1880–1950" (Ph.D. diss., New York University, 1979), p. 58; and Louise Odencrantz, *Italian Women in Industry* (New York, 1919), pp. 40–41.

113. Tape I-3, NYCILHP, Wagner Archives, Bobst Library, New York University.

114. For a different view see Tentler, *Wage-Earning Women*, p. 75.

115. On the importance of consumer items and new forms of urban entertainment for young immigrant women see Ewen, *Immigrant Women in the Land of Dollars*; Kathy Peiss, *Cheap Amusements* (Philadelphia, 1986).

116. Odencrantz, *Italian Women in Industry*, pp. 38–44, describes the ambitions of some Italian daughters, but her account does not analyze how these women negotiated the labor market.

117. Kessner, *The Golden Door*, p. 171.

118. Murtland, "A Study of the Dress and Waist Industry for the Purpose of Industrial Education," p. 172.

119. Goodman and Ueland, "The Shirtwaist Trade."

120. Hasanovitz, *One of Them*, p. 120.

121. Hadassah Kosak, "The Rise of the Jewish Working Class, New York, 1881–1905" (Ph.D. diss., City University of New York, 1987), pp. 114–15, 118–20, describes the types of apprenticeship arrangements.

122. Murtland, "A Study of the Dress and Waist Industry for the Purpose of Industrial Education," Bureau of Labor Statistics, *Bulletin* 145, p. 171.

123. Jennie Matyas interview, pp. 31–32; Pesotta, *Days of Our Lives*, p. 248.

124. Ibid.

125. Ibid.

126. *Report of the Senate Vice Committee*, State of Illinois, 48th General Assembly ([Springfield], 1916), p. 417.

127. Interview 2 with Sarah Rozner by Sherna Gluck, March 1973, p. 13, FHRP.

128. Interview 1 with Sarah Rozner by Sherna Gluck, March 1973, p. 6, FHRP.

129. Ibid.

130. Interview with Mollie Steinholtz by Taffie Viner, tape 1, side A, and tape 2, side A, March 1974, FHRP.

131. Cornelia Stratton Parker, *Working with the Working Women* (New York, 1922), p. 130.

132. Fannie Shapiro interview in Kramer and Masur, eds., *Jewish Grandmothers*, p. 11.

133. Ruth Katz interview in ibid., p. 146.

134. Records of the U.S. Department of Labor, Women's Bureau, unpub. data for *Bulletin* 74, Schedule 7-2-78, Schedule 7-2-193, Record Group 86, National Archives. For other examples see Elizabeth Howe Bliss, "Intimate Studies in the Lives of Fifty Working Girls" (M.A. thesis, Columbia University, 1915), pp. 63–64, 92.

135. Parker, *Working with the Working Women*, p. 130.

136. New York (State) Factory Investigating Commission, *Fourth Report*, 2: 521.

137. Payroll records of dress and shirtwaist factories in New York City suggest an equally high rate of turnover. Minutes of the Joint Board of Grievances in the Dress and Waist Industry, Chief Clerk's Investigation, March 19, 1914, pp. 315–17, includes selected payroll records of the Aero Waist Co. and Weisman and Son's, transcript in ILGWU Research Department, New York; Wage Scale Board Cases, Sept. 22, 1913, Minutes of the Board of Grievances between the Dress and Waist Manufacturers Association and the ILGWU, 1913 (includes Capital Waist Co., payroll record, Sept. 8, 1913), transcript in ILGWU Research Dept.

138. Caroline Manning, "The Immigrant Woman and Her Job," U.S. Department of Labor, Woman's Bureau, *Bulletin* 74 (Washington, D.C., 1930), p. 115.

139. Louise C. Odencrantz, "The Irregularity of Employment of Women Factory Workers," *The Survey* 23 (April 3, 1909): 201.

140. As quoted in Van Kleeck, *A Seasonal Industry*, p. 93.

141. Quoted in Bliss, "Intimate Studies in the Lives of Fifty Working Girls," p. 21.

Chapter 4. *"All of Us Young People"*

1. Tape I-51 (Dec. 1973), New York City Immigrant Labor History Project (NYCILHP), Wagner Labor Archives, Bobst Library, New York University.

2. Historians who have emphasized the view that immigrants were resistant to change and essentially oriented toward preserving and defending Old World habits and customs include Herbert Gutman, "Work, Culture, and Society in Industrializing America, 1815–1919," in Gutman, *Work, Culture, and Society in Industrializing America: Essays in American Working-Class and Social History* (New York,

1977); Virginia Yans-McLaughlin, *Family and Community: Italian Immigrants in Buffalo* (Ithaca, N.Y., 1977); and John Bodnar, "Immigration and Modernization: The Case of Slavic Peasants in Industrial America," *Journal of Social History* 10 (Fall 1976): 44–67. A critique of this literature which stresses the need to investigate the diversity of working-class cultures and the complex process of acculturation is Daniel T. Rodgers, "Tradition, Modernity, and the American Industrial Worker: Reflections and Critique," in *Journal of Interdisciplinary History* 7 (Spring 1977): 655–81.

3. See Louis Levine, *The Women's Garment Workers* (New York, 1924), p. 383. Levine uses the term "pre-capitalist" to describe what were actually pre-industrial methods of production and business practice.

4. Steve Fraser, "Dress Rehearsal for the New Deal: Shop-Insurgents, Political Elites, and Industrial Democracy in the Amalgamated Clothing Workers," in Michael H. Frisch and Daniel J. Walkowitz, eds., *Working Class America: Essays on Labor Community and American Society* (Urbana, Ill., 1983), p. 215.

5. The census of 1914 asked garment manufacturers whether they classified themselves as independent (inside) factories or contractors. In the women's garment industry, manufacturing firms identifying themselves as contractors employed 11 percent of all workers; in the men's clothing industry the figure was 40 percent. These figures, however, may have been too low, since some contractors probably misrepresented themselves as independent firms, and others were not counted at all. See J. M. Budish and George Soule, *The New Unionism in the Clothing Industry* (1920; repr. New York, 1968), pp. 33–34.

6. Sholem Asch, *Uncle Moses* (London, 1922), p. 64.

7. Viola Paradise, "The Jewish Immigrant Girl in Chicago," *The Survey* 30 (Sept. 6, 1913): 701.

8. Bernard Weinstein, *Fertsik yor in der Yidisher Arbeterbavegung* (1924), as quoted in Elias Tcherikower, ed., *The Early Jewish Labor Movement in the United States*, trans. and rev. Aaron Antonovsky (New York, 1961), p. 152.

9. Joseph Schlossberg, *The Rise of the Clothing Workers*, Amalgamated Clothing Workers Educational Pamphlet (New York, 1921), p. 6.

10. See, for example, Sam Liptzin, *Tales of a Tailor*, trans. Max Rosenfeld (New York, 1965), p. 35 and passim; Ephraim M. Wagner, "The Village Boy" (1939), unpub. autobiography, p. 164, YIVO Archives. A good fictional account is Abraham Cahan, "A Sweatshop Romance" (1898) in Cahan, *Yekl, the Imported Bridegroom and Other Stories of Yiddish New York* (New York, 1970).

11. See Moses Rischin, *The Promised City* (Cambridge, Mass., 1978), p. 183; Tcherikower, *The Early Jewish Labor Movement*, p. 134; and Melech Epstein, *Jewish Labor in the U.S.A.: An Industrial, Political and Cultural History, 1882–1914* (New York, 1969), pp. 96–97.

12. Interview with Mr. Gold (1939), New York City Living Lore, W.P.A. Federal Writers Project, typescript, Folklore Collection, Drawer 46-2, Library of Congress.

13. Rose Cohen, *Out of the Shadow* (New York, 1918), p. 82. On the notion that Jewish immigrant contractors acted as surrogate parents see Robert Steven Wechsler, "The Jewish Garment Trade in East London, 1875–1914: A Study of Conditions and Responses" (Ph.D. diss., Columbia University, 1979), p. 228.

14. Ernest Poole, "Task Work Bowing to Factory System," *The Outlook,* Nov. 21, 1903, quoted in Allon Schoener, ed., *Portal to America: The Lower East Side, 1870–1925* (New York, 1967), p. 170. On "merry makings" see Cohen, *Out of the Shadow,* p. 87.

15. Cohen, *Out of the Shadow,* p. 83.

16. Morris Hillquit, *Loose Leaves from a Busy Life* (New York, 1934), p. 32. For fictional insights into this work culture see Eliezer Blum-Alquit, "In the Light of Morris Rosenfeld," in Blum-Alquit, *The Revolt of the Apprentice and Other Stories,* trans. Etta Blum (South Brunswick, N.J., 1969), p. 115.

17. "The Cloakmakers in the Factories and Cloakmakers at the Contractors," *Jewish Daily Forward,* June 8, 1913, typed translation in Paul Abelson papers, Box 9, Labor Management Documentation Center (LMDC), Catherwood Library, Cornell University.

18. Annie Shapiro testimony before the Illinois Senate Committee Hearings [regarding the Chicago Clothing Strike of 1910], Feb. 3, 1911, typescript in Amalgamated Clothing Workers of America Papers, Box 39, folder 1, LMDC, Catherwood Library, Cornell University; U.S. Congress, Senate, *Report on Condition of Woman and Child Wage-Earners in the United States,* 2, 61st Cong., 2d sess. (Washington, D.C., 1911), p. 440. See also U.S. Bureau of Labor, Eleventh Special Report of the Commissioner of Labor, *Regulation and Restriction of Output* (Washington, D.C., 1904), p. 548.

19. Aaron Kiel, "Nothing to Lose," *New York Call* (July 13, 1910), p. 1.

20. Hadassah Kosak, "The Rise of the Jewish Working Class, New York, 1881–1905" (Ph.D. diss., City University of New York, 1987), p. 178.

21. "Cloakmakers in the Factories and Cloakmakers at the Contractors," *Jewish Daily Forward,* June 8, 1913.

22. William M. Leiserson, *Adjusting Immigrants and Industry* (1924; repr. New York, 1969), pp. 297, 303; Louise Odencrantz, *Italian Women in Industry: A Study of Conditions in New York* (New York, 1919), p. 32.

23. *Report on Condition of Woman and Child Wage-Earners* 2: 53.

24. U.S. Congress, House of Representatives, *Report of the Industrial Relations Commission on the Relations and Conditions of Capital and Labor Employed in Manufactures and General Business,* 7, 56th Cong., 2d sess. (Washington, D.C., 1901), pp. 190, 186–87.

25. Cohen, *Out of the Shadow,* p. 246.

26. Irving Howe, *World of Our Fathers* (New York, 1976), pp. 127–28, 169–70, 184.

27. "The Cloakmakers in the Factories and Cloakmakers at the Contractors," *Jewish Daily Forward,* June 8, 1913. See also Yitzack Yankev Doroshkin, "From Zhitkovitch—through the World," unpub. autobiography, p. 71, YIVO Archives.

28. Hannah Shapiro, as quoted in Rebecca Sive-Tomachevsky, "Identifying a Lost Leader: Hannah Shapiro and the 1910 Chicago Garment Workers' Strike," *Signs* 3 (Summer 1978): 937. Some Jewish women claimed that large factories were more desirable because they were cleaner and had better amenities than small workrooms on the Lower East Side. Tape I-109, NYCILHP, Wagner Archives.

29. Questionnaires and Letters on Factory Fire Hazards (1911), Leonora O'Reilly Papers, Reel 13, Schlesinger Library, Radcliffe College. See also Leon Stein,

The Triangle Fire (Philadelphia, 1962); New York (State) Factory Investigating Commission, *Preliminary Report,* 1 (Albany, 1912), p. 45 and passim; *Third Annual Report of the Joint Board of Sanitary Control in the Cloak, Suit and Skirt and the Dress and Waist Industries of Greater New York* (Dec. 1913), p. 47; *Special Report on Sanitary Conditions in the Shops of the Dress and Waist Industry,* May 1913, Joint Board of Sanitary Control (New York, 1913), p. 10; and George M. Price, "Factory Inspection," *The Survey* 26 (May 6, 1911), p. 227.

30. Questionnaires and Letters on Factory Fire Hazards (1911), O'Reilly Papers, Reel 13, Schlesinger Library, Radcliffe College.

31. Ibid.

32. Schlossberg, *The Rise of the Clothing Workers,* p. 7.

33. Anzia Yezierska, "America and I" (1923), in *The Open Cage: An Anzia Yezierska Reader* (New York, 1979), p. 26. Yezierska's stories and novels are perhaps the most important literary dramatizations of the cultural tensions experienced by immigrant daughters. See the remarks of Alice Kessler-Harris in her introduction to the reprint edition of Yezierska's 1925 novel *Bread Givers.*

34. See Rischin, *Promised City,* p. 146. See also Judith Greenfeld, "The Role of Jews in the Development of Clothing Manufacture," *YIVO Annual* 2–3 (1947–48), p. 200; Rabbi Solomon Foster, *The Workingman and the Synagogue* (Newark, N.J., n.d. [1910]), pp. 13–14; U.S. Congress, Senate, *Reports,* United States Commission on Industrial Relations (1912), 2, "Men's Garment Trades in New York," 64th Cong., 1st sess. (Washington, D.C., 1916), p. 1979. There were some exceptions. One immigrant man who had worked in a small shop run by religious Jews wanted to work "uptown" in what he described as one of the "better" shops. He was fortunate enough to be hired at Rueben Sadowsky's giant cloak factory, which closed its doors on Saturday and opened on Sunday instead. Tape I-101, NYCILHP, Wagner Archives.

35. Interview with Ella Wolff, Dec. 27, 1963, Amerikaner Yiddishe Geshikhte Bel-Pe, YIVO Archives. See also Julius S. Baker, "The Life Story of Yudel Shmerl, from Birsze Lithuania to Baltimore, Maryland, U.S.A.: An Autobiography," p. 48, unpub. autobiography, YIVO Archives.

36. New York (State) Factory Investigating Commission, *Fourth Report,* 4 (Albany, 1915), p. 1591.

37. Brucha Gutrajman, "A Woman's Story: The Life of a Jewish Worker" (1976), unpub. autobiography, p. 111, YIVO Archives.

38. Tape I-83, NYCILHP, Robert F. Wagner Archives, New York University. George M. D. Wolfe found that in the late nineteenth century Russian Jewish socialists and "free thinkers" considered Orthodox Jews to be "fanatics." Socialist radicals brought these ideas with them to the United States. See "A Study of Immigrant Attitudes and Problems, Based on an Analysis of the *Jewish Daily Forward*" (thesis, Training School for Jewish Social Work, New York, 1929).

39. Interview with Sarah Rozner by Sherna Gluck, Interview 4, May 11, 1973, p. 2, FHRP.

40. Tape I-51, NYCILHP, Wagner Archives.

41. Mary G. Rock, "Machine Operating on Women's Clothing, a Trade for Women," unpub. report (1910–11), p. 12, in Papers of the Women's Educational and Industrial Union, Boston, Schlesinger Library, Radcliffe College. See also

Yitzack Yankev Doroshkin, "From Zhitkovitch—through the World: Episodes from My Life," unpub. autobiography, p. 52, YIVO Archives.

42. Tape I-136, NYCILHP, Wagner Archives.

43. Sarah Rozner questionnaire, Questionnaires for Union Members (1955), Aaron Antonovsky Papers, Record Group 100, YIVO Archives.

44. Interview 6 with Lottie Spitzer by Kristine Feichtinger, Nov. 11, 1974, p. 8, FHRP. See also Elizabeth Howe Bliss, "Intimate Studies in the Lives of Fifty Working Girls" (M.A. thesis, Columbia University, 1915), pp. 35, 101.

45. Bliss, "Intimate Studies in the Lives of Fifty Working Girls," p. 18.

46. The garment industry in New York City was slowly drifting "uptown" into the world of gentile America. By 1913, 72 percent of garment shops (employing 81 percent of the workers) in the dress and shirtwaist industry were located between Fourteenth and Twenty-ninth streets. *Third Annual Report of the Joint Board of Sanitary Control in the Cloak, Suit and Skirt and Dress and Waist Industries* (New York, 1913), p. 47. See also B. M. Selekman et al., *The Clothing and Textile Industries in New York and Its Environs*, Regional Plan of New York and Its Environs (New York, 1925), table XXI.

47. This is not to suggest that immigrants who worked for contractors were uninterested in becoming Americanized, only to argue that the small-shop environment tended to be more culturally insulated than the larger, more cosmopolitan social setting of the "inside" factory.

48. Shmarya Levin, *The Arena*, trans. Maurice Samuel (New York, 1932), p. 169.

49. Etta Byer, *Transplanted People* (Chicago, 1955), p. 22.

50. Emma Goldman, *Living My Life* (1931), ed. Richard and Anna Maria Drinnon (New York, 1977), p. 15.

51. *Jewish Daily Forward*, Feb. 7, 1906, quoted in Wolfe, "A Study of Immigrant Attitudes and Problems," p. 31.

52. Cohen, *Out of the Shadow*, p. 82.

53. Interview with Rebecca Holland (Goldberg) by Patti Pricket, Nov. 12, 1974, tape 1, side A, FHRP.

54. Cohen, *Out of the Shadow*, p. 274.

55. Liptzin, *Tales of a Tailor*, p. 60.

56. Ibid.

57. *Jewish Daily Forward*, March 31, 1906, quoted in Wolfe, "A Study of Immigrant Attitudes and Problems," p. 265.

58. This point is also stressed in ibid., pp. 132–33.

59. It was probably only rarely that a woman actually had sexual relations with her boss or foreman in exchange for job security, special treatment, or other more complex motivations. See, for example, Abraham Bisno, *Union Pioneer* (Madison, Wisc., 1967), pp. 64–65.

60. Interview with Fannie Shapiro in Kramer and Masur, eds., *Jewish Grandmothers*, p. 11.

61. See Charlotte Baum, Paula Hyman, and Sonya Michel, *The Jewish Woman in America* (New York, 1977), pp. 134–35.

62. Interview with Lottie Spitzer by Kristine Feichtinger, interview 1, p. 2, FHRP.

63. Ibid., p. 10.

64. Interview with Sarah Rozner by Sherna Gluck as quoted in Gluck, ed., "'What Is It We Want, Brother Levin?': Reminiscences of a Nonconforming Shop Girl, 1892–1976," unpub. summary of interviews with Rozner, p. 11. Manuscript in possession of the author.

65. On the freedom of movement permitted by early twentieth-century textile work see Tamara K. Hareven, *Family Time and Industrial Time* (Cambridge, Mass., 1982), pp. 130–31.

66. Testimony of Morris Bernstein (1914), in U.S. Commission on Industrial Relations, *Reports*, 4, "The Women's Garment Industry in Philadelphia" (Washington, D.C., 1916), p. 3109; Rose Pesotta, "On Piece vs. Time Work" (n.d.), Rose Pesotta Papers, "Notes," Box 33, Manuscript Division, New York Public Library; and Agnes Nestor, "A Day's Work Making Gloves," *Charities and Commons* 22 (Sept. 5, 1908): 660.

67. Records of the U.S. Department of Labor, Woman's Bureau, unpub. material for *Bulletin* 74, Schedule 7-2-214, Record Group 86, National Archives.

68. Interview with Anna Weinstock Schneider, June 30, 1969, pp. 11–12, Papers of Anna Weinstock Schneider, LMDC, Catherwood Library, Cornell University.

69. Testimony of Morris Bernstein, in U.S. Industrial Relations Commission, *Reports*, 4: 3109.

70. Tape I-7, NYCILHP, Wagner Archives.

71. Annie Marion MacLean, *Wage-Earning Women* (New York, 1910), p. 35.

72. Interview with Mollie Millman by the author, Nov. 4, 1980, Oakland, Calif.

73. Interview 1 with Lottie Spitzer by Kristine Feichtinger, July 18, 1974, pp. 5–6, FHRP.

74. Interview with Mollie Linker in Kramer and Masur, eds., *Jewish Grandmothers*, p. 95.

75. Competition for "bundles" seems to have been a universal problem in piecework shops and factories regardless of the sex of the workers. Immigrants who routinely tried to monopolize the largest share of work were known in the needle trades as "bundle eaters." See Abraham Cahan, *The Rise of David Levinsky* (1917; repr. New York, 1966), p. 152. Autobiographies and oral histories reveal the dynamics of this competition. See, for example, Elizabeth Hasanovitz, *One of Them* (Boston, 1918), p. 186; Rebecca August, Sam Gelman, and Joseph Shargel questionnaires, Questionnaires for Union Members, Antonovsky Papers, YIVO Archives; Rose Schneiderman with Lucy Goldthwaite, *All for One* (New York, 1967), p. 86; and Cohen, *Out of the Shadow*, pp. 110–11.

76. Interview 4 with Lottie Spitzer by Kristine Feichtinger, Sept. 3, 1974, pp. 27–28, FHRP.

77. Ibid.

78. Anon., "My Clothing Shop," in Andrea Taylor Hourwich and Gladys L. Palmer, eds., *I Am a Woman Worker: A Scrapbook of Autobiographies*, Affiliated Schools for Workers (New York, 1936), p. 30.

79. Cooperation was probably most obvious when workers were related to one another or when neighborhood or Old-Country ties created special bonds of friendship.

80. Hasanovitz, *One of Them*, p. 45.

81. Rose Pesotta, *Days of Our Lives* (Boston, 1958), p. 248.

82. Interview with Pauline Newman (1965), Amerikaner Yiddishe Geshikhte Bel-Pe, YIVO Archives.

83. Ibid.

84. Rose Pesotta, "The Shop" (Jan. 1931), in Pesotta Papers, Box 25, Manuscripts Division, New York Public Library.

85. Interview with Becky Prescant as quoted in Elizabeth Ewen, "Immigrant Women in the Land of Dollars" (Ph.D. diss., State University of New York at Stony Brook, 1979), p. 385.

86. *Report of the Senate Vice Committee*, State of Illinois, 48th General Assembly ([Springfield], 1916), p. 380.

87. "Minutes of Meeting of Board of Grievances," Sept. 3, 1913. Case of B. Schnall and Co., pp. 41, 70, typescript in Isaac Hourwich papers, YIVO Archives. See also "Arbitration Proceedings between the Dress and Waist Manufacturers Association of New York and the I.L.G.W.U.," May 17, 1914, copy in ILGWU Research Dept., New York; "The White Goods Strike of 1913" (interviews with strikers), statement by Mary Goff, in Leonora O'Reilly Papers, Reel 13, Schlesinger Library, Radcliffe.

88. My understanding of the development of modern management in American industry has been informed by Daniel Nelson, *Managers and Workers* (Madison, Wisc., 1975), pp. 55–79 and passim. The literature on the movement to modernize management in the garment industry is thin. Suggestive, however, is U.S. Department of Labor, Bureau of Labor Statistics, *Bulletin* 135, "Wages and Hours of Labor in the Cigar and Clothing Industries, 1911 and 1912" (Washington, D.C., 1913), p. 35. Experiments between employers and the International Ladies' Garment Workers' Union to establish scientific methods for determining piece rates led to the establishment of "test shops" that utilized time-and-motion studies familiar to students of scientific management. See, for example, Nahum I. Stone, "Wages and Regularity of Employment and Standardization of Piece Rates in the Dress and Waist Industry," Bureau of Labor Statistics, *Bulletin* 146 (Washington, D.C., 1914), pp. 189ff.; M. L. Disher, *American Factory Production of Women's Clothing* (London, 1947), pp. 189–95. For an interesting discussion of the tension that arose over such experiments see Elizabeth Israels Perry, "Industrial Reform in New York City: Belle Moskowitz and the Protocol of Peace, 1913–1916," *Labor History* 23 (Winter 1982): 19–23; Steve Fraser, "Dress Rehearsal for the New Deal: Shop-Floor Insurgents, Political Elites, and Industrial Democracy in the Amalgamated Clothing Workers of America," in Michael H. Frisch and Daniel J. Walkowitz, eds., *Working Class America: Essays on Labor, Community and American Society* (Urbana, Ill., 1983), pp. 216–23.

89. Bureau of Labor Statistics, *Bulletin* 135 (Washington, D.C., 1913), p. 35.

90. Interview 1 with Lottie Spitzer by Kristine Feichtinger, July 18, 1974, p. 12; interview 2, pp. 3–4, FHRP.

91. Pauline Newman interview, Amerikaner Yiddishe Geshikhte Bel-Pe, YIVO Archives.

92. Tape I-3, NYCILHP, Wagner Archives.

93. Leslie Woodcock Tentler, *Wage-Earning Women: Industrial Work and Fam-*

ily Life in the United States, 1900–1930 (New York, 1979), p. 46, stresses that factory discipline constituted a "major" grievance in "those rare moments of women's collective protest" but argues that its major impact was to affirm women's sense of "impotence" and "low status" in the work force. Because Tentler views women's labor protest as the spontaneous and ineffectual outburst of a largely apathetic work force, she understates the ways in which disciplinary practices contributed to the growth of class consciousness and militance among immigrants.

94. Interview with Pearl Kramer (pseud.) by the author, Los Angeles, June 4, 1981; Sylvia Zwirn, "A Dress Shop," in Hilda Smith Papers, Box 3, Schlesinger Library, Radcliffe College.

95. Anna Weinstock Schneider interview, p. 8, LMDC, Catherwood Library, Cornell University; Hasanovitz, *One of Them,* p. 46; *Report on the Condition of Woman and Child Wage-Earners,* 2: 336; and Pauline Newman interview, Amerikaner Yiddishe Geshikhte Bel-Pe, YIVO Archives.

96. Interview with Mollie Millman by the author, Nov. 4, 1980; interview with May Horowitz by the author, Los Angeles, June 7, 1981.

97. Recent studies that explore the significance of factory life for adolescent socialization include Tentler, *Wage-Earning Women,* and Kathy Peiss, *Cheap Amusements: Working Women and Leisure in Turn-of-the-Century New York* (Philadelphia, 1986).

98. Grace Abbott, *The Immigrant and the Community* (New York, 1917), pp. 67–68. See also Sue Ainslie Clark and Edith Wyatt, *Making Both Ends Meet: The Income and Outlay of New York Working Girls* (New York, 1911), p. 61; Caroline Manning, "The Immigrant Woman and Her Job," U.S. Department of Labor, Women's Bureau, *Bulletin* 74 (Washington, D.C., 1930), p. 160.

99. Mary Van Kleeck, *Working Girls in Evening Schools: A Statistical Study* (New York, 1914), p. 201.

100. Max Danish, "Educational Problems of Our International," Oct. 25, 1918, typescript in Rand School of Social Science Papers, Box 1, Manuscripts Division, New York Public Library.

101. Pauline Newman interview, Amerikaner Yiddishe Geshikhte Bel-Pe, YIVO Archives.

102. Interview with Lottie Spitzer by Kristine Feichtinger, pp. 15, 10, FHRP.

103. Hasanovitz, *One of Them,* p. 310.

104. Interview with Dora Bayrack by the author, Los Angeles, June 7, 1981.

105. Peiss, *Cheap Amusements,* pp. 50–51, 178–84, and passim. On middle-class women's preferences for interacting within the "female world" see Carroll Smith-Rosenberg, "The Female World of Love and Ritual: Relations between Women in Nineteenth Century America," *Signs* 1 (Autumn 1975): 1–29; Estelle Freedman, "Separatism as Strategy: Female Institution Building and American Feminism, 1870–1930," *Feminist Studies* 5 (Fall 1979): 512–29.

106. Interview with Pearl Kramer by the author; Dorothy Richardson, *The Long Day* (1905), reprinted in William O'Neill, ed., *Women at Work* (New York, 1972); Tentler, *Wage-Earning Women,* pp. 71–74.

107. Fannie Edelman, *The Mirror of Life: The Old Country and the New,* trans. Samuel Pasner (New York, 1961), p. 25.

108. As quoted in Corinne Azen Krause, "Urbanization without Breakdown:

Italian, Jewish, and Slavic Women in Pittsburgh, 1900–1945," *Journal of Urban History* 4 (May 1978): 300.

109. Interview with Ruth Katz in Kramer and Masur, eds., *Jewish Grandmothers*, pp. 144, 147.

110. Ibid.

111. Antin, *The Promised Land*, pp. 277–78.

112. Interview with Ida Richter, quoted in Kramer and Masur, eds., *Jewish Grandmothers*, p. 132.

113. "The Life Story of a Polish Sweatshop Girl," in Hamilton Holt, ed., *The Life Stories of Undistinguished Americans as Told by Themselves* (New York, 1906), p. 42.

114. See Mari Jo Buhle, *Women and American Socialism, 1870–1920* (Urbana, Ill., 1981), pp. 186, 261–62; Sally M. Miller, "From Sweatshop Worker to Labor Leader: Theresa Malkiel, a Case Study," *American Jewish History* 68 (Dec. 1978): 197; Hasanovitz, *One of Them*, p. 102. An overview of the intellectual debate over love and marriage in late nineteenth- and early twentieth-century Russia can be found in Richard Stites, "Women and the Russian Intelligentsia: Three Perspectives," in Dorothy Atkinson, Alexander Dallin, and Gail Warshofsky Lapidus, eds., *Women in Russia* (Stanford, Calif., 1977), pp. 39–62.

115. Hasanovitz, *One of Them*, p. 102.

116. Ibid.; Miller, "From Sweatshop Worker to Labor Leader," p. 197.

117. On the lure of commercial amusements see Jane Addams, *The Spirit of Youth and the City Streets* (1909; repr. Urbana, Ill., 1972), pp. 75–103; Belle Lindner Israels, "The Way of the Girl," *The Survey* 22 (July 3, 1909): 486–97; Louise deKoven Bowen, "What Is There for Women to Do in Chicago?" lecture (1913) in *Speeches, Addresses and Letters of Louise deKoven Bowen, Reflecting Social Movements in Chicago* (Ann Arbor, Mich., 1937), pp. 320–21; Elizabeth Howe Bliss, "Intimate Studies in the Lives of Fifty Working Girls," pp. 18, 34, 38, 53–54; and interview with Ruth Katz in Kramer and Masur, eds., *Jewish Grandmothers*, pp. 146–47. For further discussion of the leisure interests and activities of young immigrant women see Ewen, *Immigrant Women in the Land of Dollars;* Peiss, *Cheap Amusements;* Tentler, *Wage-Earning Women*, pp. 109–11; and Joanne J. Meyerowitz, *Women Adrift: Independent Wage-Earners in Chicago, 1880–1930* (Chicago, 1988).

118. Israels, "The Way of the Girl," pp. 486, 491.

119. As quoted in Irving Howe, *World of Our Fathers* (New York, 1976), p. 213.

120. Andrew Heinze, *Adapting to Abundance: Jewish Immigrants, Mass Consumerism, and the Search for American Identity* (New York, 1990), p. 118.

121. I have come across no statistical survey of the degree to which young immigrant wage earners in the garment industry actually spent time and money on movies, the theater, the amusement parks, and other urban entertainment. Available studies of the leisure activities of urban youth are rarely broken down according to ethnic group and occupation. Annie Marion MacLean did try to chart the "favorite amusements" of New York working women according to nationality, but the results of that survey are inconclusive. Jewish working daughters listed their preferences as theater, dancing, music, reading. But many she interviewed gave no preference. See MacLean, *Wage-Earning Women*, p. 52; Sue Ainslie Clark and Edith Wyatt, *Making*

Both Ends Meet: The Income and Outlay of New York Working Girls (New York, 1911), p. 61. It is likely that most immigrant families and women alone in this country had little disposable income. Although they may have enjoyed an occasional visit to the theater, the movies, or the ice-cream parlor, their budgets were usually too limited to permit regular spending on leisure activities. And it is probable that rising expectations about access to such activities contributed to immigrant women's frustrations over low wages.

122. For discussions of mixed-sex social clubs on the Lower East Side, see oral interviews I-116, I-51, and I-111, NYCILHP, Wagner Archives; J. K. Paulding, "Educational Influences," in Charles Bernheimer, ed., *The Russian Jew in the United States* (New York, 1905), p. 204; Ewen, *Immigrant Women in the Land of Dollars*, p. 210; and Weinberg, *World of Our Mothers*, pp. 100–101.

123. Heinze, *Adapting to Abundance*, pp. 94, 103–4; Peiss, *Cheap Amusements*, pp. 62–63.

124. Viola Paradise, "The Jewish Immigrant Girl in Chicago," p. 704. The importance of looking like an American is a major theme in Abraham Cahan's story "Yekl: A Tale of the New York Ghetto" (1896), reprinted in Cahan, *Yekl, the Imported Bride Groom, and Other Stories of Yiddish New York* (New York, 1970). See also Hutchins Hapgood, *The Spirit of the Ghetto* (repr. Cambridge, Mass., 1967), pp. 11, 72–74.

125. Tape I-132, NYCILHP, Wagner Archives.

126. Interview with Ida Richter in Kramer and Masur, eds., *Jewish Grandmothers*, p. 130.

127. Dress and adornment are an important subtheme in Anzia Yezierska's novel *Bread Givers* (1925). Kathy Peiss devotes a chapter to this theme in *Cheap Amusements*. See also Ewen, *Immigrant Women in the Land of Dollars*, pp. 188–89, 153–54, 197–201; Elizabeth Howe Bliss, "Intimate Studies in the Lives of Fifty Working Girls," p. 29 and passim; and Heinze, *Adapting to Abundance*, chap. 5.

128. These include Ewen, *Immigrant Women in the Land of Dollars*; Tentler, *Wage-Earning Women*.

129. Tentler, *Wage-Earning Women*, pp. 73, 61.

130. Ewen, *Immigrant Women in the Land of Dollars*, pp. 210–11; Peiss, *Cheap Amusements*, p. 68.

131. Elizabeth Ewen stresses the conservative temperament of European-born mothers over most issues of leisure and consumption, arguing that mothers were hostile to the outside world of American culture. The exception she notes was the movies, "the one American institution" that "became a shared cultural experience for mothers and daughters." Ewen, "City Lights: Immigrant Women and the Rise of the Movies," *Signs* 5, no. 3 Supplement (1980), esp. pp. 50, 64–65, and *Immigrant Women in the Land of Dollars*, pp. 217–18, 223–24. More recently Andrew Heinze in *Adapting to Abundance* has argued that far from resisting consumerism, Jewish immigrant mothers enthusiastically embraced new products and new habits of consumption. Heinze makes an interesting case for the notion that Jewish mothers adapted their bargain-hunting skills to the world of urban consumer life (chap. 6). Sydney Weinberg suggests that mothers may have gained a vicarious sense of freedom and assimilation to American life through the consumer habits of their daughters. *World of Our Mothers*, p. 123.

132. As quoted in Bliss, "Intimate Studies in the Lives of Fifty Working Girls," p. 29.

133. Tape I-134, NYCILHP, Wagner Archives.

134. Lillian D. Wald, *The House on Henry Street* (1915; repr. New York, 1971), pp. 192–93.

135. Peiss, *Cheap Amusements,* p. 54.

136. As quoted in ibid., p. 38. See also New York (State) Factory Investigating Commission, *Fourth Report,* 4 (Albany, 1915), pp. 1682–83 and passim; Lee K. Frankel, "The Cost of Living in New York," *Charities and Commons* 19 (Nov. 16, 1907): 1049–54.

137. On the practice of "treating" see Peiss, *Cheap Amusements;* Meyerowitz, *Women Adrift;* and Heinze, *Adapting to Abundance.*

138. *New York Evening Journal,* Nov. 26, 1909.

139. Compare the interpretation in Tentler, *Wage-Earning Women,* pp. 61, 73. According to Tentler, "The struggles that mattered [for working women] were the struggles for adolescent autonomy; the essential victories were romantic conquests. The very success of the work group in facilitating adolescent rebellion [against parental authority] served to deflect worker dissatisfaction from overt political expression" (p. 61). A "passionate interest in social life," Tentler insists, "generated conflict with parents while it minimized conflict with the employer" (p. 73).

140. Tape I-59, NYCILHP, Wagner Archives.

141. Ibid.

Chapter 5. Uprisings

1. Jacob A. Riis, *Children of the Poor* (New York, 1892; repr. New York, 1971), p. 53.

2. Good summaries of the 1909 strike include Louis Levine, *The Women's Garment Workers* (New York, 1924), chap. 21; *The Outlook* (Dec. 11, 1909): 799–801; Helen Marot, "A Woman's Strike: An Appreciation," *Proceedings of the Academy of Political Science* 1 (Oct. 1910): 119–28; William Mailly, "The Working Girls' Strike," *Independent* 67 (Dec. 23, 1909): 1416–20; Irving Howe, *World of Our Fathers* (New York, 1976), pp. 297–300; Meredith Tax, *The Rising of the Women: Solidarity and Class Conflict, 1880–1917* (New York, 1980); and Maxine Schwartz Seller, "The Uprising of the Twenty Thousand: Sex, Class, and Ethnicity in the Shirtwaist Makers' Strike of 1909," in Dirk Hoerder, ed., *"Struggle a Hard Battle," Essays on Working Class Immigrants* (DeKalb, Ill., 1986).

3. See J. M. Budish and George Soule, *The New Unionism in the Clothing Industry* (1920; repr. New York, 1968), pp. 84–85; Leo Wolman, *The Growth of American Trade Unions* (New York, 1924), pp. 50–51; Amalgamated Clothing Workers of America, Chicago Joint Board, *The Clothing Workers of Chicago* (Chicago, 1922), chap. 4; and Joel Seidman, *The Needle Trades* (New York, 1942), pp. 115–30.

4. Wolman, *Growth of American Trade Unions,* pp. 98, 138.

5. *Life and Labor* 1 (March 1911): 67.

6. *New York Times,* July 8, 1910.

7. *The Ladies' Garment Worker* 1 (May 1910).

8. *New York Call,* Feb. 15, 1910; see also Minutes of the General Executive Board, International Ladies' Garment Workers' Union, Dec. 20, 1915, ILGWU Archives, Labor-Management Documentation Center (LMDC), Catherwood Library, Cornell University.

9. Wolman, *Growth of American Trade Unions,* pp. 98, 138.

10. Ibid., pp. 137–45, table 6. In printing and publishing 25 percent of 47,576 women workers were unionized. In the boot and shoe industry 44.6 percent of 78,558 women workers were unionized.

11. On the attitudes of the AFL and other union organizations to female membership see Alice Kessler-Harris, "Where Are the Organized Woman Workers?" *Feminist Studies* 3 (Fall 1975): 92–110.

12. Rebecca August, unpub. autobiography, p. 1, YIVO Archives.

13. "Basters' Grievances and Demands," in Papers of the National Women's Trade Union League, Reel 4, Schlesinger Library, Radcliffe College.

14. Nancy L. Green discusses the importance of *mentshlekhe bahandlung* for Jewish workers who participated in the strike movement in turn-of-the-century Paris. See *The Pletzl of Paris: Jewish Immigrant Workers in the Belle Epoque* (New York, 1986), pp. 146, 132–33. For a discussion of similar patterns of demands among workers in the Pale of Settlement, see Ezra Mendelsohn, *Class Struggle in the Pale: The Formative Years of the Jewish Workers' Movement in Tzarist Russia* (Cambridge, 1970), pp. 87–88.

15. Quoted in *New York Evening Journal,* Nov. 26, 1909.

16. *Report of the Senate Vice Committee,* State of Illinois (1916), p. 396. See also the statement by a New York white goods worker on the "coarse language" used by her employer, quoted in Harry Lang, *"62": Biography of a Union* (New York, 1940), pp. 48–49.

17. Statement by a striker quoted in "The White Goods Strike of 1913," unpub. doc., Leonora O'Reilly Papers, Reel 13, Schlesinger Library. Alice Kessler-Harris also emphasizes how women's desire to protect their special female qualities added a "moral" dimension to their strike demands. See "Problems of Coalition Building: Women and Trade Unions in the 1920s," in Ruth Milkman, ed., *Women, Work, and Protest* (Boston, 1985).

18. Report of Meeting of the Women's Trade Union League, Sept. 28, 1908, p. 2, Leonora O'Reilly Papers, Reel 12, Schlesinger Library.

19. Elias Tcherikower, *The Early Jewish Labor Movement,* trans. and rev. Aaron Antonovsky (New York, 1961), p. 313. J. B. Salutsky appears to have coined the phrase that Jews were considered "very bad unionists . . . but good strikers." See the discussion in Jonathan Frankel, *Prophecy and Politics: Socialism, Nationalism, and the Russian Jews, 1862–1917* (Cambridge, 1981), pp. 458–59.

20. See Paula E. Hyman, "Immigrant Women and Consumer Protest: The New York City Kosher Meat Boycott of 1902," *American Jewish History* 70 (1980): 91–105.

21. On the relationship between economic cycles and unionization see David Montgomery, "The 'New Unionism' and the Transformation of Workers' Consciousness in America," in Montgomery, *Workers' Control* (Cambridge, 1979). On the influence of progressive ideology among manufacturers and reformers see Melvyn Dubofsky, *When Workers Organize: New York City in the Progressive Era*

(Amherst, Mass., 1968), p. 48. The idea that large inside manufacturers saw union-ization as a means of gaining more control over a chaotic industry must be qualified at every step. Even those firms who cooperated with the garment unions to establish contractual forms of "control" such as the Protocols of Peace remained extremely suspicious of, if not hostile to, the unions. For more extended discussion, see Elizabeth Israels Perry, "Industrial Reform in New York City: Belle Moskowitz and the Protocol of Peace, 1913–1916," *Labor History* 23 (Winter 1982): 5–31, and Steve Fraser, "Dress Rehearsal for the New Deal: Shop-Floor Insurgents, Political Elites, and Industrial Democracy in the Amalgamated Clothing Workers," in Michael H. Frisch and Daniel Walkowitz, eds., *Working Class America: Essays on Labor, Community, and American Society* (Urbana, Ill., 1983), pp. 212–55.

22. Moses Rischin, *The Promised City: New York's Jews, 1870–1914* (Cam-bridge, Mass., 1962; repr. 1978), chap. 12; Dubofsky, *When Workers Organize*, pp. 27, 47–48; N. Sue Weiler, "The Uprising in Chicago: The Men's Garment Workers Strike, 1910–1911," in Joan Jensen and Sue Davidson, eds., *A Needle, a Bobbin, a Strike: Women Needleworkers in America* (Philadelphia, 1984), pp. 114–45.

23. Interview with Rebecca Holland by Patti Pricket, 1974, interview III-A, Feminist History Research Project, Topanga, Calif. Hereafter cited as FHRP.

24. On the role of the WTUL in organizing immigrant women workers see Nancy Schrom Dye, *As Equals and as Sisters: Feminism, the Labor Movement and the Women's Trade Union League* (Columbia, Mo., 1980); Nancy MacLean, "The Culture of Resistance: Female Institution Building in the International Ladies' Garment Workers Union, 1905–1925," Michigan Occasional Papers 21 (Ann Ar-bor, Winter 1982); and Carolyn Daniel McCreesh, "On the Picket Line: Militant Women Campaign to Organize Garment Workers, 1880–1917" (Ph.D. diss., Uni-versity of Maryland, 1975). Karen Mason, "Feeling the Pinch: The Kalamazoo Corset Makers' Strike of 1912," in Milkman, ed., *Women, Work, and Protest*, compares middle-class League members' emphasis on "women's" issues in garment strikes with working-class members' emphasis on "economic" issues. For a discus-sion of the undermining impact of the withdrawal or absence of League support see Lois Scharf, "The Great Uprising in Cleveland: When Sisterhood Failed," in Jensen and Davidson, eds., *A Needle, a Bobbin, a Strike*, pp. 146–67.

25. Mendelsohn, *Class Struggle in the Pale*; Henry Tobias, *The Jewish Bund in Russia from Its Origins to 1905* (Stanford, Calif., 1972); and Nora Levin, *While Messiah Tarried: Jewish Socialist Movements, 1871–1917* (New York, 1977).

26. Mendelsohn, *Class Struggle in the Pale*, pp. 85, 87–88, 52–53, 46, 31; Yitzack Doroshkin, "From Zhitkovitch—through the World," unpub. autobiogra-phy, pp. 43–46, YIVO Archives; and E. Eisenberg, ed., *Plotzk: A History of an Ancient Jewish Community* (Tel Aviv, 1967), p. 53.

27. Tobias, *Jewish Bund in Russia*, pp. 339, 140, 239–40, 246; Levin, *While Messiah Tarried*, pp. 348–59.

28. Mendelsohn, *Class Struggle in the Pale*, pp. 27, 98, 107, 157.

29. For a fuller treatment of these tensions see Chapter 1 and Mendelsohn, *Class Struggle in the Pale*, p. 153.

30. Rischin, *The Promised City*, p. 166. For other interpretations see Arthur Liebman, *Jews and the Left* (New York, 1979), pp. 1–37; Mendelsohn, *Class*

Struggle in the Pale, p. 153. This is also a major theme in Gerald Sorin's study of Jewish radicalism, *The Prophetic Minority: American Jewish Immigrant Radicals, 1880–1920* (Bloomington, Ind., 1985).

31. Mary Kingsbury Simkhovitch, *Neighborhood* (New York, 1938), p. 63.

32. Tape I-83, NYCILHP, Wagner Archives, New York University.

33. Tape I-136, side 2, NYCILHP, Wagner Archives; Ephraim M. Wagner, "The Village Boy," unpub. autobiography, p. 161, YIVO Archives; and Harry Roskolenko, "America the Thief," in Thomas Wheeler, ed., *The Immigrant Experience* (Baltimore, Md., 1971), pp. 167–68. Charles Leinenweber provides an evocative portrait of the political culture of Jewish immigrant socialism in "Socialists in the Streets: The New York City Socialist Party in Working Class Neighborhoods, 1908–1918," *Science and Society* 41 (1977): 152–77.

34. As quoted in George M. D. Wolfe, "A Study of Immigrant Attitudes and Problems" (M.A. thesis, Training School for Jewish Social Work, New York, 1929–33), pp. 173–74.

35. White Goods Strike (1913) testimony, Reel 11, Leonora O'Reilly Papers, Schlesinger Library.

36. Fannia Cohn interview, Aaron Antonovsky Papers, Record Group 100, YIVO Archives.

37. Howe, *World of Our Fathers,* p. 310. For a superb analysis of the relationship between "grass-roots" and "immigrant" socialism and the intersection between the socialist and feminist movements see Mari Jo Buhle, *Women and American Socialism* (Urbana, Ill., 1981).

38. Sorin, *Prophetic Minority,* provides many examples of the fervor with which immigrant radicals embraced socialist ideals.

39. Sorin, *Prophetic Minority,* pp. 162–64.

40. Melvyn Dubofsky, "The Success and Failure of Socialism in New York City," *Labor History* 9 (Fall 1968): 361–75.

41. Ibid.

42. Howe, *World of Our Fathers,* p. 307; Sorin, *Prophetic Minority.*

43. See Dubofsky, "The Success and Failure of Socialism"; Dubofsky, *When Workers Organize,* pp. 33–35; Charles Leinenweber, "The Class and Ethnic Bases of New York City Socialism, 1904–1915," *Labor History* 22 (Winter 1981): 31–56.

44. On the United Hebrew Trades see Tcherikower, *Early Jewish Labor Movement,* pp. 330–32.

45. Numerous writers have stressed the link between the post-1905 influx of Jewish radicals from Russia and the growth of Jewish unionism in the United States. See, for example, Howe, *World of Our Fathers,* pp. 292–93; Budish and Soule, *The New Unionism,* chap. 7; and J. H. M. Laslett, "Jewish Socialism and the Ladies' Garment Workers," in Laslett, *Labor and the Left* (New York, 1970).

46. Tape I-9, NYCILHP, Wagner Archives.

47. Tape I-135, NYCILHP.

48. Interview with Bessie Udin by Sherna Gluck, FHRP.

49. Rose Schneiderman with Lucy Goldthwaite, *All for One* (New York, 1967), p. 49.

50. Ibid., p. 47.

51. As quoted in Levine, *The Women's Garment Workers,* p. 157.

52. For other examples of the role of skilled workers in protest and unioniza-tion see David Brody, *Steel Workers in America: The Non-Union Era* (Cambridge, Mass., 1960); Ronald Schatz, "Union Pioneers: The Founders of Local Unions at General Electric and Westinghouse, 1933–1937," *Journal of American History* 66 (1979): 586–602.

53. Levine, *The Women's Garment Workers,* p. 158.

54. Woods Hutchinson, "Hygienic Aspects of the Shirtwaist Strike," *The Survey* 13 (Jan. 22, 1910): 545.

55. "Girl Strikers Tell Rich Women Their Woes," *New York Times,* Dec. 16, 1909, p. 3. See also Helen Sumner, "The Spirit of the Strikers," *The Survey* 23 (Jan. 22, 1910): 554.

56. Jennie Matyas interview, p. 34, transcript in Industrial Relations Library, University of California, Berkeley.

57. For an example of this kind of rhetoric, see Helen Marot, "A Woman's Strike: An Appreciation of the Shirtwaist Workers of New York," *Proceedings of the Academy of Political Science of New York* 1, no. 1 (Oct. 1910). For further discussion of the WTUL concept of "women's strikes" see Seller, "The Uprising of the Twenty Thousand." Seller too describes these strikes as examples of female "solidarity and feminism," as does MacLean in "The Culture of Resistance." The concept of a "united front of women" is a central framework in Meredith Tax, *The Rising of the Women: Feminist Solidarity and Class Conflict, 1880–1917* (New York, 1980), pp. 11–22 and passim.

58. Alice Kessler-Harris, "Where Are the Organized Women Workers?" *Feminist Studies* 3 (Fall 1975): 92–110.

59. Alice Kessler-Harris, "Organizing the Unorganizable: Three Jewish Women and Their Union," *Labor History* 17 (Winter 1976): 5–23.

60. A description of this incident, probably the most famous in the history of the 1909 strike, is found in F. E. Sheldon, *Souvenir History of the Shirtwaist Makers Strike* (New York, 1910). Many secondary accounts describe the scene at Cooper Union, but the most interesting discussion of Lemlich's background appears in Sorin, *Prophetic Minority,* pp. 81–82.

61. Hutchinson, "Hygienic Aspects of the Shirtwaist Strike."

62. Constance D. Leupp, "The Shirtwaist Makers' Strike," *The Survey* 23 (Dec. 18, 1909): 384. The garment industry was not the only context in which shared work and ethnic cultures led to cooperation during strikes. See Nancy A. Hewitt, "'The Voice of Virile Labor': Labor Militancy, Community Solidarity, and Gender Identity among Tampa's Latin Workers," in Ava Baron, ed., *Work Engendered: Toward a New Understanding of Men, Women, and Work* (Ithaca, N.Y., forthcoming).

63. Gertrude Barnum, "The Children's Crusade," *The Ladies Garment Worker* 4, no. 2 (Feb. 1913).

64. *The Outlook,* Feb. 25, 1911, p. 376.

65. New York Women's Trade Union League, Minutes of the Executive Board, Sept. 15, 1909. New York State Dept. of Labor Library, New York City.

66. See "Girl Strikers Tell Rich Women Their Woes," *New York Times,* Dec. 16, 1909; Schneiderman, *All for One,* pp. 87–89; and Special Meeting of a Committee

to Investigate All of the Grievances of the Firm and the Workers of Joseph Rosenberg and Co., Feb. 8, 1915, Paul Abelson Papers, Box 19, LMDC, Cornell University.

67. Elizabeth Hasanovitz, *One of Them* (New York, 1918), pp. 45–46; interview with May Horowitz by the author.

68. Interview 2 with Lottie Spitzer by Kristine Feichtinger, p. 4, FHRP.

69. Interview with Rebecca August, Aaron Antonovsky Papers, YIVO Archives.

70. Interview with Dora Bayrack by the author.

71. Interview 2 with Lottie Spitzer by Kristine Feichtinger, pp. 2–5; interview 3, pp. 3–4, FHRP.

72. *Life and Labor* 1 (Sept. 1911); "Report," New York Women's Trade Union League, Sept. 8, 1908, Organization Files, New York State Dept. of Labor Library, New York City. See also Mary Van Kleeck, *A Seasonal Industry* (New York, 1917), p. 68, and Elias Tobenkin, "The Immigrant Girl in Chicago," *The Survey* 23 (Nov. 6, 1909): 194.

73. Mary Van Kleeck, *Working Girls in Evening Schools* (New York, 1914), p. 24.

74. "A New York Worker," *Life and Labor* 1 (Dec. 1911).

75. Hasanovitz, *One of Them*, p. 49. See also *The Message* (Local 25, ILGWU) 2 (Nov. 26, 1915); *Justice* (ILGWU), Feb. 22, 1919.

76. Interview with Bessie Mintz by Janice Adelstein, tape 1A, June 1, 1974, FHRP.

77. Interview with Bessie Udin by Sherna Gluck, tape 1A, FHRP.

78. Estimates on the percentages of each ethnic group on strike appear in Marot, "A Woman's Strike," p. 123. Data on the ethnic composition of the female work force in the shirtwaist industry are unavailable for the year of the strike, but the official industry census, completed in March 1913 by the Joint Board of Sanitary Control in the Dress and Waist Industry, provided the approximate figures for this chapter. See "Special Report on Sanitary Conditions in the Shops of the Dress and Waist Industry," May 1913, table II, p. 7. Meredith Tax, who lists no source for her data, provides figures on ethnic labor force participation in 1909 that are very close to the Joint Board's estimates for 1913. See *The Rising of the Women* (New York, 1980), p. 211.

79. Tape I-132, NYCILHP, Wagner Archives.

80. For important discussions of the construction of ethnic group myths see Micaela di Leonardo, *The Varieties of Ethnic Experience: Kinship, Class and Gender among California Italian-Americans* (Ithaca, N.Y., 1984), and James N. Gregory, *American Exodus: The Dust Bowl Migration and Okie Culture in California* (New York, 1989), pp. 146–49.

81. See Carole Turbin, "And We Are Nothing but Women: Irish Working Women in Troy," in Carol Ruth Berkin and Mary Beth Norton, eds., *Women of America: A History* (Boston, 1979); Susan Levine, *Labor's True Woman: Carpet Weavers, Industrialization, and Labor Reform in the Gilded Age* (Philadelphia, 1984); Patricia Cooper, *Once a Cigar Maker: Men, Women, and Work Culture in American Cigar Factories* (Urbana, Ill., 1987); Philip S. Foner, *Women and the American Labor Movement: From the First Trade Union to the Present* (Boston,

1979); and Barbara M. Wertheimer, *We Were There: The Story of Working Women in America* (New York, 1977).

82. Leslie Woodcock Tentler, *Wage-Earning Women: Industrial Work and Family Life in the United States, 1900–1930* (New York, 1979), p. 78.

83. Joan Jensen, "The Great Uprising at Rochester," in Jensen and Davidson, eds., *A Needle, a Bobbin, a Strike.*

84. The most comprehensive studies of Italian immigrant participation in the unionization of the garment industry are Columba Marie Furio, "Immigrant Women and Industry: A Case Study. The Italian Women and the Garment Industry, 1880–1950" (Ph.D. diss., New York University, 1979); Edwin Fenton, "Immigrants and Unions, a Case Study: Italians and American Labor, 1870–1980" (Ph.D. diss., Harvard University, 1957; repr. New York, 1975).

85. On the movement of second-generation Italian immigrants into the union movement see Furio, "Immigrant Women and Industry," and Steve Fraser, "Landslayt and Paesani: Ethnic Conflict and Cooperation in the Amalgamated Clothing Workers of America," in Hoerder, ed., *"Struggle a Hard Battle."*

86. Virginia Yans-McLaughlin, *Family and Community: Italian Immigrants in Buffalo, 1880–1930* (Ithaca, N.Y., 1977), pp. 83–84, 224, 246, 234–35; Furio, "Immigrant Women and Industry," p. 130 and passim.

87. As quoted in Dye, *As Equals and as Sisters,* p. 112.

88. For a critique of this paradigm, see di Leonardo, *The Varieties of Ethnic Experience,* chap. 3. For a more conventional view, see Furio, "Immigrant Women and Industry," pp. 318, 329; Yans-McLaughlin, *Family and Community,* pp. 224, 234–37; Richard Gambino, *Blood of My Blood: The Dilemma of the Italian-Americans* (New York, 1974).

89. See Elizabeth Ewen, *Immigrant Women in the Land of Dollars: Life and Culture on the Lower East Side, 1890–1925* (New York, 1985), pp. 210–11, and Furio, "Immigrant Women and Industry," pp. 27–28.

90. Furio, "Immigrant Women and Industry," pp. 84, 123.

91. Interview with Tina Gaeta, quoted in ibid., p. 447.

92. Interview with Grace de Luise-Natarelli, quoted in ibid., p. 274.

93. Interview with Grace Grimaldi, quoted in Ewen, *Immigrant Women in the Land of Dollars,* p. 256.

94. Furio, "Immigrant Women and Industry," pp. 121, 201, 208 and passim.

95. Hasanovitz, *One of Them,* pp. 48–49.

96. Interview with Rose Priola Falk by Kristine Feichtinger, Sept. 5, 1975, p. 7, FHRP.

97. Furio, "Immigrant Women and Industry," p. 326.

98. See "Whistle Blasts Send 40,000 Girls on Strike," New York *World,* Dec. 2, 1909, p. 4.

99. Jennie Matyas interview, p. 35.

100. Interview with Rebecca Holland by Patti Pricket, tape 1A, FHRP.

101. Interview with Sarah Rozner, in Questionnaires for Union Members, Aaron Antonovsky Papers, YIVO Archives.

102. See Rudolph Vecoli, "The Italian Immigrants in the United States Labor Movement from 1880 to 1929," in Franco Angeli, ed., *Gli italiani fuori d'Italia* (Milan, 1983), pp. 270–71; Eugene Miller and Gianna Panovsky, "Radical Italian

Unionism: Its Development and Decline in Chicago's Men's Garment Industry, 1910–1930," paper presented at Illinois Labor History Society conference "One Hundred Years of Organized Labor in Illinois," Oct. 9–10, 1981 (my thanks to Joe Costigan of the Chicago Joint Board of the ACWA for bringing this paper to my attention); Fenton, "Immigrants and Unions," chap. 9.

103. Vecoli, "The Italian Immigrants in the United States Labor Movement," pp. 274–75; Fraser, "Landslayt and Paesani"; Fenton, "Immigrants and Unions," chap. 9.

104. Fenton, "Immigrants and Unions," pp. 292, 484–85; 527–30; Vecoli, "The Italian Immigrants in the United States Labor Movement," pp. 278–79.

105. Fenton, "Immigrants and Unions," pp. 527–33.

106. Minutes of the General Executive Board, ILGWU Sixth Quarterly Report, 1916, ILGWU Archives, LMDC, Cornell University; Nancy Schrom Dye, "The Women's Trade Union League of New York, 1903–1920" (Ph.D. diss., University of Wisconsin, 1974), pp. 274–81; Furio, "Immigrant Women and Industry," p. 234 and passim; *The Ladies' Garment Worker* 1 (Jan. 9, 1911).

107. Furio, "Immigrant Women and Industry," pp. 244–45.

108. See Fraser, "Landslayt and Paesani"; Miller and Panofsky, "Radical Italian Unionism"; Fenton, chap. 9; and Vecoli, "Italian Immigrants in the United States Labor Movement."

109. Fraser, "Landslayt and Paesani."

110. See Hutchins Hapgood, *The Spirit of the Ghetto* (New York, 1902; repr. Cambridge, Mass., 1967), pp. 76–84. Nancy Schrom Dye, in *As Equals and as Sisters,* discusses the WTUL stereotypes of Jewish radical women. Mari Jo Buhle notes the romantic images of the radical woman popularized by Jewish poets and journalists; *Women and American Socialism,* pp. 178–79, 196–97.

111. On "Alrightniks" see Howe, *World of Our Fathers,* p. 132; Baum et al., *The Jewish Woman,* pp. 199–214. On Austro-Hungarian and Romanian women see Elias Tobenkin, "The Immigrant Girl in Chicago," *The Survey,* Nov. 6, 1909, p. 194.

112. Interview with Ida Richter in Sydelle Kramer and Jenny Masur, eds., *Jewish Grandmothers* (Boston, 1976), p. 131.

113. Charles Bernheimer, ed., *The Russian Jew in the United States* (New York, 1905), p. 153.

114. On the Jewish press see Mordecai Soltes, *The Yiddish Press: An Americanizing Agency* (New York, 1925), pp. 14–29; Howe, *World of Our Fathers,* chap. 16; and Ronald Sanders, *The Downtown Jews* (New York, 1969), p. 384.

115. Interview with Fannie Shapiro in Kramer and Masur, eds., *Jewish Grandmothers,* p. 7.

116. Howe, *World of Our Fathers,* p. 520.

117. *Jewish Daily Forward,* April 1, 1906, quoted in George M. D. Wolfe, "A Study of Immigrant Attitudes and Problems, Based on Analysis of Four Hundred Letters in the 'Bintl Brief' of the *Jewish Daily Forward*" (thesis, Training School for Jewish Social Work, New York, 1920–1933), part I.

118. "Second-Hand Tailors Rest over Sabbath," *New York Call,* July 9, 1910, p. 2.

119. See Sorin, *Prophetic Minority,* pp. 89–91, and Howe, *World of Our Fa-*

294 Notes to Chapter 5

thers, pp. 112, 108–9. For a good example of this mixing of secular and religious values, see Melech Epstein, *Jewish Labor in the U.S.A.: An Industrial, Political, and Cultural History of the Jewish Labor Movement* (New York, 1969), pp. 173–74. Bernard Weinstein, secretary of United Hebrew Trades, once attended a meeting of children's jacket pressers at a small East Side synagogue, where the chairman of the local told his audience that Moses was "the first walking delegate among the Jews."

120. Rischin, *Promised City,* pp. 250, 178–79, 234, 246.

121. Howe, *World of Our Fathers,* p. 520; Epstein, *Jewish Labor in the U.S.A.,* p. 154.

122. This conclusion is based on the *Yiddishes Tageblatt* coverage of the 1909 shirtwaist strike, the 1910 cloakmakers' strike, and the 1913 white goods strike. *Tageblatt,* Nov. 23, 1909–Feb. 15, 1910; July 28, 1910–Sept. 6, 1910; Jan. 8, 1913–Feb. 24, 1913. Mordecai Soltes's survey of Yiddish press attitudes toward strikes and unionization also concludes that most newspapers supported labor's right to organize for self-protection and to raise living standards, though some of the more conservative papers advocated the avoidance of "unnecessary strikes" through arbitration. *The Yiddish Press: An Americanizing Agency,* pp. 139–41.

123. Unsigned editorials, *Tageblatt,* July 28, 1910, p. 4, and Aug. 3, 1910, p. 4. On the conciliatory role of the Jewish Orthodox press in Chicago's strike movement see Seymour J. Pomerenze, "Aspects of Chicago Russian-Jewish Life," in Simon Rawidowicz, ed., *The Chicago Pinkas* (Chicago, 1952), pp. 125–26.

124. See Moses Rischin, *The Promised City* (Cambridge, Mass., 1977), pp. 245–46.

125. Chicago *Daily Courier,* Aug. 27, 1912; April 27, 1917; July 18, 1919. Typed translations in Works Progress Administration (WPA) Foreign Language Press Survey, Regenstein Library, University of Chicago.

126. *Naye Post,* Dec. 7, 1910, p. 1, copy in Paul Abelson Papers, LMDC, Cornell University.

127. Bernard Drachman to Benjamin Schlesinger, May 5, 1916, Schlesinger Correspondence, Box 1, Folder 12, ILGWU Archives, LMDC, Cornell University.

128. On the relationship between shared occupational culture and political behavior of immigrants see Elinor Lerner, "Family Structure, Occupational Patterns, and Support for Women's Suffrage," in Judith Friedlander et al., eds., *Women in Culture and Politics* (Bloomington, Ind., 1986), pp. 223–36; Judith E. Smith, *Family Connections: A History of Italian and Jewish Immigrant Lives in Providence, Rhode Island, 1900–1940* (Albany, N.Y., 1985), pp. 154–57. Nancy L. Green's study of the strike movement among Jewish immigrant workers in turn-of-the-century Paris also underscores the centrality of immigrant occupational and local community networks for labor organization, as does Hadassah Kosak's discussion of the community context of industrial strikes and consumer boycotts among immigrant Jews in New York in the late nineteenth century. See Greene, *The Pletzl of Paris,* pp. 172–94, and Hadassah Kosak, "The Rise of the Jewish Working Class, New York, 1881–1905" (Ph.D. diss., City University of New York, 1987), pp. 227–58.

129. Isidore Wisotsky, "Such a Life," unpub. autobiography, p. 11, YIVO Archives. See also Charles Zimmerman interview, p. 5, YIVO Amerikaner Yiddish Geshikhte Bel-Pe, YIVO Archives, and Rose Cohen, *Out of the Shadow* (New York, 1918).

130. For further elaboration, see Leinenweber, "Socialists in the Streets." For similar findings on the community nature of Jewish immigrant strikes in Paris see Greene, *The Pletzl of Paris,* pp. 190–91. The interconnections between strikes and daily life in working-class communities as well as the role of non–wage earners in strikes have been documented in other contexts. See, for example, Ardis Cameron, "Bread and Roses Revisited: Women's Culture and Working Class Activism in the Lawrence Strike of 1912," and Priscilla Long, "The Women of the Colorado Fuel and Iron Strike, 1913–14," both in Milkman, ed., *Women, Work, and Protest;* Temma Kaplan, "Female Consciousness and Collective Action: The Case of Barcelona, 1910–1918," *Signs* 7 (Spring 1982): 545–66.

131. *New York Call,* Dec. 25, 1909, p. 2.

132. *New York Call,* Nov. 23, 1909, p. 1.

133. *New York Call,* Nov. 25, 1909, p. 1.

134. Lang, *"62": Biography of a Union,* p. 101.

135. Abraham Rosenberg to Officers of the Executive Board of the Women's Trade League, Aug. 4, 1911, Box 2, Folder 4, Rose Schneiderman Papers, Wagner Archives, New York University.

136. Pauline Newman, "Types of Jewish Girls Active in the Cloak Makers' Strike," *New York Call,* July 15, 1910, p. 2.

137. Interview with Pearl Spenser by Elizabeth Balanoff, June 8, 1976, Oral History Collection, Roosevelt University, Chicago.

Chapter 6. "As We Are Not Angels"

1. Mollie Schepps's speech was reprinted in *Life and Labor,* July 1912, pp. 215–16.

2. For a discussion of the Wage Earners' Suffrage League, see Nancy Schrom Dye, *As Equals and as Sisters: Feminism, Unionism, and the Women's Trade Union League of New York* (Columbia, Mo., 1980), pp. 127, 133, and Elinor Lerner, "Immigrant and Working Class Involvement in the New York City Woman Suffrage Movement, 1905–1917: A Study in Progressive Era Politics" (Ph.D. diss., University of California, Berkeley, 1981), p. 191.

3. See Linda Gordon Kuzmak, "The Emergence of the Jewish Women's Movement in England and the United States, 1881–1933: A Comparative Study" (Ph.D. diss., George Washington University, 1986), pp. 524–28. Kuzmak concludes that most active suffragists tended to be middle-class German Jews rather than Russian Jewish immigrants. Jewish women's support for suffrage is discussed in Lerner, "Immigrant and Working Class Involvement." Support for suffrage was strong in the eastern European Jewish community, though this was (with the exception of the Wage Earners' Suffrage League) not expressed in organizations whose chief goal was winning the vote for women.

4. There is an extensive literature on the New Woman. Especially useful are Carroll Smith-Rosenberg, "The New Woman as Androgyne: Social Disorder and Gender Crisis, 1870–1936," in Smith-Rosenberg, *Disorderly Conduct: Visions of Gender in Victorian America* (New York, 1985); Jill K. Conway, "Female Reformers and American Culture," in Jean E. Friedman and William G. Shade, eds., *Our American Sisters* (Lexington, Mass., 1982); Mary P. Ryan, *Womanhood in America,* 2d ed. (New York, 1979), pp. 152–82; Sheila M. Rothman, *Woman's*

Proper Place: A History of Changing Ideals and Practices, 1870 to the Present (New York, 1978); June Sochen, *The New Woman in Greenwich Village, 1910–1920* (New York, 1972); Elaine Tyler May, *Great Expectations: Marriage and Divorce in Post-Victorian America* (Chicago, 1980); and Nancy F. Cott, *The Grounding of Modern Feminism* (New Haven, Conn., 1987). The image and style of the flapper are discussed in Paula S. Fass, *The Damned and the Beautiful* (New York, 1977).

5. Hutchins Hapgood, *The Spirit of the Ghetto: Studies of the Jewish Quarter in New York* (New York, 1902; repr. Cambridge, Mass., 1967), pp. 76–85.

6. The wording is Joanne Meyerowitz's. Writing of the subcultures of single working women, Meyerowitz goes further, suggesting that middle-class "bohemians" in America in the 1920s learned about new sexual possibilities not only from "highbrow" sexologists but also from the "lowbrow" sexual exploits of working-class women. See *Women Adrift: Independent Wage Earners in Chicago, 1880–1930* (Urbana, Ill., 1988), pp. 115–16 and chap. 5. Kathy Peiss has argued that changes in feminine demeanor and attitudes were a result not simply of upper-class styles "trickling down" to working women but of workers "pioneering" new styles of mixed-sex public behavior: *Cheap Amusements: Working Women and Leisure in Turn-of-the-Century New York*. See also Lewis Erenberg, *Steppin' Out: New York Nightlife and the Transformation of American Culture* (Chicago, 1981). For an important analysis of working-class New Womanhood as it evolved in the context of labor organization, see Jacqueline Dowd Hall, "Disorderly Women: Gender and Labor Militancy in the Appalachian South," *Journal of American History* 73 (Sept. 1986): 354–82.

7. Cott, *The Grounding of Modern Feminism*, pp. 42, 27–34, 35–41, 151, 236–37. See also Ellen Carol DuBois, "Working Women and Suffrage Militance: Harriot Stanton Blatch and the New York Woman Suffrage Movement, 1894–1909," *Journal of American History* 74 (June 1987), esp. pp. 66–68. Dye, *As Equals and as Sisters*, pp. 9, 55–56, also notes the tendency of middle-class women to romanticize the lives of wage earners.

8. I use the term "civic" to refer to the constellation of public responsibilities, rights, and activities associated with protecting and bettering the welfare of the immigrant community. Civic concerns extend beyond issues of wages and hours for workers and reflect working people's larger concerns for a voice in the polity.

9. Consumer protests are discussed in Paula Hyman, "Immigrant Women and Consumer Protest: The New York City Kosher Meat Boycott of 1902," *American Jewish History* 70 (1980): 91–105; Elizabeth Ewen, *Immigrant Women in the Land of Dollars: Life and Culture on the Lower East Side, 1890–1925* (New York, 1985), pp. 126–27, 176; Dana Frank, "Housewives, Socialists, and the Politics of Food: The 1917 Cost of Living Protests," *Feminist Studies* 11 (Summer 1985): 255–86; Judith Smith, *Family Connections: A History of Italian and Jewish Immigrant Lives in Providence, Rhode Island, 1900–1940* (Albany, N.Y., 1985), pp. 156–57; Hadassah Kosak, "The Rise of the Jewish Working Class, New York, 1881–1905" (Ph.D. diss., City University of New York, 1987), pp. 228–39; Leon Stein, "The Great Flanken War of 1902," presented at the New York State Labor History Association, Albany, June 1, 1978, unpub. ms. in author's possession.

10. Hyman, "New York City Kosher Meat Boycott," and Kosak, "Rise of the Jewish Working Class," show the strong class-conscious language of these protests.

Kosak argues that consumer protest and strike activity were mutually reinforcing, both of them parts of the quest for collective social justice in defiance of capitalist individualism.

11. My thinking on this issue has been influenced by Temma Kaplan, "Female Consciousness and Collective Action: The Case of Barcelona, 1910–1918," *Signs* 7 (Spring 1982): 545–66, and Sheila Rowbotham, *Women, Resistance, and Revolution* (London, 1972), pp. 102–4. Virginia Yans-McLaughlin follows a similar interpretive tack when she asserts that Italian women used radical protest methods to carry out the "conventional expectations" of females to feed the family. See *Family and Community: Italian Immigrants in Buffalo, 1880–1930* (Ithaca, N.Y., 1971), pp. 250–51.

12. As quoted in Mary Brown Sumner, "Spirit of the Strikers," *The Survey* 23 (Jan. 22, 1910): 551.

13. Interview with Fannia Cohn, in Questionnaires for Union Members, Aaron Antonovsky Papers, YIVO Archives, New York.

14. Jennie Matyas interview, pp. 36–37, transcript at Industrial Relations Institute, University of California at Berkeley.

15. On female-centered reformers and "homosocial" networks see Conway, "Female Reformers and American Culture." See also Ryan, *Womanhood in America*, pp. 135–44; Carroll Smith-Rosenberg's comment in "Politics and Culture in Women's History: A Symposium," *Feminist Studies* 6 (Spring 1980); Estelle Freedman, "Separatism as a Strategy: Female Institution Building and American Feminism, 1870–1930," *Feminist Studies* 5 (Fall 1979): 512–29.

16. For an extended discussion of German Jewish reform and feminist movements and their woman-centered approach to activism, see Kuzmack, "The Emergence of the Jewish Women's Movement in England and the United States," pp. 389, 564, and passim.

17. Paula E. Hyman, "Gender and Culture: Women in the Immigrant Jewish Community," in David E. Berger, ed., *The Legacy of Jewish Migration: 1881 and Its Impact* (New York, 1983).

18. For an important discussion that stresses the need to pay attention to the ways in which race, class, and ethnicity mediate women's culture, see Nancy A. Hewitt, "Beyond the Search for Sisterhood: American Women's History in the 1980's," *Social History* 10 (Oct. 1985): 299–321.

19. The complexion of the Progressive Reform movement was changing in this period as radical feminists who wanted both heterosexual relationships and careers entered the fray, but many women who chose reform careers still found themselves closely bound to the female community, living and working with other women. On the radicals see Cott, *Grounding of Modern Feminism*. Alice Kessler-Harris shows the tensions in the careers of Jewish unionists in "Organizing the Unorganizable: Three Jewish Women and Their Union," *Labor History* 17 (Winter 1976): 5–23, noting that the choice to remain single was a painful one that went against personal inclination and ethnic values.

20. On this pattern see Harriet Davis-Kram, "Jewish Women in Russian Revolutionary Movements" (M.A. thesis, Hunter College, 1979), and "The Story of the Sisters of the Bund," *Contemporary Jewry* 5 (Winter 1980): 27–43.

21. I am borrowing from Mari Jo Buhle's terminology to distinguish between

native-born or grass-roots varieties of feminism that grew out of the separate spheres traditions of middle-class womanhood in the United States and the urban-immigrant (in this case, Jewish socialist) contributions to political culture in the late nineteenth and early twentieth centuries. Buhle, *Women and American Socialism*.

22. On the tradition of the "woman movement" in American feminism see Cott, *Grounding of Modern Feminism;* Freedman, "Separatism as a Strategy"; and Buhle, *Women and American Socialism*.

23. Lerner, "The New York City Woman Suffrage Movement," p. 348.

24. Ibid., pp. 351–68. These findings are conveniently summarized by Lerner in "Family Structure, Occupational Patterns, and Support for Women's Suffrage," in Judith Friedlander et al., eds., *Women in Culture and Politics: A Century of Change* (Bloomington, Ind., 1986).

25. Lerner, "New York City Woman Suffrage Movement," p. 351, also stresses that in the climate of anti-Semitism Jewish immigrants saw the vote for women as protection against potential threats to the community, such as immigration restriction.

26. For an overview of the problem see Alice Kessler-Harris, "Where Are the Organized Women Workers?" *Feminist Studies* 3 (Fall 1975): 92–110. For an example of the disastrous situation that could result when male workers failed to organize women in their trade, see Patricia A. Cooper, *Once a Cigar Maker: Men, Women, and Work Culture in American Cigar Factories* (Urbana, Ill., 1987).

27. The rate of membership turnover in Local 25 is discussed in Alice Kessler-Harris, "Problems of Coalition-Building: Women and Trade Unions in the 1920s," in Ruth Milkman, ed., *Women, Work and Protest: A Century of Women's Labor History* (Boston, 1985).

28. See Kessler-Harris, "Problems of Coalition-Building"; Nancy MacLean, "The Culture of Resistance: Female Institution Building in the International Ladies' Garment Workers' Union, 1905–1925," Michigan Occasional Papers 21 (Ann Arbor, Winter 1982).

29. On the new unionism see J. M. Budish and George Soule, *The New Unionism in the Clothing Industry* (New York, 1920); Steven Clark Fraser, "Sidney Hillman and the Origins of the New Unionism, 1890–1933" (Ph.D. diss., Rutgers University, 1983); and Louis Levine, *The Women's Garment Workers* (New York, 1924).

30. Levine, *Women's Garment Workers,* p. 485. Rose Schneiderman spoke of the need to give the labor movement a "social as well as an economic attraction." See "Women's Trade Union League, Report of an Organizer, 1908–1909," Schneiderman Papers, Box 6, Folder 2, Wagner Labor Archives, Bobst Library, New York University. For further commentary on this issue, see Hattie Goodman, letter to editor in *The Message* [Local 25, ILGWU] 2 (May 28, 1915): 6–7. See also MacLean, "Culture of Resistance," pp. 68–69, and Kessler-Harris, "Problems of Coalition-Building."

31. Anna Rudnitzky, "Time Is Passing," *Life and Labor* 2 (April, 1912), n.p.

32. Budish and Soule, *The New Unionism,* pp. 215–16; Levine, *The Women's Garment Workers,* pp. 487–88; Robert J. Schaeffer, "Educational Activities of the Garment Unions, 1890–1948" (Ph.D. diss., Columbia University, 1951); Ricki Carole Myers Cohen, "Fannia Cohn and the International Ladies' Garment Work-

ers Union" (Ph.D. diss., University of Southern California, 1976), p. 124 and passim.

33. Levine, *The Women's Garment Workers,* pp. 492–93. MacLean, "Culture of Resistance," pp. 67–77, 88–91, discusses both education and recreation in the ILGWU as though these were exclusively "female" institutions, thus implying they were of little interest to men. My point is that while women initiated these programs, the programs had a wide appeal.

34. See Levine, *Women's Garment Workers,* p. 338.

35. Budish and Soule, *The New Unionism,* pp. 214–20.

36. On the Progressive reformers' attitudes toward urban amusements for working-class women see Peiss, *Cheap Amusements.* Colette Hyman notes the propensity of middle-class League members in Chicago to build programs that would promote "acceptable social activities" for union women, though she does not tie this to the Progressive reform ethos. See "Labor Organizing and Female Institution-Building: The Chicago Women's Trade Union League, 1904–24," in Milkman, ed., *Women, Work, and Protest.*

37. See Levine, *Women's Garment Workers,* pp. 500–502.

38. Vernon L. Lidtke, *The Alternative Culture: Socialist Labor in Imperial Germany* (New York, 1985). Well before the ILGWU got its educational programs off the ground, the socialists were busy establishing programs for workers' education such as the Rand School, founded in New York in 1906. See Schaeffer, "Educational Activities of the Garment Unions," p. 55.

39. Unpub. doc. J-R 34, vol. 2, pp. 8–9, Columbia University Research on Contemporary Cultures Collection, Manuscripts Division, Library of Congress.

40. Ibid. See also Max Danish, "Educational Problems of Our International," Oct. 25, 1918, pp. 1–2, ms. in Rand School of Social Science Papers, New York Public Library.

41. This is the central theme in her autobiographical novel *Bread Givers* (New York, 1925).

42. Interview with Fannia Cohn, Questionnaires for Union Members, Antonovsky Papers, YIVO Archives. This issue is also discussed in Schaffer, "Educational Activities in the Garment Unions," pp. 69–71.

43. See, for example, Rose Pesotta, *Days of Our Lives* (Boston, 1958), p. 169; Brucha Gutrajman, "A Woman's Story," unpub. autobiography, p. 100, YIVO Archives; and Yitzack Yankev Doroshkin, "From Zhitkovitch—through the World: Episodes from My Life," unpub. autobiography, YIVO Archives. See also Henry Tobias, *The Jewish Bund in Russia, from Its Origins to 1905* (Stanford, Calif., 1972), p. 29, and Maxine Seller, "The Education of the Immigrant Woman, 1900–1935," *Journal of Urban History* 4 (May 1978): 307–31.

44. Interview with Bessie Udin by Sherna Gluck, tape 1, side 1, Feminist History Research Project (FHRP), Topanga, Calif.

45. Esther Frumkin as quoted in Nora Levin, *While Messiah Tarried: Jewish Socialist Movements, 1871–1917* (New York, 1977), p. 248.

46. Fannia Cohn to Rebecca Holland, Oct. 22, 1924, Fannia Cohn Papers, Box 4, Manuscripts Division, New York Public Library.

47. Gus Tyler is quoted in Cohen, "Fannia Cohn and the International Ladies' Garment Workers' Union," p. 128.

48. Mollie Friedman is quoted in Schaeffer, "Educational Activities of the Garment Unions," pp. 67–68.

49. Tape I-21, New York City Immigrant Labor History Collection (NYCILHP), Wagner Labor Archives, Bobst Library, New York University.

50. Fannie Shapiro interview in Kramer and Masur, eds., *Jewish Grandmothers*, p. 12. See also S. Adele Shaw, "Organized Stitching," *The Survey*, April 29, 1922, pp. 141–45, and Amalgamated Clothing Workers of America, Chicago Joint Board, *The Clothing Workers of Chicago, 1910–1922* (Chicago, 1922), pp. 274–76.

51. Quoted in Shaw, "Organized Stitching," p. 143.

52. Ibid.

53. Quoted in Charles H. Winslow, "Conciliation, Arbitration, and Sanitation in the Dress and Waist Industry of New York City," U.S. Bureau of Labor Statistics, *Bulletin* 145 (Washington, D.C., 1914). See also Julius Henry Cohen, "The Revised Protocol in the Dress and Waist Industry," April 1916, typescript in Charles Bernheimer Papers, Box 4, New York Historical Society; Minutes of the General Executive Board, ILGWU, Special Meeting of the New York GEB, Dec. 20, 1915, copy in ILGWU Archives; and ACWA, *The Clothing Workers of Chicago*, pp. 196–281. See also Hyman Berman, "Era of Protocol: A Chapter in the History of the International Ladies' Garment Workers' Union, 1910–1916" (Ph.D. diss., Columbia University); Levine, *The Women's Garment Workers;* Budish and Soule, *The New Unionism;* and Elizabeth Israels Perry, "Industrial Reform in New York City: Belle Moskowitz and the Protocol of Peace, 1913–1916," *Labor History* 23 (Winter 1982): 5–31.

54. Tape I-108, New York City Immigrant Labor History Project (NYCILHP), Wagner Archives, Bobst Library, New York University.

55. Tape I-132, NYCILHP, Wagner Archives.

56. Tape I-3, NYCILHP, Wagner Archives.

57. Interview 3 with Sarah Rozner by Sherna Gluck, p. 22, and interview 4, p. 5, FHRP. Italics added.

58. The term was used by Julius Henry Cohen, attorney for the Dress and Shirtwaist Manufacturers Association. See "Revised Protocol . . . Dress and Waist Industry" (1916), p. 10, Bernheimer Papers, Box 4, New York Historical Society. The assertive behavior of women workers is best viewed in the context of arbitration and mediation proceedings. See, for example, Arbitration Proceedings between the Dress and Waist Manufacturers Association of New York and the ILGWU, May 17, 1914; Arbitration Proceedings between the Ladies Dress and Waist Manufacturers Association and the ILGWU, Feb. 6 and 7, 1916, transcripts in ILGWU Research Dept., New York City.

59. On this point see Steve Fraser, "Dress Rehearsal for the New Deal: Shop-Floor Insurgents, Political Elites, and Industrial Democracy in the Amalgamated Clothing Workers," in Michael H. Frisch and Daniel J. Walkowitz, eds., *Working Class America: Essays on Labor, Community, and American Society* (Urbana, Ill., 1983).

60. Interview 2A with Mollie Steinholtz by Taffie Viner, May 5, 1974, FHRP. Other women tell of workers violating union rules in order to follow shop customs that would keep up their earning level. Interview 4 with Lottie Spitzer by Kristine

Feichtinger, p. 30; and interview with Rebecca Holland by Patti Pricket, both in FHRP.

61. Minutes of the Joint Board of Grievances in the Dress and Waist Industry, New York City, January–May, 1914, Case 4854, Feb. 13, 1914, Aero Waist Co., pp. 193–99. Transcript in Paul Abelson Papers, Labor-Management Documentation Center (LMDC), Catherwood Library, Cornell University. See also Arbitration Proceedings between the Dress and Waist Manufacturers Association of New York and the ILGWU, May 17, 1914, pp. 7, 43–54. Transcript in ILGWU Research Dept., New York.

62. Arbitration Proceedings between the Dress and Waist Manufacturers Association of New York and the ILGWU, May 17, 1914, pp. 24–25 and passim. With regard to such protocol violations, Socialist politician and garment union lawyer Meyer London observed that workers would fight harder against an "unreasonable rule" than for better wages and hours.

63. Report of the general secretary John A. Dyche, Proceedings of the Tenth Annual Convention of the ILGWU, June 1910. See also Berman, "Era of Protocol," p. 424.

64. Arbitration Proceedings between the Dress and Waist Manufacturers Association of New York and the International Ladies' Garment Workers' Union, Nov. 8 and 9, 1913, pp. 152–54, Abelson Papers, LMDC, Catherwood Library, Cornell University. For other examples see Arbitration Proceedings between the Ladies' Dress and Waist Manufacturers Association and the ILGWU, Feb. 6 and 7, 1916, p. 389, copy in ILGWU Research Dept.; Board of Grievances under the Protocol of Peace, Decision of Chief Clerk, New York, May 2, 1916, in Matter of Union Complaint no. 1064, against Adler and Ast, Charge of Lockout. Transcript in Bernheimer Papers, Box 4, New York Historical Society.

65. For the classification of the kind of complaints that women had against employers in union shops, see Arbitration Proceedings between the Ladies' Dress and Waist Manufacturers Association and the ILGWU, Feb. 26, 1916, New York, p. 1411a. Copy in ILGWU Research Dept. See also Winslow, "Conciliation and Arbitration and Sanitation in the Dress and Waist Industry of New York City."

66. Winslow, "Conciliation and Arbitration," p. 20; Chicago Joint Board, ACWA, Clothing Workers of Chicago, p. 127; Charlotte Baum, Paula Hyman, and Sonya Michel, The Jewish Woman in America (New York, 1976), p. 147.

67. Interview 7 with Lottie Spitzer by Kristine Feichtinger, p. 8, FHRP.

68. Nina Lynn Asher, "Dorothy Jacobs Bellanca: Feminist Trade Unionist, 1894–1946" (Ph.D. diss., State University of New York at Binghamton, 1982), pp. 100, 107–8. See also Carolyn McCreesh, "On the Picketline: Militant Women Campaign to Organize Garment Workers, 1880–1917" (Ph.D. diss., University of Maryland, 1975), pp. 251–52.

69. Levine, Women's Garment Workers, annotated "Index of Names," suggests the lopsided distribution of power between the sexes. See also McCreesh, "On the Picketline," pp. 246–47.

70. On the dilemmas of socialist women see Mari Jo Buhle, Women and American Socialism, 1870–1920 (Urbana, Ill., 1981). For an excellent study of a Jewish unionist grappling with this problem, see Nina Asher, "Dorothy Jacobs Bellanca: Women Clothing Workers and Runaway Shops," in Joan M. Jensen and Sue David-

son, eds., *A Needle, a Bobbin, a Strike: Women Needleworkers in America* (Philadelphia, 1984). Alice Kessler-Harris also focuses on these issues in "Organizing the Unorganizable" and "Problems of Coalition Building."

71. Buhle, *Women and American Socialism*, pp. 105–22. For a somewhat different interpretation, see Sally M. Miller, "Socialism and Women," in John H. M. Laslett and Seymour Martin Lipset, eds., *Failure of a Dream? Essays in the History of American Socialism*, rev. ed. (Berkeley, Calif., 1984). Miller argues that Socialist women quite consciously "chose to enter a men's club." Thus unlike Buhle, who stresses the differences between separatists and integrationists, Miller underplays the degree to which separatism was a critical issue for women in the party. See the two authors' "replies" to one another's arguments in *Failure of a Dream*.

72. For an analysis of the League's influence on Jewish unionists, see MacLean, "Culture of Resistance," pp. 53–63 and passim.

73. Report of Secretary, April 27, 1911, Minutes of the Executive Board, Papers of the Women's Trade Union League of New York, New York State Dept. of Labor Library, New York City.

74. On this point see Dye, *As Equals and as Sisters*, p. 85. Dye insists that the League rejected separatist schemes for fear of alienating the AFL. It seems clear from other accounts, however, that what the League endorsed in public and what they privately favored were not always the same. For an analysis of the separatist issue in the garment workers' union and of League influence, see MacLean, "Culture of Resistance." The garment workers' unions were not the only ones to experiment with separatist tactics. Sue Cobble's "Rethinking the Troubled Relation between Women and Unions: The Exceptional Case of Waitress Activism," forthcoming in *Feminist Studies*, traces the history of separate women's locals and the reasons for their success.

75. Alice Henry, *The Trade Union Woman* (New York, 1915), p. 155.

76. Ibid., p. 285.

77. Constance Denmark, "Our Women Workers," *The Ladies' Garment Worker* 5 (Aug. 1914).

78. John Andrews and W. D. P. Bliss, *History of Women in Trade Unions* [Report on Condition of Women and Child Wage-Earners in the United States], (Washington, D.C., 1911), p. 223.

79. "Cloak Finishers of New York," *The Ladies Garment Worker* 4 (May 1913): 23–24.

80. As quoted in MacLean, "Culture of Resistance," p. 44.

81. See MacLean, "Culture of Resistance," p. 63. Indeed, it was not until the 1920s that German Jewish women, whose cultural orientation in some ways was closer to that of American middle-class women than to Russian Jewish immigrants, began to adopt separatism, doing so for reasons similar to those of the "social housekeepers." On Jewish women's organizations in the 1920s see Norma Fain Pratt, "Transitions in Judaism: The Jewish American Woman through the 1930s," *American Quarterly* 30 (Winter 1978): 681–702.

82. Buhle, *Women and American Socialism*, pp. 131, 188–89, 206, and passim.

83. Raissa Lomonossoff to Joseph Schlossberg, April 2, 1920, ACWA Papers, Box 12, Folder 24, LMDC, Catherwood Library, Cornell University.

84. Letter to Sam Levin, Manager of Chicago Joint Board, n.d. [c. 1920], as

quoted in Sherna Gluck, ed., " 'What Is It We Want, Brother Levin?' Reminiscences of a Nonconforming Shop Girl, 1892–1976," pp. 28–30, oral history summary based on Gluck's interviews with Rozner from the Feminist History Research Project as well as Rozner's letters and diary entries. Unpub. ms. in author's possession.

85. Interview 1 with Rose Priola Falk and Agnes Budilovsky by Kristine Feichtinger, p. 5, Sept. 5, 1974, FHRP.

86. Constance Denmark, "Our Women Workers," *The Ladies Garment Worker* 5 (Aug. 1914). See also MacLean, "Culture of Resistance," pp. 64–66.

87. Interview with Rose Kaplan [Himmelfarb] by Sherna Gluck, tape 1B, FHRP. See also "Cloak Finishers of New York," *The Ladies' Garment Worker* 4 (May 1913): 23–24.

88. Asher, "Dorothy Jacobs Bellanca: Feminist Trade Unionist," p. 95.

89. See the *Advance* [ACWA] 1 (July 27, 1917); Sept. 28, 1917.

90. *Advance,* March 9, 1917.

91. See Nettie Richardson to Jacob Potofsky, April 27, 1920, File 52, Box 31, ACWA Papers, LMDC, Catherwood Library, Cornell University. Sherna Gluck, "Socialist Feminism between the Two World Wars: Insights from Oral History," in Lois Scharf and Joan M. Jensen, eds., *Decades of Discontent: The Women's Movement, 1920–1940* (Westport, Conn., 1983), claims that seven women ran as delegates in Chicago. Rozner recalled in her oral interviews that all of the Chicago women including herself were defeated in the election but that to "bribe" her to "forget about the women's local" she was allowed to sit as a delegate for coatmakers' Local 39. See Gluck, ed., " 'What Is It We Want, Brother Levin?' " p. 24.

92. As quoted in Gluck, ed., " 'What Is It We Want, Brother Levin?' " p. 23.

93. Rozner's account in ibid., pp. 24–28.

94. Ibid., p. 23. Rozner served as business agent for Local 275 from 1922 to 1923.

95. Interview with Rose Kaplan [Himmelfarb] by Sherna Gluck, tape 1B, FHRP.

96. See Kessler-Harris, "Problems of Coalition Building." Sherna Gluck argues that it was the women in the left wing of the ILGWU who first supported the branches and who also led the move to abolish them when they had outlived their usefulness. See "Socialist Feminism," pp. 285–86.

97. Raissa Lomonossoff to Joseph Schlossberg, April 22, 1920, Box 12, Folder 24, ACWA Papers, LMDC, Catherwood Library, Cornell University.

98. Interview 1 with Rose Priola Falk and Agnes Budilovsky by Kristine Feichtinger, p. 4, FHRP.

99. Nettie Richardson to Jacob Potofsky, Aug. 21, 1920, File 52, Box 31, ACWA Papers, LMDC, Cornell University.

100. Falk and Budilovsky interview 1 by Kristine Feichtinger, p. 3, FHRP.

101. Ibid., p. 15; Feichtinger interview 3 with Agnes Budilovsky, p. 9, FHRP.

102. Hortense Powdermaker to Dorothy Jacobs Bellanca, Aug. 22, 1924, Box 31, Folder 53, ACWA Papers, LMDC, Cornell University. Correspondence and organizers' reports in the ACWA papers suggest that ethnic insularity and inter-ethnic rivalries kept tensions high and foreign-language locals alive all through the interwar period. In Chicago, for example, the coatmakers were divided into Polish, Italian, Lithuanian, and Bohemian locals.

103. Interview 3A with Mollie Wexler by Sherna Gluck, FHRP.

104. This attitude emerges in the NYCILHP interviews. For further comment on this issue, see Ewen, *Immigrant Women in the Land of Dollars*, pp. 230–31.

105. Quoted in Ewen's dissertation, "Immigrant Women in the Land of Dollars," p. 348.

106. Interview with Dora Bayrack by the author, Santa Monica, Calif., June 7, 1981. For other examples see Ewen, *Immigrant Women in the Land of Dollars*, pp. 230–31, and Ewen's dissertation of the same title, pp. 347–49.

107. Tape 2, I-2, NYCILHP, Wagner Archives.

108. Interview with Lottie Spitzer by Kristine Feichtinger, FHRP.

109. Interview with Mollie Linker in Kramer and Masur, *Jewish Grandmothers*, p. 100. Other oral interviews provide similar statements. See for example, Interview I-2, tape 2, NYCILHP, Wagner Archives.

110. For good examples of American women's activism in the interwar period see the essays in Scharf and Jensen, *Decades of Discontent*, and Cott, *Grounding of Modern Feminism*. For a discussion of the activities of German and Russian Jewish women see Pratt, "Transitions in Judaism."

111. Hutchins Hapgood, *The Spirit of the Ghetto* (1902; repr. Cambridge, Mass., 1967), p. 77.

112. Interview I-21, NYCILHP, Wagner Archives.

113. Tape 3, Interview I-111, NYCILHP. Similar experiences were recalled by Bessie Udin, interview 1A by Sherna Gluck, Dec. 16, 1974, FHRP. See also Ewen, *Immigrant Women in the Land of Dollars*, pp. 424–26.

114. Maxine Seller, "Defining Socialist Womanhood: The Women's Page of the *Jewish Daily Forward* in 1919," *American Jewish History* 76 (June 1987): 416–38; Morris Ziskind, "The First Cultural Organization by Jewish Working Women in Chicago," *Jewish Daily Forward*, Jan. 6, 1923, copy in WPA, Chicago Foreign Language Press Survey, Regenstein Library, University of Chicago. Rose Chernin's story provides some sense of the way women in the Communist party reconciled homemaking and activism. See Kim Chernin, *In My Mother's House* (New York, 1983).

115. This was especially, though not exclusively, true for women with Communist affiliations or sympathies.

116. *Jewish Daily Forward*, Jan. 6, 1923, copy in Chicago Foreign Language Press Survey.

117. Interview with Ruth Katz in Kramer and Masur, *Jewish Grandmothers*, p. 149.

Index

Library of Congress Cataloging-in-Publication Data

Glenn, Susan Anita.
    Daughters of the Shtetl: Life and labor in the immigrant generation / Susan A. Glenn.
        p. cm.
    Includes bibliographical references (p.).
    ISBN 0-8014-1966-2 (alk. paper)
    1. Women clothing workers—United States—History. 2. Women, Jewish—Europe,
Eastern—Social conditions. 3. Women, Jewish—United States—Social conditions. 4. Jews,
East European—United States—Social conditions. 5. Women immigrants—United States—
History. I. Title.
HD6073.C62U54 1990
331.4'81687'089924—dc20   90-1557